Welcome to *Guinness World Records 2025*
This year, GWR celebrates its platinum anniversary – that's 70 years of fact-finding, adjudicating and curating all things extreme. Our unique view of the world – through the lens of the superlative – has enabled us to honour the widest and most diverse group of people, and pictured here are some of the record holders who've attained GWR ICON status over the years – among them some of the most recognized and celebrated figures in the world. In this edition, in honour of our platinum jubilee, we salute some more of these embodiments of record breaking...

GUINNESS WORLD RECORDS 2025

ICON

How many of these ICONS do you recognize? Find out who's who and the records that they hold on our website via the QR code!

Contents

To celebrate GWR's 70th birthday, we're throwing a party with a feast of new features in our opening chapter that look back over our last seven decades. We're also highlighting the very best of record breaking from the past 12 months...

We've had a complete makeover for our platinum birthday, starting with a fun new cover design that continues into the pages of the book. This fresh new look is packed with facts, stats, trivia and infographics, plus over 1,000 eye-catching images.

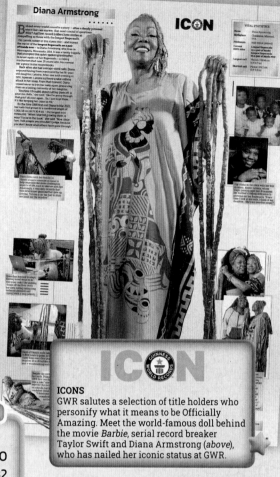

ICONS
GWR salutes a selection of title holders who personify what it means to be Officially Amazing. Meet the world-famous doll behind the movie *Barbie*, serial record breaker Taylor Swift and Diana Armstrong (*above*), who has nailed her iconic status at GWR.

Dear GWR...

As part of our 70th anniversary celebrations, the *Guinness World Records* editors have dipped into the archives to choose some favourite record submissions that didn't quite meet our rigorous criteria. These applications are full of enthusiasm and out-of-the-box thinking, qualities that we cherish at GWR. So a big thank-you for getting in touch over the years – keep those applications coming!

Flashbacks
New to *GWR 2025*, these poster-like pages trace the progression of some popular superlatives. Join us on a deep dive into the histories of records ranging from the **tallest building** and the **most expensive soccer player** to the **fastest 3x3x3 puzzle solve**.

Kids' Zone
Continuing GWR's ongoing mission to inspire record breakers of all ages, we introduce an entire chapter dedicated to junior record setters. It contains five brand-new Under-16 titles for you to take on and the latest batch of Young Achievers, including a trailblazing skateboarder, a quick-fire magician and a troupe of hoopers with more than 30 records.

Continue the story online at guinnessworldrecords.com
Whenever you see this symbol, visit guinnessworldrecords.com/2025 for bonus video content. Our video team has curated a selection of clips from the world's most awe-inspiring record holders. Don't miss the opportunity to see the records explode into life!

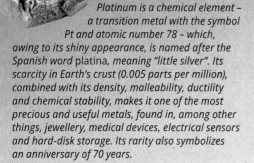

Platinum

Platinum is a chemical element – a transition metal with the symbol Pt and atomic number 78 – which, owing to its shiny appearance, is named after the Spanish word platina, meaning "little silver". Its scarcity in Earth's crust (0.005 parts per million), combined with its density, malleability, ductility and chemical stability, makes it one of the most precious and useful metals, found in, among other things, jewellery, medical devices, electrical sensors and hard-disk storage. Its rarity also symbolizes an anniversary of 70 years.

Largest platinum nugget
A chunk of platinum weighing 7,860.5 g (277.27 oz) – heavier than a typical bowling ball – was found in 1904 at the Ivov mine in Yekaterinburg, Russia. It was christened "The Ural Giant". It is now thought to be kept in the Diamond Fund at the Kremlin in Moscow.

Most PlayStation Platinum trophies won
Virtual awards are earned by players of PlayStation games, with Platinum trophies reserved for those who unlock all other trophies in a game. As of 8 Dec 2023, gamer dav1d_123 (CAN) had won a record 9,190 Platinum trophies from playing more than 10,761 games.

Largest atlas
Earth Platinum is a book of maps published by Millennium House (AUS) that measures 1.854 m high, 1.45 m wide (closed) and 6 cm thick (6 ft x 4 ft 9 in x 2.3 in). It was first presented at the British Library in London, UK, on 13 Jul 2012. Platinum in name only, the tome contains 61 pages and weighs *c.* 200 kg (440 lb). Only 31 copies were printed, with a purchase price of $100,000 (£64,650).

Most expensive bottle
A private collector in Mexico splashed out $225,000 (£122,958) for a bottle of Platinum & White Gold Tequila sold by Tequila Ley .925 on 20 Jul 2006. The contents – a blue agave tequila – were worth "just" $2,500 (£1,366); the 5 lb (2.26 kg) of platinum and 4,100 white diamonds used to create the bottle accounted for 98.8% of the price.

Most expensive...
Sari: A silk sari bejewelled with diamonds, emeralds, sapphires and topazes – and stitched with gold, silver and platinum – was sold for 3,931,627 rupees ($99,990; £50,658) on 5 Jan 2008. It was made by Chennai Silks (IND) and features reproductions of paintings by the celebrated Indian artist Raja Ravi Varma.
Cufflinks: In a private sale in Nov 1996, the "King of Pop" Michael Jackson paid $39,750 (£23,643) for a pair of cufflinks made by the designer Arfaq, aka Arfaq Hussain of Batley, West Yorkshire, UK. The links – named "V2" – were made from diamonds and sapphires set in platinum and 18-karat gold.
Wallet: A platinum-cornered, diamond-studded crocodile-skin creation made by Louis Quatorze of Paris, France, and Mikimoto of Tokyo, Japan, sold in Sep 1984 for £56,000 ($69,895).

Smallest handmade chess set
On 22 Aug 2020, the Armenian-American artist Ara Davidi Ghazaryan unveiled a playable chess set that measured a minuscule 8 x 8 mm (0.32 x 0.32 in). The board is made from yellow and white gold with Armenian apricot wood, resting on a frame made of platinum, yellow gold, rubies and diamonds.

Platinum records
According to the Recording Industry Association of America (RIAA), a single or album "goes platinum" when it registers *audited* sales of 1 million physical copies, or is streamed 150 million times for singles and 1.5 billion times for albums. Sales/streams of double these amounts are recognized as "multi-platinum". The **most platinum certificates awarded** is 82, for the "King of Rock 'n' Roll", Elvis Presley (USA) – 57 platinum and 25 multi-platinum. Barbra Streisand (USA) holds the **women's** record, with 42 (30 platinum, 12 multi), and the **group** record is held by The Beatles (UK), with 68 (42 platinum, 26 multi).

100%

MOST EXPENSIVE MATERIALS USED IN A PIECE OF CONTEMPORARY ART

For the Love of God is a jewelled skull created in 2007 by Damien Hirst (UK, *below*) – manufactured by the British jewellers Bentley & Skinner – using raw materials costing £12 m ($23.7 m). A human skull – thought to be that of a European male who died in his mid-30s – was cast in 2,156 g (76 oz) of platinum, and set with 8,601 ethically sourced flawless diamonds. The work of art was revealed at the White Cube gallery in London, UK, on 1 Jun 2007, and described as a *memento mori*, or reminder of the inevitability of death. It was originally displayed with a price tag of £50 m ($98.8 m).

Flawless diamonds
The skull is covered in 8,601 brilliant-cut flawless pavé diamonds totalling 1,106.18 carats (221.236 g)

"Skull Star"
In the middle of the forehead lies an internally flawless light-fancy pink pear-shaped brilliant-cut diamond weighing 52.4 carats (10.48 g); it represents the "third eye", according to Hirst

Centrepiece surround
The Skull Star is encircled with 14 D-coloured (pure-white) flawless brilliant-cut pear-shaped diamonds, weighing a total of 37.81 carats (7.56 g)

Original teeth
The human skull was bought from a "London taxidermy and natural-history artefacts" shop in 2007, and radio carbon-dated to somewhere between 1720 and 1810; the original teeth were extracted and inset into the platinum cast

Smooth operator
Platinum is "low grain" (i.e., smooth), making it ideal for revealing details in electron microscopy. The **smallest greetings card**, for example, was made at the UK's National Physical Laboratory from silicon nitride coated in platinum; it measured just 15 x 20 micrometres (0.0006 x 0.0008 in). The **smallest snowman** – made by Todd Simpson (CAN) at the Western University Nanofabrication Facility in Ontario, Canada – stands a mere 3 micrometres (0.0001 in) tall and has platinum rods for arms.

Most expensive crab cake
Among the many luxury ingredients in the $310 (£243) crab cake dished up by chef Lazarius Leysath Walker (USA) at The Twist in Columbia, South Carolina, USA, in 2019 was a gilding of platinum. Because the metal is biologically inert, it passes straight through the body.

Editor's Letter

This year, Guinness World Records celebrates its platinum jubilee – seven decades documenting the Officially Amazing! But we've hardly any time to blow out our birthday candles – not with more than 29,000 applications to review from this year alone…

Seventy years ago, two identical twins (*below*) – each with a photographic memory – set up a small office in a disused gym in London's Fleet Street. Their task was to "turn the heat of argument into the light of knowledge" and produce a reference book that could be used to settle arguments in British pubs (and promote some rather famous stout, of course!) What they ended up producing was nothing short of a publishing phenomenon.

The Guinness Book of Records, as their little green hardback was then called, was bound with a beer-proof coating and duly given out free to publicans. It proved to be a big hit with customers and, after much public demand, was soon released in book stores. That year, it became a Christmas best-seller and kickstarted a publishing business that has expanded into a global media enterprise, with record-breaking annual book sales in up to 40 languages, a vast social-media network that engages with millions of fans online every year, and a consultancy venture that has opened up record breaking to everyone on the planet.

SUPERLATIVE SUCCESS

With this special 70th anniversary edition of the book, we want to celebrate this incredible heritage and explore how our horizons have expanded, particularly when viewed through the lens of the superlative. This way of seeing the world, through the "ests" – longest, highest, strongest and smallest – gives us a unique insight into how the world turns, and offers us all the opportunity to make our mark and have our achievements, great and small, celebrated.

But we also want to look forward to the next 70 years.

Most push-ups in one minute (male, CID1, CID2)
Joe Bird completed 61 press-ups in 60 sec on 29 Sep 2023. "CID1" and "CID2" are GWR impairment classifications for the loss or lack of smooth body motion in both arms and both legs. Born with cerebral palsy, Joe trained himself to move without assistance, and eventually became a Paralympic rower. He's a walking (and running and jumping!) challenge to stereotypes about disability.

The thousands of applications we still receive every year attest to the power of the world record as a way of describing and classifying amazing feats. And as long as people continue to push themselves towards ever-more challenging goals, we'll be there with our stopwatches and tape measures, poised to document it all.

LOOKING BACK…

One way of chronicling the story of record breaking is by plotting the progressive history of certain categories. Within each chapter, then, you'll find a "Flashback" feature that explores how a record has changed over the

>>> Continued on p.8

GWR royalty: the McWhirters
As we celebrate our 70th anniversary this year, it seems only fitting to pay tribute to GWR's original editors, Norris and Ross McWhirter. The twin brothers helped to imbue the **best-selling annual** with its unique character, right from our very first edition in 1955 (*see p.10–11*). They became a pivotal part of the BBC's legendary *Record Breakers* show, with a studio audience putting them on the spot with questions about world records. Ross passed away in 1975, but Norris (d. 2004) remained a presiding presence at GWR until 1996. Their superlative influence on the book you're reading cannot be overstated.

On 23 Apr 2023, the London Marathon saw thousands of athletes taking to the streets to raise money for charities close to their hearts. In total, 44 new records were set, here listed in order from the fastest…

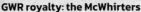

- **London Marathon** Kelvin Kiptum (KEN) 2:01:25
- **Boxer (m)** Alex Grady (USA) 2:38:52
- **Lifeguard (m)** Thomas Hall 2:42:22
- **In pyjamas (m)** Julian Rendall 2:46:46
- **In Malay dress (m)** Mohd S Bin Alias (MYS) 2:49:22
- **Badminton player (m)** Pawel Czudec (POL) 2:53:01
- **Handcuffed pair (m)** Jack Meegan, Daniel Gallagher 2:53:33
- **Scientist (m) ▲** Robert Walsh 2:55:40
- **Golfer (m)** Andrew Tarrant 2:57:26
- **Non-racing wheelchair – front wheel (f)** Claudia Burrough 3:00:56
- **Fairy-tale character (f)** Victoria Hill 3:01:59
- **Lucha-libre wrestler (m) ▲** Ben Molyneux 3:10:30
- **Savoury food (f)** Larissa Kolasinski (USA) 3:11:34
- **In a safari suit (m)** Stuart Cable 3:14:52
- **In suit and dress shoes (m)** Masakazu Konno (USA) 3:23:24
- **In AFL kit (m)** Guillaume Perin (AUS) 3:26:43
- **In Kung Fu kit** Matthew Friend 3:28:10
- **Postal worker (m)** Nickolaj Kennett 3:28:38
- **Star (m)** Peter Banks 3:30:09
- **With a stoma (f)** Adele Roberts 3:30:22
- **Pirate (f)** Eva Ellis 3:31:27
- **In pyjamas (f) ▲** Emanuela Pizzoni (ITA) 3:34:20
- **Body part (f)** Amy Ellett (CAN) 3:37:16

▲ *Record since broken*   * *All record holders UK unless otherwise stated*

Blue Peter sets sail with GWR

This year, the **longest-running children's TV show** once again played host to a tranche of fun GWR titles. *Left to right*: Eurovision hopeful Olly Alexander set the record for the **most objects caught while spinning on a chair in one minute**, grabbing 27 beach balls; Shini Muthukrishnan, *Blue Peter*'s newest presenter, managed the **most clown noses worn in one minute** – 33; Lucy Underdown completed the **fastest 50 m yoke carrying two people (female)** – 37.47 sec. And the show's Joel Mawhinney (*in green*) beat TV host Stephen Mulhern to the **fastest time to put on five jackets** – 28.63 sec.

Most kilts put on in one minute

In celebration of St Andrew's Day on 30 Nov 2023, broadcaster Jennifer Reoch donned five kilts in 60 sec in the studios of Heart Radio in Glasgow, UK. GWR's Editor-in-Chief Craig Glenday was on hand to commemorate the feat. Fellow Scot Lorraine Kelly first set this record back in 2007 by wrapping herself in three kilts.

Fastest time to put on five jumpers (team)

Presenters Josh Widdicombe, Adam Hills (AUS) and Alex Brooker (*second left to right below*) each pulled on five festive sweaters in 34.43 sec on the New Year's Eve Special of Channel 4's *The Last Leg*. Filmed on 31 Dec 2023, this was the trio's second attempt, having failed to attain the title the week before during their Christmas special.

Most hugs by an individual in one minute

On 15 Jan 2024, TV-host Sam Thompson embraced 88 people in just 60 sec on ITV's *This Morning*, in Shoreham-by-Sea, UK. Sam was on a mission to spread some joy on the UK's "Blue Monday", regarded as the most depressing day of the year. As if that weren't reason enough for a hug, the town has been found by the Office for National Statistics to be the saddest in the country.

Monarch (m) ▲ Gilles Dufosse (FRA) 3:38:13

Lumberjack (m) Kirk Millikan (USA) 3:39:12

In Thai dress (f) Kanchanasevee Charinya (THA) 3:45:34

Insect (m) David Church 3:49:38

Glass (m) Daniel Bent 3:50:21

Milk deliverer (m) Gary Qualter 3:52:12

In wellington boots (f) Becky Lafford 3:59:57

3D aircraft (m) ▲ Martin Gear 4:03:02

Christmas cracker (f) Lucy Price 4:05:57

Glass (f) Caroline Lear 4:09:26

Candy (f) Annelise Broussard (USA) 4:14:36

Carrying golf clubs (m) Jeremy Wright 4:14:59

Full-body inflatable costume (m) Steven Waters 4:15:02

3D plant (m) Michael Daniels 4:15:23

Road vehicle (m) ▲ Jem Smith 4:27:52

3D aircraft (f) Fiona Betts 4:33:32

3D dinosaur (m) Richard Allison 4:36:43

Knight (m) Paul Evans 4:50:27

Carrying white goods (m) Sam Hammond 4:52:10

Book (m) ▲ Shane Owen 5:19:15

In clogs (m) Johannes A Teunissen 7:08:37

Editor's Letter

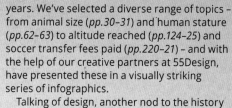

Making history on St David's Day
Welsh-language broadcaster S4C once again oversaw a host of record breaking for St David's Day. *Clockwise, from top right*: Ski4All completed the **greatest distance adaptive skiing in one hour by a relay team** – 13.75 km (8.54 mi). Leporine-loving Tom Jackson unveiled the **most rabbit tattoos** – 69. Rhianna Loren bounced her way into the record books in 11.77 sec with the **fastest 20 m on a space hopper (female)**. And Beth Grice, Lisa Marie Hassall, Sam Taylor and Nicola Walters notched up the **fastest time to pull a truck 20 m by a team (female)**, hauling a 20.2-tonne (44,620-lb) lorry in just 20 sec.

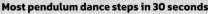

Most pendulum dance steps in 30 seconds
On 10 Nov 2023, Lauren Oakley completed 15 of these dance moves, alternating between legs, in the allotted time on the set of BBC TV's *Strictly Come Dancing: It Takes Two*. Light-footed Lauren began dancing at the age of two, and went on to become Under–21 British National Champion.

years. We've selected a diverse range of topics – from animal size (*pp.30–31*) and human stature (*pp.62–63*) to altitude reached (*pp.124–25*) and soccer transfer fees paid (*pp.220–21*) – and with the help of our creative partners at 55Design, have presented these in a visually striking series of infographics.

Talking of design, another nod to the history of record breaking can be found in the very first chapter. Here, we recreate seven book spreads inspired by the layout of *Guinness World Records* at 10-year intervals. It's been fascinating to see how the styles – and the record categories – have evolved over the decades… and to see that some records have remained unbeaten!

LOOKING FORWARD
The continuing success of GWR is due partly to its ongoing mission to reflect what's actually happening in the world (and beyond). The content is dictated by the claims we receive and the records we approve, and with upwards of 30,000 applications a year, we're never short of new ideas. So, thank you to everyone who has been in touch – even those whose submissions didn't make it (*see Dear GWR… on p.2*).

Fastest time to complete five stunts in a car
Paul Swift notched up a quintet of vehicle stunts in just 57.21 sec at The British Motor Show in Farnborough, Hampshire, on 20 Aug 2023. They were: driving on two wheels for 50 m (164 ft); J-turning between two cars separated by a gap just 1.5 m (5 ft) wider than the car's length; ramp-jumping over a distance at least as long as the car; parallel parking into a space just 1 m (3 ft 3 in) longer than the car; and performing three donuts.

On 21 Apr 2024, the London Marathon saw thousands of athletes taking to the streets to raise money for charities close to their hearts. In total, 47 new records were set, here listed in order from the fastest…

Marathon (women-only) Peres Jepchirchir (KEN) 2:16:16
Marathon (LA3, m) ◊ Richard Whitehead 2:42:01
Type 1 diabetic (m) Simone Carniglia (ITA) 2:44:33
Scientist (m) Stephen Cochrane (IRL) 2:48:51
Videogame character (m) Simon Killen 2:52:57
Tennis player (m) Sam Hull 2:59:38
Cheerleader (m) Warren Parish 3:03:51
In pyjamas (f) Holly Brownlee 3:06:18
Multiple sclerosis (m) Jonathan Astle 3:07:34
Tap/faucet (m) Marcus Mumford 3:10:50
Harlequin (m) James Whistler 3:12:00
Videogame character (f) Alison Stewart 3:19:10
Pilot (m) James Applegarth 3:20:25
Rotating puzzle cube (m) Ian Howard 3:20:31
Inflatable costume (m) Lee Baynton 3:21:07
Traffic cone (m) Matt Everett 3:22:16
Sweet food (m) Douglas O'Neill 3:28:16
Monarch (m) Gilles Dufosse (FRA) 3:32:16
Star Wars character (f) Kate Baldock 3:33:12
3D aircraft (m) Toby Norman 3:34:27
Body part (m) Ollie Shortt (IRL) 3:43:00
Sweet food (f) Laura Baker 3:45:57
Emoji (m) Tom Hall 3:50:17
Skeleton (f) Claire Casselton 3:51:01

*◊ GWR's impairment classification criteria can be found at **guinnessworldrecords.com***   ** All record holders UK unless otherwise stated*

Longest train drawing (II)
Harvey Price created a 21.3-m (69-ft 10-in) sketch of a train, as verified on 13 Jul 2023. A true train aficionado (his favourite is the Gatwick Express), he spent a month on the drawing, which was part of the Mencap Myth Busters campaign to challenge fallacies about disability. (The "II" category denotes an ongoing limitation to learning or adaptive behaviour.) He's shown above with his mother, celebrity Katie Price.

Largest ceilidh band
The Late Late Show (IRL) brought together 384 musicians from all over Ireland on 15 Mar 2024 for its St Patrick's Day show. Staged at the iconic Croke Park stadium in Dublin, which has hosted Gaelic sports since 1891, the event was a joyful celebration of traditional music, with a dance troupe adding to the atmosphere.

I want to give special thanks to all those under-16-year-olds who've earned that official GWR certificate. We're proud to celebrate our Young Achievers, and for the first time ever, we've dedicated a whole chapter to our junior superlative stars. Meet them – and be inspired by them – in the Kids' Zone on pp.174–91.

RECORD-BREAKING ICONS
Lastly, we're using this anniversary edition to introduce our ICONS. These are role models like YouTube sensation MrBeast, basketball legend LeBron James, polar pioneer Preet Chandi and even the cultural phenomenon that is Barbie! Record holders who truly symbolize and embody the spirit of Guinness World Records, and whose values resonate with those originally celebrated by our founding Editors all those years ago. I want to thank them – and all of our readers and expert contributors – for being a part of GWR's ongoing story.

Craig Glenday
Editor-in-Chief

Find out more...

We simply can't fit all the record-breaking action into *GWR 2025*... so we're offering you a treasure trove of extra bonus content on our website (*see QR code above*)!

As you journey through the book, keep your eyes peeled for other QR codes; scan them with your phone's camera and you'll be directed straight to GWR Facebook and Instagram posts as well as related web articles.

Watch out too for the play button (▶) – it means that a record is accompanied by a video from our YouTube channel. Scan the QR code above and you'll be able to access our most-loved videos.

Finally: if you want to see what goes on behind the scenes at GWR HQ, be sure to give us a follow on BeReal (gwr). You'll also find us on TikTok (@guinnessworldrecords), Snapchat (Guinness World Records) and X (@GWR).

Riding the waves with Guinness World Records
In 2023, GWR took to the high seas in partnership with MSC Cruises, giving passengers the chance to become Officially Amazing! On 25 Sep, Gianluca Pascale (ITA) achieved the **fastest time to pull 100 m of rope (male)** – 37.68 sec – on MSC *Euribia* (*left*). Sadly, an attempt to record the **most balls caught on a Velcro suit in one minute (team of two)** didn't quite hit the mark, but they still had fun trying!

Steve Edwards set the fastest **aggregate time to run 1,000 marathons** – 3,363 hr 4 min 2 sec, aged 61. He ran his first official marathon in 1981.

Record	Holder	Time
Carrying a bicycle	Ben Kellett	3:54:52
In a safari suit (f)	Kimberly Siano (USA)	3:54:58
In Mongolian dress (f)	U Bodikhuu (MNG)	3:59:56
Flag (f)	Jennifer Stack (USA)	4:01:02
Snowperson (f)	Charlie Fitton	4:05:52
Mobile phone (f)	Karen Stebel	4:08:42
House (f)	Dawn Williams	4:09:12
Clown (f)	Joanne Bridle	4:16:36
Non-racing wheelchair (f)	Jani Barré (CAN)	4:19:21
Road vehicle (m)	Adrian Bebb	4:21:41
In chainmail (upper body)	Andrew Roberts	4:22:24
In Mongolian boots (m)	G Ulaankhuu (MNG)	4:22:59
Most puzzle cubes solved	George Scholey	520 (4:25:00)
Mechanic (f)	Alexandra Fresco-Sumner	4:28:58
In a flight suit (f)	Caroline Duncan	4:36:16
Road vehicle (f)	Emma Whatley (USA)	4:38:30
Rocking horse (m)	Andy Fountain	5:04:52
Book (m)	Philip Beer	5:08:04
Full-body inflatable costume (f)	Georgina Box	5:10:31
Marathon (CIH, m) ◊	Anthony Bryan	5:49:04
Most T-shirts worn (m)	Brendan Matthews	100 (5:49:33)
10-person costume △		6:32:05
Youngest person (II2, m) ◊	Lloyd Martin	19 y 195 d (6:46:10)

△ Jackie Scully, Frances Walker, Petr Maslov, Aileen Rice-Jones (IRL), Michael Edwards, Daniel Smith, Alex Weight, James Read, Kate Rham and Cameron Sharpe

This is where it began. The first *Guinness Book of Records* was a promotional item given free to British pubs to settle drunken debates. Its runaway success and best-seller status was ascribed by Rupert Guinness to "the brilliance of the editorship" in reference to its creators, Norris and Ross McWhirter, whose book helped to "turn the heat of argument into the light of knowledge".

1. The Artistic World

ACADEMY AWARDS
MOST POSTHUMOUS
NOMINATIONS

In the months prior to his untimely death in Sep 1955, American actor James Dean made two films, *East of Eden*, in which he played the wayward Caleb Trask, and *Giant*, which saw him take on the part of Jett Rink, a Texas ranch-hand. These roles earned him posthumous Best Actor nominations at the 28th and 29th Academy Awards.

POPULAR MUSIC
FIRST MILLION-
SELLING SINGLE (UK)

"Rock Around the Clock" by hit-makers Bill Haley & His Comets (USA) spent five weeks at No.1 on the UK singles chart after becoming the first record to sell more than 1 million copies in the country. The *world* record was a 1902 recording of "Vesti la giubba" from Ruggero Leoncavallo's opera *I Pagliacci* by Enrico Caruso (ITA).

SCULPTURE
LARGEST SOLID GOLD

On 29 May 1955, the statue of Buddha known as the "Phra Phuttha Maha Suwan Patimakon" was dropped during renovation works at the temple of Wat Traimit in Bangkok, Thailand. The damage revealed that the statue was a thin layer of plaster over a long-hidden gold sculpture, measuring 9 ft 10 in (3 m) in height and comprising 6 tons (5,450 kg) of solid gold.

2. The Technological World

TELEVISION
FIRST WIRELESS
REMOTE CONTROL

Released on 22 Jan 1955, the "Bismarck" series of television receivers, made by the Zenith Radio Company of Chicago, Illinois, USA, featured four photo-resistors on the edge of the screen. A device called the "Zenith Flash-Matic" allowed users to remotely mute the speakers or tune to a different channel without wires.

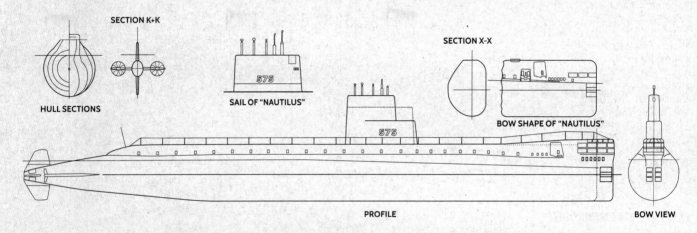

SECTION K+K
HULL SECTIONS
SAIL OF "NAUTILUS"
575
SECTION X-X
BOW SHAPE OF "NAUTILUS"
575
PROFILE
BOW VIEW

SUBMARINES
FIRST ATOMIC

The US Navy submarine "Nautilus" (SS-571) made the first atomic-powered ocean voyage on 17 Jan 1955, setting out from New London, Connecticut, and covering the 1,200-nautical-mi (1,381-mi; 2,200-km) journey to San Juan, Puerto Rico, in just 90 hours – a feat that also made it the *fastest* submarine in service. *See diagram above.*

FLYING BOATS
FASTEST

The XP6M-1 "Seamaster", manufactured by the Glenn L Martin Company of Santa Ana, California, USA, achieved a speed of 646 mph (1,040 km/h) during testing in southern Maryland in Aug 1955. Both prototypes were lost in fatal crashes shortly after, however, so the jet bomber would not enter service for several years.

The British record holder in this category, and the previous holder of the world record, was the experimental Saunders-Roe SR.A/1 flying boat, which flew to 512 mph (824 km/h) over the Solent in Jul 1947.

3. The Sporting World

MOTOR RACING
OLDEST GRAND PRIX
DRIVER

The Monaco F1 Grand Prix, held on 22 May 1955, saw Monégasque driver Louis Chiron finish sixth at the age of 55 years 292 days. On his way to the chequered flag, he overtook the highest-finishing British driver, Stirling Moss, who was less than half his age.

BOXING
MOST UNDEFEATED
HEAVYWEIGHT BOUTS

The American pugilist Rocco Francis Marchegiano, aka "Rocky Marciano", successfully defended his heavyweight title for a sixth time on 21 Sep 1955, recording his 49th consecutive win since his professional debut. Marciano recovered from a second-round knock-down to overcome challenger Archie Moore with a ninth-round knockout. Previous unsuccessful challengers to Marciano's title included Ezzard Charles, aka "The Cincinnati Cobra", and British heavyweight champion Don Cockell.

SNOOKER
FIRST 147 BREAK

In snooker, a score of 147 points can be achieved in a single frame, provided the player can pot all the balls on the table in the following order: all 15 reds (15 points) each followed by the black (105 points), and then all six colours (27 points). The 15-time champion Joe Davis (UK) performed this feat for the first time in an exhibition match against Willie Smith at Leicester Square Hall in London, UK, on 22 Jan 1955.

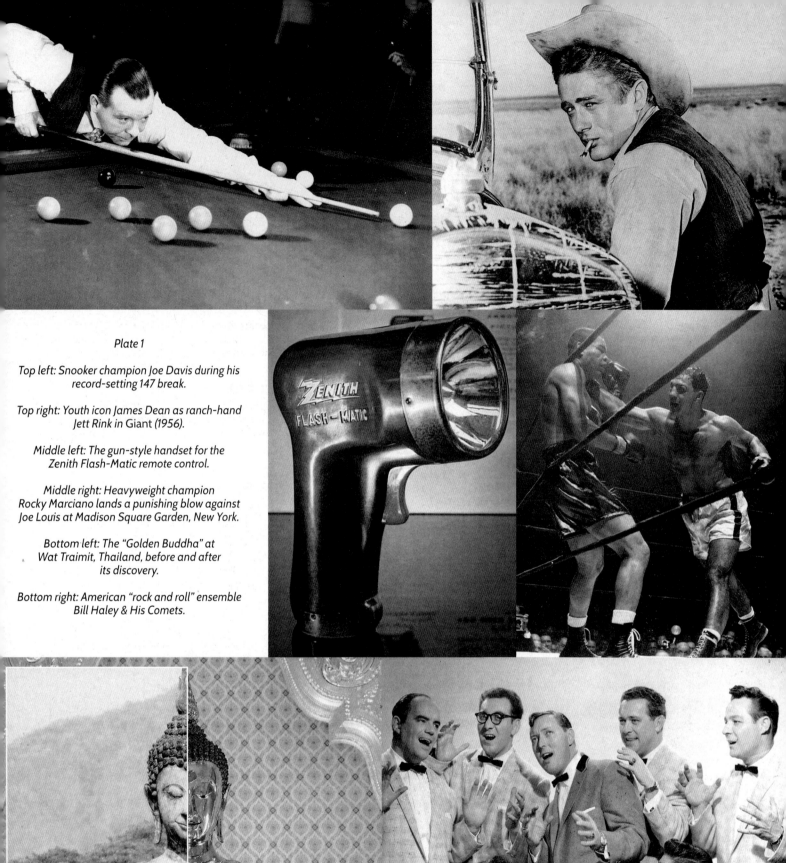

Plate 1

Top left: Snooker champion Joe Davis during his record-setting 147 break.

Top right: Youth icon James Dean as ranch-hand Jett Rink in Giant (1956).

Middle left: The gun-style handset for the Zenith Flash-Matic remote control.

Middle right: Heavyweight champion Rocky Marciano lands a punishing blow against Joe Louis at Madison Square Garden, New York.

Bottom left: The "Golden Buddha" at Wat Traimit, Thailand, before and after its discovery.

Bottom right: American "rock and roll" ensemble Bill Haley & His Comets.

HISTORY OF GWR: 1965

In the 1960s, the editorial team at Guinness Superlatives Ltd found themselves at the heart of Swinging London. The great rivalries of the age – whether the Soviet Union versus the United States or The Rolling Stones versus The Beatles – battled it out in the pages of the *Guinness Book of Records*. The publication was now a global phenomenon with more than 1 million copies sold and translated editions in French, German, Japanese and Spanish.

1. The Animal Kingdom

SPIDERS
Largest species

Native to the coastal rainforests of northern South America, the goliath bird-eating tarantula (*Theraphosa blondi*) typically reaches a weight of 6.2 oz (175 g) and a leg-span of around 9 in (23 cm) by the time it reaches adulthood. This is about the same weight as a billiard ball or a high-quality deck of playing cards.

Largest specimen

In Apr 1965, naturalists from the Pablo San Martin Expedition caught a goliath bird-eater with a leg-span of 11 in (28 cm) near Rio Cavro, Venezuela.

SNAKES
Most milked

Bernard Keyter, a supervisor at the South African Institute for Medical Research in Johannesburg, personally milked 780,000 venomous snakes and obtained 1,046 gal (3,960 litres) of venom over a 14-year period ending in Dec 1965. He was never bitten.

2. Human Achievements

FASTING
Longest without
solid food

Angus Barbieri (b. 1940) of Tayport in Fife, UK, lived on tea, coffee, water, soda water and vitamins in Maryfield Hospital, Dundee, UK, from Jun 1965 to Jul 1966. During this time, his weight declined from 472 lb (33 st 10 lb; 214 kg) to a healthy 178 lb (12 st 10 lb; 80.74 kg). Barbieri maintained his weight loss and died in Sep 1990.

JUDICIARY
Oldest serving judge

Judge Albert Alexander (b. 8 Nov 1859) of Plattsburg, Missouri, USA, retired from the courtroom on 9 Jul 1965, having presided over probate hearings until the age of 105 years 243 days. Alexander had been elected to the position in 1950, when he was already 90 years old, and won re-election a further three times before ill health finally forced his retirement.

3. Mechanisms and Structures

LAND VEHICLES
First to 600 mph

On 15 Nov 1965, American racing driver Craig Breedlove became the first person to exceed 600 mph (965.6 km/h) in a four-wheeled automobile at the Bonneville Salt Flats in Utah, USA. Breedlove achieved an average speed of 600.601 mph (966.573 km/h) in *Spirit of America Sonic I*, which was powered by a 15,000-hp (11,032-kW) J79 engine reclaimed from an F-4 Phantom supersonic fighter jet.

Fastest crash survived

With this record, Breedlove won a decisive victory in his years-long rivalry with Art Arfons (USA). Over the preceding two years, the two had traded the land-speed record back and forth seven times. A few months after Breedlove's 600-mph run, Arfons crashed his *Green Monster* jet-powered car at 610 mph (981 km/h). He walked away unharmed. Breedlove would go on to break the record in 1977, surviving a crash clocked at 675 mph (1,086 km/h).

Heaviest self-powered

Each of the two Crawler-Transporter vehicles, built for NASA by the Marion Power Shovel Company of Ohio, USA, weighed 5.95 million lb (2,700 tonnes). These baseball-field-sized mobile platforms are driven by a pair of 2,750-hp (2,022-kW) ALCO locomotive engines. They were originally designed to move the Saturn V rocket at the Kennedy Space Center in Florida; subsequent upgrades have increased their weight to 6.65 million lb (3,016 tonnes).

MONUMENTS
Tallest commemorative

Completed on 28 Oct 1965, the Gateway Arch in St Louis, Missouri, rises 630 ft (192 m) above the banks of the Mississippi River. The striking stainless-steel arch was designed by Finnish modernist architect Eero Saarinen to celebrate the westward expansion of the United States, and St Louis's pivotal role as the "gateway to the west".

4. Arts and Culture

ACADEMY AWARDS
Most Supporting
Actress wins

At the 38th Academy Awards, Shelley Winters (USA) became the first performer to win the Oscar for Best Supporting Actress twice. Her wins were for roles in *The Diary of Anne Frank* (1959) and *A Patch of Blue* (1965). This record was later equalled by Dianne Wiest (USA) for her parts in *Hannah and Her Sisters* (1986) and *Bullets Over Broadway* (1994).

First actor with dwarfism
to be nominated

The star-studded 1965 Columbia movie *Ship of Fools* (USA) received eight Oscar nominations, including a Best Supporting Actor nod to Michael Dunn (USA). A talented character actor and musician, the 1.17-m-tall (3-ft 10-in) Dunn played the role of Glocken, a first-class passenger on an ocean liner bound for pre-World War II Nazi Germany. Dunn, a Tony nominee and New York Film Critics Circle award winner for his stage work, was credited with raising the profile of Little People performers who, prior to this, were typically cast as novelty background characters.

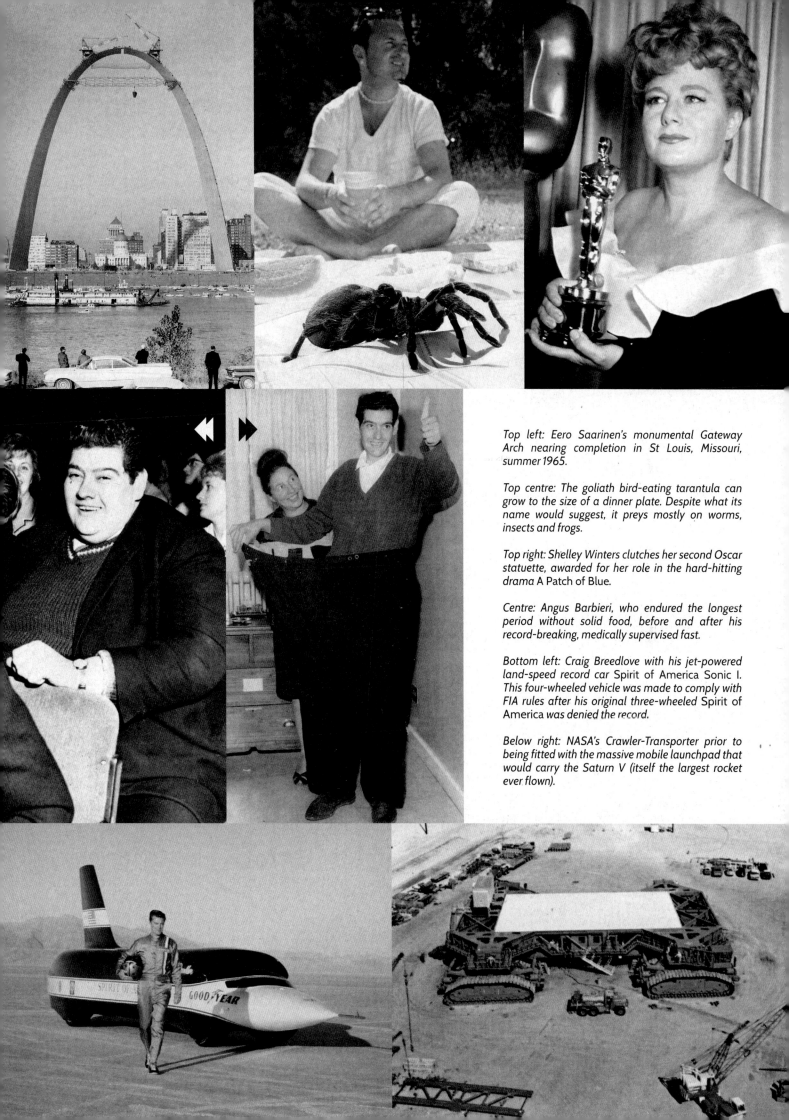

Top left: Eero Saarinen's monumental Gateway Arch nearing completion in St Louis, Missouri, summer 1965.

Top centre: The goliath bird-eating tarantula can grow to the size of a dinner plate. Despite what its name would suggest, it preys mostly on worms, insects and frogs.

Top right: Shelley Winters clutches her second Oscar statuette, awarded for her role in the hard-hitting drama A Patch of Blue.

Centre: Angus Barbieri, who endured the longest period without solid food, before and after his record-breaking, medically supervised fast.

Bottom left: Craig Breedlove with his jet-powered land-speed record car Spirit of America Sonic I. This four-wheeled vehicle was made to comply with FIA rules after his original three-wheeled Spirit of America was denied the record.

Below right: NASA's Crawler-Transporter prior to being fitted with the massive mobile launchpad that would carry the Saturn V (itself the largest rocket ever flown).

HISTORY OF GWR: 1975

The 1970s saw the founding of Microsoft and Apple, heralding a new era in home computing; movies achieved "blockbuster" status thanks to hits such as *Jaws* and *Star Wars*; and the launch of the *Voyager* probes expanded our horizons ever farther. Back down on Earth, countless millions were frustrated by the invention of the Rubik's Cube...

Artwork from the "Natural World" chapter of the 1975 edition.

1. THE NATURAL WORLD

Oldest canary
On 8 Apr 1975, a male canary (*Serinus canaria*) called Joey died at the age of 34 at the home of its owner, Kathleen Ross of Hull, East Yorkshire, UK. Joey had been purchased in Calabar, Nigeria, in 1941 by Ms Ross's father, who was in the Merchant Navy.

Deepest sponge
Soviet research vessel *Vityaz* discovered living sponges from the family Cladorhizidae at a depth of 9,990 m (32,776 ft) during its 1975 survey of the Philippine Trench. In its more than 30 years of service, the *Vityaz* and its crew of scientists discovered 1,176 new species of deep-sea animals and plants.

2. SCIENCE & TECHNOLOGY

First digital camera
In Dec 1975, Kodak engineer Steven Sasson (USA) took a digital photograph using a prototype that combined a cassette tape deck, several layers of circuit boards and a bulky movie-camera lens. At the heart of this toaster-sized camera was a 100-x-100-pixel electronic sensor, which recorded pictures that were then saved to the magnetic cassette tape.

Best-selling videogame console
The Magnavox Odyssey made its last appearance on Christmas lists in 1975. In the three years since its release on 14 Sep 1972, the wood-grained box had sold more than 330,000 copies, a sales record that would stand until the 1977 launch of the Atari VCS.

First food grown in space
On 8 Jul 1975, Soviet cosmonaut Vitaly Sevastyanov celebrated his 40th birthday on board the *Salyut 4* space station. The centrepiece of his birthday meal, prepared by crewmate Pyotr Klimuk, was a garnish of spring onions that were grown in the station's Oasis 1M grow-lamp greenhouse.

3. ENTERTAINMENT

First album to debut at No.1 on the *Billboard* chart
Elton John's ninth studio album, *Captain Fantastic and the Brown Dirt Cowboy*, reached No.1 on the US chart within the first week of its release on 7 Jun 1975. The previous four Elton John albums had all climbed to the top of the chart, and *Captain Fantastic* was hotly anticipated, despite having no lead single ("Someone Saved My Life Tonight" wasn't released until later in the month).

Best-selling album by a group
Their Greatest Hits (1971–1975), which collates material from the first four albums by American country-rock band the Eagles, was released shortly after the departure of founding guitarist Bernie Leadon in Dec 1975. It has gone on to sell 38 million copies in the US alone. The album showcases the country-influenced sound of their first three albums.

Most bones broken
On 26 May 1975, American daredevil Evel Knievel attempted to jump 13 city buses on a motorcycle at Wembley Stadium in London, UK. He cleared the vehicles but lost control of his bike on landing, breaking his pelvis. This was reportedly the 433rd time he'd broken or fractured a bone in his career.

Highest attendance at a circus performance
For their 1975 engagement in the city of New Orleans, Louisiana, USA, the Ringling Bros. and Barnum & Bailey Circus shunned their usual big top in favour of the newly opened Louisiana Superdome. On 14 Sep 1975, they drew a crowd of 52,385 people to see a show that included acrobats, trapeze artists and high-wire walker Philippe Petit – who had crossed the gap between the twin towers of the World Trade Center in New York City the previous year.

4. SPORTS & GAMES

First century at the Cricket World Cup (male)
England batter Dennis Amiss hit 137 off 147 balls against India during the opening game of the inaugural Cricket World Cup on 7 Jun 1975. His innings included 18 boundaries. The tournament was won by the West Indies, led by Clive Lloyd, who defeated Australia by 17 runs in the final.

Longest-reigning checkers champion
In Jul 1975, Walter Hellman (USA, b. SWE) vacated the title of World Checkers Champion due to his failing health. The steelworker from Gary, Indiana, had dominated the game since he first took the crown in 1948. He only lost one title match in the following 27 years, to Marion Tinsley in 1955, and was undefeated from 1958 until his retirement.

A yellow canary similar to Joey (see above left). The average lifespan of these tiny songbirds is around 10–15 years.

Above: The Magnavox Odyssey was sold with circuit cards that allowed users to play different games on their televisions. Screen overlays added some detail to the system's crude graphics.

Above right: The first self-contained digital camera, assembled by Steven Sasson at Kodak. His superiors didn't think the idea had any potential.

Centre: British performer Elton John in 1975. *Captain Fantastic and the Brown Dirt Cowboy* was his seventh album in a row to go platinum (*for more platinum performances, turn to p.4*).

Far right: The Eagles at a press conference organized for the launch of *Their Greatest Hits*.

Below: Evel Knievel soars over a line of cars on his custom Harley-Davidson during one of his potentially bone-crunching stunt performances.

Below right: English batter Dennis Amiss hits another shot to the boundary during his century against India at the 1975 Cricket World Cup.

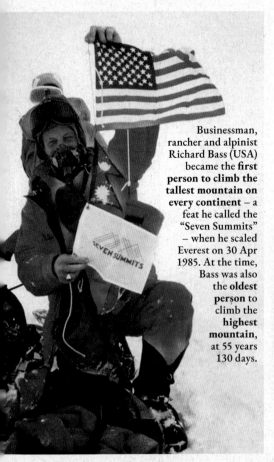

Businessman, rancher and alpinist **Richard Bass (USA)** became the **first person to climb the tallest mountain on every continent** – a feat he called the "Seven Summits" – when he scaled Everest on 30 Apr 1985. At the time, Bass was also **the oldest person to climb the highest mountain**, at 55 years 130 days.

hadrosaur *Maiasaura peeblesorum* lived in what is now the US state of Montana during the Late Cretaceous period, and a few fossilized bones and eggshells from a nesting site were taken into space by Montana-born astronaut Loren Acton.

First royal in space
Prince Sultan bin Salman bin Abdulaziz Al Saud (SAU) flew as a payload specialist on board the STS-51-G mission of the Space Shuttle *Discovery* on 17–24 Jun 1985. He was also the first Arab and first Muslim in space.

The stained-glass knight from *Young Sherlock Holmes* (USA, 1985) was the **first entirely computer-generated movie character**. It was animated by John Lasseter, who would go on to co-write and direct Pixar's *Toy Story* (USA, 1995).

British entertainer, and long-time presenter of the *Record Breakers* TV show, Roy Castle took just 23 hr 44 min to complete 1 million tap-dancing steps. His dance-athon took place at a Guinness World Records event in London, UK, on 31 Oct–1 Nov 1985.

The 1980s saw GWR expand to monitor the rise of MTV and the big-budget music video, the advent of CGI movies and the launch of the videogame that drove everyone to distraction: Tetris. The fall of the Berlin Wall symbolized the end of the Cold War, and it was also the end of the McWhirter era, with GWR's founding editor Norris stepping down after 30 years at the helm.

SCIENCE & TECHNOLOGY

First dinosaur in space
On 29 Jul 1985 – around 76 million years after its death – a few bones from a maiasaur were taken into orbit on board the *Challenger* Space Shuttle mission STS-51-F. The duck-billed

スーパーマリオブラザーズ™ (Nintendo)

The success of *Super Mario Bros.* fuelled Nintendo's rise from Japanese toymaker to global entertainment giant. The 1985 platformer sold 40 million copies for the Famicom and NES, making it the **best-selling platformer of all time.**

First "people" sim
Little Computer People, released on various home-computer platforms by Activision (USA) in 1985, tasked the player with looking after a man and his dog living in a three-storey house. One of the most innovative aspects of the videogame was that every disk featured a serial number, which was typed in before the game first booted up; the result was a little digital avatar with a unique appearance and personality.

First domain name
Symbolics.com was the first domain name ever registered, according to NetNames Ltd. It was established on 15 Mar 1985.

NATURAL WORLD

Heaviest garlic bulb
A head of garlic grown by Robert Kirkpatrick of Eureka, California, USA, in 1985 weighed 1.19 kg (2 lb 10 oz).

Heaviest rhubarb
A stick of rhubarb weighing 2.67 kg (5 lb 14 oz) was grown by Eric Stone of East Woodyates, Dorset, UK, in 1985. Stone chalked up his green-fingered success to 30 years of manuring his garden with horse dung.

Longest poultry flight
Chickens are not good flyers, owing to their small wings and enlarged pectoral muscles. However, Sheena, a barnyard bantam owned by twins Bill and Bob Knox (both USA), flew 192.07 m (630 ft 2 in) at Parkesburg, Pennsylvania, USA, on 31 May 1985. Bob, a former figure-skating instructor, became an expert in all things fowl after founding a company that rents swans and cleans up goose droppings.

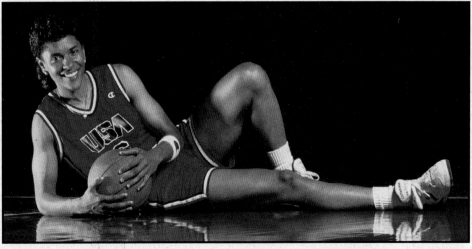

In 1985, Lynette Woodard (USA) became the **first woman to play for the Harlem Globetrotters (USA).** One of the greatest female players of all time, the 6-ft (1.83-m) guard was captain of the 1984 US Olympic gold-medal-winning team. She would go on to be inducted into the prestigious Naismith Basketball Hall of Fame and the Women's Basketball Hall of Fame.

ENTERTAINMENT

First movie based on a board game

The comedy whodunnit *Clue* (USA, 1985) was based on the board game Cluedo. It starred Tim Curry as the butler, Wadsworth, aiming to finger the killer of his employer, Mr Boddy. The six suspects are all characters from the game: Mrs Peacock (Eileen Brennan), Mrs White (Madeline Kahn), Professor Plum (Christopher Lloyd), Mr Green (Michael McKean), Colonel Mustard (Martin Mull) and Miss Scarlet (Lesley Ann Warren). Three endings were filmed, and a different one shown at different theatres.

Longest time between a movie and its sequel

A total of 46 years passed before the release of Walt Disney Productions' *Return to Oz* (USA, 1985), which resumed the story six months after the end of MGM's *The Wizard of Oz* (USA, 1939). The lead role of Dorothy Gale passed from Judy Garland to Fairuza Balk.

SPORT

Youngest winner of the Gentlemen's Singles at the Wimbledon Championships

Boris Becker (DEU, b. 22 Nov 1967) won the men's title on 7 Jul 1985 aged 17 years 227 days – the **first unseeded player** to do so. In 1984, aged 16 years 216 days, he'd become the **youngest man to win a game at Wimbledon**, beating America's Blaine Willenborg in the first round.

Most points scored in a Stanley Cup series

Ice hockey legend Wayne Gretzky (CAN) scored 47 points for the Edmonton Oilers in the 1985 playoff season. This comprised 17 goals and 30 assists – also both records at the time.

Most base hits in an MLB career

On 11 Sep 1985, Pete Rose (USA) overtook Ty Cobb with his 4,192nd hit (reaching or passing first base). His career total would rise to an unbeaten 4,256 by his retirement in Nov 1986.

Tetris made its debut in 1985, courtesy of Soviet computer engineer Alexey Pajitnov. The falling blocks began life as a series of simple text characters on a laboratory computer, but its addictive simplicity inspired a franchise that would go on to become the world's **biggest-selling puzzle videogame** (*c.* 520 million units) and the **most ported videogame** of any kind (at least 70 different platforms).

Deadliest lahar

On 13 Nov 1985, the Nevado del Ruiz volcano in Colombia erupted, sending pyroclastic flows down the mountainside. The ash and molten rock mixed with the ice and snow on the slopes and created four separate volcanic mudflows or "lahars", which raced down the volcano's flanks at 60 km/h (37.3 mph), growing as they picked up clay and soil from eroding the river valleys they travelled in. Four hours after the initial eruption, the lahars had travelled 100 km (62 mi) and killed an estimated 23,000 people. The worst-affected town was Armero, which was hit by several lahar pulses up to 5 m (16 ft 5 in) deep. Three-quarters of the town's 28,700 inhabitants were killed.

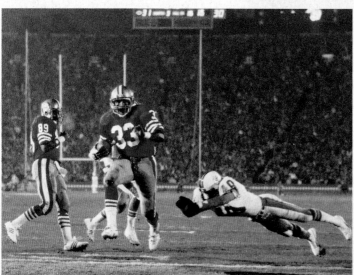

At Super Bowl XIX on 20 Jan 1985, running back Roger Craig scored three touchdowns as the San Francisco 49ers overcame the Miami Dolphins. This remains a Super Bowl record, equalled six times but never beaten.

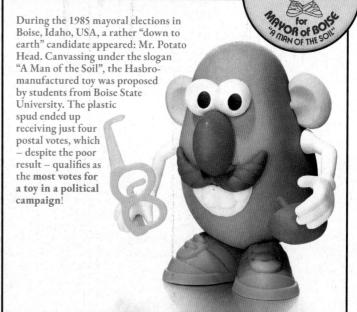

During the 1985 mayoral elections in Boise, Idaho, USA, a rather "down to earth" candidate appeared: Mr. Potato Head. Canvassing under the slogan "A Man of the Soil", the Hasbro-manufactured toy was proposed by students from Boise State University. The plastic spud ended up receiving just four postal votes, which – despite the poor result – qualifies as the **most votes for a toy in a political campaign!**

Introduction

The 1990s saw the end of the Cold War, the emergence of the World Wide Web, the launch of Google (or BackRub, as it was first known), the cloning of Dolly the sheep, and an explosion in videogaming thanks to the PlayStation®, Nintendo® 64 and Sega® Saturn gaming consoles. The world's population hit 6 billion...

Animal Kingdom

Fastest snail The World Snail Racing Championships (established 1967) are held each July at Congham in Norfolk, UK, and conducted on a 33-cm-wide (13-in) circular course. The all-time record holder is a snail named Archie – trained by Carl Bramham (UK) – who, in 1995, sprinted from the centre to the edge in exactly 2 min.

> "Runners" in the Congham snail race are typically put out to pasture after a race. At the annual snail-racing event in Lagardère, France, however, the losers are tossed into the cooking pot!

First predatory sponge In Jan 1995, while exploring a shallow-water Mediterranean cave off La Ciotat, France, researchers from the Centre d'Océanologie de Marseille found a sponge that preyed on small crustaceans. *Asbestopluma hypogea* employs long, tendril-like structures to seize prey swimming nearby, which is then hauled inside its body and digested. Until this discovery, sponges were thought to be passive filter-feeders.

Longest service for a hearing guide dog Donna, a support dog owned by John Hogan of Pyrmont Point, New South Wales, Australia, completed 18 years of service before her death on 6 May 1995 at the age of 20 years 2 months.

Hop, Skip and a Jump!

British athlete Jonathan Edwards landed the **longest triple jump** at the IAAF World Championships in Gothenburg, Sweden, on 7 Aug 1995 – an as-yet-unbeaten 18.29 m (60 ft 0.07 in). Edwards broke the world record with both of his first two efforts in the final, recording 18.16 m (59 ft 6.96 in) before going out even farther in the next round. Earlier that year, Edwards – nicknamed "Titch" at school for his diminutive stature – had made a wind-assisted jump of 18.43 m (60 ft 5.59 in) at the European Cup that was ineligible for the world record.

Longest cock-crow A rooster (a male chicken, *Gallus domesticus*) named Tugaru-Ono-94 was recorded crowing for 23.6 sec in Ueda City, Nagano, Japan, on 8 May 1995. A sound meter placed next to a crowing cock can register up to 142 decibels (a chainsaw is about 120 decibels).

Human Achievements

Farthest distance to spit a watermelon seed Jason Schayot (USA) expelled a seed a distance of 22.91 m (75 ft 2 in) – almost a quarter of an American football field – at the annual De Leon Peach and Melon Festival (established 1914) in Texas, USA, on 12 Aug 1995. The hybridization of *Citrullus lanatus* means that only a small percentage of watermelons sold in US stores now have seeds, suggesting that the death knell has sounded for seed-spitting contests.

THEN & NOW

The **first eBay transaction** was made in Sep 1995, when Pierre Omidyar (FRA) sold a broken laser pointer to Mark Fraser (USA) – a self-confessed "collector of broken laser pointers" – for $14.83 (£9.52). Omidyar, a French-born Iranian-American programmer, had launched his person-to-person transaction site in the USA on 3 Sep 1995 as a personal project under the name of AuctionWeb. The service was renamed eBay in 1997 and went public shortly after, riding on the success of its lucrative role in the Beanie Babies craze.

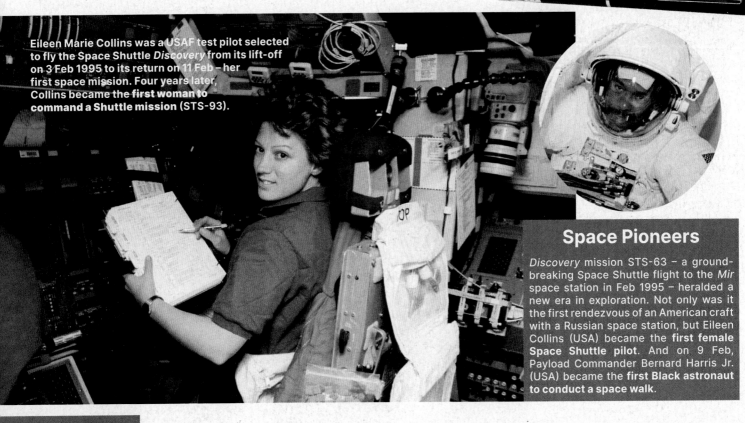

Eileen Marie Collins was a USAF test pilot selected to fly the Space Shuttle *Discovery* from its lift-off on 3 Feb 1995 to its return on 11 Feb – her first space mission. Four years later, Collins became the **first woman to command a Shuttle mission** (STS-93).

Space Pioneers

Discovery mission STS-63 – a groundbreaking Space Shuttle flight to the *Mir* space station in Feb 1995 – heralded a new era in exploration. Not only was it the first rendezvous of an American craft with a Russian space station, but Eileen Collins (USA) became the **first female Space Shuttle pilot**. And on 9 Feb, Payload Commander Bernard Harris Jr. (USA) became the **first Black astronaut to conduct a space walk**.

Tallest object ever moved: Despite weighing 683,600 tonnes (753,540 tons), the 472-m-high (1,548-ft) Troll A gas installation was towed 200 km (124 mi) from Vats in Rogaland, Norway, to the Troll field in the North Sea on 10–17 May 1995. The rig – about three-and-a-half times taller than the Great Pyramid of Giza (*see p.148*) – began production for Statoil (now Equinor, NOR) in 1996.

Largest teddy-bears' picnic On 24 Jun 1995, Dublin Zoo (IRL) welcomed 33,573 stuffed bears – plus their owners – for an *al fresco* feast of cake, potato crisps and, in celebration of their centenary, Jacob's Mikado biscuits.

Farthest throw of a spear The record distance achieved chucking a spear is 258.63 m (848 ft 6.5 in) by David Engvall in Aurora, Colorado, USA, on 15 Jul 1995. In competitive spear-throwing, an *atlatl* (Aztec: "throwing stick") is used; this handheld device comprises a length of wood that fits between the throwing hand and the back end of the spear shaft, conveying additional power to the launch – sufficient, at least, to pierce 16th-century Spanish armour.

Science

Coldest naturally occurring temperature The Boomerang Nebula – a cloud of dust and gas 5,000 light years from Earth – has a temperature of less than -272°C (-457.6°F). The low temperature is the result of the rapid expansion of gas and dust flowing away from the nebula's central ageing star. The discovery was made in 1995 by astronomers using data obtained by the Swedish-European Southern Observatory Submillimeter radio telescope in La Silla, Chile.

Longest-standing maths problem to be solved In 1995, Andrew Wiles (UK) proved Fermat's Last Theorem, finally showing that $x^n+y^n=z^n$ has no solutions in integers for n being equal to or greater than 3. The theorem was posed by Pierre de Fermat in 1637, and stood for 358 years.

Sport

First X Games gold medallist Waterskier Justin Seers (AUS) won the Barefoot Jumping event at the inaugural Extreme Games on 25 Jun 1995 in Providence, Rhode Island, USA. The action-sports event was renamed the X Games the next year.

Highest-scoring Super Bowl On 29 Jan 1995, the San Francisco 49ers beat the San Diego Chargers 49–26 at Super Bowl XXIX – the highest aggregate score in the history of American football's biggest game

First PlayStation game to sell 1 million copies
One-on-one fighting game *Tekken* (Namco, 1995) had sold 1,728,556 copies by Christmas 1995 in Japan and the USA alone. It was also a Christmas best-seller in the UK.

Most consecutive Oscar wins for Best Actor: At the 1995 American Academy Awards, Tom Hanks (USA) took home his second Best Actor statuette, for his starring role in *Forrest Gump* (USA, 1994). Having won the previous year for *Philadelphia* (USA, 1993), he became only the second movie star to win two Best Actor Oscars back to back, a record he shares with Spencer Tracy (USA) for *Captains Courageous* (USA, 1937) and *Boys Town* (USA, 1938).

Between 17 and 21 Feb 1995, American stockbroker and adventurer Steve Fossett made the **first solo crossing of the Pacific Ocean in a balloon**. He launched from the Olympic Stadium in Seoul, South Korea, and landed at Mendham in Saskatchewan, Canada. He travelled 8,738 km (5,430 mi) in *Spirit of Freedom* – a gondola suspended beneath a 45-m-tall (150-ft) helium balloon.

GUESS WHAT?

Q Which three movies have each won a record 11 Oscars?
A See page 208.

History of GWR: 2005

The Golden Anniversary of Guinness World Records

« First video uploaded to YouTube

On 24 Apr 2005, a 19-sec clip of YouTube co-founder Jawed Karim (USA, b. DEU) and two elephants at San Diego Zoo became the inaugural upload to the video-sharing platform. "Me at the Zoo" has gone on to receive more than 296 million views, earning 15 million likes (as of 5 Dec 2023).

⌃ Heaviest apple

In 2005, farmer Chisato Iwasaki (JPN) grew an astonishing apple big enough to satisfy Godzilla.

A specimen of the appropriately named "Stark Jumbo" cultivar, the scale-busting fruit weighed 1.849 kg (4 lb 1 oz) – about the same as three basketballs. It was picked by Chisato on 24 Oct. His farm is situated in Hirosaki City in Aomori, Honshu, which is famous across Japan for its apples.

Largest egg beater »

This 14-ft 3-in-tall (4.36-m) utensil was whisked up by Canadian folk artist Kerras Jeffery.

The egg beater was made from recycled parts: a truck rear axle provided the main working mechanism, while a ring from a store clothes rack was repurposed as the round handle. It was verified on 1 Apr 2005.

Kerras, who died in 2017 at the age of just 51, was a folk artist known for his creative, playful spirit. He would typically repurpose found materials, crafting them in his backyard studio in Prince Edward Island into something unexpected, such as turning a Volkswagen Beetle into a chicken coop or fashioning a sideboard from a bulldozer shovel.

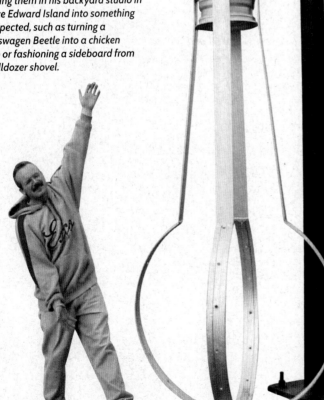

★ Highest railway line

Completed in Oct 2005, most of the 1,956-km-long (1,215-mi) Qinghai–Tibet railway in China lies 4,000 m (13,123 ft) above sea level. Its highest point, at 5,072 m (16,640 ft), is more than half the height of Mount Everest. Passenger carriages are pressurized and oxygen masks are available.

★ Tallest rollercoaster

Kingda Ka at Six Flags Great Adventure in New Jersey, USA, reaches a height of 139 m (456 ft). It opened to the public on 21 May 2005 and was, at the time, the world's **fastest rollercoaster**, clocking in at 206 km/h (128 mph).

★ First cloned dog

Snuppy the Afghan hound owed his existence to a team of scientists at South Korea's Seoul National University (after which the puppy was named). Snuppy's growth was stimulated when a donor egg cell was fused with DNA from the ear of a three-year-old male Afghan hound called Tie. The egg was then transferred to a surrogate golden Labrador female for 60 full days of pregnancy, before being born on 25 Apr 2005. Snuppy, who lived to the age of 10 years, was named by *TIME* magazine as the "Invention of the Year".

★ Largest focaccia

Pietro Catucci and Antonio Latte (both ITA) baked a loaf of flat leavened Italian bread weighing 2.8 tonnes (6,172 lb) – the weight of six grand pianos – in Mottola, Taranto, Italy, on 6 Aug 2005.

★ Largest bar of gold

On 11 Jun 2005, Mitsubishi Materials (JPN) manufactured a pure gold bar weighing 250 kg (551 lb). Ounce for ounce, the ingot – about the size of a desktop printer – would be worth around £13.1 m ($15.8 m) if based on current gold prices (as of 5 Dec 2023).

★ Fastest 100 m by a pantomime horse (female)

On 18 Aug 2005, Samantha Kavanagh and Melissa Archer (both UK, front and rear, respectively) completed a 100-m course inside their four-legged costume in 18.13 sec. They were racing at Harrow School in Middlesex, UK.

★ Largest simultaneous whoopee-cushion sit

On 6 Oct 2005, a total of 5,983 people filled the air with the sound of flatulence. The practical jokers let rip at the Catalyst Conference in Atlanta, Georgia, USA, where they beat the previous record by more than 1,600.

⌃ First film in digital 3D

The Walt Disney animation *Chicken Little* (USA, 2005) was shown in "Disney Digital 3-D" at 85 cinemas across the USA. It was the first mainstream release to be distributed in a digital stereographic 3D format, which required cinemas to upgrade to a digital projection system. As with traditional 3D screenings, cinema-goers were required to wear polarized glasses.

⌃ Most hurricanes in one year

In 2005, a record 15 hurricanes caused *c.* $170 bn (£98.8 bn) of damage and left more than 3,400 people dead across Mexico, the Caribbean and the Gulf States of the USA.

Worst affected was the Mississippi coast, and in particular the Louisiana city of New Orleans, 80% of which was flooded in just one day (29 Aug) as the storm surge resulting from Hurricane Katrina overwhelmed the levees (*pictured*). The National Hurricane Center attributed 1,836 fatalities to Katrina alone.

★ Most expensive poster

An original poster for Fritz Lang's groundbreaking sci-fi movie *Metropolis* (DEU, 1927) was sold by the Reel Poster Gallery in London, UK, to a US collector for $690,000 (£396,963) on 15 Nov 2005. The Art Deco poster was designed by Heinz Schulz-Neudamm and is one of only four copies known to exist.

★ Youngest winner of a BRIT award

Joss Stone (UK, b. 11 Apr 1987) was aged 17 years 304 days when she was honoured at the British Phonographic Industry's annual music awards on 9 Feb 2005. Stone won two categories: Best Female Solo Artist and Best Urban Act.

★ Youngest signed gamer

Lil Poison, aka Victor De Leon III (USA, b. 6 May 1998), was a mere six years old when he was signed by professional esports organization Major League Gaming. The precocious talent first picked up a controller aged two to play *NBA 2K*.

★ First woman to lead the Indianapolis 500

Danica Patrick (USA) made history at the 89th Indy 500 on 29 May 2005, sweeping into the lead on lap 56. Driving for Rahal Letterman Racing, Patrick led the race for a total of 19 laps, finishing in fourth place and winning the Indianapolis 500 Rookie of the Year award.

★ Youngest goalscorer in the English Premier League

James Vaughan (UK, b. 14 Jul 1988) was aged just 16 years 270 days when he scored for Everton during their 4–0 win against Crystal Palace on 10 Apr 2005 at Goodison Park on Merseyside, UK.

★ Fastest men's indoor 400 m

On 12 Mar 2005, Kerron Clement (USA, b. TTO) ran two laps of an indoor running track in 44.57 sec. The 19-year-old was competing for the University of Florida at the NCAA Division I Men's Indoor Track and Field Championships in Fayetteville, Arkansas, USA.

First digital track ⟫ to sell 1 million copies

In Oct 2005, "Hollaback Girl" by Gwen Stefani (USA) hit 1 million paid downloads in the USA.

The No Doubt singer teamed up with producers The Neptunes (Pharrell Williams and Chad Hugo) for the hip-hop smash, which featured on her solo album *Love. Angel. Music. Baby.*

Tina Ackles (USA) had the **most bridesmaids** at her wedding on 18 Apr 2015 – a total of 168!

In the last decade, Facebook celebrated its 1 billionth user and TikTok welcomed its first; Amazon turned 20 just as Jeff Bezos's net worth surpassed $200 bn; the Curiosity rover found water on Mars; and back here on Earth, a new generation of environmental activists found a champion in the Swedish teenager Greta Thunberg.

Most wool in a single shearing

On 3 Sep 2015, Chris – an errant overgrown sheep rescued by animal charity RSPCA ACT (AUS) – was shorn of 41.1 kg (90 lb 9.7 oz) of wool by Ian Elkins in Weston Creek, Australia.

Most car-crash tests

W R "Rusty" Haight (USA) has endured more than 1,000 automobile collisions in the course of his career as a teacher of accident investigation. The "crash reconstructionist" and his vehicle are fitted with sensors to gather data on the impact. Despite driving at speeds of up to 85 km/h (53 mph), his worst injury to date is a small cut from an airbag.

First skull-and-scalp transplant

Treatment for a rare form of cancer left James Boysen (USA) without the top of his skull. On 22 May 2015, he received partial skull and scalp grafts during a groundbreaking 15-hr operation at Houston Methodist Hospital in Texas, USA.

Youngest golfer ranked world No.1

Lydia Ko (NZ, b. KOR, 24 Apr 1997) reached the top of the Women's World Golf Rankings aged 17 years 284 days on 2 Feb 2015. Already the **youngest LPGA Tour winner** – aged 15 years 124 days, on 26 Aug 2012 – Ko went on to become the **youngest winner of a women's major**, aged 18 years 142 days, at the Evian Championship on 13 Sep 2015.

FACT
A hooping craze in 14th-century England left people suffering with exhaustion and heart failure!

Most hula hoops spun simultaneously

Marawa the Amazing, aka Marawa Ibrahim (AUS), kept 200 hoops moving for at least three spins in Los Angeles, California, USA, on 25 Nov 2015.

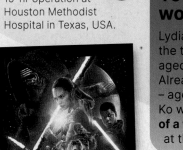

Highest-grossing *Star Wars* movie

With total worldwide box-office takings of $2,064,615,817 (£1.7 bn) according to The Numbers, *Star Wars: Episode VII – The Force Awakens* (USA, 2015) is the most lucrative instalment of the sci-fi franchise (and fifth-highest-grossing movie of all time).

Largest...

• **Sock monkey**: On 7 Feb 2015, Jody Lewis (UK) introduced the world to her homemade 3.19-m-tall (10-ft 5.6-in) stuffed toy in Bridgwater, Somerset, UK. She stitched together the hollow-fibre-filled simian from 66 pairs of socks.

• **TV remote control**: Brothers Suraj and Rajesh Kumar Meher (both IND) channel hop in record style using a 4.5-m-long (14-ft 9.1-in) controller, as measured in Odisha, India, on 21 Sep 2015.

• **Twister mat**: To promote the launch of his new album *Tangled Up*, country music star Thomas Rhett (USA) invited his fans to a game of Twister using a mat covering 2,521.01 m² (27,136 sq ft). The finished playing surface took up half of the AT&T Stadium pitch in Arlington, Texas, USA, on 23 Sep 2015.

Largest asteroid

Between 6 Mar 2015 and 31 Oct 2018, NASA's Dawn mission orbited 1 Ceres in the Asteroid Belt between the orbits of Mars and Jupiter. With an average diameter of 952 km (591 mi), 1 Ceres is massive enough to now also be classified as a dwarf planet.

> ## OUTSIZED INSECTS, MYRIAPODS AND ARACHNIDS

Largest ant: fulvous driver ant (*Dorylus fulvus*) – 5 cm (2 in) long

Largest centipede: giant centipede (*Scolopendra gigantea*) – 26 cm (10 in) long

Largest aquatic insect (length): giant water bug (*Lethocerus maximus*) – 11.5 cm (4.5 in) long

Largest spider: Goliath bird-eating tarantula (*Theraphosa blondi*) – 28 cm (11 in) leg span (*see also pp.12–13*)

Longest insect: *Phryganistria chinensis* – 64 cm (2 ft 1.2 in) outstretched

Longest beetle (body): titan beetle (*Titanus giganteus*) – 16.7 cm (6.5 in)

Largest aquatic insect (wingspan): *Acanthacorydalis fruhstorferi* dobsonfly – 21.6 cm (8.5 in)

First flyby of Pluto

On 14 Jul 2015, the *New Horizons* probe achieved its closest approach to Pluto during its flyby. It passed the minor planet 12,472 km (7,749 mi) from the surface, at a velocity of 49,600 km/h (30,820 mph). Just 10 days earlier, NASA had lost contact with the probe but reconnected in time for the flyby.

Most wins of the Ballon d'Or

In 2015, Argentinian striker Lionel Messi secured his status as the most celebrated recipient of soccer's "Golden Ball" trophy with his fifth win – two ahead of Cristiano Ronaldo. Messi would go on to win again in 2019, 2021 and 2023.

Tallest superhero cosplay costume

Iron Man's Hulkbuster suit – first seen on the big screen in *Avengers: Age of Ultron* (USA, 2015) – was brought to life in gigantic fashion by cosplay designer Thomas DePetrillo (USA). First unveiled at New York Comic Con in Oct 2015, it stands an impressive 8 ft (2.44 m) tall and is fully articulated.

Longest-reigning queen

As of 5:30 p.m. on 9 Sep 2015, Her Majesty Queen Elizabeth II (UK) – who succeeded to the throne on 6 Feb 1952 following the death of her father, King George VI – had reigned for 23,226 days, 16 hr and *c*. 30 min, surpassing the reign of her great-great-grandmother Queen Victoria. She would remain on the throne until her death on 8 Sep 2022 – an uninterrupted reign of a record 70 years 214 days.

Most individual points in an NBA quarter

Klay Thompson (USA) of the Golden State Warriors dropped 37 points against the Sacramento Kings

Most balloons blown up in one hour

Hunter Ewen (USA) overcame his long-time globophobia by inflating 910 party balloons in 60 min in Allenspark, Colorado, USA, on 4 Sep 2015. "Part of the reason I wanted to attempt this record comes from my childhood fear of balloons," he said. "I didn't blow up a balloon for 15 years and I thought this might be a fun way to get over that fear."

Youngest male solo artist to debut at No.1 on the Hot 100

Canadian pop superstar Justin Bieber (b. 1 Mar 1994) was just 21 years 202 days old when "What Do You Mean?" – the first single from his fourth studio album – debuted at No.1 on the *Billboard* Hot 100 on 19 Sep 2015. Bieber has enjoyed a superlative career at the top of the charts, and since 2010 has broken more than 40 GWR titles – 18 of which he still currently holds.

during the third quarter of their clash on 23 Jan 2015. He went a perfect 13-for-13 from the field, 9-for-9 from beyond the three-point line and 2-for-2 from the free-throw line. His nine field goals from behind the arc also broke the NBA record for **most three-point baskets in a quarter**. The Warriors won 126–101.

Oldest competitive sprinter

Hidekichi Miyazaki (JPN, b. 22 Sep 1910) was 105 years 1 day old when he competed in the Kyoto Masters Athletics Autumn Competition in Japan on 23 Sep 2015. Miyazaki – known as the "Golden Bolt" – ran 100 m in 42.22 sec.

 ## Bearing fruit

On 2 Jan 2015, science teacher Dinesh Shivnath Upadhyaya (IND) broke the record for the **most grapes eaten in three minutes**, wolfing down 205 in short order. He has since focused on more fruity feats, earning himself GWR certificates for the **fastest time to peel and eat three oranges** (1 min 7.94 sec) and the **most grapes stuffed in the mouth** (94).

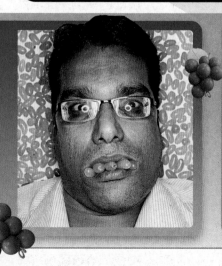

Small town, **big ambitions**

The **largest mailbox** (internal volume: 162.63 m³; 5,743.22 cu ft) is just one of the record-breaking roadside attractions you'll find in Casey, Illinois, USA (population: 2,376). During a visit there in 2015, we found – among other things – the **largest pitchfork** (length: 18.65 m; 61 ft 2 in), the **largest rocking chair** (height: 17.09 m; 56 ft 1 in) and the **largest clogs** (length: 3.5 m; 11 ft 5 in).

The 19th annual day dedicated to record breaking took place on 16 Nov 2023. In a bid to earn GWR glory, people from around the world took on an array of challenges centred on the theme of "super skills". Their dazzling (and varied!) feats just go to show that, whatever your passion or skill, there's a record out there with your name on it.

Zhou Quan (CHN) performed the **most consecutive single-leg full-twist back somersaults** – 11 – in front of the Wuling Pavilion in his hometown of Chenzhou in Hunan, China. Zhou is a world champion in "tricking", which combines moves from martial arts, gymnastics and capoeira.

In Abu Dhabi, UAE, fire artist Sara Spadoni (ITA) blazed into the record books with the women's title for **highest flame blown** – 5.4 m (17 ft 8 in). Sara, a trained rhythmic gymnast, also set a record for the **most fire hoops spun while in the splits position** – four. *Check out more pyro feats on pp.112–13.*

Christian Rodríguez (ESP) ran the **fastest mile controlling a table-tennis ball** – 6 min 4.41 sec – in Toledo, Spain (*left*). He added to his impressive portfolio of sporty GWR titles by setting a new benchmark for the **fastest mile dribbling a basketball** – 4 min 23.32 sec (*right*).

In Karachi, Pakistan, Muhammad Rashid (PAK) racked up the **most green coconuts smashed with the head in one minute** – 43. The black-belt martial artist is a serial record breaker who uses his head, hands and elbows to dispatch everything from pencils and walnuts to bottle caps.

Germany's most prolific record setter André Ortolf (*right*) teamed up with countryman Tobias Wittmeir to assemble the **most tacos in one minute (team of two)** – 17. The duo prepared their Mexican *fast* food in the village of Langweid am Lech in Germany.

In Saitama, Japan, Masakazu Hashimoto and Nene Kaneko (both JPN) completed the **most consecutive Double Dutch-style handstand skips (team of two)** – 32. Masakazu is Nenc's Double Dutch teacher and is part of the pro skipping team Capliore.

GWR's Editor-in-Chief Craig Glenday visited the UK's Silverstone circuit to bear witness to the **tightest gap driven through by a pick-up truck on side wheels**. Paul Swift (UK) guided his 2.7-tonne (2.9-ton) Ford Raptor through a space just 88 cm (2 ft 10 in) wider than the height of the vehicle. Breathe in!

In 2022, Paul executed the tightest parallel park by electric car – a clearance of just 30 cm (11.8 in)!

In Chennai, India, a pair of precocious gymnasts claimed one-minute GWR titles. Aadhav Sugumar (IND, *left*) performed the **most hula-hoop rotations around the neck on a balance board** – 153. Myra Chetan Pophale (IND, *above*) completed the **most hula-hoop rotations around the neck while in the splits position** – 158.

Henry Cabelus (USA) bounced his way to the **highest backflip pogo-stick jump**, soaring over a 3.07-m-tall (10-ft 1-in) bar in Pittsburgh, Pennsylvania, USA. Henry went up against his Xpogo teammate Michael Mena (USA) to take on this long-standing record, which had remained at 2.82 m (9 ft 3 in) since it was set by Curt Markwardt (USA) in 2012. Up first was Michael, who beat the record with a 2.92-m (9-ft 7-in) jump; his triumph was short-lived, though, as Henry followed up with an even higher bounce, beating Michael's mark by 15 cm (5.9 in).

In Tokyo, Japan, Yu-dama – aka Yutaro Fukushima (JPN) – achieved three world records using traditional cup-and-ball toys, known as kendamas. They included the **most consecutive catches**, using his specially modified 10-cup kendama – he landed all 10 balls 17 times in a row.

25

ICON

Robert Wadlow

Who better to introduce the Guinness World Records ICONS project than arguably the most iconic record holder of them all? Robert Pershing Wadlow: the tallest human who has ever lived.

In looking to celebrate those record holders who most embody the spirit of GWR – individuals who have achieved significant firsts, made pioneering strides forward in their chosen field, or who've left an indelible impression on society – the selection committee was unanimous in naming Bob Wadlow as their first choice. Throughout this year's edition, you'll find profiles on a number of GWR ICONS, but none whose record is as instantly identifiable as the tallest man of all time.

Wadlow was born on 22 Feb 1918 in Alton, Illinois, USA, weighing a typical 8 lb 5 oz (3.8 kg). However, it took just eight years for Bob to surpass his father's height of 5 ft 11 in (180.3 cm). The cause of his rapid growth spurt was diagnosed as hypertrophy (enlargement) of his pituitary gland – the organ in the brain that regulates the production of growth hormone. With surgery too risky, Bob continued to grow, peaking at 8 ft 11 in (272 cm).

A quiet young man, Bob eschewed a life on the stage; he toured briefly with the Ringling Bros. Circus in 1936, but refused to dress up in a top hat and tails, like his predecessor, Albert Kramer (see pp.62–63). He soon left and took to the road as a promoter for the International Shoe Company. It was while on a trip to Michigan that the leg brace he needed to wear rubbed at his ankle, resulting in a blister that became infected. Despite doctors' best efforts, the infection spread and Bob died in his sleep on 15 Jul 1940 at the age of just 22 years old.

Wadlow's resilience and dignity in the face of adversity has captivated every new generation who reads his story. And the archival photography documenting his tragically short life provides a lasting legacy celebrating this iconic individual.

VITAL STATISTICS

Name	Robert Pershing Wadlow
Birthplace	Alton, Illinois, USA
Nickname	The Alton Giant
Current GWR titles	Tallest person ever Tallest teenager ever Largest hands ever Largest feet ever
Height	8 ft 11.1 in (272 cm)
Weight	491 lb (223 kg)
Hand size	12.75 in (32.3 cm) from wrist to middle fingertip
Shoe size	USA: 37 AA (UK: 36, Europe: 75)

Bob was the eldest of five children. This family snap shows the 18-year-old with (*left to right*) his brother Eugene (14), mother Addie, youngest brother Harold Jr (4), sister Betty (12), father Harold and sister Helen (15).

In 1936, Bob achieved celebrity status when he signed to the Ringling Bros. Circus. He's pictured here recreating a scene from *Gulliver's Travels* with a troupe of short-stature performers.

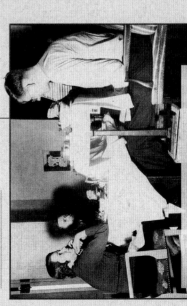

The Wadlows adapted their home to accommodate their supersized son. Here, Bob dines with his family from the comfort of a specially made chair and a raised side table.

Bob at the age of 13, comparing shoe sizes with an adult man of average height. He made more than 800 appearances – and covered c. 300,000 mi (482,800 km) – as an ambassador for the International Shoe Company. In return, he received free footwear; each pair cost around $100 at the time – the equivalent today of $2,200 (£1,800).

According to the Hartmann's clothing store in Alton, it took nine yards (27 ft; 8.22 m) of fabric to make Bob a suit. Here, two employees – Walter Hanlon (*left*) and store manager Carl Hartmann – hold aloft a pair of Bob's newly cut titanic trousers.

At just 10 years old – and standing 6 ft 6 in (198.1 cm) – Bob was already taller than his father (*right*). The Alton Giant never stopped growing, becoming the **tallest person of all time** in 1939 when he surpassed fellow American John "Bud" Rogan (1868–1905, *see pp.62–63*).

Find out more about Robert in the ICON section at www.guinnessworldrecords.com/2025

The giant padma is a national plant of Indonesia, along with white jasmine and the moon orchid.

CONTENTS

The Oxford Botanic Garden's Chris Thorogood went on a hunt for *Rafflesia* in 2022 as part of a drive to protect them.

LARGEST FLOWER

No single flowers grow bigger than those of the parasitic plant *Rafflesia arnoldii*, aka the giant padma. One specimen – recorded in the tropical rainforest of West Sumatra, Indonesia, in Jan 2020 – spanned 111 cm (3 ft 7.7 in), twice the width of a typical bicycle wheel. Their superlative size is not the only noteworthy thing about these blooms: they also emit a foul odour likened to rotting meat, hence their nickname "corpse lilies". Drawn to the stench, carrion flies enter the inner chamber (*right*) and unwittingly transfer pollen as they go. All 40 or so species of *Rafflesia* are deemed at high risk owing to habitat degradation.

29

Largest Animals Ever

The very **first life-forms** – marine bacteria that emerged *c.* 3.5 billion years ago – were just a few micrometres long. With no rivals, they were nevertheless the biggest organisms of their day. Slowly but surely, those tiny creatures would evolve into mind-bogglingly colossal megafauna. Here, we spotlight some of the most prodigious beasts of their eras, on land and in water, culminating with the **largest animal** alive today.

Pneumodesmus newmani (428 million years ago [MYA]) This mini millipede is the **earliest land animal**, so by default was also the biggest terrestrial beast of its time – despite being a mere 1 cm (0.4 in) long!

Basal synapsids (308–252 MYA) These carnivorous tetrapods, exemplified by the 4.5-m-long (15-ft) sail-backed *Dimetrodon*, were the largest land animals until the Permian-Triassic extinction event. Despite a reptilian appearance, they were, in fact, the precursor to mammals.

Riojasaurus (228–208.5 MYA) A herbivorous sauropodomorph measuring 6.6–10 m (22–33 ft) in length and weighing up to 1 tonne (1.1 ton), this was among the biggest dinosaurs living in the Triassic. By the Jurassic period, its descendants would have scaled up to be giant sauropods, such as *Brontosaurus* and *Diplodocus* – then later the next-level titanosaurs (*see right*).

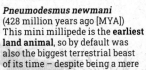

Arthropleura armata (345–295 MYA) Millipedes weren't always mini-beasts like *P. newmani* (*above*). This 2.6-m-long (8-ft 6-in) bug – 10 times heavier than a domestic cat – was the **largest arthropod ever**.

Prionosuchus plummeri (299–272 MYA) This croc-fish-blend creature of the Early Permian was actually a temnospondyl, a primitive group of amphibious tetrapods. Up to 9 m (30 ft) long, it represents the **largest amphibian ever** – five times the size of its extant counterpart (*see p.41*).

Tiktaalik roseae (375 MYA) Among the first vertebrates to transition from water to land, this species – the **earliest land-walking fish** – measured up to 2.75 m (9 ft).

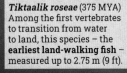

Aegirocassis benmoulai (480 MYA) Double the size of the next biggest animal in the Early Ordovician, at 2 m (6 ft 6 in), this radiodont arthropod was the **first giant filter feeder**.

Edestus scissor-tooth sharks (313–307 MYA) So named for their saw-blade-like gnashers, these 6.7-m-long (22-ft) sharks were the apex predators of the Carboniferous seas.

Albertonectes vanderveldei (83.5–70.6 MYA) While not the bulkiest plesiosaur, this Cretaceous marine reptile did boast one superlatively sized feature. Its 7-m (23-ft) neck, with 76 vertebrae, makes it the **longest-necked animal ever** (based on neckbone count). Humans have a mere seven cervical vertebrae.

Dickinsonia (558 MYA) Reaching 1.4 m (4 ft 7 in) long, these soft-bodied, shallow-water dwellers are the **oldest animal megafossils** (creatures visible without a microscope).

Jaekelopterus rhenaniae (460–255 MYA) Devonian-era sea scorpions (eurypterids) are among the largest arthropods of all time, growing up to 2.5 m (8 ft 2 in) – close to the size of *Arthropleura* (*above*).

Triassic ichthyosaurs (237–202 MYA) Some of these dolphin-like predators could be longer than a bowling alley, making them the **largest marine reptiles ever**. One species, named *Ichthyotitan severnensis* in Apr 2024, is estimated to have measured 25–26 m (82–85 ft) based on its jawbone.

Spinosaurus (99–93.5 MYA)
Forget *T. rex* – this meat-eating predecessor was 4 m (13 ft) longer, making it the **largest carnivorous dinosaur**. It reached up to 17 m (56 ft) nose to tail and weighed *c.* 9 tonnes (9.9 tons) – the equivalent of 18 polar bears (*Ursus maritimus*), which are today's **largest terrestrial carnivores**.

Sarcosuchus (110 MYA)
The forebears of today's biggest crocs (*see p.39*) were more than double their average size at *c.* 12 m (40 ft). The prehistoric caiman *Purussaurus* attained similar lengths, so is also in contention to be the **largest crocodyliform ever**.

Titanosaurs (140–66 MYA)
Although there is as yet no consensus as to which was the **largest dinosaur**, all experts agree it was a sauropod. This group of gargantuan reptiles – the **tallest**, **longest** and **heaviest land animals ever** to walk on Earth – are typified by titanosaurs such as *Argentinosaurus*, *Bruhathkayosaurus* and *Patagotitan*, though there are other candidates such as the diplodocoid *Maraapunisaurus*.

Based on fossilized bones – some bigger than humans! – these behemoths grew to at least 30–40 m (98–131 ft) long and weighed conservatively 50–75 tonnes (55–83 tons), akin to between four and six double-decker buses. Admittedly, with skeletal remains varying in completeness, comparisons are tricky. New bones and also new ways to interpret them are coming to light all the time, however it's unlikely that any land animal will ever emerge to surpass the superlative sauropods.

In 2023, new research posited that some "super sauropods" may even have rivalled the blue whale in mass!

Otodus megalodon (23–3.6 MYA)
At 18–20 m (59–65 ft) – about three times the length of the largest great whites (*see p.36*) – the "Meg" was easily the **largest shark ever**. It could well be the all-time **largest fish** too.

Perucetus colossus (40–38 MYA)
Reported in Aug 2023, this early form of cetacean has already made a big splash, being pitched as the **heaviest animal ever**, with a weight range of 85–340 tonnes (94–375 tons). Although several metres shorter than a typical blue whale (*right*) – the long-uncontested holder of this title – *Perucetus*'s bones are thought to have been much denser. Some have contested such a high mass estimate, though.

Balaenoptera musculus (1.5 MYA–present)
No animal alive comes close in scale to a blue whale. Adults average 25 m (82 ft) and 160 tonnes (176 tons), dwarfing today's **largest land animal**: the African elephant (*Loxodonta africana*) at 5.5 tonnes (6 tons).

The all-time largest specimen, measured in 1909, was a 33.57-m (110-ft 1-in) female – longer than a basketball court. Although no weight was logged for her, a 27.6-m (90-ft 6-in) female found in 1947 was 190 tonnes (209 tons). These supersized cetaceans have long been deemed the **largest animal ever** to live on our planet, though recently a few extinct rivals for the title have emerged (*see left and above*)...

Mammals

Earliest mammal

The oldest mammal currently known to science is *Brasilodon quadrangularis*, which existed 225.42 million years ago, during the Late Triassic, in what is now Brazil. Presently identified from fossilized teeth, skull and bone samples, it is believed to have been a small shrew-like creature that measured 12–20 cm (4.7–7.9 in), and probably ate insects. It was formally described in the *Journal of Anatomy* on 5 Sep 2022.

Largest order of mammals

Of the 6,500 or so known mammal species, rodents (Rodentia) comprise around 2,552, or 39%. Of these, 834 (13%) fall into the sub-group of Muridae (true rats and mice), making them the **largest mammal family**.

Longest tongue for a land mammal

The licker of the giant anteater (*Myrmecophaga tridactyla*) can reach 61 cm (2 ft) – about one-third of the animal's total body length. Covered in super-sticky saliva and hooked bumps (papillae), the tongue nimbly infiltrates the nests of ants and termites in Central and South America. In a day, an anteater can eat 30,000 insects!

Tallest animal

Giraffes (*Giraffa camelopardalis*) stand head and shoulders above all other living creatures, reaching 4.6–5.5 m (15–18 ft) from hoof to horn tips (ossicones). Found across savannah and woodland in sub-Saharan Africa, their numbers have dropped by 30% since the 1980s, owing largely to habitat loss and illegal hunting.

Farthest head rotation by a mammal

Owing to their spinal morphology, tarsiers (Tarsiidae) – arboreal primates from south-east Asia – are able to twist their heads nearly 180° in each direction. The Philippine tarsier (*Carlito syrichta*; *pictured*) boasts the **largest mammal eyes relative to body size**. Its 16-mm-wide (0.6-in) eyeballs are akin to a human having eyes the size of grapefruits!

Only one other animal can turn heads to a greater extent than the tarsier (find out which one on p.34).

Smallest mammal (mass)

The Etruscan shrew (*Suncus etruscus*), of the Mediterranean region and southern Asia, is the most minute mammal by mass. The thumb-sized rodent averages 1.8 g (0.06 oz) – 20 times lighter than a mouse.

Highest-living mammal

A *Phyllotis vaccarum* leaf-eared mouse was collected at the top of Volcán Llullaillaco on the Chile/Argentina border, 6,739 m (22,110 ft) above sea level, in Feb 2020. The record was logged in the *Journal of Mammalogy* on 5 Apr 2022.

Deepest dive by a mammal

The greatest depth plunged to by a mammal is 2,992 m (9,816 ft), by a Cuvier's beaked whale (*Ziphius cavirostris*) in 2013. The record descent – almost 12 times greater than the deepest human freedive – took place off California, USA.

Fastest pinniped

California sea lions (*Zalophus californianus*) can cut through the water at 40 km/h (25 mph) in short bursts – faster than a galloping horse. They are not the **fastest marine mammal** overall, though: that title goes to the orca (*Orcinus orca*), aka killer whale, with a male clocked at 55.5 km/h (34.5 mph) on 12 Oct 1958.

Fastest mammal in flight

In Texas, USA, in 2009, Brazilian free-tailed bats (*Tadarida brasiliensis*) fitted with radio transmitters were clocked flying for short bursts at a ground speed of 44.5 m/s (160.2 km/h; 99.5 mph). This means these bats potentially rival the fastest birds in level flight.

Texas is, in fact, home to the world's **largest bat colony**: an estimated 15 million free-tailed bats often congregate in Bracken Cave, near the city of San Antonio.

The state also once hosted the **largest mammal colony** outright. In 1901, American zoologist and ecologist C H Merriam found a prairie dog "town" that spanned an area of 65,000 km² (25,100 sq mi) – almost the size of Ireland – in west Texas. It was estimated to be home to more than 400 million black-tailed prairie dogs (*Cynomys ludovicianus*).

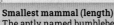

Smallest mammal (length)

The aptly named bumblebee bat (*Craseonycteris thonglongyai*) is 3 cm (1.2 in) long and weighs about 2 g (0.07 oz). It's native to caves in Thailand and Myanmar.

Largest land mammal

Adult male bush elephants (*Loxodonta africana*) from sub-Saharan Africa average 5.5 tonnes (6 tons) and up to 3.7 m (12 ft 1 in) to the shoulder.

Largest mammal

Widely regarded as the **largest animal ever** (see pp.30–31), a typical blue whale (*Balaenoptera musculus*) is 25 m (82 ft) long and c. 160 tonnes (176 tons).

LARGEST WILD CAT

Apocryphally, the lion is known as the "king of the jungle", but the title really ought to go to its Asian counterpart: the Siberian or Amur tiger (*Panthera tigris altaica*). (Though, of course, neither of these big cats technically lives in the jungle!) An inhabitant of mountain forests in eastern Russia, northern China and North Korea, the biggest tigers can reach 3.3 m (10 ft 9 in) from nose to tail tip and top 300 kg (660 lb) – about the same weight as 70 domestic moggies!

To withstand colder climes, this northerly subspecies of tiger has denser fur, a mane and a thick layer of fat.

Smallest wild cat

At the other end of the feline scale is the rusty-spotted cat (*Prionailurus rubiginosus*) of south India and Sri Lanka. It can measure as little as 50 cm (1 ft 7 in) long – tail included – with adults weighing one-third that of a typical pet cat. A close contender for this tiny crown is the black-footed cat (*Felis nigripes*) of southern Africa.

Oldest mammal
Several specimens of bowhead whale (*Balaena mysticetus*) have been assessed to be centenarians. One was even calculated to be 211 years old!

Slowest mammal
Three-toed sloths (*Bradypus tridactylus*) like to live in the slow lane: their peak speed while on the ground is 2.4 m (8 ft) per minute (0.14 km/h; 0.09 mph).

Fastest land mammal
Over short distances, the cheetah (*Acinonyx jubatus*) is the top mammalian sprinter, with registered speeds of 28.7 m/s (103.5 km/h; 64.3 mph) in 1965.

Birds

First bird

It's generally agreed among ornithologists that all of today's birds, from majestic eagles to the humble house sparrow, descend from theropod dinosaurs. The question of *when* precisely that evolutionary split occurred is more debatable.

The earliest undisputed bird is *Archaeopteryx lithographica*, a 153-million-year-old crow-sized avian unearthed from Jurassic sediments near Solnhofen, Germany. There is an older contender called *Protoavis texensis*, which was found in 220-million-year-old rocks in Texas, USA. However, many palaeontologists are sceptical that its remains represent a true bird, or even necessarily a single animal.

Largest bird ever

Vorombe titan, the largest of Madagascar's extinct elephant birds, was a towering 3 m (9 ft 10 in) tall. These giants, which died out *c.* 1,000 years ago, weighed as much as 860 kg (1,895 lb); that's more than five times the mass of today's **largest bird** (*see opposite*).

Largest order of birds

By far and away the most diverse taxonomic avian group is Passeriformes (perching, or sparrow-like, birds), hosting 6,533 species. This equates to around 58% of all birds.

They include the **largest family of birds**: the tyrant flycatchers (Tyrannidae) native to the Americas, with 450 species (4% of all birds).

Highest-living bird

The alpine chough (*Pyrrhocorax graculus*), a species of red-legged crow (corvid), habitually breeds at altitudes of 6,500 m (21,325 ft) in the Himalayas, but specimens have been sighted by mountaineers scavenging as far up as 8,235 m (27,018 ft).

The **highest-flying bird**, meanwhile, is a Rüppell's vulture (*Gyps rueppellii*) that collided with an aircraft at 11,300 m (37,000 ft) over the Ivory Coast on 29 Nov 1973.

Longest beak

The bill of an Australian pelican (*Pelecanus conspicillatus*) stretches up to 47 cm (1 ft 6 in), akin to a human newborn.

Greatest avian mimic

The marsh warbler (*Acrocephalus palustris*) is capable of imitating the songs of more than 80 other species of bird.

Greatest head rotation by an animal

No group of animals can twist their heads farther than owls (Strigiformes). Some species have a range of 270° in each direction! This is made possible by additional neck vertebrae (14, compared with seven in humans), as well as the size, structure and position of their carotid arteries, so blood supply to the brain doesn't get cut off.

Largest pigeon species

The Victoria crowned pigeon (*Goura victoria*) of New Guinea can exceed 80 cm (2 ft 7.5 in) long from beak to tail and weigh *c.* 3.5 kg (7 lb 11 oz). This is around 10 times heavier than a common pigeon (*Columba livia*). These birds – along with three related species – are distinguished by the "crown" of lace-like feathers on their heads.

Deepest-diving bird

The emperor penguin (*Aptenodytes forsteri*) – today's **largest penguin species** at up to 1.3 m (4 ft 3 in) tall – is the most accomplished avian diver. It can attain depths of 564 m (1,850 ft) while hunting fish off Antarctica, and can remain submerged on a single breath for over 32 min, also making it the **longest-diving bird**.

Oldest wild bird

A Laysan albatross or mōlī (*Phoebastria immutabilis*) named Wisdom was *c.* 73 years old as of 2024. She was ringed at the age of at least five on the Midway Atoll in the Pacific Ocean in 1956. Still returning there to breed, she has laid around 40 eggs and reared some 30 chicks over her lifetime.

Loudest bird

Calls of male white bellbirds (*Procnias albus*) have been recorded at 125.4 dB during courtship displays. They live in northern South America.

Fastest bird in flight

In ideal conditions, during a stoop (dive), the peregrine falcon (*Falco peregrinus*) can attain a terminal velocity of at least 320 km/h (200 mph).

Smallest bird

Bee hummingbirds (*Mellisuga helenae*) of Cuba can measure 57 mm (2.24 in) in total length – half of which is bill and tail. They weigh *c.* 1.6 g (0.056 oz).

Its beak is so long that the swordbill has had to find another way to preen its feathers: using its feet!

MOST BIRD SPECIES (COUNTRY)

According to BirdLife International, Colombia plays host to 1,866 species of bird – 16.7% of the 11,188 global total as of Oct 2023. Prominent groups include toucans, such as the keel-billed toucan (*Ramphastos sulfuratus*, *above*), hummingbirds (*left*), trogons, tanagers, owls, antbirds, vultures (*below*), ovenbirds, herons and woodpeckers. Its bonanza of bird biodiversity places it just ahead of two of its neighbours: Peru (with 1,860 species) and Brazil (1,816). Not surprisingly, South America as a whole boasts the **most bird species (continent)**: 3,557.

Longest beak (relative to body size)

An inhabitant of cloud forests in the Andes, the sword-billed hummingbird (*Ensifera ensifera*) is the only bird whose bill can exceed its body length! It can reach 12 cm (4.7 in), akin to a ballpoint pen. This behemoth beak enables it to reach the nectar in tube-shaped flowers, such as those of *Passiflora mixta*.

Heaviest bird of prey

Among the 500 or so bird of prey species, the Andean condor (*Vultur gryphus*) looms large over all its raptor rivals. Adult males average 9–12 kg (20–27 lb), with wings longer than ironing boards – a total span in excess of 3 m (9 ft 10 in). Riding mountain thermals, these vultures glide over vast distances in search of carrion, including the carcasses of deer, llamas and sheep.

Oldest bird
Cookie – a Major Mitchell's cockatoo (*Cacatua leadbeateri*) at Brookfield Zoo in Illinois, USA – was 82 years 89 days old when he died on 27 Aug 2016.

Largest wingspan
Among extant species, the wandering albatross (*Diomedea exulans*) is the wing king. Tip to tip, the wings of a male specimen in 1965 were 3.63 m (11 ft 11 in).

Largest bird
Birds don't get any bigger today than Africa's ostrich (*Struthio camelus*) at 2.74 m (9 ft) tall. Its 0.9-m (3-ft) neck and 5-cm-wide (2-in) eyes are also avian records.

Fish

100%

Smallest seahorse
Fully grown, Satomi's pygmy seahorses (*Hippocampus satomiae*) have an average length of 13.8 mm (0.5 in) from snout to tail tip – small enough to fit on a fingernail. Seahorses (Syngnathidae) are the **slowest fish**. Smaller species, such as the Satomi's, can't exceed 0.016 km/h (0.001 mph); that's 7 sec to move an inch.
The **largest seahorse** is the pot-bellied seahorse (*H. abdominalis*) of Australasian waters, which grows to 35 cm (1 ft 2 in).

First fish
In 1999, two fossilized fish species dating back c. 530 million years were discovered near Kunming in Yunnan, China. *Haikouichthys ercaicunensis* and *Myllokunmingia fengjiaoa* were jawless chordates (a group that includes all vertebrates). They were around 50 million years earlier than fish were previously thought to have evolved.

Largest order of fish
As of Oct 2023, Cypriniformes (goldfish-like fishes) had 4,825 species (14% of all fish). Almost all of them live in fresh water, including tenches, minnows and loaches. The order contains the **largest family of fish**, Cyprinidae, with 1,790 species such as carps and barbels.

Most venomous fish
Stonefish (*Synanceia*) possess up to 15 dorsal spines, each with two sacs containing 5–10 mg of venom. The estuarine stonefish (*S. horrida*) has venom that can cause the highest levels of pain known to be delivered by any fish. It lives in muddy bays and reefs around China, south-east Asia and Australia.

Largest fish colony
In Feb 2021, a research team discovered a breeding ground of Jonah's icefish (*Neopagetopsis ionah*) on the seafloor under an ice shelf in the southern Weddell Sea, near Antarctica. The colony covers at least 240 km² (93 sq mi) – larger than Washington, DC – and is thought to have more than 60 million active nests. Each nest comprises one adult fish and 1,500–2,000 eggs, giving an estimated 100 billion eggs in this single mega-colony.

Most electric animal
Electrophorus voltai, a species of electric eel or poraquê native to rivers in northern Brazil, can discharge 860 volts – enough to stun a human. These fish produce electricity by means of three dedicated paired organs along their elongated bodies.

Smallest natural range for a vertebrate
The Devils Hole pupfish (*Cyprinodon diabolis*) is endemic to the eponymous water-filled chasm in the Amargosa Desert, Nevada, USA. The pool's surface is just 3.5 x 22 m (11 x 72 ft) and the pupfish venture no deeper than 24 m (80 ft).

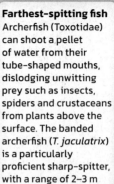

Farthest-spitting fish
Archerfish (Toxotidae) can shoot a pellet of water from their tube-shaped mouths, dislodging unwitting prey such as insects, spiders and crustaceans from plants above the surface. The banded archerfish (*T. jaculatrix*) is a particularly proficient sharp-spitter, with a range of 2–3 m (6 ft 6 in–9 ft 10 in).

Fastest fish
During speed trials, a sailfish (*Istiophorus platypterus*) in Florida, USA, is said to have taken out 300 ft (91 m) of line in 3 sec, which was equated to a velocity of 68 mph (109 km/h). Under natural conditions, it is far more difficult to assess fish swimming speed. In more recent studies, bluefin tuna (*Thunnus thynnus*) have asserted a claim to this title, logging a g-force acceleration of 3.27 *g*, compared with a peak of 1.79 *g* for sailfish. For context, astronauts experience 3 *g* during a rocket launch.

Shortest-lived fish
The seven-figure pygmy goby (*Eviota sigillata*) lives for no more than 59 days – c. 2,400 times briefer than the **longest-lived fish** (*see opposite*).

Largest predatory fish
Great white sharks (*Carcharodon carcharias*) average 4.3–4.6 m (14–15 ft) long, and weigh some 520–770 kg (1,150–1,700 lb). As of 2022, the largest-known living specimen is "Deep Blue", a female estimated to be 6.1 m (20 ft) long and weigh more than 2 tonnes (4,400 lb). She was first filmed off Guadalupe Island, Mexico, in 2014.

Heaviest bony fish
Sunfish (*Mola*) average c. 1,000 kg (2,200 lb). One bump-head sunfish (*M. alexandrini*) caught in 2021 weighed 2,744 kg (6,049 lb).

Largest fish
Whale sharks (*Rhincodon typus*) grow 9–12 m (29–39 ft) long. In 2001, one exceptional 18.8-m (61-ft 8-in) female was logged in the Arabian Sea.

Smallest fish
Just 6.2 mm (0.24 in) long, male *Photocorynus spiniceps* anglerfish latch on to females (which are significantly larger) to mate, then remain for life!

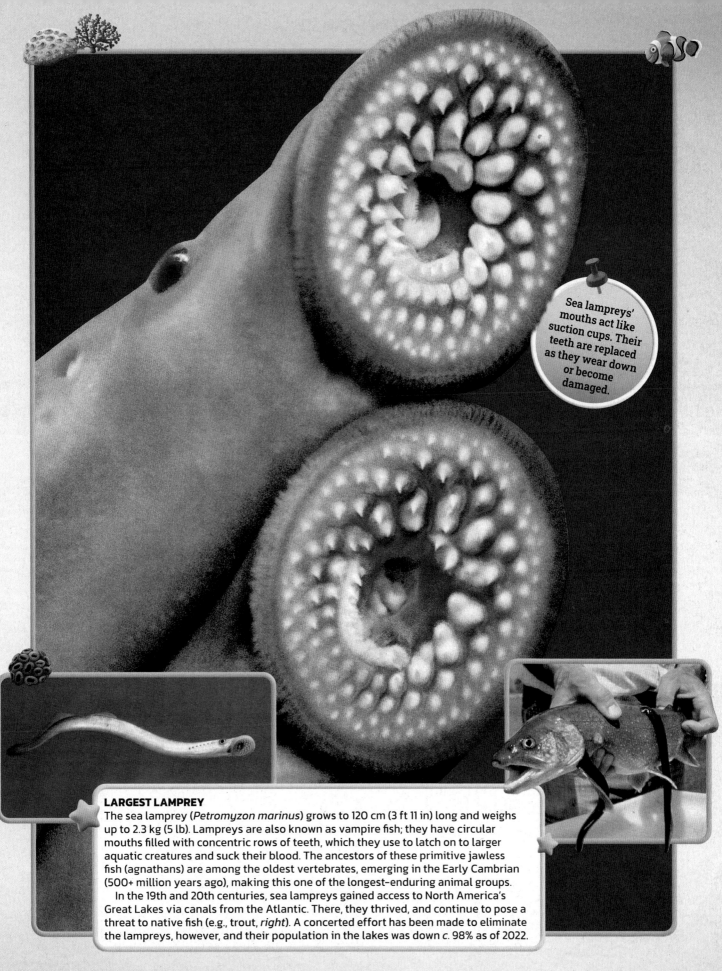

> Sea lampreys' mouths act like suction cups. Their teeth are replaced as they wear down or become damaged.

LARGEST LAMPREY

The sea lamprey (*Petromyzon marinus*) grows to 120 cm (3 ft 11 in) long and weighs up to 2.3 kg (5 lb). Lampreys are also known as vampire fish; they have circular mouths filled with concentric rows of teeth, which they use to latch on to larger aquatic creatures and suck their blood. The ancestors of these primitive jawless fish (agnathans) are among the oldest vertebrates, emerging in the Early Cambrian (500+ million years ago), making this one of the longest-enduring animal groups.

In the 19th and 20th centuries, sea lampreys gained access to North America's Great Lakes via canals from the Atlantic. There, they thrived, and continue to pose a threat to native fish (e.g., trout, *right*). A concerted effort has been made to eliminate the lampreys, however, and their population in the lakes was down *c.* 98% as of 2022.

Largest freshwater fish
A giant freshwater stingray (*Urogymnus polylepis*) found in Cambodia in 2022 weighed *c.* 300 kg (661 lb). It was 3.98 m (13 ft) long, including tail.

Deepest fish
Pseudoliparis snailfish dwell as deep as 8,336 m (27,349 ft) within trenches in the Pacific Ocean. That's 94% the vertical extent of the **highest mountain**, Everest.

Longest-lived fish
Living for up to 392 years (and perhaps longer), the Greenland shark (*Somniosus microcephalus*) is also the **longest-lived vertebrate**.

Reptiles

Earliest reptile

Animal tracks dating back 315 million years to the Carboniferous period have been discovered in sea cliffs on Canada's Bay of Fundy. Prints clearly show five digits and the presence of scales, marking them as those of a reptile. Although their creator has not been universally agreed upon, they are widely attributed to the lizard-like *Hylonomus* ("forest dweller").

Largest order of reptiles

As of Oct 2023, Squamata included 11,671 from a total of 12,060 reptile species. It comprises all lizards, snakes and worm lizards.

The **largest family of reptiles** is Colubridae, with 2,105 species across 249 genera. This worldwide, largely non-venomous group includes corn snakes and grass snakes.

Heaviest reptile

The saltwater crocodile (*Crocodylus porosus*, *see opposite*) of south-east Asia and northern Australia can weigh 1,200 kg (2,645 lb) – more than two grand pianos.

Deepest dive by a reptile

On 16 Dec 2006, a satellite-tagged leatherback turtle (*Dermochelys coriacea*) plunged to 1,280 m (4,199 ft) – four times the human scuba dive record – off Cape Verde in the Atlantic Ocean.

Fastest reptile on land

In tests conducted on a special "lizard racetrack" at the University of California, a Costa Rican spiny-tailed iguana (*Ctenosaura similis*) was clocked at 34.9 km/h (21.7 mph).

Most venomous terrestrial snake

Just 1 mg of venom (about one-third of a sesame seed) from an inland taipan (*Oxyuranus microlepidotus*) is enough to kill a person. Native to Queensland, Australia, this serpent mainly hunts rats, so has evolved extra-potent venom to dispatch them quickly in order to avoid injury. No human fatalities have been documented.

Fastest-evolving animal

The tuatara (*Sphenodon punctatus*) is a reptile endemic to New Zealand; its name in Māori means "peaks on the back". The species is making about 1.37 tiny genetic adaptations every million years; while this may not sound a lot, it compares to an average of 0.2 for other creatures.

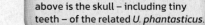

100%

Smallest chelonian

The shell of the speckled Cape tortoise, or speckled padloper (*Chersobius signatus*), measures as little as 6 cm (2.3 in) long. "Padloper" means "path runner", and refers to the South African trails that this reptile frequents. Its size allows it to hide from predators in cracks in the rocks.

Most teeth in a land animal

The common leaf–tailed gecko (*Uroplatus fimbriatus*) of Madagascar possesses 317 teeth. This lizard feeds on invertebrates, in particular snails. When threatened, it opens its mouth wide and emits a distress call. Inset above is the skull – including tiny teeth – of the related *U. phantasticus*.

Heaviest species of snake

Female green anacondas of tropical South America and Trinidad can weigh in excess of 300 kg (660 lb), especially during pregnancy or after a large meal, such as a caiman (*below*)! In Feb 2024, a genetic study revealed that this mega constrictor has two species – *Eunectes murinus* and *E. akayima*. Both on occasion can credibly exceed 7 m (22 ft 11 in) in length; *see the **longest snake species** below*.

Largest water walker

The Indonesian giant sailfin dragon (*Hydrosaurus microlophus*) can measure 1.07 m (3 ft 6 in) from snout to tail tip. It lives on the island of Sulawesi, often in mangrove swamps. The sailfin dragon can dash short distances on top of water thanks to flat, elongated toes that trap pockets of air on the surface and a long tail that provides balance.

Longest reptile

Reticulated pythons (*Malayopython reticulatus*) of south-east Asia regularly exceed 6.25 m (20 ft 6 in). A specimen found in 1912 measured 10 m (32 ft 9 in).

Fastest turtle

The leatherback (*Dermochelys coriacea*) – the **largest turtle** – can swim at 10–15 km/h (6.2–9.3 mph). Unlike all other sea turtles, it lacks a bony shell.

Cassius might have been a ferocious predator in the wild, but at Marineland Melanesia he's shown his softer side. When a baby croc named Zina (*circled right*) found her way into his enclosure, Cassius became a surrogate dad, taking care of her for the next 15 years.

LARGEST CROCODILE IN CAPTIVITY

Cassius the saltwater crocodile (*Crocodylus porosus*) measures 5.48 m (17 ft 11 in) from snout to tail tip. He is the largest of the 16 current residents at Marineland Melanesia, a wildlife habitat on Australia's Green Island founded by George Craig (*above*), which takes care of crocodiles that pose a threat to humans if left in the wild. Cassius was brought to the sanctuary in 1987 after attacking boat engines, but despite a missing leg and damage to his snout and tail, the 1-tonne (2,200-lb) predator is described as a "happy, healthy boy".

Cassius is estimated to be more than 110 years old, so he could have been born before the outbreak of WWI!

Largest lizard
Found on Indonesian islands, male Komodo dragons (*Varanus komodoensis*) weigh up to 166 kg (366 lb). On average, they are as long as a Smart car.

Smallest reptile
Madagascar's *Brookesia* dwarf chameleons measure just 21.9 mm (0.86 in) long, tail included – small enough to fit on the tip of a matchstick!

Oldest land animal
Living on St Helena, a Seychelles giant tortoise (*Aldabrachelys gigantea hololissa*) named Jonathan (born *c.* 1832) was at least 192 years old as of 2024.

Amphibians

Earliest amphibian

The transition from fish to four-footed animals (tetrapods) occurred at least 393 million years ago (MYA), based on fossil tracks discovered at a quarry in Zachełmie, Poland. As to when the first true amphibian emerged, that is more contested depending upon criteria.

A prime contender – unearthed from East Kirkdon Limestone in West Lothian, Scotland, UK, by fossil collector Stan Wood in the 1980s – is the temnospondyl *Balanerpeton*, dating back to the Early Carboniferous (*c.* 336 MYA).

Largest order of amphibians

Anura (frogs and toads) includes some 7,647 species, constituting 88% of all known living amphibians as of Oct 2023.

Largest toad

Cane toads (*Rhinella marina*) average 15–25 cm (6–10 in) long and weigh *c.* 650 g (1 lb 7 oz). However, occasionally supersized specimens come to light: in Jan 2023, a ranger at Conway National Park in Queensland, Australia, stumbled upon "Toadzilla" (*right*), a female said to weigh 2.7 kg (5 lb 15 oz), akin to a pet rabbit.

Also the **most fecund amphibian**, cane toads can lay 35,000 eggs (*below*) per clutch, and sometimes breed twice a year!

100%

Sitting within that group, the **largest amphibian family** is Hylidae (tree frogs) with 1,050 species across 51 genera.

Some of Hylidae's quirkiest members are the paradoxical frogs, such as *Pseudis paradoxa* of South America. They are unique in that their tadpoles outsize the adults by as much as 10 cm (3.9 in) post-metamorphosis – a decrease of more than 60%. This is the **greatest size reduction from tadpole to frog**.

Most amphibian species (country)

Of the 8,688 known species of amphibian in the world, 1,222 resided naturally within the borders of Brazil – a share of 14% – as of Oct 2023.

Most poisonous salamander

Found in streams and wetlands in western North America, Pacific newts (*Taricha*) all contain the powerful nerve poison tetrodotoxin (TTX). A single rough-skinned newt (*T. granulosa, above*) can harbour as much as 14 mg (0.0005 oz) of TTX; less than 1 mg (0.00004 oz) is enough to kill a typical adult man if ingested.

Highest-living amphibians

Three species of anuran live at 5,400 m (17,720 ft) above sea level in Peru's Cordillera Vilcanota. The marbled water frog (*Telmatobius marmoratus*), Andean toad (*Rhinella spinulosa*) and marbled four-eyed frog (*Pleurodema marmoratum*) have moved into ponds recently formed as a result of melting glacial ice.

Longest gestation period

At higher elevations (>2,500 m; 8,200 ft) in the Swiss Alps, alpine salamanders (*Salamandra atra*) can be pregnant for four to five years – up to six times longer than humans. In fact, it may be the longest gestation in the animal kingdom.

Most cold-tolerant amphibians

Natural "anti-freeze" in the blood enables the Siberian newt (*Salamandrella keyserlingii*) and the closely related three-toed newt (*S. tridactyla*) to withstand lows of -35°C (-31°F), and perhaps more, in permafrost soil in north-east Asia.

The **most heat-tolerant amphibian**, on the other hand, is the Japanese stream tree frog (*Buergeria japonica*), whose tadpoles can survive in hot springs with 46.1°C (114.9°F) water.

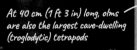

At 40 cm (1 ft 3 in) long, olms are also the largest cave-dwelling (troglodytic) tetrapods

Dear GWR...

My son, who is 2 years and 6 months old, he made a sound just like frogs do. His mouth was closed and he was making a sound similar to frogs. We were amazed to see that. We tried to do the same but couldn't. After a few days, when he was showing it to everyone at a family gathering, we all felt that he is amazing and his talent needs to be appreciated.

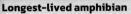

Longest-lived amphibian

Endemic to Croatia, Italy and Bosnia–Herzegovina, the olm (*Proteus anguinus*) is a blind, pigmentless salamander that spends its whole life in dark, water-filled caves. Specimens in zoos or semi-wild conditions have lived for up to 70 years.

But ecophysiologist Yann Voituron has estimated a potential maximum lifespan of 102 years – almost double that of any other amphibian.

Largest amphibian genome
The genetic make-up of Mexico's axolotl (*Ambystoma mexicanum*) comprises 32 billion base pairs; that's more than 10 times the size of the human genome.

Fastest animal tongue
A giant palm salamander (*Bolitoglossa dofleini*) can fully flick out its tongue in just 7 milliseconds – 50 times faster than the blink of an eye!

The huge webbed feet of the Wallace's flying frog essentially turn into four adjustable parachutes when it splays out its long limbs.

Supersized pads at the end of each digit help to soften the landing and also with sticking to vertical surfaces

FARTHEST-GLIDING AMPHIBIAN

Frogs may not have been blessed with wings, but that hasn't stopped a few from taking to the air. The most proficient amphibious aviator is thought to be the Wallace's flying frog (*Rhacophorus nigropalmatus*), capable of covering more than 15 m (50 ft) horizontally during leaps between trees in the rainforests of south-east Asia. There are approximately 380 species of gliding frogs, all of which use extra-large webbed feet and flaps of skin to create air resistance and thus sustain their flight time. A descent angle of 45° or less has to be achieved to be considered "gliding"; anything steeper than that is deemed "parachuting".

Males guard the tadpoles, with females returning about once a week to lay unfertilized eggs as food. Yum!

Largest amphibian
Chinese giant salamanders (*Andrias*) reach lengths of 1.75 m (5 ft 9 in), akin to the height of an adult man. They are highly endangered.

Smallest amphibian
At 7.1 mm (0.27 in) long from snout to vent, male Brazilian flea toads (*Brachycephalus pulexis*) – see p.57 – are among the world's smallest vertebrates.

First monogamous amphibian
Traditionally, amphibians aren't known for pair-bonding, with most only meeting briefly to reproduce. However, the mimic poison frog (*Ranitomeya imitator*) of Peru turned that stereotype on its head with a report published in 2010. Males and females of this species partner for life and also share parental duties. This close relationship appears to increase the odds of survival for their progeny.

Invertebrates

Smallest starfish
The asterinid sea star (*Parvulastra parvivipara*) has a maximum diameter of just 9 mm (0.35 in). Discovered in 1975, this tiny echinoderm dwells in rock pools in South Australia.

100%

Earliest invertebrates
Fossilized remains of archaeocyathids – primitive reef-dwelling sponges resembling hollow horn corals – date to the Early Cambrian, c. 525 million years ago (MYA). However, there are numerous trace fossils of possible soft-bodied and shelled animals dating back further, to at least 560 MYA.

Largest taxonomic group
The order Coleoptera comprises approximately 400,000 species of beetle and weevil, including *Goliathus goliatus* (*left*), one of the biggest beetles at 40–50 g (1.4–1.8 oz) as adults. This group accounts for roughly one in every five living animal species.

Heaviest insect
Despite several large beetles long vying for this title, the heaviest verified specimen was a pregnant 71-g (2.5-oz) Little Barrier Island giant wētā (*Deinacrida heteracantha*), a grasshopper-like bug from New Zealand. Juvenile beetles can be even heftier, though – the **heaviest insect larvae** are those of Actaeon beetles (*Megasoma actaeon*): one was 228 g (8 oz) – akin to a rat!

Fastest...
• **Invertebrate on land**: Solifugids, aka camel spiders (*Solpuga*), can scurry at 4.4 m/s (16 km/h; 10 mph) for brief spurts. These desert arachnids inhabit North Africa and the Middle East.
• **Spider**: the Moroccan flic-flac spider (*Cebrennus rechenbergi*) can move at 1.7 m/s (6.12 km/h; 3.8 mph). It rolls down sand dunes using a technique similar to circus tumblers.
• **Insect**: *Cicindela (Rivacindela) hudsoni* – a species of Australian tiger beetle – attains running speeds of 2.5 m/s (9 km/h; 5.6 mph).

Longest insect
A specimen of *Phryganistria chinensis* (*see p.22*) was 64 cm (2 ft 1 in) with its legs fully outstretched in Aug 2017. The supersized stick insect was bred at the Insect Museum of West China in Chengdu, Sichuan.

Most legs on an animal
The 95-mm-long (3.7-in) millipede *Eumillipes persephone* possesses 1,306 legs (653 pairs). It was found in 2020 inside a 60-m-deep (200-ft) drill hole in Western Australia.

Greediest animal
In its first 56 days, the larva of the polyphemus moth (*Antheraea polyphemus*) of North America eats an amount of foliage equal to 86,000 times its own birthweight. This is equivalent to a human baby consuming 247 tonnes (272 tons) of food in its first two months!

Most venomous cephalopod
The blue-ringed octopuses *Hapalochlaena maculosa* and *H. lunulata* are equipped with a deadly neurotoxic venom called tetrodotoxin – a bite imparting just 0.87 mg can be fatal to humans. Fortunately, these creatures are not aggressive, and prefer to warn away threats by making the patterns on their skin glow.

Largest moth
The atlas moth (*Attacus atlas*, *below*) of south-east Asia has a wingspan of 30 cm (11.8 in) – as wide as a dinner plate. This short-lived insect has no mouth, so only survives for about four days. The **heaviest moth** is the giant wood moth (*Endoxyla cinereus*) of Australia. It can weigh 31.2 g (1.1 oz), about the same as a standard light bulb.

Loudest insect
The calling song of the African cicada (*Brevisana brevis*) can measure 106.7 decibels from 50 cm (1 ft 7 in) away. That's almost as loud as a chainsaw!

Fastest flying insect
The Australian dragonfly (*Austrophlebia costalis*) is capable of short bursts in flight of 58 km/h (36 mph) – faster than a galloping horse.

Largest invertebrates
Giant squid (*Architeuthis dux*) can grow close to 13 m (42 ft 8 in) long; colossal squid (*Mesonychoteuthis hamiltoni*) weigh up to 495 kg (1,091 lb).

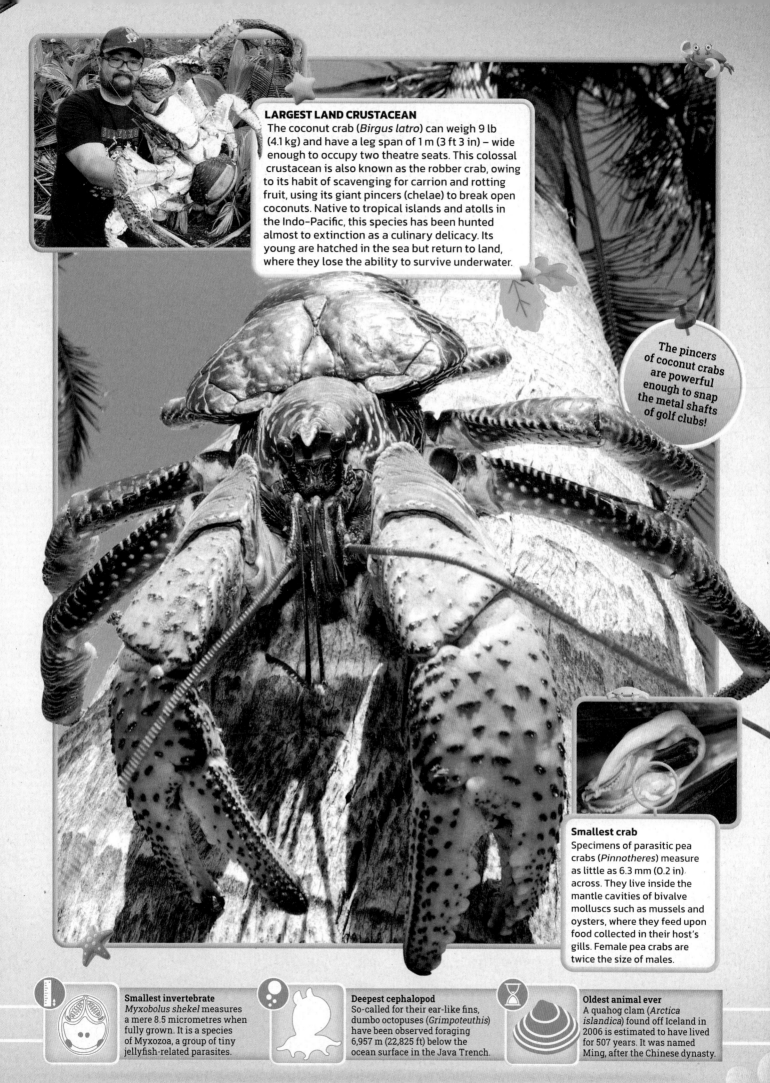

LARGEST LAND CRUSTACEAN
The coconut crab (*Birgus latro*) can weigh 9 lb (4.1 kg) and have a leg span of 1 m (3 ft 3 in) – wide enough to occupy two theatre seats. This colossal crustacean is also known as the robber crab, owing to its habit of scavenging for carrion and rotting fruit, using its giant pincers (chelae) to break open coconuts. Native to tropical islands and atolls in the Indo–Pacific, this species has been hunted almost to extinction as a culinary delicacy. Its young are hatched in the sea but return to land, where they lose the ability to survive underwater.

The pincers of coconut crabs are powerful enough to snap the metal shafts of golf clubs!

Smallest crab
Specimens of parasitic pea crabs (*Pinnotheres*) measure as little as 6.3 mm (0.2 in) across. They live inside the mantle cavities of bivalve molluscs such as mussels and oysters, where they feed upon food collected in their host's gills. Female pea crabs are twice the size of males.

Smallest invertebrate
Myxobolus shekel measures a mere 8.5 micrometres when fully grown. It is a species of Myxozoa, a group of tiny jellyfish-related parasites.

Deepest cephalopod
So-called for their ear-like fins, dumbo octopuses (*Grimpoteuthis*) have been observed foraging 6,957 m (22,825 ft) below the ocean surface in the Java Trench.

Oldest animal ever
A quahog clam (*Arctica islandica*) found off Iceland in 2006 is estimated to have lived for 507 years. It was named Ming, after the Chinese dynasty.

Animals in Action

Highest jump by a miniature horse

Zephyr Woods Storming Treasure cleared a bar set at 117 cm (3 ft 10 in) in Bargemon, France, on 2 May 2020. It's even more impressive considering that he only stands 85 cm (2 ft 9 in) from hoof to shoulder. Owned by Célia Limon (FRA), Zephyr is a three-time show-jumping champion; as 2020's contest was cancelled owing to COVID-19, Célia decided to take on this record instead.

Fastest 5 m on a scooter by a parrot

A Triton cockatoo named Chico rolled 5 m (16 ft 4 in) in 14.58 sec on 15 Feb 2022. He improved on his own record – set just five days earlier – by 3 sec. On hand to congratulate Chico was his owner, bird trainer Kaloyan Yavashev (BGR). The multi-talented parrot can also pedal a mini bicycle and slam-dunk balls into a tiny hoop.

Longest jump by a cat

Sputnik nimbly leaped 2.3 m (7 ft 6 in) between two platforms on 20 Feb 2024, encouraged by owner Melissa Arleth (USA). A former contestant on TV series such as *America's Got Talent* and *World Pet Games*, animal trainer Melissa is pictured here showing off Sputnik's long-jumping skills as part of their touring show, *Cirque du Sewer*.

On the same day, Melissa's pet rodent – and fellow *Sewer* star – Palsy performed the **most jumps through a hoop by a rat in 30 seconds** – 12 – beating the previous record by four.

Fastest 10 m on a scooter by a dog and cat

Bengal cat Sashimi and Boston terrier Lollipop scooted 10 m (32 ft 9 in) in 13.55 sec on 4 Feb 2023. Trainer Melissa Millett (CAN) reveals that they actually devised the trick on their own. "Sashimi jumped on the scooter first, then Lollipop jumped on and started pushing her. We were shocked!"

On 19 Sep 2020, the dynamic duo had achieved the equivalent **5-m** record with a time of 4.37 sec.

Most legs passed through on a skateboard by a dog

On 27 Feb 2024, Coda the cocker spaniel glided beneath a line of 40 people, cheered on by owner Satomi Asano (JPN). He surpassed the existing record, which had stood for seven years, by a count of seven. Satomi gave Coda a board when he was aged two, and says that he'd taught himself to ride in just two weeks.

FASTEST 10 SIDE-LEAPFROG JUMPS BY TWO DOGS

Simba the border collie and Bonnie the springer spaniel each hopped over the other five times in 16.78 sec in Reading, Berkshire, UK, on 31 Aug 2023. They were guided by owner Olga Jones (UK; *see Q&A below*). Within a month, Simba had racked up three more canine one-minute records, starting with the **most bottles deposited in a recycling bin** – 16. He went on to achieve the **most clothes hung on a washing line** – 17 socks – followed by the **most coins deposited into a bottle** – 13. The precocious pooches are pictured below with Olga and their four GWR certificates.

Earlier in 2023, the doggy double act had auditioned with Olga for hit TV show *Britain's Got Talent.*

GWR talks to...

What drew you to teaching your dogs advanced tricks?
For me, trick training is a way of communicating and building understanding on a deeper level. The more words and commands the dog knows, the larger your joint vocabulary, and the more things you can tell each other.

Of the four records you've set, which was the most challenging?
The hardest was probably the **most clothes hung on a washing line in one minute**. But it was also really fun for me to figure out how to get Simba to go faster and to be more accurate. I was hoping that it would encourage my kids to do the same with their clothes... but I concluded that dogs are easier to train than kids!

How did it feel performing on *Britain's Got Talent*?
That was a great experience. My personal highlight was when Bonnie was playing the grand piano and a ukulele on that huge stage in Manchester's Lowry theatre. The audience loved her and many of them gave her a standing ovation at the end of our performance, including Simon [Cowell, the show's creator and one of the judges].

Do you have any tips for teaching dogs complex tricks?
The main one is to break tricks into simple steps that build on each other, rather than trying to teach the whole action in one go. How many steps will depend on the dog, the previous training and the trick itself.
And another key tip is to *listen* to your dog. Dogs are great at giving feedback. We just need to learn to read it and take it on board.

Unless otherwise stated, all records were achieved on TV show Lo Show dei Record *in Milan, Italy*

45

Pet Pals

Oldest animal-welfare charity

The Royal Society for the Prevention of Cruelty to Animals (RSPCA) formed – as the SPCA – on 16 Jun 1824 in London, UK; patron Queen Victoria granted its "royal" status in 1840. Over its 200-year history, the charity has spearheaded new legislation, brought animal abusers to justice, as well as rescuing, rehabilitating and championing the welfare of pets, livestock and wildlife. Pictured are two RSPCA workers with rescued dogs from *c.* 1940 and 2024.

Most dogs at a film screening

On 24 Sep 2023, a pack of 219 pooches and their humans descended on Griffith Park in Los Angeles, California, USA, to watch *PAW Patrol: The Mighty Movie* (CAN, 2023). The event was organized by US studio Paramount and presented by TV host Kevin Frazier, while stars from the movie – including Chase and Marshall (*right*) – added a touch of canine celebrity. The *paw*some premiere also sought to promote animal adoption.

Tallest steer

Six-year-old Holstein Romeo measures 1.94 m (6 ft 4.5 in) at the withers (shoulders), as verified on 17 Dec 2023. Rescued as a calf, he now lives with Misty Moore (USA) at the Welcome Home Animal Sanctuary in Creswell, Oregon, USA.

Most expensive cow

A Nelore cow named Mara (aka Viatina-19 FIV Mara Imóveis) was sold for 21 million Brazilian reals ($4.38 m; £3.33 m) in Arandu, São Paulo, Brazil, on 1 Jul 2023. Nelores are highly prized for their ability to cope in tropical climates.

Fastest duck-herding dog

Overseen by Matteo Carboni (ITA), unflappable border collie Glen guided a waddling of five ducks around an agility course – including a slalom, bridge and tunnel – in 2 min 55.55 sec on 5 Feb 2024. The feat took place on the TV show *Lo Show dei Record* in Milan, Italy.

Most tricks in one minute by a...

• **Cow**: 10, by Ghost, a four-year-old Charolais, and Megan Reimann (USA) in Hay Springs, Nebraska, USA, on 4 Mar 2023.
• **Horse**: 13, by Rose – a miniature horse – and Noeline Cassettari (AUS) in Somersby, New South Wales, Australia, on 6 May 2023.
• **Pig**: 15, by dwarf pig Pongo and his owner Iris Brun (ITA) in Fondi, Italy, on 15 Apr 2023. Pongo and Iris "cleaned up" with a further record on *Lo Show dei Record* on 25 Jan 2024: the **fastest time to transfer 10 socks from a foot to a washing machine by a pig**: 1 min 55 sec.

Oldest chicken

GWR was sad to hear that Peanut – the most recent holder of this record – passed away on Christmas Day 2023, aged at least 21 years 238 days. We offer our condolences to Marsi Darwin of Michigan, USA, who had raised her since she was a chick. New applications for the title are now welcomed.

Most items identified by a parrot in three minutes

Apollo, an African grey, named 12 objects – including a block (*above*), a rock and a sock – in St Petersburg, Florida, USA, on 18 Dec 2023. Trained by Dalton and Victoria Mason (both USA), the perspicacious parrot with a penchant for pistachios is an online star, with more than 1 million fans on YouTube alone.

 ## Loudest purr by a domestic cat

Bella registered a 54.59-decibel purr from a distance of 1 m (3 ft 3 in) in Huntingdon, Cambridgeshire, UK, on 30 Aug 2023. Her owner, Nicole Spink (UK), says she sometimes has to turn up the volume of her TV when Bella's in a happy mood!

Largest horn spread on a goat ever
A Sempione goat named Albino boasted horns that stretched 1.46 m (4 ft 9 in) from point to point, as verified in Naters, Switzerland, on 16 Oct 2021. Albino lived on Roland Fercher's (CHE) farm, where his outsized appendages saw him assume leadership of his herd, as well as become something of a local celebrity (*he is pictured with a floral crown and presentation bell*). Sadly, Albino passed away on 17 Apr 2022, so GWR is now on the lookout for a new living holder.

Longest horns on a yak ever
Jericho, a Tibetan native trim yak, had spiral-shaped horns with a combined length of 3.23 m (10 ft 7 in) on 23 Dec 2018, as confirmed in Welch, Minnesota, USA. Their increasing weight as they grew made them gradually curve forwards and down. His owners Hugh and Melodee Smith (both USA) had to duct-tape the points of the animal's superlative horns to stop them from rubbing his chest. Jericho died from natural causes in Dec 2019.

To mark Jericho's GWR title, the Smiths arranged for monks from Tibet (the native home of yaks) to bless the feat.

▶ Largest horn spread on a steer ever
Poncho Via is a Texas longhorn – with the emphasis on *long*. His horns measure 3.23 m (10 ft 7 in) from tip to tip – more than twice the width of a grand piano – as verified in Goodwater, Alabama, USA, on 8 May 2019. Poncho Via's proud owners are the Pope family (USA).

Cacti

Most mobile cactus

Creeping devil (*Stenocereus eruca*) can spread across the desert floor by as much as 60 cm (2 ft) in a year. This recumbent (horizontal-growing) species is endemic to the Magdalena Plains in Mexico. It effectively "moves" across the sandy soil by promoting new growth at one end as the other end slowly dies.

Oldest cactus fossils

There are very few remains of cacti (family: Cactaceae) in the fossil record, making their origins difficult to pin down. However, fossilized seeds and spines of prickly pear plants (*Opuntia*) have been radiocarbon-dated to 30,800 years. The remains were recovered from the dung heaps of packrats in desert and brushland areas of modern-day North America.

Largest genus of cactus

There are some 140 confirmed species of *Mammillaria* – aka pincushion cacti – among the total *c.* 1,600 formally recognized as of Aug 2023. Around 99% of *Mammillaria* can be found in Mexico, which boasts the **most cactus species (country)**: in excess of 850.

Most widely distributed cactus

Thought to have originated in the Americas, the mistletoe cactus (*Rhipsalis baccifera*), a type of jungle cactus, now grows in tropical forests across much of equatorial and southern Africa, and as far as Sri Lanka – a longitudinal range

Most invasive cactus

The Indian fig (*Opuntia ficus-indica*) has become naturalized in 22 countries beyond its native range in Mexico, from Australia to Italy (*it's shown below in Sicily*). This species of prickly pear thrives in both arid and semi-arid habitats and has no natural predators outside of Mexico. It is often used for ornamental purposes or as a formidable boundary plant.

Largest cactus flowers

The nocturnal blooms of the genus *Selenicereus*, aka moonlight cacti, can span as much as 30 cm (11.8 in) across – bigger than this page! These short-lived, often scented flowers are pollinated by moths and occasionally bats. They can be found across Central America, northern South America and islands in the Caribbean.

Longest spines on a cactus

Specimens of *Tephrocactus* (*example, left*), *Echinopsis* and *Eulychnia* have all been documented with spines reaching 30 cm (11.8 in) – equivalent to standard knitting needles! Cacti's spiky protrusions serve a range of critical functions, such as providing shade, deterring predators and offering a degree of camouflage.

of around 196°. There are indications that this epiphyte (a plant that grows on other plants) may have established itself even farther east, perhaps on the Indonesian island of Java.

Most northerly cactus

The cold-tolerant pygmy prickly pear (*Opuntia fragilis*) has been found growing in the Peace River Valley of Alberta and British Columbia, Canada, at a latitude of 56.28°N. This places it farther north than Moscow, Russia.

The **most southerly cactus**, meanwhile, is likely *Austrocactus aonikenkensis*. First described in *CactusWorld* in Jun 2018, the succulent subshrub is endemic to the Patagonian province of Santa Cruz in Argentina, with a range that extends to at least 50.86°S.

Largest barrel cactus species

Named for their distinctive ribbed, rounded form, barrel cacti can be found throughout south-west USA and Mexico. The candy barrel or giant barrel cactus (*Echinocactus platyacanthus*) of the Chihuahuan Desert grows up to 2.5 m (8 ft 2 in) tall and achieves a diameter of 1 m (3 ft 3 in). Known locally as *biznaga*, this plant has been harvested and consumed by humans since prehistoric times. Its pith is boiled to make the traditional Mexican candy *acitrón*.

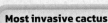

TALLEST CACTUS SPECIES
The cardón or elephant cactus (*Pachycereus pringlei*) commonly reaches more than 10 m (33 ft), with one towering 19.2-m (63-ft) specimen discovered by hikers in Baja California, Mexico, in Apr 1995. This is almost as tall as the White House in Washington, DC, USA.

Reaching similar heights is the saguaro (*Carnegiea gigantea*, right), a close relative of the cardón native to southern USA. Both of these giants are considered the **longest-lived cacti**, able to grow for *c.* 300 years; the largest examples tend to also represent the oldest.

A cardón is able to grow with no soil thanks to bacteria on its roots that can extract nutrients from bare rock!

In a landscape where trees are scarce, such as the Sonoran Desert, the saguaro provides a welcome home for the elf owl (*Micrathene whitneyi*), which nests inside cavities drilled out by woodpeckers. The tiny tenant is the **smallest owl**, with an average length of 12–14 cm (4.7–5.5 in) and weighing about the same as an apricot.

100%

Smallest cactus species
The button-like *Blossfeldia liliputana* measures as little as 10 mm (0.3 in) in diameter when fully mature. Its name is derived from the tiny people of Lilliput in the 1726 novel *Gulliver's Travels*. The spineless species grows in the Andes mountains of northern Argentina and southern Bolivia, unusually often in moist areas around waterfalls. It is monotypic – i.e., the only documented species within its genus.

Fungi

them at the tip of a long stalk. This is pumped with fluid to become pressurized. Once the pressure reaches a threshold, or the stalk is disturbed, the spores are catapulted into the air, accelerating at up to 1.8 million m/sec^2. That's about 60,000 times the g-force experienced at a rocket launch!

Longest lichen

Lichens are symbiotic organisms formed from at least a fungus, a photosynthetic partner (algae or cyanobacteria) and a complex microbiome. One species, old man's beard (*Usnea longissima*), can grow to 10 m (32 ft 10 in). It typically hangs in the canopies of coniferous forests across the northern hemisphere.

Most lives saved by fungi

Since its inception, the antibiotic penicillin has revolutionized the treatment of bacterial infections and has prevented around 200 million deaths. Isolated by scientist Alexander Fleming (UK) on 28 Sep 1928, it is derived from *Penicillium* fungi (*P. digitatum* is the mould that grows on decaying fruit).

Heaviest fungus

The Malheur National Forest in Oregon, USA, is home to an *Armillaria ostoyae* honey mushroom estimated to weigh 7,500–35,000 tons (6,800–31,750 tonnes). Dubbed the "Humongous Fungus", it occupies 9.6 km^2 (3.7 sq mi) – almost three times the size of New York City's Central Park – also making it the **largest fungus**.

Fastest-accelerating organism

Often found on cow dung, *Ascobolus immersus* bundles up spores into balls, then sets

Most poisonous fungus

The death cap (*Amanita phalloides*) is responsible for 90% of fatal fungi poisonings and has no known antidote. Its primary toxin – alpha-amanitin – destroys the liver's cells then passes through the kidneys and is recirculated, leading to further catastrophic damage. Adding to its danger, this fungus is easily mistaken for several harmless edible mushrooms.

Most diverse bioluminescent fungus

Of the 81 fungi species known to generate their own light (bioluminesce), 84% are represented by the genus *Mycena*, aka bonnet mushrooms. The leading school of thought is that these fungi glow in order to attract insects that help to spread their spores.

GWR talks to...

...Giuliana Furci, founder of the Fungi Foundation.

Why did you set up the foundation?
To provide a legal platform to everybody who is interested in mycology. The main aims are the conservation of fungi, their habitats and the people who rely on them.

Why do you think fungi have historically been so overlooked?
The fungi kingdom was only classified in 1969. And it was only possible to identify how different it is to plants and animals after the technical development of microscopes.

What current potential applications of fungi most interest you?
The possibility that they might replace plastic packaging is exciting. Also, the idea of using fungi to replace animal leathers, which goes back to practices developed in eastern Europe hundreds of years ago.

Is there one particular field of fungi research that you feel is most urgent?
One of the key topics in mycology right now is understanding underground fungal communities. Through this, we'll be able to better comprehend subterranean fungal diversity hotspots around the world and implement policies for their protection. Everything indicates that they have a pivotal role in combating climate change.

Tell us something about fungi that you'd like our readers to take away.
That although death, decay and decomposition seem to mark an ending, through fungi they actually become the beginning of life.

Zombifying Cordyceps inspired the outbreak in the game and TV series The Last of Us.

Largest animal to be "zombified" by a fungus

A 20-cm-long (7.8-in) green bean stick insect (*Diapherodes gigantea*) found in Ecuadorian rainforest in 2004 was infested with *Cordyceps diapheromeriphila*. Many *Cordyceps* species are known to manipulate their host insects' behaviour, effectively turning them into a zombie for their own procreative purposes.

On 19 Jun 2023, a Rao's intermediate golden-backed frog (*Hylarana intermedia*) was spotted in India's Western Ghats by Lohit YT, Chimnay C Maliye and a team of naturalists with what appeared to be a *Mycena spp.* fruiting body on its side. The frog was seemingly unaffected by what is thought to be the **first mushroom growing on living animal tissue** on record.

LARGEST PHYLUM OF FUNGI

Ascomycota is the largest of the seven recognized phyla (highest taxonomic groups) of fungi, with more than 64,000 named species. Its members are known as ascomycetes, or sac fungi, owing to a pouch-like structure called the ascus in which their spores develop.

Despite sharing similar biology, ascomycetes come in a vast variety of sizes, colours and forms. These range from morels and the yeast used to make bread to cup fungi (*Cookeina, pictured*) and the so-called dead man's fingers (*Xylaria polymorpha, inset above*). It also includes the world's **most expensive fungi** (*see both below*).

Most expensive fungus
Found in the Himalayas, the caterpillar fungus (*Ophiocordyceps sinensis*) – aka *yartsa gunbu* – can cost as much as $63,000 (£50,200) per pound (450 g). Like other parasitic fungi (*see opposite*), its existence depends on infecting a host insect in order to propagate its spores. The rarity of the fungus, its gruelling harvesting process and prestige within Chinese medicine all contribute to its eye-watering price tag.

Most expensive edible fungus
Native to parts of Italy and the Istrian Peninsula in Croatia, the white truffle (*Tuber magnatum*) regularly fetches up to $6,985 (£5,500) per kilogram, or $3,175 (£2,530) per pound. The price varies with size and how bountiful the season's harvest is.

Above is the **most expensive truffle sold at auction**: a 1.3-kg (2-lb 13-oz) specimen bought by businessman Stanley Ho for $330,000 (£160,000) in Macau, China, on 1 Dec 2007.

Dynamic Earth

Largest prehistoric landslide

Around 13,000 years ago, the Green Lake Landslide saw a 27-km³ (6.4-cu-mi) section of the Hunter Mountains on New Zealand's South Island collapse. It is believed to have been caused by an earthquake.

One-tenth of the size, the **largest modern-day landslide** occurred on 18 May 1980, when *c.* 2.8 km³ (0.7 cu mi) of rock slipped off Mount St Helens in Washington, USA, after a 5.1-magnitude quake. The ensuing eruption resulted in the USA's deadliest volcanic event, with 57 lives lost.

Highest tsunami wash

On 9 Jul 1958, a giant wave passed through Lituya Bay in Alaska, USA, flattening trees up to 524 m (1,719 ft) – almost the height of New York City's One World Trade Center – above the fjord's shoreline. The 160-km/h (100-mph) surge was produced by a huge earthquake-induced rockslide.

Most powerful volcanic eruption recorded with modern equipment

On 15 Jan 2022, the largely submarine Hunga Tonga–Hunga Ha'apai volcano in the South Pacific erupted with an energy equivalent of 15–200 megatons of TNT. That upper limit is four times greater than the **most powerful nuclear explosion**, resulting from a test of the Tsar Bomba in 1961. The largest volcanic event since Krakatoa in 1883, the small part of the peak that did lie above the ocean surface (*right*) was left decimated (*inset*).

The Tongan eruption broke many records, including the **highest volcanic plume** – *c.* 57 km (35.4 mi) – and the **fastest atmospheric waves** – with peak speeds of up to 269 m/s (968 km/h; 602 mph); the waves would circle Earth six times!

First identified impact crater

Located in Arizona, USA, the Barringer Crater was created when an iron–nickel asteroid crashed into the Colorado Plateau 50,000 years ago. The 4,150-ft-diameter (1,265-m) hole was initially thought to have been formed by a volcanic steam explosion. It was first theorized to have been created via a meteor by engineer Daniel Barringer in 1906.

Most seismically active region on Earth

The "Ring of Fire" is a 40,000-km-long (24,850-mi) tectonic belt that surrounds most of the Pacific Ocean (*inset*). It is responsible for some 90% of all our planet's earthquakes and 75% of all volcanic eruptions. Tonga (*above*) and Japan are two countries that feel its effects. On 1 Jan 2024, a 7.5-magnitude quake struck the Noto Peninsula in Japan, causing extensive damage (*right*) and up to 200 deaths.

Nov 2023

Aug 2011

Most powerful earthquake

On 22 May 1960, a tremor measuring 9.5 M_w on the moment magnitude scale hit Chile, killing more than 2,000 people. It triggered tsunamis that caused destruction and loss of life as far away as Japan and Hawaii.

Country with the most earthquakes

Indonesia experienced 2,212 earthquake events (measuring magnitude 4 or above) in 2023. Mexico was in second place, with 1,834.

Fastest-rising mountain

The 8,126-m (26,660-ft) Nanga Parbat in Pakistan grows by 7 mm (0.27 in) per annum. This is due to the ongoing collision between the Eurasian and Indian continental plates.

Largest iceberg

A floating mass of ice designated A23A has an area of *c.* 3,900 km² (1,500 sq mi) – around three times the size of New York City – as of Feb 2024. The iceberg was calved from Antarctica's Filchner–Ronne Ice Shelf in 1986 and remained stuck in the Weddell Sea for 30 years. But in 2023, it finally broke free. Currents have now pushed A23A beyond the tip of the Antarctic Peninsula (*inset*), where the warmer air and surface waters will melt it away.

LARGEST ISLAND CREATED BY VOLCANIC ERUPTIONS

Measuring 103,000 km² (39,768 sq mi), Iceland was formed about 70 million years ago from volcanic activity on the Mid–Atlantic Ridge, a seam under the North Atlantic Ocean where the Eurasian and North American tectonic plates meet. Molten lava poured to the surface and began to cool, creating land – a process that is ongoing to this day. There are currently 32 active volcanoes on Iceland, which experiences an average of one eruption every five years. However, this rate has markedly increased since 2021, when the eruption of Fagradalsfjall (*right*) signalled a new era of geological activity; this looks set to continue as the tectonic plates beneath Iceland steadily move apart.

Largest glacial meltwater flood

On 5 Nov 1996, an underground lake burst through Iceland's largest ice cap, Vatnajökull, sending forth meltwater at a peak rate of 45,000 m³ (1.58 million cu ft) – or about 18 Olympic-sized swimming pools – every second. The lake had been formed by an eruption of the Grímsvötn volcano, which lies underneath Vatnajökull. The flood was the largest recorded, although an eruption in 1918 beneath the Mýrdalsjökull ice cap may have generated as much as 400,000 m³ (14.12 million cu ft) per sec.

Fagradalsfjall volcano had been dormant for 6,000 years before its eruption in Mar 2021.

Pictured left are scientists working by a volcanic fissure following an eruption near Iceland's Sundhnúkur crater on 18 Dec 2023. Around 320 earthquakes were recorded by the Icelandic Meteorological Office in the aftermath of the eruption, which produced 100-m-high (330-ft) lava flumes that were visible from the capital Reykjavik, 42 km (26 mi) away. Residents of the nearby fishing town of Grindavík had to be evacuated, with up to 200 m³ (7,060 cu ft) of lava issuing from the fissure every second (*right*).

Extreme Weather

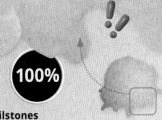

100%

Greatest rainfall in...
• **One hour**: 304.8 mm (12 in), in Holt, Missouri, USA, on 22 Jun 1947.
• **24 hours**: 1,825 mm (71.8 in; 5 ft 11 in), at Foc-Foc on the Indian Ocean island of Réunion on 7–8 Jan 1966.

Heaviest hailstones
Occasionally hail can agglomerate into much larger chunks of ice, such as above, which fell in Vivian, South Dakota, USA, on 23 Jul 2010. At 0.88 kg (1 lb 15 oz) and 20.3 cm (8 in) wide, it is the USA's largest hailstone. According to the World Meteorological Organization (WMO), 1.02-kg (2-lb 4-oz) hailstones fell in Bangladesh's Gopalganj district on 14 Apr 1986.

Largest snowflake
On the night of 27 Jan 1887, snowflakes (clusters of snow crystals) reported to be 38 cm (1 ft 3 in) wide and 20 cm (8 in) thick fell across the Clark Fork River valley near Missoula, Montana, USA.
The **largest snow crystal** was 10 mm (0.39 in) from tip to tip, found by Kenneth Libbrecht in Cochrane, Ontario, Canada, on 30 Dec 2003.

Most named storms in a single year
To help with public communication, weather events are named once they reach the status of tropical storm – i.e., sustained winds of 39 mph (63 km/h) or more. In 2020, a total of 104 occurred globally; 30 of these arose in the **Atlantic Ocean**, also an annual record.

Hottest temperature on Earth
On 10 Jul 1913, a temperature of 56.7°C (134°F) was registered at Greenland Ranch (now Furnace Creek) in Death Valley, California, USA. This was ratified by the WMO on 13 Sep 2012, after the former holder was disqualified by a panel led by Randall Cerveny (*see right*).
On 21 Jul 1983, a record low of -89.2°C (-128.6°F) was logged at the Vostok research station in Antarctica, the **coldest temperature on Earth**.

Deadliest...
• **Lightning strike (direct)**: 21 fatalities, in Manica Tribal Trust Lands in eastern Rhodesia (now Zimbabwe) on 23 Dec 1975.
• **Lightning strike (indirect)**: 469 fatalities, after a flash of lightning over Dronka, Egypt, ignited three railway tanker cars containing some form of petrol on 2 Nov 1994. The line beneath the cars collapsed in a flood, whose waters then carried the blazing fuel into the town.
• **Hailstorm**: 246 fatalities, as the result of an icy downpour near Moradabad in Uttar Pradesh, India, on 30 Apr 1888.

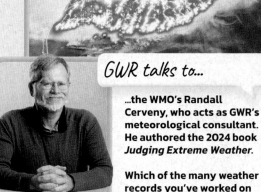

GWR talks to...

...the WMO's Randall Cerveny, who acts as GWR's meteorological consultant. He authored the 2024 book *Judging Extreme Weather*.

Which of the many weather records you've worked on has most shocked you?
That's a good way to put it, as the records that have most "shocked" me are those to do with lightning extremes! The **longest lightning flash** (*above*) covered 768 km (477 mi) across southern USA in 2020 – equivalent to the distance from London to Hamburg in Germany – while the **longest-lasting lightning flash** endured for 17.1 sec.

Why does ratification of climate records sometimes take so long?
We need to ensure that all of the correct procedures were followed in taking the observation, and that the equipment was working properly. Unfortunately, such detailed investigations take time.

Climate change seems to be driving ever-more extreme weather: how concerned are you?
Yes, I'm quite concerned. We know that climate change is caused by numerous factors, each of which has its own particular time scale. For example, volcanic eruptions can cause climate change that lasts one to four years. Orbital fluctuations of the Earth can cause climate change over the course of thousands of years. Anthropogenic [human-influenced] climate change works on a time frame of decades. All of these affect weather and climate. The direction that we're moving over the next few decades is alarming.

Why are we obsessed with the weather?
Weather is something that impacts each and every one of us every day. It's such an integral part of who we are and how we live. In particular, we love talking about – and hearing about – weather extremes.

Longest-lasting rainbow
On 30 Nov 2017, atmospheric scientists at the mountaintop Chinese Culture University in Yangmingshan, Taiwan, China, observed a rainbow continuously for 8 hr 58 min, between 6:57 a.m. and 3:55 p.m. Ideal conditions included scattered clouds, light wind and moisture in the air from a monsoon.

Warmest month on record
In Jul 2023, the average global surface air temperature was 16.95°C (62.51°F), which is 0.72°C (1.29°F) above the 1991–2020 average for that month, according to the Copernicus Climate Change Service. One consequence of rising temperatures is more volatile wildfires, which raged across numerous locations during this heatwave, including the Greek island of Rhodes (*pictured*), leading to the evacuation of 19,000 people.

LONGEST-LASTING TROPICAL STORM

Although still to be officially ratified by the WMO, it's probable that Tropical Cyclone Freddy endured longer than any other storm of its kind. Its estimated lifespan of 33 days, from 6 Feb to 11 Mar 2023, saw it cross the southern Indian Ocean, from its inception off Australia's north-west coast to its final landfall near the city of Quelimane in Mozambique. The current holder, Hurricane/Typhoon John, lasted 31 days, crossing the eastern Pacific Ocean between 11 Aug and 11 Sep 1994. The inset satellite image shows Freddy over Mozambique on 24 Feb 2023.

The storm left a trail of destruction in its wake, causing floods that ripped apart roads in Malawi (*main picture*). It also devastated communities in Madagascar and Mozambique's Zambezia Province (*inset, below*).

Pending investigation, Freddy may also have set a record for the most accumulated cyclone energy (ACE).

Tropical Cyclone Freddy began north-west of the Australian coast, first made landfall at Madagascar and went on to strike Mozambique twice. The colours of the dots below reflect its estimated sustained wind speeds. At its peak, as a Category-5 tropical cyclone, Freddy generated wind speeds of around 270 km/h (167 mph). Although the storm covered more than 11,000 km (6,835 mi), it fell short of the 13,280 km (8,250 mi) traversed by the current **farthest-travelled tropical cyclone**, Hurricane/Typhoon John, in 1994.

KEY
Saffir–Simpson hurricane wind scale

- Tropical depression: ≤38 mph (≤62 km/h)
- Tropical storm: 39–73 mph (63–118 km/h)
- Category 1: 74–95 mph (119–153 km/h)
- Category 2: 96–110 mph (154–177 km/h)
- Category 3: 111–129 mph (178–208 km/h)
- Category 4: 130–156 mph (209–251 km/h)
- Category 5: ≥157 mph (≥252 km/h)
- Start / ● End / ➔ Direction of travel

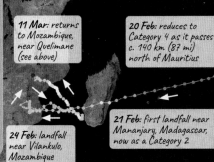

11 Mar: returns to Mozambique, near Quelimane (see above)

20 Feb: reduces to Category 4 as it passes c. 140 km (87 mi) north of Mauritius

6 Feb: classed as a Category-1 tropical cyclone

14 Feb: upgraded to a Category-5 tropical cyclone

24 Feb: landfall near Vilankulo, Mozambique

21 Feb: first landfall near Mananjary, Madagascar, now as a Category 2

Round-Up

Earliest bat skeleton

The microbat *Icaronycteris gunnelli* is known from two fossil skeletons dating back to the Early Eocene, some 52 million years ago. The remains were unearthed from the Fossil Lake deposits of the Green River Formation in Wyoming, USA, as documented in the journal *PLOS ONE* on 12 Apr 2023.

Longest animal cryobiosis

Specimens of *Panagrolaimus kolymaensis*, a previously unknown species of nematode (roundworm), have survived in suspended animation for 46,000 years. The worms were collected in a frozen state from permafrost located near north-east Siberia's Kolyma River. They were later revived in a laboratory.

Highest density of fairy circles

Natural growth patterns, insect colonies and toxic soil have all been posited as causes for these unusually uniform bare patches that occur in grasslands in southern Africa and Australia. But for now their precise origin remains a mystery. The densest-known proliferation of fairy circles is in the Pilbara region of Western Australia, near the town of Newman. A spatial-analysis study in 2016, led by Dr Stephan Getzin, noted as many as 78 circles per ha (193 per acre).

Oldest fossilized forest

The remnants of a *c.* 390-million-year-old woodland were uncovered by chance by scientists studying sediments in the Hangman Sandstone Formation in Somerset, UK. The Mid Devonian trace fossils of cladoxylopsids (extinct plants thought to be related to ferns) included a series of tree trunks as well as fallen branches. The findings were published in the *Journal of the Geological Society* on 23 Feb 2024.

Most complete *Pliosaurus* skull

In 2022, a remarkably intact cranium belonging to one of these Jurassic marine reptiles was extracted from a cliff in Dorset, UK. It came to light after the tip of its snout was found by amateur fossil hunter Phil Jacobs on the beach. Now cleaned and restored by local palaeontologist Dr Steve Etches (*right*), the skull is about 95% complete and includes 130 teeth. Just under 2 m (6 ft 6 in) long, it dates back some 150 million years.

Most venomous spiders

Neotropical wandering spiders (*Phoneutria*) and Australia's funnel-web spiders (Atracidae) are deemed the most toxic of their kind; a single bite from either can be fatal. One of the most common culprits are male Sydney funnel-webs (*Atrax robustus*). Above is the largest documented specimen – Hercules – with a leg span of 7.9 cm (3.1 in). Found in early 2024, he was donated to a park that runs an antivenom programme which helps to save spider-bite victims.

The skull is now on show at the Etches Collection museum in Kimmeridge, Dorset, close to where it was excavated.

Longest neck on a dinosaur

The sauropod *Mamenchisaurus sinocanadorum* was a herbivore whose neck measured an estimated 15.1 m (49 ft 6 in), according to research published in 2023. This is about six times greater than the **longest neck on a living animal** – that of male giraffes (*Giraffa camelopardalis*). *M. sinocanadorum* lived about 162 million years ago, during the Late Jurassic period. Its remains were first unearthed in China's Xinjiang Uyghur Autonomous Region in 1987.

First RNA recovered from an extinct animal

Present in all living cells, and similar to DNA, ribonucleic acid (RNA) is essential to most biological processes. In Sep 2023, a Swedish research team revealed that they had extracted RNA from a 132-year-old museum specimen of the thylacine (*Thylacinus cynocephalus*). Also known as the Tasmanian tiger, this was a wolf-like carnivorous marsupial, the last-known living specimen of which died at Hobart Zoo in Tasmania, Australia, in 1936.

Largest faecal impaction (relative to size)

A female northern curly-tailed lizard (*Leiocephalus carinatus*) found in Cocoa Beach, Florida, USA, on 21 Jul 2018 contained a 22-g (0.77-oz) faecal bolus in its gastrointestinal tract. The agglomeration of semi-digested matter, thought to be a mix of greasy food and sand, comprised 78.5% of the reptile's total weight. This is believed to be the largest poo-to-body mass ratio ever documented in a living animal.

Farthest-gliding insect

In a 2023 study, nymph (juvenile) orchid mantises (*Hymenopus coronatus*) were documented gliding an average horizontal distance of 6.09 m (20 ft); one travelled as far as 14.7 m (48 ft 2 in). The first wingless arthropod ever observed to glide, they achieved this by reorienting their petal-shaped legs while falling through the air in order to generate uplift.

Highest-ranking penguin

Sir Nils Olav III, a king penguin (*Aptenodytes patagonicus*), was promoted to Major General of His Majesty the King's Guard of Norway and Baron of Bouvet Island on 21 Aug 2023 at Edinburgh Zoo, UK. The Norwegian King's Guards adopted a penguin as their mascot on a visit to the zoo in 1972; they named him after two of the guards and made him an honorary lance corporal. Since then – together with two succeeding mascots, both of whom were also named "Nils Olav" – the unflappable birds have been steadily climbing up the ranks.

Smallest frog

The 7.7-mm-long (0.3-in) *Paedophryne amauensis* lost its diminutive crown, worn since 2012, to an even tinier frog in Feb 2024. Male Brazilian flea toads (*Brachycephalus pulex*) have an average snout-to-vent length of 7.1 mm (0.27 in) – and as little as 6.5 mm (0.25 in) in one case – as reported in *Zoologica Scripta*. This also makes it the **smallest amphibian**, the **smallest tetrapod** and among the smallest of all vertebrates.

Rarest egg-laying mammal

For decades, the Attenborough's long-beaked echidna (*Zaglossus attenboroughi*) was known only from a dead specimen found in Papua, Indonesia, in 1961. However, in Nov 2023, video was released of a live adult foraging in Papua's remote Cyclops Mountains. The footage was captured on a camera trap by scientists from Oxford University (UK). Its total population size remains unknown.

Most birds spotted in a lifetime

Peter Kaestner (USA) sighted his 10,000th unique bird species on 9 Feb 2024. He reached the landmark with an orange-tufted spiderhunter (*Arachnothera flammifera*), observed in Mindanao, Philippines. Retired, well-travelled diplomat Kaestner has been a committed bird-spotter for 64 years and uses the IOC World Bird List as his guide. A major highlight thus far has been having a new species of antpitta – *Grallaria kaestneri* – that he recorded in Colombia named in his honour.

Most flowers on an orchid (monopodial)

A *Phalaenopsis* orchid grown by Kevin Englisch (CAN) bore 131 blooms on 30 Mar 2023, as verified in Waterloo, Ontario, Canada. Monopodial orchids grow single upright "stems", with one leaf following another on alternating sides. *Phalaenopsis* species are commonly known as moth orchids and include the flowers that appear to be mimicked by *H. coronatus* (*above*).

Tallest poison ivy

On 12 Mar 2023, Robert Fedrock (CAN) discovered a 20.75-m-tall (68-ft) specimen of *Toxicodendron* growing in Paris, Ontario, Canada. Known for leaves that can irritate the skin, these clambering plants are native to woodland in North America and Asia.

Oldest (in captivity)...

• **Gorilla**: a female western lowland gorilla (*Gorilla gorilla gorilla*) named Fatou has lived at Zoo Berlin in Germany since May 1959. She was judged to be two years old on arrival and celebrated her 67th year in 2024 (the zoo has designated 13 Apr as her birthday).

• **Sloth**: Jan, a male Linne's two-toed sloth (*Choloepus didactylus*), was aged at least 53 as of 2023. He has lived at Krefeld Zoo in Germany since 30 Apr 1986. In the wild, the typical lifespan for two-toed sloths is *c*. 20 years.

• **Wombat**: Wain, a common wombat (*Vombatus ursinus*), was at least 34 years 86 days old on 31 Jan 2024, as verified at Satsukiyama Zoo in Ikeda, Osaka, Japan.

Oldest orangutan in captivity

Born in the wild *c*. 1961 and collected in 1964, Bella the Sumatran orangutan (*Pongo abelii*) was estimated to have reached a superlative 63 years of age in 2024. She has lived at Tierpark Hagenbeck in Hamburg, Germany, since 15 Apr 1964. These great apes of south-east Asia typically live for 35–40 years in the wild.

Zeus

Great Danes are famous for their size, among the largest of all breeds. But even so, some are decidedly *greater* than others. Step forward Zeus (*right*), the tallest dog ever recorded by GWR.

This prodigious pooch's parents were both of average size, so nothing prepared his owners – the Doorlag family of Otsego, Michigan, USA – for Zeus's superlative stature. He proved to be the epitome of a "gentle giant". "He loved to sit on people's laps – it was his favourite place to be," Denise Doorlag told GWR. "He was a pet therapy dog at the hospital that I work at and people loved it when he sat on the bed next to them."

Of course, caring for such a humongous hound presented challenges aplenty. For one thing, the Doorlags had to strike a balance between accommodating Zeus's large appetite and – on vets' advice – keeping him slim, on account of his height.

Zeus is pictured here alongside Morgan, the **tallest female dog ever**, at 98.15 cm (3 ft 2.6 in), owned by Canada's Dave and Cathy Payne. Morgan was around 10 cm (3.9 in) taller than average for female Great Danes, and needed around 80 min of daily exercise – which often included squirrel chasing!

Sadly, Zeus and Morgan both passed away, within a month of each other, in 2014. But to this day, they continue to stand tall and proud among the *pantheon* of GWR ICONS.

VITAL STATISTICS

Name	Zeus
Lifespan	26 Nov 2008–3 Sep 2014
Breed	Great Dane
Current GWR titles	◐ Tallest dog ever – 111.8 cm (3 ft 8 in), to the shoulder
Height when standing on hind legs	223 cm (7 ft 4 in)
Favourite food	Cooked chicken (mixed in with cottage cheese and canned meat)

The family picked Zeus out of a litter of 15 puppies. Although he was certainly one of the bigger pups, they actually chose him for his colouring. "We wanted a black puppy," Denise told us, "and he had the least amount of white."

Zeus with Kevin in the family's hometown of Otsego, Michigan. At 7 ft-plus standing on his hind legs, this canine colossus was so large that small children often mistook him for a horse!

The Doorlags with their supersized, record-breaking pet. Left to right: Nicholas, Denise, Kevin and Miranda.

"Zeus got along well with everyone and all dogs that he was around," Denise told GWR. He's pictured below with two dogs belonging to Denise's parents – Ox, a black Labrador, and Bear, a Pomeranian.

Zeus weighed in at 81 kg (180 lb) – c. 30 times heavier than a Chihuahua, such as Boo Boo (see 2004 below).

Find out more about Zeus in the ICON section at www.guinnessworldrecords.com/2025

A HISTORY OF HIGH HOUNDS

2004

Gibson (and Boo Boo): On GWR Day 2007, the 107-cm (3-ft 6.1-in) Great Dane Gibson met the then **shortest dog**, 10.16-cm-tall (4-in) Boo Boo.

2012

Bella: A former **tallest female dog**, Bella measured 94.93 cm (3 ft 1.3 in). Her achievements included winning four obedience trial titles.

2014

Lizzy: Another one-time **tallest female dog**, 96.4-cm (3-ft 1.9-in) Lizzy lived with her owner, Greg Sample, in Florida, USA.

2016

Freddy: Owned by Claire Stoneman, Great Dane Freddy stood 103.5 cm (3 ft 4.75 in) tall. Amazingly, he was the runt of a litter of 13 puppies!

2022

Zeus: Shown with owner Brittany Davis – also called Zeus – this Great Dane was the most recent **tallest living dog**, at 104.6 cm (3 ft 5.1 in).

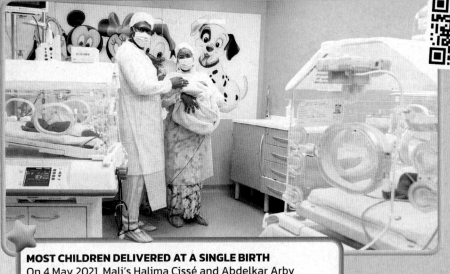

MOST CHILDREN DELIVERED AT A SINGLE BIRTH

On 4 May 2021, Mali's Halima Cissé and Abdelkar Arby became the proud parents of nonuplets when Halima gave birth to five girls and four boys at the Ain Borja Clinic in Casablanca, Morocco. The babies were born prematurely, at 30 weeks, and delivered by Caesarean section. They spent the first 19 months of their life being cared for in Morocco before going home to Mali. In May 2023, the family celebrated the nonuplets' second birthday with a party themed around their favourite TV show, *Miraculous*. The children's names are Adama, Bah, Elhadji, Fatouma, Hawa, Kadidia, Mohammad VI, Oumar and Oumou.

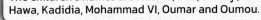

For most of her pregnancy, Halima thought that she was carrying "only" seven babies!

Tallest Person

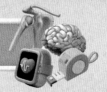

Few records are as frequently disputed as the title of **tallest person**. Even Guinness World Records hasn't always been able to filter out those whose heights have been "distorted for the financial considerations of promoters" (as our 1955 edition put it). To set the record straight, here we present a progressive history of the 14 men and 2 women who have irrefutably held the title since 1900, including the **tallest person ever** recognized by GWR (*see pp.26–27*).

John "Bud" Rogan (USA)
Was unable to stand as an adult; his height was calculated after a medical examination.
1867–1905
267 cm (8 ft 9.1 in)
1900–05

Fyodor Makhnov (BLR)
Was billed as "Feodor Machnow" during his career as a touring attraction.
1878–1912
239 cm (7 ft 10 in)
1905–12

Frederick Kempster (UK)
1889–1918
237 cm (7 ft 9.3 in)
1912–18

Bernard Coyne (USA)
1897–1921
254 cm (8 ft 4 in)
1918–21

Albert Kramer (NLD)
Often went by "Jan van Albert" during his career as a circus performer.
1897–1976
237.5 cm (7 ft 9.5 in)
1921–33

Robert Wadlow (USA)
1918–40
272 cm (8 ft 11.1 in)
1933–40

Väinö Myllyrinne (FIN)
Was also the tallest soldier; enjoyed the longest reign as tallest person.
1909–63
251 cm (8 ft 2.8 in)
1940–59

John Carroll (USA)
Actual standing height was 243.8 cm (7 ft 11.9 in) owing to a curved spine.
1932–69
263.5 cm (8 ft 7.7 in)
1959–69

*Years of birth and death; Height; Reign as **tallest living person***

Donald Koehler (USA)
- 1925–81
- 248.9 cm (8 ft 1.9 in)
- 1969–81

Zeng Jinlian (CHN)
- 1964–82
- 246.3 cm (8 ft 0.9 in)
- 1981–82

*Still the **tallest woman ever**, and the only known woman to have exceeded 8 ft in height.*

Gabriel Estêvão Monjane (MOZ)
- 1944–90
- 245.7 cm (8 ft 0.7 in)
- 1982–90

Emerged in the early 1970s as a circus performer with a claimed height of 265 cm (8 ft 8.3 in), but was not measured until 1982.

Mohammad Alam Channa (PAK)
- 1953–98
- 231.7 cm (7 ft 7.2 in)
- 1990–98

Was initially reported in 1982 as standing 251 cm (8 ft 3 in) tall. When measured, his height was identical to that of Sandy Allen.

Sandy Allen (USA)
- 1955–2008
- 231.7 cm (7 ft 7.2 in)
- 1990–98

*Also the **tallest living woman** from 1982 until her passing in 2008.*

Radhouane Charbib (TUN)
- 1968–
- 235.9 cm (7 ft 8.8 in)
- 1998–2005

Xishun Bao (CHN)
- 1951–
- 236.1 cm (7 ft 8.9 in)
- 2005–09

Sultan Kösen (TUR)
- 1982–
- 251 cm (8 ft 2.8 in)
- 2009–present

Stood 246.5 cm (8 ft 1 in) when first measured by GWR; reached current height in 2011.

The GWR adjudicator (*below right*) stands 175 cm (5 ft 9 in) tall – the average height of a British man.

63

Size Matters

Guinness World Records has maintained a keen interest in the extremes of the human form since our first edition in 1955 (which opened its HUMAN BEING chapter with a discussion of "giants" and "giantesses"). Over the subsequent 70 years, we've tracked the heights of the world's tallest and shortest people, and been fortunate enough to meet, measure and befriend these remarkable individuals, six of whom we introduce here.

All these title holders have attained the status of a GWR ICON. It's an honour bestowed both for the distinctive status of their records and because they embody superlative determination and strength of character.

⊘ Tallest woman

Rumeysa Gelgi measured 215.16 cm (7 ft 0.7 in) as of 23 May 2021. Like her lofty peer Sultan, she hails from Türkiye. She owes her remarkable stature to a rare condition called Weaver syndrome, which causes accelerated growth.

Despite the difficulties this creates, Rumeysa loves to travel and meet new people. Her 2023 GWR documentary *Rumeysa: Walking Tall (left)* took her around the world to meet other remarkable record holders.

⊘ Tallest man

In 2011, Sultan Kösen (TUR) became the first 8-ft-plus (2.43-m) man to be measured by GWR in over 20 years. (*You can trace the progression of the record for history's real-life giants on the Tallest Person flashback – see p.62.*) The former farmer tops out at a towering 251 cm (8 ft 2.8 in). He also boasts the **largest hands** – 28.5 cm (11.22 in), from the wrist to the tip of the middle finger.

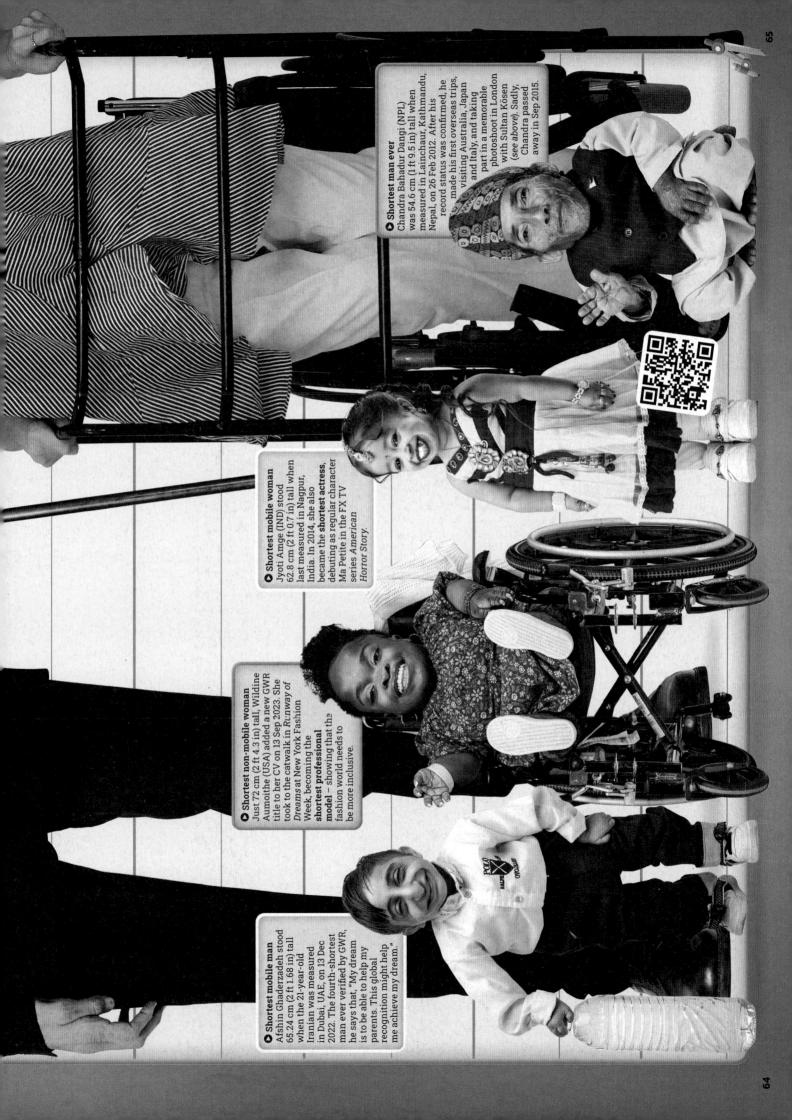

❍ **Shortest man ever**
Chandra Bahadur Dangi (NPL) was 54.6 cm (1 ft 9.5 in) tall when measured in Lainchaur, Kathmandu, Nepal, on 26 Feb 2012. After his record status was confirmed, he made his first overseas trips, visiting Australia, Japan and Italy, and taking part in a memorable photoshoot in London with Sultan Kösen (*see above*). Sadly, Chandra passed away in Sep 2015.

❍ **Shortest mobile woman**
Jyoti Amge (IND) stood 62.8 cm (2 ft 0.7 in) tall when last measured in Nagpur, India. In 2014, she also became the **shortest actress**, debuting as regular character Ma Petite in the FX TV series *American Horror Story*.

❍ **Shortest non-mobile woman**
Just 72 cm (2 ft 4.3 in) tall, Wildine Aumoithe (USA) added a new GWR title to her CV on 13 Sep 2023. She took to the catwalk in *Runway of Dreams* at New York Fashion Week, becoming the **shortest professional model** – showing that the fashion world needs to be more inclusive.

❍ **Shortest mobile man**
Afshin Ghaderzadeh stood 65.24 cm (2 ft 1.68 in) tall when the 21-year-old Iranian was measured in Dubai, UAE, on 13 Dec 2022. The fourth-shortest man ever verified by GWR, he says that, "My dream is to be able to help my parents. This global recognition might help me achieve my dream."

Senior Citizens

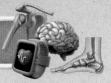

Oldest gaming streamer (male)
"Gamer Grandpa" Yang Binglin (CHN, b. 10 Dec 1935) was sharing his gaming exploits with the world at 88 years 15 days old, as verified on 25 Dec 2023 in Luzhou, Sichuan, China. An active content creator on Chinese platform Bilibili, Binglin regularly posts videos on his page, which boasts more than 273,000 subscribers.

COLETTE MAZE

109 ANS DE PIANO

Oldest professional pianist ever
On 1 Jul 2023, Colette Maze (FRA, 16 Jun 1914–19 Nov 2023) launched a new CD of classical music at the age of 109 years 15 days. This also makes her the **oldest person to release an album**. Titled *109 ans de piano* ("*109 Years of Piano*"), it was the seventh and final release of her recording career, which only began in 2004, aged 90. In Apr 2023, she enjoyed a spell in the social-media limelight after an interview about the album.

OLDEST...

Twin Holocaust survivors
Peter Somogyi and Thomas Simon (HUN, b. 14 Apr 1933) were aged 90 years 179 days as of 10 Oct 2023. The twins were imprisoned in the Auschwitz-Birkenau concentration camp in Poland from 9 Jul 1944 until the camp's liberation in Jan 1945. Peter and Thomas now live in Canada and the USA respectively.

The oldest singleton twin to have survived the Holocaust is Yugoslav-born Annetta Able (b. 4 Feb 1924), who turned 100 in 2024. Her sister, Stephanie, died aged 96 in 2019.

Triplets (male)
On 2 Nov 2023, Larry A Brown, Lon B Brown and Gene C Brown (all USA, b. 1 Dec 1930) had their age verified at 92 years 336 days in Raymore, Missouri, USA. *For more senior siblings, turn to p.72.*

Tandem parachute jumper
Rut Linnéa Ingegärd Larsson (SWE, b. 12 Sep 1918) was 103 years 259 days old when she leapt from a plane over Motala, Östergötland, Sweden, on 29 May 2022. Rut discovered parachuting late in life, and paraglided for the first time on her 90th birthday.

The **oldest person to indoor skydive** is Ivar Kristoffersen (NOR, b. 8 Jan 1921), who was aged 102 years 171 days on 28 Jun 2023 in Voss, Vestland, Norway.

Wing walker
Aged 95 years 138 days, John Symmonds (UK, b. 2 Feb 1928) took to the skies above Cirencester, Gloucestershire, UK, on 20 Jun 2023. "Wingman John" performed the daredevil stunt to raise funds for a local hospice.

Competitive motorcycle racer
Leslie Harris (NZ, b. 26 Feb 1925) was 97 years 344 days old when he took part in the Pukekohe 43rd Classic Motorcycle Festival in Auckland, New Zealand, on 5 Feb 2023. He rode his BSA Bantam 175cc against a field that included both his son and granddaughter.

Dentist
Japan's Etsuro Watanabe (b. 31 Oct 1924) was conducting dental check-ups aged 99 years 133 days old, as verified in Minamitsuru, Yamanashi, Japan, on 12 Mar 2024.

Train driver
At the age of 81 years 233 days on 20 Feb 2024, Helen Antenucci (USA, b. 2 Jul 1942) still worked for the Department of Transportation in Boston, Massachusetts, USA.

Oldest waterskier (female)
On 8 Aug 2023, Dwan Jacobsen Young (USA, b. 1 May 1931) waterskied 1 km (0.6 mi) across Bear Lake in Idaho, USA, aged 92 years 99 days. Dwan took up the sport in 1961, at the age of 29, and takes to the water every summer. Now she skis with her great-grandchildren. "Do not be afraid to try a new sport when you are older," advises Dwan. "You are more capable than you think."

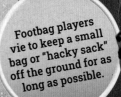

Footbag players vie to keep a small bag or "hacky sack" off the ground for as long as possible.

Oldest competitive footbag player
Ken Moller (USA, b. 14 Jul 1947) was 75 years 331 days old when he lined up for the 2023 US Open Footbag Championships. He took part in the Intermediate Freestyles Routine event on 10 Jun in Erie, Pennsylvania, USA – and finished first! The veteran hacky-sack champ aims to compete until he is 80.

TOP 10 OLDEST PEOPLE EVER

Name	Age
Jeanne Calment (FRA, 21 Feb 1875–4 Aug 1997)	122 y 164 d
Kane Tanaka (JPN, 2 Jan 1903–19 Apr 2022)	119 y 107 d
Sarah Knauss (USA, 24 Sep 1880–30 Dec 1999)	119 y 97 d
Lucile Randon (FRA, 11 Feb 1904–17 Jan 2023)	118 y 340 d
Marie-Louise Meilleur (CAN, 29 Aug 1880–16 Apr 1998)	117 y 230 d
Violet Brown (JAM, 10 Mar 1900–15 Sep 2017)	117 y 189 d
Emma Morano (ITA, 29 Nov 1899–15 Apr 2017)	117 y 137 d
Chiyo Miyako (JPN, 2 May 1901–22 Jul 2018)	117 y 81 d
Delphia Welford (USA, 9 Sep 1875–14 Nov 1992)	117 y 66 d
María Branyas Morera (ESP, b. USA, 4 Mar 1907)	117 y 51 d

All ages confirmed by the Gerontology Research Group and correct as of 24 Apr 2024.

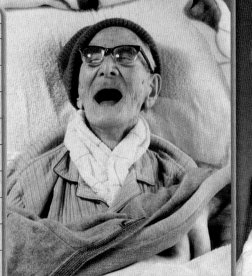

María ascribes her age to many factors, including a balanced, positive outlook and "staying away from toxic people".

OLDEST PERSON EVER

Jeanne Calment (FRA, 21 Feb 1875–4 Aug 1997) lived to the age of 122 years 164 days – the greatest fully authenticated age to which any human has ever survived. Born 14 years before the Eiffel Tower (*see p.149*) was completed, Jeanne met the artist Vincent van Gogh as a teenager and cycled until she was 100. She attributed her longevity in part to a diet rich in olive oil.

The **oldest man ever** was Jiroemon Kimura (JPN, b. 19 Apr 1897, *above left*), who passed away on 12 Jun 2013 aged 116 years 54 days. He was survived by 25 great-grandchildren and 15 great-great-grandchildren.

TOP 10 OLDEST LIVING PEOPLE

Name	Age
María Branyas Morera (ESP, b. USA, 4 Mar 1907)	117 y 51 d
Tomiko Itooka (JPN, b. 23 May 1908)	115 y 337 d
Inah Canabarro Lucas (BRA, b. 8 Jun 1908)	115 y 321 d
Elizabeth Francis (USA, b. 25 Jul 1909)	114 y 274 d
Ethel Caterham (UK, b. 21 Aug 1909)	114 y 247 d
Okagi Hayashi (JPN, b. 2 Sep 1909)	114 y 235 d
Masa Matsumoto (JPN, b. 29 Nov 1909)	114 y 147 d
Charlotte Kretschmann (DEU, b. 3 Dec 1909)	114 y 143 d
Ina Okazawa (JPN, b. 10 Mar 1910)	114 y 45 d
Hisako Shiroishi (JPN, b. 19 May 1910)	113 y 341 d

All ages confirmed by the Gerontology Research Group and correct as of 24 Apr 2024.

OLDEST LIVING PERSON

US-born María Branyas Morera (ESP, b. 4 Mar 1907) was aged 117 years 51 days as of 24 Apr 2024. She became the oldest person on Earth in Jan 2023. María, who has lived in the same nursing home for 23 years, is in remarkable physical health and can recall events from when she was four – 113 years ago! She even has an X account. Her bio reads: "I'm old, very old, but not an idiot."

As this year's book was being compiled, GWR was saddened to hear of the death of Venezuela's Juan Vicente Pérez Mora (b. 27 May 1909, *inset*) on 2 Apr 2024, aged 114 years 311 days – making him the fourth-oldest man ever verified. With Juan's demise, the title of **oldest living man** passed to a British citizen (*see right*).

OLDEST LIVING MAN

John Tinniswood (UK, b. 26 Aug 1912) was aged 111 years 242 days as of 24 Apr 2024. The WWII veteran, who lives in a care home in Southport, Merseyside, UK, says the secret to his long life is "pure luck". He eats fish and chips every Friday and is a diehard supporter of Liverpool FC, which was founded just 20 years before he was born. John's advice to younger generations? "Give it all you've got!"

Tattoos

Most rabbit tattoos
Craig Evans (UK) had his 69th unique rabbit tattoo applied in Cardiff, UK, on 20 Nov 2023. It was created by artist Ash Davies, who has inked many of the leporine designs. Craig, who began his bunny bonanza way back in Jul 2009, likes to give individual tattoo artists free rein to interpret his request in whatever artistic style they wish.

Most tattoos of the same band
Tom M Engelbrecht (NOR) is a committed Metallica fan – and has 43 tattoos of the group to prove it. They include portraits of the band's legendary guitarists Kirk Hammett (*inset right*) and James Hetfield (*bottom inset*) in full shredding mode. Tom's Metallica tats were counted in Bergen, Vestland, Norway, on 5 Dec 2023.

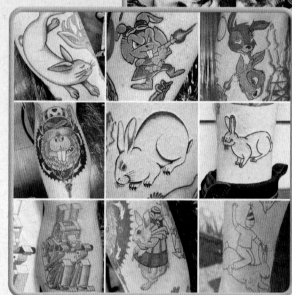

Dear GWR...
I bet I could set the record for the most tattoo cover-ups undergone. Why I thought it would be a wise idea to get my ex-girlfriend's name on my ▇▇▇▇▇, I'll never know!

Most tattooed man
Lucky Diamond Rich (AUS, b. NZ) has spent more than 1,000 hr under the tattooist's needle. Having achieved a full-body set of colourful designs, he opted for a 100% cover of black ink. With ongoing white and coloured tattoos on top, his coverage is now estimated at 200%-plus.
In 2024, GWR encountered Max Max, who has a similar all-over body coverage – but entirely inked by himself. Could he be a record holder? Watch this space!

Largest tattoo artwork
Atlanta Ink, Iron Palm Tattoos and Pèse Noir (all USA) created a 7.39-m² (79.54-sq-ft) tribute to the late rapper Takeoff (Kirsnick Ball), as confirmed in Atlanta, Georgia, USA, on 5 Jul 2023. The portrait of the musician – a founding member of hip-hop group Migos – was inked on silicone skin.

ICON

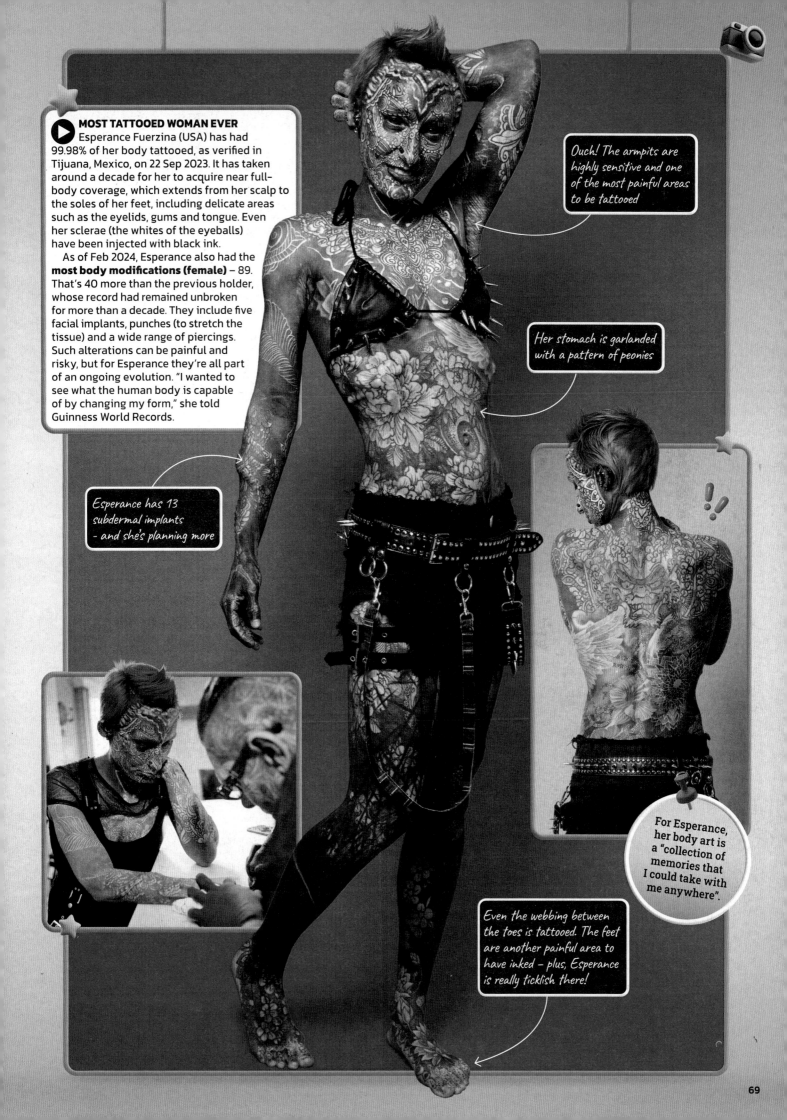

MOST TATTOOED WOMAN EVER

Esperance Fuerzina (USA) has had 99.98% of her body tattooed, as verified in Tijuana, Mexico, on 22 Sep 2023. It has taken around a decade for her to acquire near full-body coverage, which extends from her scalp to the soles of her feet, including delicate areas such as the eyelids, gums and tongue. Even her sclerae (the whites of the eyeballs) have been injected with black ink.

As of Feb 2024, Esperance also had the **most body modifications (female)** – 89. That's 40 more than the previous holder, whose record had remained unbroken for more than a decade. They include five facial implants, punches (to stretch the tissue) and a wide range of piercings. Such alterations can be painful and risky, but for Esperance they're all part of an ongoing evolution. "I wanted to see what the human body is capable of by changing my form," she told Guinness World Records.

Esperance has 13 subdermal implants – and she's planning more

Ouch! The armpits are highly sensitive and one of the most painful areas to be tattooed

Her stomach is garlanded with a pattern of peonies

For Esperance, her body art is a "collection of memories that I could take with me anywhere".

Even the webbing between the toes is tattooed. The feet are another painful area to have inked – plus, Esperance is really ticklish there!

Hair

Longest beard on a woman

Erin Honeycutt's (USA) facial hair was 30 cm (11.8 in) long when measured in Caro, Michigan, USA, on 8 Feb 2023. Erin has polycystic ovary syndrome, a condition whose side effects include excess hair growth.

Sarwan Singh (CAN) holds the **men's** record – 2.54 m (8 ft 4 in) – as verified in Surrey, British Columbia, Canada, on 15 Oct 2022.

Longest handmade wig

Helen Williams (NGA; *circled*) created a hairpiece that measured 351.28 m (1,152 ft 5 in) long – more than three soccer pitches – in Abule Egba, Lagos, Nigeria, on 7 Jul 2023. She was effectively training for this record in her day job – Helen has worked as a professional wig maker for eight years. It took 11 days to make and required 1,000 bundles of hair, 6,250 hair clips, 35 tubes of glue and 12 cans of hairspray.

Tallest hairstyle

Dani Hiswani (SYR) decked out a model with a 2.9-m-high (9-ft 6.1-in) hairdo in the shape of a Christmas tree in Dubai, UAE, on 16 Sep 2022. In a final festive flourish, Hiswani added baubles.

Tallest Mohican spike

On 16 Apr 2021, Joseph Grisamore (USA) unveiled a 1.29-m (4-ft 2-in) pointed Mohican hairstyle in Park Rapids, Minnesota, USA. Two years previously he'd achieved the record for the **tallest full Mohican** – 1.08 m (3 ft 6.5 in). Key to its gravity-defying success was half a can of got2b Glued Blasting Freeze Hairspray.

Largest afro

Aevin Dugas (USA) boasted a voluminous afro measuring 26 cm (10.2 in) from scalp to tip and 1.65 m (5 ft 4 in) in circumference, as verified in Gonzales, Louisiana, USA, on 11 Sep 2022. Aevin is on a mission to encourage everyone to embrace their natural hair.

Widest wig

Artist Dani Reynolds (AUS) presented a 2.58-m-wide (8-ft 6-in) wig in Adelaide, South Australia, on 12 Nov 2022. Its frame includes a bike helmet and pool noodles, while the colour and texture are based on Dani's own locks.

Most candy canes in a beard

Joel Strasser (USA) fitted 187 cane-shaped sweets into his whiskers in Meridian, Idaho, USA, on 9 Dec 2023. A multiple record holder, Joel has adorned his facial fuzz with the **most BBQ skewers** (600), **beard baubles** (710), **pipe cleaners** (1,150) and **cotton buds** (2,470), among other objects.

Largest single donation of hair

On 26 Aug 2021, Zahab Kamal Khan (USA) gave 1.55 m (5 ft 1 in) of her own tresses to the charity Children with Hair Loss in McLean, Virginia, USA. Zahab had been growing her luxuriant locks for 17 years.

The **men's** record – 83 cm (2 ft 8.6 in) – was achieved by Kodai Fukushima (JPN), as confirmed in Bunkyō, Tokyo, Japan, on 17 Apr 2023.

US National Beard and Moustache Championships

On 3 Nov 2023, fuzzy-faced folks joined *fur*-ces to set three records at Daytona Beach in Florida, USA. A total of 86 competitors linked to form the **longest beard chain** (*below*) – 195 ft 3 in (59.51 m). Records were also set for:
• **Longest moustache chain** (*right*): 20 ft 4 in (6.19 m), by 27 competitors.
• **Longest chain of partial beards** (defined as non-full beards, such as goatees, sideburns, imperial whiskers and musketeers): 42 ft 8 in (13 m), by 24 competitors.

▶ LONGEST HAIR

Aliia Nasyrova's (UKR) cascading tresses are 2.57 m (8 ft 5.2 in) long, as confirmed in Milan, Italy, on 25 Feb 2024. Perhaps unsurprisingly, Rapunzel was one of Aliia's favourite fairytale characters as a child and she hasn't had a hair cut for around 20 years. Her majestic mane has its downsides – not least its weight, which Aliia compares to that of the family's cat, and the fact that it takes a whole day to air–dry her luxurious locks. On the upside, she receives an abundance of haircare products from companies proud to be associated with this GWR title holder.

The record for **longest hair** doesn't generally change hands – or should that be heads?! – very often. Yet in the past year, the record has been broken twice. Prior to Aliia Nasyrova, the title was held by Smita Srivastava of India, whose tresses extended for 2.36 m (7 ft 9 in), as confirmed in Prayagraj, Uttar Pradesh, on 20 Aug 2023. Smita was partly influenced by her love of 1980s Hindi cinema, in which many actresses favoured long hairstyles, as well as Indian culture: "Goddesses traditionally had very long hair," she told GWR. "It is considered inauspicious to cut it."

GUINNESS WORLD RECORDS

CERTIFICATE

The longest hair on a living person (female) is 257.33 cm (8 ft 5.3 in) and was achieved by Aliia Nasyrova (Ukraine) in Milan, Italy on 25 February 2024

OFFICIALLY AMAZING

RECORD HOLDER

Superlative Siblings

Most family members born on the same day

As verified in 2019, nine people in the Mangi family of Larkana, Pakistan, celebrate birthdays on the same calendar day: 1 Aug. These are dad Ameer (1968), mum Khudeja (1973) and their seven children: Sindhoo (1992), twin sisters Sasui and Sapna (1998), Aamir (2001), Ambar (2002), and twin brothers Ammar and Ahmar (2003). This also represents the **most siblings born on the same day**.

First twins born in different decades

Joslyn Grace Guilen Tello was born at 11:37 p.m. on 31 Dec 2019, at Ascension St Vincent Carmel Hospital in Indiana, USA. Her brother, Jaxon DeWayne Mills Tello, followed just 30 min later, at 12:07 a.m. but in a new decade, on 1 Jan 2020.

The **first twins born in different countries** were Katherine and Heidi Roberts (both UK). Heidi arrived at 9:05 a.m. on 23 Sep 1976 at Welshpool Hospital in Wales. Katherine followed at 10:45 a.m., after their mother was transferred across the border to the Royal Shrewsbury Hospital in England, owing to complications.

Most premature...

• ▶ **Twins**: Adiah Laelynn and Adrial Luka Nadarajah (both CAN) were born 126 days before their due date on 4 Mar 2022.
• ▶ **Triplets**: Rubi-Rose, Payton-Jane and Porscha-Mae Hopkins (all UK) were born at a gestational age of 159 days – making them 121 days premature – on 14 Feb 2021.

Longest separated twins

After 77 years 289 days apart, Elizabeth Ann Hamel (née Lamb, USA) and Ann Patricia Hunt (née Wilson, UK) were reunited on 1 May 2014. They were born on 28 Feb 1936 in Aldershot, Hampshire, UK, to unmarried mother Alice Lamb, and were parted for adoption soon after.

In Feb 2024, reports emerged of a potentially even longer-delayed twin reunion: 90-year-olds Maurilia Chavez and Andrea Lopez (both USA) met in Dec 2023 after 81 years apart. GWR was examining the case as the book went to press.

Oldest craniopagus conjoined twins to be separated

On 8–9 Jun 2022, Arthur and Bernardo Lima (both BRA, b. 29 Aug 2018) were surgically separated at the age of 3 years 284 days. They were born joined at the head, with a fused brain; craniopagus twins are the rarest among conjoined twins, representing only 2–6% of cases. The series of procedures, lasting more than 27 hr, took place at the Instituto Estadual do Cerebro Paulo Niemeyer in Rio de Janeiro, Brazil. Some 100 medical staff were involved, led by paediatric neurosurgeon Professor Noor ul Owase Jeelani (*left, with parents Adriely and Antonio*) and Dr Gabriel Mufarrej.

Oldest conjoined twins ever

When Ronnie and Donnie Galyon (both USA, b. 25 Oct 1951) passed away from heart failure on 4 Jul 2020, they were aged 68 years 253 days.

The **oldest female-born conjoined twins ever** were Lori Lynn and George (b. Dori) Schappell (both USA, b. 18 Sep 1961). The craniopagus twins (*see above*) were aged 62 years 202 days when they died on 7 Apr 2024. In 2007, Dori declared that he was transgender, identifying as George.

Highest twinning rate (country)

About 1.6 million twins are born globally each year. Ivory Coast registered a rate of 24.9 twins for every 1,000 deliveries in 2010–15, according to a study of 135 countries published in 2020.

Oldest quadruplets

Ann, Ernest, Paul and Michael Miles (all UK, b. 28 Nov 1935) were aged 87 years 316 days as of 10 Oct 2023. Dubbed the "St Neots Quads", they were delivered by Dr Ernest Harrison (after whom one of the boys was named) some seven weeks premature. Owing to their exceptional needs in the early months, Dr Harrison took them into his own home, to better administer around-the-clock care with the support of nurses. Among the first quads to survive, they captured global media attention, as well as featuring in adverts, such as those by Cow & Gate milk.

Oldest non-identical mixed twins

Elsie Parkinson and George Bradley (both UK, b. 9 Apr 1927) were 96 years 112 days old, as verified on 30 Jul 2023. They were born at home in Weeton, Lancashire, UK. George was a farmer and Elsie a nursery-school teacher.

▶ **GREATEST HEIGHT DIFFERENCE IN NON-IDENTICAL FEMALE TWINS**

Yoshie Kikuchi is 75 cm (2 ft 5.5 in) taller than her sister Michie (both JPN), as confirmed in Okayama, Japan, on 23 Feb 2023. Michie has congenital spinal epiphyseal dysplasia – a rare genetic disorder. Once an introverted character, she was given a confidence boost after the twins were chosen to be torchbearers at the 2020 Tokyo Olympics. She was also inspired to apply to GWR after reading about the **shortest man ever** – 54.6-cm-tall (1-ft 9.5-in) Chandra Bahadur Dangi from Nepal.

▶ **Greatest height difference in identical female twins**

A disparity of 38 cm (1 ft 3 in) separates US twins Sienna "Sinny" Bernal (132 cm; 4 ft 4 in) and her sister Sierra (170 cm; 5 ft 7 in), as verified in Tomball, Texas, USA, in 2018. Both were 20 years old at the time. Sinny's diminutive stature is the result of a form of primordial dwarfism so uncommon that it isn't yet formally classified.

The girls' father is the chief priest at a temple, where the family also lives. Michie likes to help out there.

Amazing Anatomy

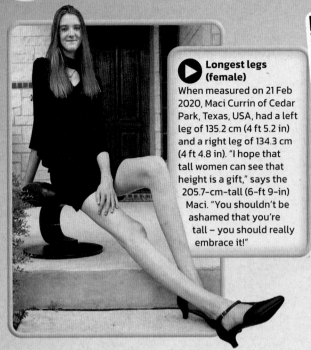

▶ Longest legs (female)

When measured on 21 Feb 2020, Maci Currin of Cedar Park, Texas, USA, had a left leg of 135.2 cm (4 ft 5.2 in) and a right leg of 134.3 cm (4 ft 4.8 in). "I hope that tall women can see that height is a gift," says the 205.7-cm-tall (6-ft 9-in) Maci. "You shouldn't be ashamed that you're tall – you should really embrace it!"

▶ Largest tongue circumference

Braydon McCullough (USA, *right*) has a rare ability: he can "inflate" his tongue, swelling it to 16 cm (6.3 in) – larger than a golf ball. The outsized organ was measured in Grafton, West Virginia, USA, on 23 May 2023.

The **women's** record is 13.25 cm (5.21 in) and held by Jenny DuVander (USA). She was reading *GWR 2023* with her son when they spotted the previous holder and decided to apply. Her record was ratified in Portland, Oregon, USA, on 17 May 2023.

Dear GWR...

After years of practice, I can fart the first verse of the *Star-Spangled Banner*. This is a very challenging song for a flatulist (fart-artiste) to attempt due to its range. Reaching the high notes requires tremendous control and a special diet to be eaten in the days before. I have offered to perform it at the opening game of the season for my local baseball team, the ▮▮▮▮▮▮▮▮. Perhaps you could send an official judge.

Largest kidney stone

On 1 Jun 2023, a 13.37–cm–long (5.26–in) nephrolith was removed from Canistus Coonghe (LKA) in Colombo, Sri Lanka. Weighing in at 800 g (1 lb 12 oz) – equivalent to around five billiard balls – it is also the **heaviest**. Kidney stones are common, affecting 1 in 10 people; these hard deposits are a combination of salt and minerals that form within the organ and are typically anywhere in size between a grain of sand and a pea.

Longest nose ever

According to historical accounts, Thomas Wedders (UK), a circus sideshow performer who toured England in the 18th century, had a 19-cm-long (7.5-in) nose. The most recent holder of the **living** record (8.80 cm; 3.46 in), Mehmet Özyürek, has passed away, leaving the category vacant. Large-nosed claimants should apply at **guinnessworldrecords.com**.

Smallest waist ever

Between 1929 and 1939, Ethel Granger (UK) reduced her midriff from a natural size of 56 cm (22 in) to 33 cm (13 in). A body-modification pioneer, Granger shrank her waist by wearing progressively tighter corsets. The French actress Polaire (aka Émilie Marie Bouchaud; 1874–1939) also claimed to have achieved a 33-cm "wasp waist".

Cathie Jung (USA) holds the **living** record, with a 38.1-cm (15-in) corseted midriff.

Largest hands ever (female)

The hands of Zeng Jinlian (CHN) had a wrist-to-fingertip length of 25.4 cm (10 in). For the **men's** record, *see p.26,* while to discover more about Zeng – who was also the **tallest woman ever** – *see p.63*.

▶ Widest mouth (female)

Samantha Ramsdell (USA) has a 10.33-cm-wide (4.07-in) mouth – broad enough to accommodate an entire large portion of McDonald's French fries. Her capacious maw was measured in Norwalk, Connecticut, USA, on 29 Nov 2022.

Samantha also has the **largest gape (female)** – 6.52 cm (2.56 in) separates her upper and lower incisors, as confirmed on 15 Jul 2021.

Oldest milk tooth

On 14 Mar 2023, at the age of 90 years 192 days, Leonard Murray (b. 3 Sep 1932) of Chattanooga, Tennessee, USA, was confimed as still having a healthy lower-right T deciduous ("baby") tooth.

▶ Farthest eyeball pop

Tio Chico Brasil (aka Sidney de Carvalho Mesquita, BRA) can protrude his eyeballs by 18.2 mm (0.71 in), as measured in São Paulo, Brazil, on 10 Jan 2022.

The **women's** record – 12 mm (0.47 in) – has been held by Kim Goodman (USA) since 2 Nov 2007. Before she learned how to control them properly, Kim's eyes would even propel forwards when she yawned!

100%

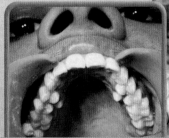
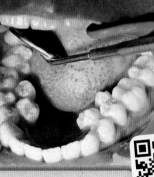

▶ Most teeth (female)

Kalpana Balan (IND, *above*) has 38 teeth – six more than most adults – as verified in Thanjavur, Tamil Nadu, India, on 24 Jun 2023. The supernumerary teeth form a partial row within her mouth.

The **overall** hyperdontia record – 41 – is held by Evano Mellone (CAN), as confirmed in Montreal, Quebec, Canada, on 11 Nov 2021.

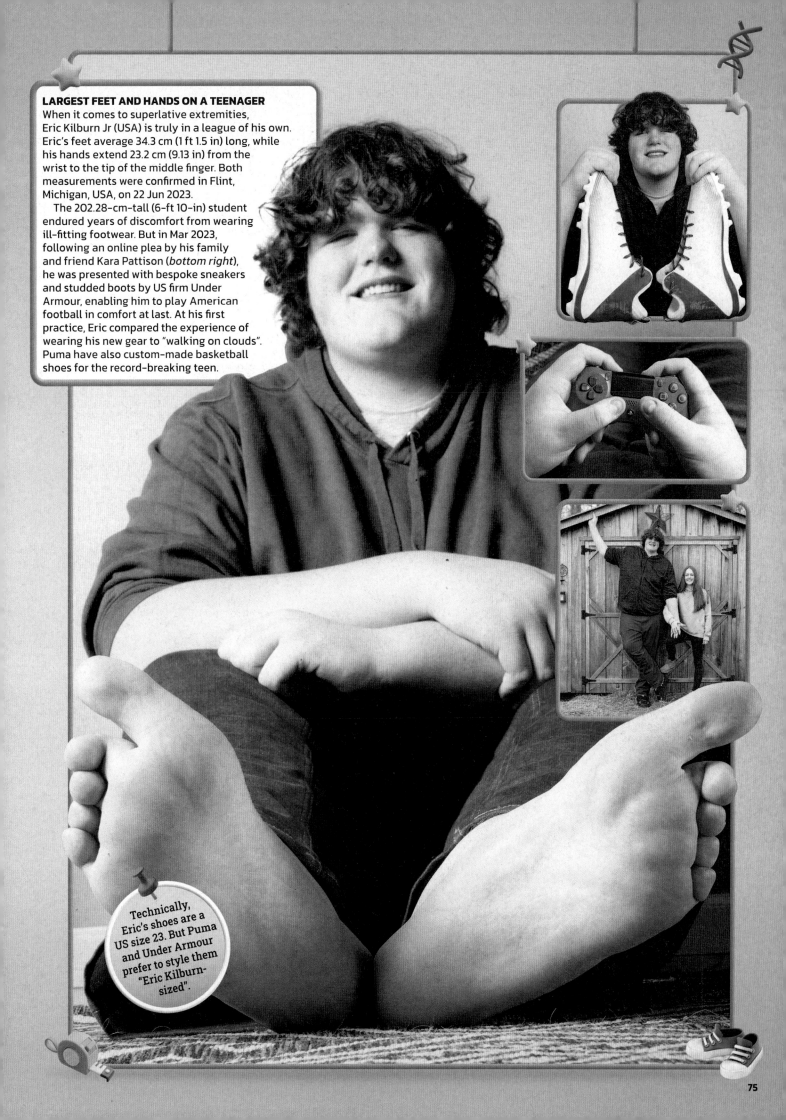

LARGEST FEET AND HANDS ON A TEENAGER
When it comes to superlative extremities, Eric Kilburn Jr (USA) is truly in a league of his own. Eric's feet average 34.3 cm (1 ft 1.5 in) long, while his hands extend 23.2 cm (9.13 in) from the wrist to the tip of the middle finger. Both measurements were confirmed in Flint, Michigan, USA, on 22 Jun 2023.

The 202.28-cm-tall (6-ft 10-in) student endured years of discomfort from wearing ill-fitting footwear. But in Mar 2023, following an online plea by his family and friend Kara Pattison (*bottom right*), he was presented with bespoke sneakers and studded boots by US firm Under Armour, enabling him to play American football in comfort at last. At his first practice, Eric compared the experience of wearing his new gear to "walking on clouds". Puma have also custom-made basketball shoes for the record-breaking teen.

Technically, Eric's shoes are a US size 23. But Puma and Under Armour prefer to style them "Eric Kilburn-sized".

Bodybuilders

First bodybuilding contest

"The Great Competition" was held at the Royal Albert Hall in London, UK, on 14 Sep 1901. Competitors posed in a leopard-skin loincloth and tights to display their physique for the judges – who included Sherlock Holmes author Arthur Conan Doyle and Eugen Sandow (DEU, *left*), a famed strongman who is thought of as the father of modern bodybuilding. Around 15,000 people attended, with many others turned away. The winner was a track athlete and professional footballer called William Murray. He was presented with a gold statuette of Sandow and a cash prize of £1,050 – equivalent to around £107,000 ($136,000) in 2024.

Greatest prize money for bodybuilding

Staged annually in the USA since 1965, Mr Olympia is regarded as the most prestigious award in professional men's bodybuilding. The 2023 competition, held on 2–5 Nov, offered a purse of $400,000 (£322,950) for the winner of the Men's Open. Derek Lunsford (USA) walked away with the top prize. A previous winner of the "212" category in 2021, he became Mr Olympia's first two-division winner.

Most Mr Olympia titles

Two men have won eight Open titles, both consecutively: Lee Haney (USA), from 1984 to 1991; and Ronnie Coleman (USA), between 1998 and 2005. Coleman also won the Arnold Classic in 2001, becoming the first bodybuilder to claim both titles in the same year.

Most Ms Olympia titles

Between 2004 and 2014, Iris Kyle (USA) won 10 editions of the IFBB's blue-riband women's event. A college basketball All-American, Iris discovered bodybuilding when her family moved to Orange County, California. She dominated the sport, also claiming seven Ms International titles at the Arnold Sports Festival.

Most wins of Wheelchair Olympia

Harold Kelley (USA) won the first five editions of this event between 2018 and 2022. A professional bodybuilder, Harold was left paralysed from the waist down after a car accident in 2007. After completing his medical rehabilitation he returned to the sport he loved, and began a new training regimen adapted to his condition.

Shortest male competitive bodybuilder

Indian iron-pumper Pratik Mohite stands just 102 cm (3 ft 4 in) tall. Born short-statured, with undersized hands and feet, doctors feared he would not be able to walk. But Pratik took up weight training at the age of 18 and has competed in more than 40 bodybuilding events.

On 30 Jul 2023, Pratik set the record for the **most push-ups in one minute (male)** in GWR's short-statured category – 84, in Raigad, Maharashtra, India.

Shortest Mr Olympia contestant

Flavio Baccianini (ITA) measured 147 cm (4 ft 10 in) at the 1993 event in Atlanta, Georgia, USA. He placed 13th out of 22 competitors.

Tallest male professional bodybuilder

Olivier Richters (NLD) measured 218.3 cm (7 ft 1.9 in) on 27 Apr 2021. The "Dutch Giant" is also an actor who appeared in *Indiana Jones and the Dial of Destiny* (USA, 2023).

The confirmed **female** record is held by Maria Wattel (NLD), who stood 182.7 cm (5 ft 11.9 in) tall as of 15 Jan 2021.

Oldest female bodybuilder ever

Edith Wilma Conner (USA, 5 Sep 1935–28 Nov 2020) was aged 75 years 349 days when she competed in the Armbrust Pro Gym Warrior Classic on 20 Aug 2011. The great-grandmother took up bodybuilding in her 60s and triumphed in her very first event – the Grand Masters – on her 65th birthday.

Youngest Mr Olympia

Arnold Schwarzenegger (USA, b. AUT; 30 Jul 1947) was 23 years 65 days old when he won his first Mr Olympia title on 3 Oct 1970. He went on to win seven overall, coming out of retirement to reclaim his crown in 1980. His star turn in bodybuilding documentary *Pumping Iron* (USA, 1977) helped propel "Arnie" to Hollywood stardom in movies such as *The Terminator* (UK/USA, 1984).

In Mar 2024, Arnie's chiselled physique was immortalized as the largest action figure (see p.206).

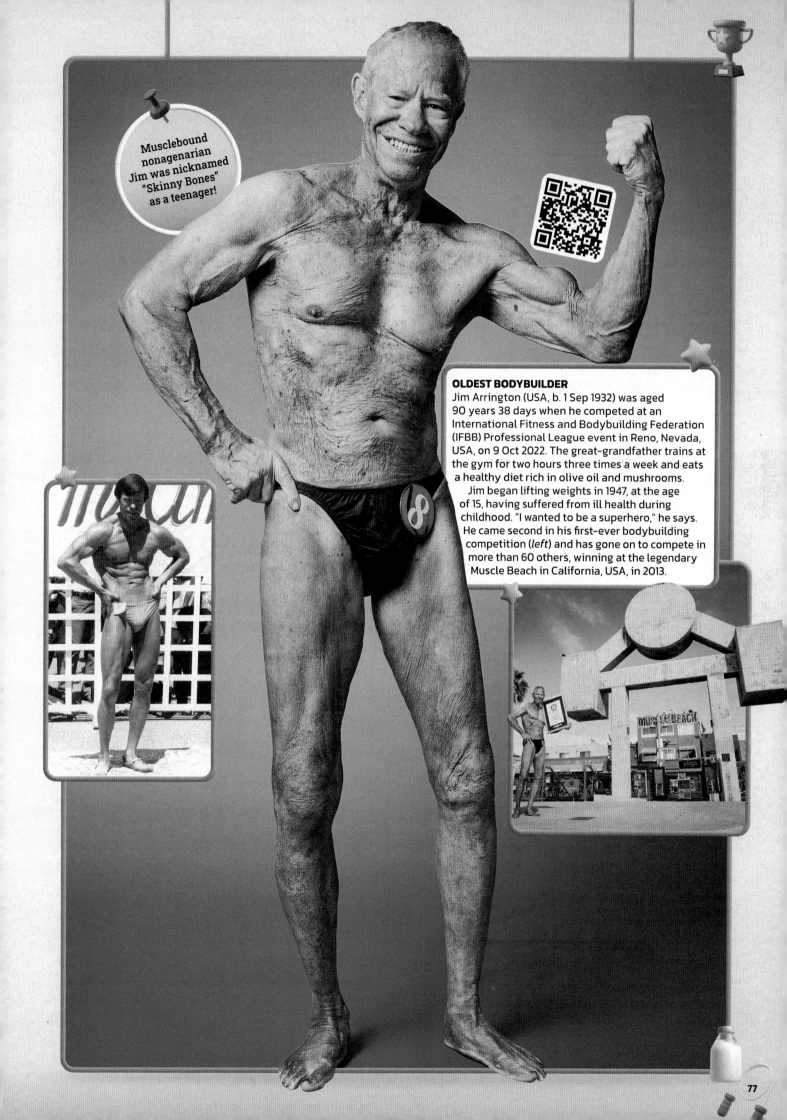

Musclebound nonagenarian Jim was nicknamed "Skinny Bones" as a teenager!

OLDEST BODYBUILDER

Jim Arrington (USA, b. 1 Sep 1932) was aged 90 years 38 days when he competed at an International Fitness and Bodybuilding Federation (IFBB) Professional League event in Reno, Nevada, USA, on 9 Oct 2022. The great-grandfather trains at the gym for two hours three times a week and eats a healthy diet rich in olive oil and mushrooms.

Jim began lifting weights in 1947, at the age of 15, having suffered from ill health during childhood. "I wanted to be a superhero," he says. He came second in his first-ever bodybuilding competition (*left*) and has gone on to compete in more than 60 others, winning at the legendary Muscle Beach in California, USA, in 2013.

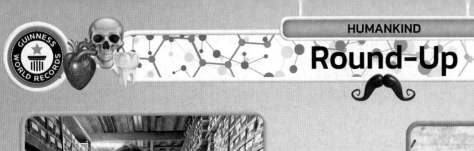

Round-Up

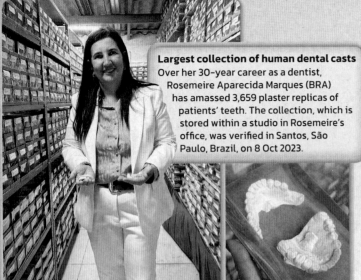

Largest collection of human dental casts
Over her 30-year career as a dentist, Rosemeire Aparecida Marques (BRA) has amassed 3,659 plaster replicas of patients' teeth. The collection, which is stored within a studio in Rosemeire's office, was verified in Santos, São Paulo, Brazil, on 8 Oct 2023.

Largest human image of an organ
On 16 Mar 2024, a group of 5,596 people dressed in red or green recreated a pair of lungs in Manila, Philippines. The event was organized by the country's Department of Health to highlight the need for collective action to end tuberculosis (TB), ahead of World TB Day on 24 Mar.

First successful human eye transplant
After being injured in a high-voltage electrical accident, Aaron James (USA) underwent 21 hr of surgery to receive a new eye in May 2023 in New York City, USA. Doctors have observed direct blood flow to the retina of the replacement eye, although Aaron has not yet regained vision in it.

Longest-surviving heart-transplant patient
Fifty-seven-year-old Bert Janssen (NLD) has lived with a donated heart for 39 years 100 days, as verified on 14 Sep 2023. His operation took place at Harefield Hospital in London, UK, on 6 Jun 1984.

Oldest fashion model
Daphne Selfe (UK, b. 1 Jul 1928), who is signed to the Models 1 agency, was aged 95 years 158 days as of 6 Dec 2023. In a career that has spanned more than 70 years, she has modelled for the likes of Dolce & Gabbana, appeared in *Vogue* and been snapped by renowned photographers such as Mario Testino and David Bailey.

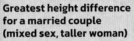

Greatest height difference for a married couple (mixed sex, taller woman)
A gap of 86.36 cm (2 ft 10 in) separates Larry McDonnell and Jessica Burns-McDonnell (both USA), as verified in South Charleston, West Virginia, USA, on 5 Dec 2023. The couple had originally met in elementary school and later became neighbours. They have been married for almost 15 years and have four children.

Oldest kidney-transplant recipient
On 11 Jun 2023, Walter Tauro (IND, b. 22 Sep 1935) received a new kidney at the age of 87 years 262 days. The operation took place at St Michael's Hospital in Toronto, Ontario, Canada. Despite the risk of surgery at his age, Walter was adamant that he didn't want to continue having dialysis every day.

Oldest septuplets
Born to Kenny and Bobbi McCaughey in Des Moines, Iowa, USA, on 19 Nov 1997, Kenneth (Kenny), Alexis, Natalie, Kelsey, Nathan, Brandon and Joel celebrated their 26th birthday in 2023.

Most whole blood donated
By 11 Nov 2023, Josephine Michaluk (CAN) had given blood 208 times, as confirmed in Red Deer, Alberta, Canada. Her first donation was on 25 Mar 1987, since when she has provided more than 99 litres (209 pints).

▶ Loudest burp
Neville Sharp (AUS) unleashed a belch registering 112.4 decibels (dB) in Darwin, Northern Territory, Australia, on 29 Jul 2021. That's louder than a chainsaw at a distance of 1 m (3 ft 3 in).
The **women's** record eructation – 107.3 dB – was delivered by Kimberly Winter (USA) in Rockville, Maryland, USA, on 28 Apr 2023. In preparation, she ate breakfast, washed down with a coffee and a beer.

▶ Loudest nose whistle
LuLu Lotus (CAN) produced a 44.1-dB whistle through her nose in Mississauga, Ontario, Canada, on 3 Jun 2022. She creates the high-pitched sound using her throat muscles; with her mouth closed, the noise exits through her nostrils. One of LuLu's young sons has the same ability. "It would be a dream come true if he beat my record one day," she said.

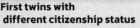

First twins with different citizenship status
On 16 Sep 2016, married couple Andrew (USA/CAN, *left*) and Elad Dvash-Banks (ISR, *right*) had fraternal twin sons via surrogacy. But despite the boys being born within minutes of each other in Canada, only Aiden (*centre left*) was granted US citizenship. The application for their other son, Ethan (*centre right*), was rejected in 2017, as the twins had been conceived with the sperm of different fathers: Aiden from Andrew's and Ethan from Elad's. After years of legal action, the fathers were finally granted US citizenship for both of their sons in Feb 2021.

Highest combined age of 13 living siblings

The Beers siblings (all NLD) had an aggregate age of 1,106 years 105 days as of 25 Feb 2023. They are: Riek (b. 26 Feb 1928), Nick (b. 26 Feb 1928), Gré (b. 5 Apr 1930), Ali (b. 24 Jul 1931), Riet (b. 5 Dec 1932), Truus (b. 25 Aug 1935), Wout (b. 3 Jan 1938), Siem (b. 5 Aug 1940), Cor (b. 30 Mar 1942), Harm (b. 18 Jan 1944), Wil (b. 7 Nov 1945), Nel (b. 2 Sep 1947) and Jos (b. 27 Jul 1949). To keep everyone updated on each other's lives, the family produce a newspaper, titled *Beersenkrant*. They are shown below in 1953 with parents Johannes Beers and Aaltje Mooij. Two other siblings who have since passed away are also pictured.

Most couples married in 12 hours

A mass wedding saw 2,143 couples tie the knot in Baran, Rajasthan, India, on 26 May 2023, in a ceremony arranged by non-profit organization Shri Mahaveer Gaushala Kalyan Sansthan (IND). Both Hindu and Muslim marriages were conducted at the event, which attracted more than 1 million attendees.

Most henna tattoos completed in one hour

On 15 Jul 2021, teacher Samina Hussain (UK) applied 600 temporary armbands at Wensley Fold CE Primary Academy in Blackburn, Lancashire, UK. Samina was assisted by pupils and sponsored by community group One Voice Blackburn.

Shortest band

MINIKISS (USA) have an average height of 138.55 cm (4 ft 6.5 in), as confirmed on 4 Feb 2023. Currently comprising Arturo Knight, Zach Morris, Andrew Jacobs and Leif Manson, they are a tribute act to US rock legends KISS, with whom they teamed up for a Dr Pepper commercial during Super Bowl XLIV in 2010.

Longest arm hair

• **Female**: 18.4 cm (7.24 in), set by Macie Davis-Southerland (USA) in Tracy, California, USA, on 5 Dec 2023.
• **Male**: 21.7 cm (8.54 in), set by David Reed (USA) in Los Angeles, California, USA, on 26 Aug 2017.

Greatest foot rotation (male)

Renato Bayma Gaia (BRA) twisted his right foot 210.66° from its natural position in São José dos Campos, São Paulo, Brazil, on 21 Jan 2024.

Highest combined age of five living siblings

France's Paulette (b. 3 Feb 1921), Ginette (b. 30 Jul 1923), Mireille (b. 20 Dec 1924), Christiane (b. 3 Jun 1926) and Philippe (b. 17 Oct 1927) Toutée had a total age of 495 years 352 days, as verified on 18 Dec 2023.

Largest nasal septum flesh tunnel

Colton Pifer (USA) has a 2.6-cm-thick (1-in) item of jewellery inserted between his nostrils, as confirmed in Monroe, Michigan, USA, on 17 Aug 2023. He's not averse to performing party tricks with his modified nasal passageways, such as removing the flesh tunnel and passing a hot dog through the gap!

Most facial flesh tunnels

James Goss (UK) has 17 holes in his face created by plug piercings – as verified in London, UK, on 28 Mar 2023. Already the record holder with a count of 15, James increased his tally with two 4.5-mm-diameter (0.1-in) piercings on his nostrils, added just above an existing pair. He had his very first piercing – in his earlobe – aged 13.

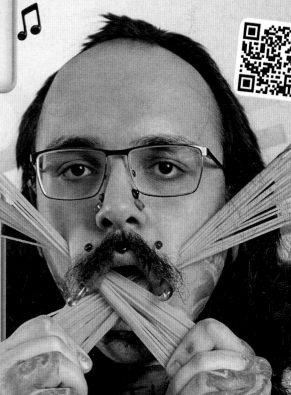

ICON

Diana Armstrong

Behind every world record is a story – often a deeply personal story that can answer that most crucial of questions: *Why?* And few record holders have stories as compelling as those with the longest fingernails.

The current holder of this iconic title – and indeed the owner of the **longest fingernails on a pair of hands ever** – is Diana Armstrong, who lives in Minneapolis, Minnesota, USA. It was a family tragedy that prompted this quiet-spoken grandmother to never again cut her fingernails – a coping mechanism that now, 25 years later, has earned her a place in the record books.

Back when she had average-sized nails, Diana enjoyed having them manicured by her 16-year-old daughter, Latisha. After one such evening in 1997, however, Latisha suffered a fatal asthma attack in her sleep. From that moment, Diana vowed never to trim her nails again, preserving them as a lasting memento of her daughter.

"Anytime I thought about cutting them off, it gave me chills," she said, "like I'm going through that grief all over again... So, I just kept them. It's like keeping her close to me."

By the time GWR first met Diana in Mar 2022, her nails had grown to a combined length of 1,306.58 cm (42 ft 10.4 in) – the longest ever measured. "When I started growing them, it wasn't to be in the book," she said. "Now, since I am, I tell people you shouldn't judge, because you don't know what others have gone through."

Diana lives with her family, so there's always someone on hand to help negotiate the more challenging aspects of life, such as sleeves and zips. Amazingly, it was only recently that this determined grandmother gave up driving. "I drove a car but had to stick my hand out the window."

Top: Diana in the 1990s with her four children. *Above:* Latisha, whose tragic passing aged just 16 inspired her mother's lifelong dedication to growing out her fingernails. "Every time I look at my nails, I think of my daughter... She's my guardian angel."

Diana with her daughter Rania (*top*) and granddaughter Dafyiness (*above*). In the decade following the death of Latisha, Diana battled with depression and kept the reason why she didn't trim her nails a secret from her family. "Mind your business," she'd tell them when asked. "When she told us the backstory, it kind of changed my feelings towards it," said Rania. "If that's her way of holding on to Tisha, then I accept."

Find out more about Diana in the ICON section at **www.guinnessworldrecords.com/2025**

Diana has learned to adapt, finding novel ways to do everyday tasks like picking things off the floor (with her toes), eating (using long barbecue utensils) and typing (with a long pencil).

Each of Diana's nails takes around four to five hours to paint, so she only has them done every few years. The process requires 15 to 20 bottles of nail polish – and a woodworking tool for filing.

Despite the extraordinary length of her nails, Diana was surprised when GWR first reached out. "I thought it was a joke," she admitted. She initially rejected the record for fear of criticism or ridicule, but has since come to feel confident about her unique status. "I think my nails are pretty. To somebody else, they might not be, but to me, they are."

LARGEST COLLECTION OF SQUISHMALLOWS

Sabrina Dausman (USA) had accumulated 1,523 cuddly plushies as of 17 Dec 2023. She spotted her first Squishmallow in 2018 in the run-up to Valentine's Day, and it was love at first sight. Sabrina will drive for hours and wait outside stores if it means she can track down a certain Squishmallow – although ultra-rare editions of cattle Connor and Cliff still elude her. Her favourite is Sam the dog, as it reminds her of a childhood pet. "What I love most about Squishmallows is how comforting they are," Sabrina told GWR, adding that they help her deal with anxiety. She has collected toys from a young age, including ranges such as Bratz and Webkinz.

Squishmallows creator Jonathan Kelly was inspired by kawaii-style cute toys in Japan.

CONTENTS

Sabrina has two dedicated "Squish Rooms" at home, which she has crammed with the soft toys.

Fastest 3x3x3 Puzzle Solve

Ever since the appearance of the Rubik's Cube in 1974, cubers have steadily shaved seconds – and now milliseconds – off the time it takes to solve it. And since the first official event in 1982, the record has fallen by a factor of *seven*!

It took Hungarian inventor Ernő Rubik a whole month to unscramble his own twisty puzzle. Yet today, cubers are logging unofficial times under 3 sec! (E.g., Patrick Ponce – see #6 below – reported 2.99 sec in 2019, and one cuber in Jun 2023 claimed 2.47 sec!)

What really matters, though, is the time logged in competition. Here, we visualize the history of those official fastest solves, using a cube for every second (and, for the 20 fastest results, "cubies" for the fractions). Cubers are influenced by many things: the physical limits of the human hand, the manufacturing tolerance of the cube and pure luck, as the computer-generated random scramble might give an advantage. So, will anyone officially break that elusive 3-sec barrier?

KEY
1 cube = 1 sec

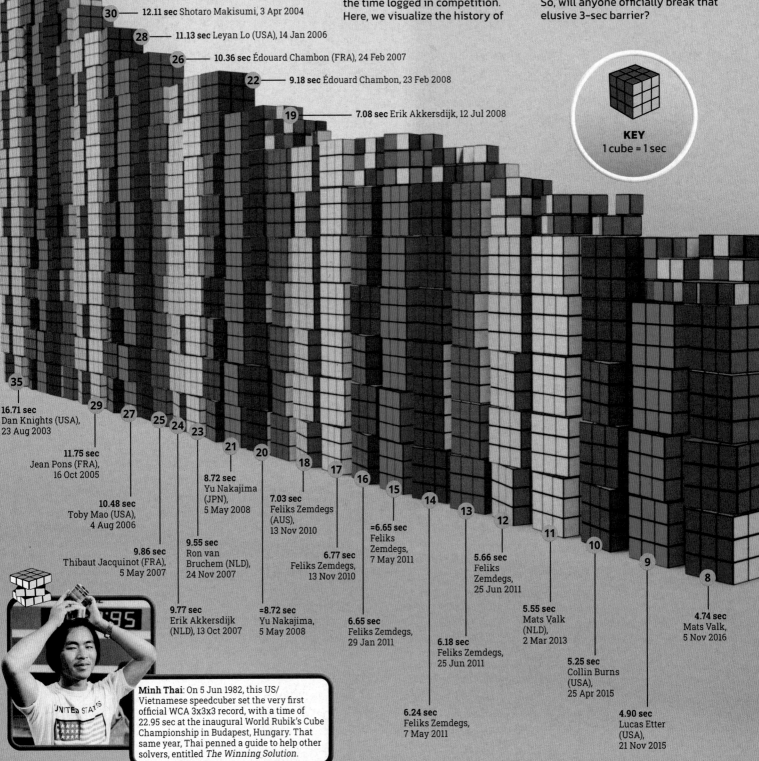

36 — 22.95 sec
Minh Thai
(USA, b. VNM),
5 Jun 1982
(*see below*)

34 — 16.53 sec Jess Bonde (DNK), 23 Aug 2003

33 — 15.07 sec Shotaro Makisumi (JPN), 24 Jan 2004

32 — 14.76 sec Shotaro Makisumi, 24 Jan 2004

31 — 13.93 sec Shotaro Makisumi, 3 Apr 2004

30 — 12.11 sec Shotaro Makisumi, 3 Apr 2004

28 — 11.13 sec Leyan Lo (USA), 14 Jan 2006

26 — 10.36 sec Édouard Chambon (FRA), 24 Feb 2007

22 — 9.18 sec Édouard Chambon, 23 Feb 2008

19 — 7.08 sec Erik Akkersdijk, 12 Jul 2008

35
16.71 sec
Dan Knights (USA),
23 Aug 2003

29
11.75 sec
Jean Pons (FRA),
16 Oct 2005

27
10.48 sec
Toby Mao (USA),
4 Aug 2006

25
9.86 sec
Thibaut Jacquinot (FRA),
5 May 2007

24
9.77 sec
Erik Akkersdijk
(NLD), 13 Oct 2007

23
9.55 sec
Ron van
Bruchem (NLD),
24 Nov 2007

21
8.72 sec
Yu Nakajima
(JPN),
5 May 2008

20
=8.72 sec
Yu Nakajima,
5 May 2008

18
7.03 sec
Feliks Zemdegs
(AUS),
13 Nov 2010

17
6.77 sec
Feliks Zemdegs,
13 Nov 2010

16
6.65 sec
Feliks Zemdegs,
29 Jan 2011

15
=6.65 sec
Feliks
Zemdegs,
7 May 2011

14
6.18 sec
Feliks Zemdegs,
25 Jun 2011

13
5.66 sec
Feliks
Zemdegs,
25 Jun 2011

12
5.55 sec
Mats Valk
(NLD),
2 Mar 2013

11
5.25 sec
Collin Burns
(USA),
25 Apr 2015

10
4.90 sec
Lucas Etter
(USA),
21 Nov 2015

9

8
4.74 sec
Mats Valk,
5 Nov 2016

6.24 sec
Feliks Zemdegs,
7 May 2011

Minh Thai: On 5 Jun 1982, this US/Vietnamese speedcuber set the very first official WCA 3x3x3 record, with a time of 22.95 sec at the inaugural World Rubik's Cube Championship in Budapest, Hungary. That same year, Thai penned a guide to help other solvers, entitled *The Winning Solution*.

Most wins of the WCA World Championship
Competitive cubing is governed by the World Cube Association (WCA), and two speedcubers have won the WCA World Championship twice – close friends Feliks Zemdegs (AUS, *left,* in 2013 and 2015) and Max Park (USA, *right,* in 2017 and 2023). Zemdegs is a cubing legend, having set the 3x3x3 single-solve record 10 times. He also previously claimed the **fastest *average* time to solve a 3x3x3 cube** on several occasions, but that record has now passed to Yiheng Wang (*below*).

When Max was just 10 years old, he won his second cubing competition, beating two college graduates.

Fastest 3x3x3 (average)
On 20 Jun 2023, Yiheng Wang (CHN) clocked an average 3x3x3 solve of 4.48 sec. His final time came from five attempts: 4.72 sec, 4.72 sec, 3.99 sec, 3.95 sec and 5.99 sec, with the fastest and slowest solves discounted as per WCA rules. The nine-year-old achieved the fleet-fingered feat during the final at the Mofunland Cruise Open event in Singapore.

Fastest 3x3x3 (single)
Speedcubing colossus Max Park (USA) took just 3.13 sec to unscramble a 3x3x3 cube at the Pride in Long Beach 2023 event in California, USA. Proving he is no one-trick pony, the official Rubik's Ambassador also currently holds the **single-solve** and **average-time** records for **4x4x4**, **5x5x5** and **7x7x7** cubes (*see p.99*).

4.22 sec
Feliks Zemdegs,
6 May 2018
(*see above*)
3

3.47 sec
Yusheng Du (CHN),
24 Nov 2018
2

3.13 sec
Max Park (USA),
11 Jun 2023
(*see above*)
1

7
4.73 sec
Feliks
Zemdegs,
11 Dec 2016

6
4.69 sec
Patrick Ponce
(USA),
2 Sep 2017

5
4.59 sec
SeungBeom Cho
(KOR), 28 Oct 2017

4
=4.59 sec
Feliks Zemdegs,
27 Jan 2018

Kites

Oldest kite

An example of a "French pear-top" discovered in 1985 dates back at least 250 years to 1773. It was found during renovations of a property in Leiden, Netherlands, and is inscribed "RB and TB 1773". Despite its age, the kite is still thought to be flyable and is now part of a collection in New Zealand that is being curated by Peter Lynn (*see opposite*).

Largest leaf kite flown

Kites made from interwoven leaves may have been the first ever flown, and are still made in Indonesia to this day. On 7 Oct 2016, Yayasan Masyarakat Layang (IDN) unveiled one with an area of 10.75 m² (115.71 sq ft) at Jakarta Garden City. The leaf kite took two weeks to make and stood 5 m (16 ft 4 in) tall and 4.3 m (14 ft 1 in) wide.

First kites

Scholars have long attributed the invention of kites to China in the 5th century BCE. Philosopher Mozi (*c.* 470–*c.* 391 BCE) and engineer Lu Ban (*c.* 507–444 BCE) are credited as being among the first to create "flying birds" – initially out of wood, then lighter bamboo and silk.

A rival theory contends that a Mesolithic cave painting (*c.* 9000–9500 BCE) on the Indonesian island of Muna, off Sulawesi, depicts a figure flying a kite. Yet while kites have played a role in Indonesian and Pacific island culture for centuries – including as tools for fishing – this origin story remains disputed.

First kite-powered vehicle

British inventor George Pocock patented the first "horseless carriage" in the form of a kite-drawn buggy in 1826. It could attain speeds of 25 mph (40 km/h) for short bursts. His "charvolant" attracted some attention as a novelty but never caught on as everyday transport.

Largest kite museum

The Weifang World Kite Museum in Shandong, China, has a floor area of 8,100 m² (87,190 sq ft) spread across 12 halls. It houses approximately 1,300 exhibits dedicated to the craft and culture of kite-making and flying, including more than 1,000 unique kites from around the globe.

The city has a long and illustrious history in this field, as the **first kites** (*see left*) are believed to have emerged in the region some 2,500 years ago. It also hosts the Weifang International Kite Festival each year, which celebrated its 40th edition in 2023 (*below*).

Highest altitude for a kite

With assistance, Robert Moore (AUS) flew a 12.3-m² (132.4-sq-ft) DT Delta to a height of 4,879.54 m (16,009 ft) in the skies above a remote sheep station in New South Wales, Australia, on 23 Sep 2014. Around 12.4 km (7.7 mi) of line was used.

The **highest altitude for a train of kites** is 9,740 m (31,955 ft), set by a team from the Prussian Meteorological Institute on 1 Aug 1919 in Lindenberg, Germany. The "Schirmdrachen" comprised eight modified box-kites. Multi-kite designs can attain greater heights as more evenly distributed weight along the line increases stability.

Fastest speed by a flying kite

A modified Flexifoil Super 10 flown by Pete DiGiacomo (USA) hit 193 km/h (120 mph) in Ocean City, Maryland, USA, on 22 Sep 1989.

Most kites flown at once by one person

Ma Qinghua (CHN) flew 43 kites off the same string in Weifang, Shandong, China, on 7 Nov 2006. Ma, a kite designer, set the record on Chinese TV.

The **most kites flown on one line (team)** is 15,585, by students from Toyohashi Municipal Inami Junior High School in Aichi, Japan, on 14 Nov 1998.

The Weifang festival's show kites come in many forms, from dragons and sea creatures to space stations!

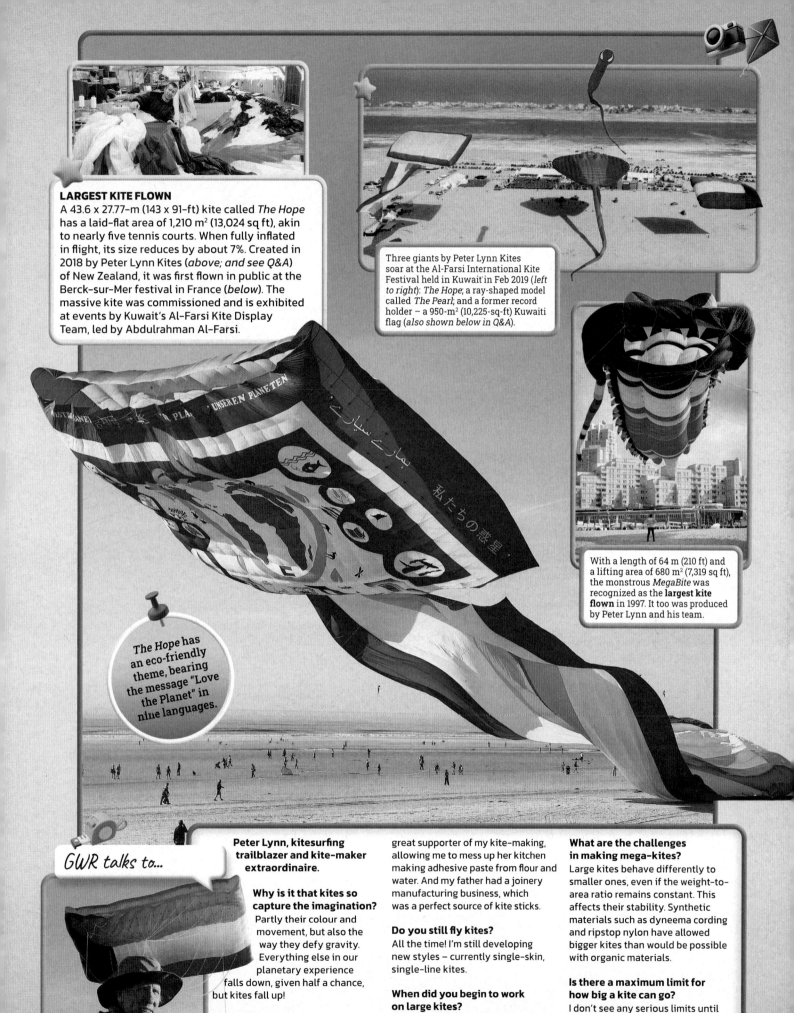

LARGEST KITE FLOWN

A 43.6 x 27.77-m (143 x 91-ft) kite called *The Hope* has a laid-flat area of 1,210 m² (13,024 sq ft), akin to nearly five tennis courts. When fully inflated in flight, its size reduces by about 7%. Created in 2018 by Peter Lynn Kites (*above; and see Q&A*) of New Zealand, it was first flown in public at the Berck-sur-Mer festival in France (*below*). The massive kite was commissioned and is exhibited at events by Kuwait's Al-Farsi Kite Display Team, led by Abdulrahman Al-Farsi.

Three giants by Peter Lynn Kites soar at the Al-Farsi International Kite Festival held in Kuwait in Feb 2019 (*left to right*): *The Hope*; a ray-shaped model called *The Pearl*; and a former record holder – a 950-m² (10,225-sq-ft) Kuwaiti flag (*also shown below in Q&A*).

The Hope has an eco-friendly theme, bearing the message "Love the Planet" in nine languages.

With a length of 64 m (210 ft) and a lifting area of 680 m² (7,319 sq ft), the monstrous *MegaBite* was recognized as the **largest kite flown** in 1997. It too was produced by Peter Lynn and his team.

GWR talks to...

Peter Lynn, kitesurfing trailblazer and kite-maker extraordinaire.

Why is it that kites so capture the imagination?
Partly their colour and movement, but also the way they defy gravity. Everything else in our planetary experience falls down, given half a chance, but kites fall up!

When did you build your first kite?
Around three/four years old – with help from my mother. She was a great supporter of my kite-making, allowing me to mess up her kitchen making adhesive paste from flour and water. And my father had a joinery manufacturing business, which was a perfect source of kite sticks.

Do you still fly kites?
All the time! I'm still developing new styles – currently single-skin, single-line kites.

When did you begin to work on large kites?
I made the *MegaBite* (*above*) in the 1990s. Since then we have escalated the sizes slowly, to give each new large kite its time in the spotlight.

What are the challenges in making mega-kites?
Large kites behave differently to smaller ones, even if the weight-to-area ratio remains constant. This affects their stability. Synthetic materials such as dyneema cording and ripstop nylon have allowed bigger kites than would be possible with organic materials.

Is there a maximum limit for how big a kite can go?
I don't see any serious limits until around 5,000 m² [53,819 sq ft]. However, diagonal stresses in fabric panels begin to be an issue even at 1,250 m² [13,454 sq ft].

Numismatics

Smallest paper money
In 1917, amid the turmoil of World War I, Romania issued a series of emergency notes to replace coins. The smallest 10-bani note had a printed area of just 27.5 x 38 mm (1.08 x 1.49 in).

100%

First paper money
During China's Song Dynasty (960–1279), merchants in Sichuan printed promissory notes called "Jiaozi". They included secret cyphers and marks intended to reveal forgeries.

The **oldest surviving banknotes** are examples of the "Great Ming Circulating Treasure Note" from c. 1375. There were no restrictions on the printing of these notes by local governors, so they soon lost 99% of their value due to oversupply. When the currency collapsed, bundles of the useless notes were stowed away, meaning they are quite common in collections today.

Largest legal banknote
In 2017, Bank Negara Malaysia issued an 814-cm² (126-sq-in) banknote to mark the 60th anniversary of the Federation of Malaya Independence Act of 1957. All 15 of the country's leaders since that year are depicted on the bill, which has a face value of 600 Malaysian ringgit (approximately £100; $127).

Most expensive error banknote
The "Del Monte Note" is a $20 bill that sold for $396,000 (£288,811) at Heritage Auctions (USA) on 22 Jan 2021. The note acquired its unique name after a Del Monte fruit sticker became stuck to it between printing passes. Experts believe that the sticker was likely placed deliberately by a bored employee.

Largest counterfeiting operation
During World War II, the German Third Reich instigated "Operation Bernhard", a plan to ruin the British economy with a flood of bogus currency. It involved more than 9 million counterfeit British notes valued at £130 m ($520 m) in £5, £10, £20 and £50 bills. At the end of the war, the equipment and remaining notes were deliberately sunk in Lake Toplitz, Austria.

The **largest counterfeiting operation by an individual** saw Frank Bourassa (USA) forge about $250 m (£194 m) in US currency between 2008 and 2010. Using an illegal print shop on a farm in Quebec, Canada, Bourassa printed 12.5 million faked $20 bills and sold them for 30% of their face value.

Most expensive coin sold at auction
The 1933 Double Eagle sold for $18,872,250 (£13.3 m) at Sotheby's in New York City, USA, on 8 Jun 2021. This was the final US gold coin to be struck for circulation before President Franklin D Roosevelt removed the USA from the gold standard – separating the value of the dollar from that of gold – and ordered all copies of the coin to be destroyed.

100%

Largest replica coin
The Big Nickel is a 9.1-m-wide (30-ft), 0.6-m-thick (2-ft) likeness of a 1951 Canadian five-cent coin. It dominates the Dynamic Earth science facility in Sudbury, Ontario, Canada, and was unveiled to the public on 27 Jul 1964. The coin was chosen because 1951 marked the bicentennial of the chemical isolation and classification of nickel, the mining of which had greatly contributed to the city's growth.

Highest denomination banknote ever
The Hungarian million billion pengő note was first printed on 3 Jun 1946, while the country's finances were in crisis. During World War II, 40% of its assets were stripped by occupying forces and it was made to pay $300 m (c. £74 m) in war reparations. All this fuelled hyperinflation.

In Jul 1946, Hungary recorded the **highest inflation rate ever**, with a consumer price index inflation rate of 41,900,000,000,000,000%. A daily inflation rate of 207% saw the prices of everyday items double every 15 hr.

The million billion pengő note was withdrawn on 31 Jul. Later that year, Hungary issued a new currency, the forint, which could be exchanged at a rate of one for 400 octillion pengő (4 with 29 zeros). Major tax and banking reforms subsequently helped to stabilize the economy.

Oldest coins
The earliest recorded coins were issued in c. 620 BCE, under King Gyges (or Kukaś) of Lydia – an ancient nation in what is now western Türkiye. They are made from electrum, a natural amalgam of gold and silver. Lydia's location on trade routes between Europe and Asia was a key factor in the development of its coinage.

100%

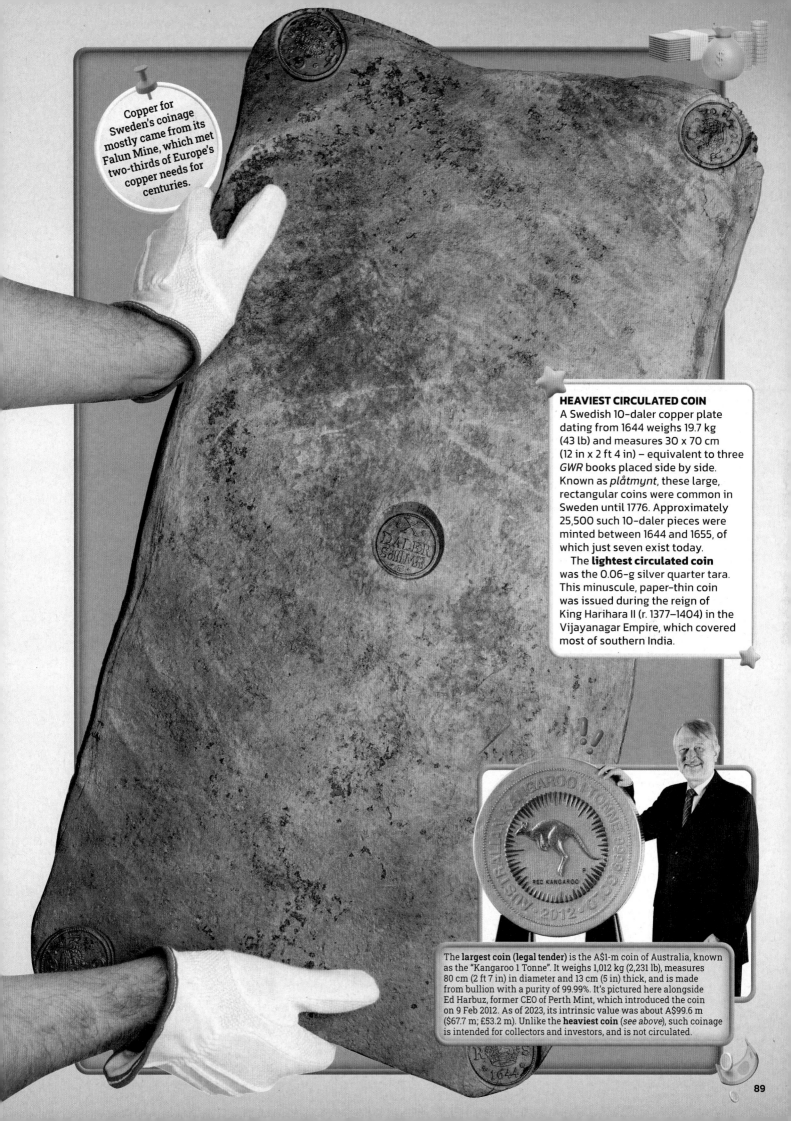

Copper for Sweden's coinage mostly came from its Falun Mine, which met two-thirds of Europe's copper needs for centuries.

HEAVIEST CIRCULATED COIN

A Swedish 10-daler copper plate dating from 1644 weighs 19.7 kg (43 lb) and measures 30 x 70 cm (12 in x 2 ft 4 in) – equivalent to three *GWR* books placed side by side. Known as *plåtmynt*, these large, rectangular coins were common in Sweden until 1776. Approximately 25,500 such 10-daler pieces were minted between 1644 and 1655, of which just seven exist today.

The **lightest circulated coin** was the 0.06-g silver quarter tara. This minuscule, paper-thin coin was issued during the reign of King Harihara II (r. 1377–1404) in the Vijayanagar Empire, which covered most of southern India.

The **largest coin (legal tender)** is the A$1-m coin of Australia, known as the "Kangaroo 1 Tonne". It weighs 1,012 kg (2,231 lb), measures 80 cm (2 ft 7 in) in diameter and 13 cm (5 in) thick, and is made from bullion with a purity of 99.99%. It's pictured here alongside Ed Harbuz, former CEO of Perth Mint, which introduced the coin on 9 Feb 2012. As of 2023, its intrinsic value was about A$99.6 m ($67.7 m; £53.2 m). Unlike the **heaviest coin** (*see above*), such coinage is intended for collectors and investors, and is not circulated.

Brick Masters

Largest LEGO®-brick recreation of a painting

Water Lilies #1, a 41.31-m² (444.7-sq-ft) reimagining of Claude Monet's 1914–26 masterpiece by Chinese artist Ai Weiwei, comprises 650,000 studs in 22 different colours. It was unveiled for an exhibition at the Design Museum in London, UK, in Apr 2023. Weiwei has used LEGO since 2007, creating artworks such as portraits of animals of the zodiac, but this is by far his largest piece in this medium to date.

Largest gaming-themed LEGO set

The Mighty Bowser is a 2,807-piece homage to the villainous King of the Koopas from the *Super Mario Bros.* franchise. Released on 1 Oct 2022, Bowser stands just over 32 cm (1 ft) tall and comes with snapping jaws and a fireball launcher. He is flanked by two flaming torches, one of which conceals a secret "POW" block.

Largest LEGO-brick playing card

On 5 Sep 2023, Faith Howe (CAN) unveiled a Queen of Hearts made from almost 50,000 bricks and measuring 3.69 x 2.59 m (12 ft 1 in x 8 ft 5 in). The 21-year-old, who hopes to become a professional LEGO artist, spent nine days building the card at her local library in Fredericton, New Brunswick, Canada.

Cooper formerly set the fastest time to build the LEGO World Map – the largest 2D LEGO set, with 11,695 pieces.

Fastest time to build the LEGO Eiffel Tower

Comprising 10,001 pieces, this model of the famous Parisian landmark is currently the **largest 3D LEGO set**. On 29 Apr 2023, Cooper Wright (USA) topped out the 1.49-m (4-ft 10-in) structure – the same height as him! – in 9 hr 14 min 35 sec. He now has his sights on speed-building the 9,036-piece LEGO Colosseum.

Fastest time to build the LEGO *Titanic*

Sebastian Haworth (USA) assembled a model of the ill-fated ocean liner in 8 hr 42 min 12 sec on 22 May 2022 in Springfield, Virginia, USA. The 15-year-old beat the previous record by 2 hr. Featuring 9,090 pieces and measuring 1.35 m (4 ft 5 in) long, *Titanic* was the **largest 3D LEGO set** on its release in 2021, until it was surpassed by the Eiffel Tower (*see left*).

Ben had to spend a night on the LEGO bed inside his caravan after locking himself in his workroom!

Largest LEGO-brick caravan

Australian artist Ben Craig (*above*) has found a novel way to channel his lifelong love of LEGO. As "The Brick Builder", he has created scale models of everything from airports to lighthouses. But in 2018, he took his brick game to another level: he spent five weeks building a life-size 1973 Viscount Royal caravan from 288,630 bricks. The mobile home was fully kitted out with a stove top (*below*), refrigerator, sink (with running water!), drawers filled with cutlery and even that Aussie staple: a tub of Vegemite. The project was supported by Caravanning Queensland, Top Parks (now G'day Parks) and John Cochrane Advertising (all AUS).

Largest LEGO-brick truck

In May 2023, Ben built on his previous success with replica LEGO vehicles and took it up a gear. His actual-size Mack truck measured 7.03 m (23 ft) long and 3.54 m (11 ft 7 in) tall. The big rig was made from around 1 million bricks and took two months to construct in Brisbane, Australia.

Ready, Steady, Cook!

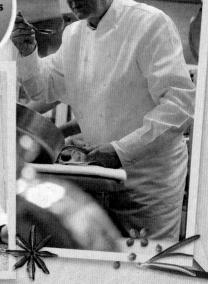

In 2016, Joël Robuchon (FRA, 1945–2018) held the most Michelin stars by an individual ever – 31.

Most expensive French fries
A portion of Crème de la Crème Pommes Frites will set you back $200 (£157.33). They're served with black truffle, a Mornay dipping sauce and dusted with 23-karat gold at the New York eatery Serendipity3. The restaurant's creative director, Joe Calderone, has concocted several record-setting luxury dishes.

Oldest printed cookbook
De honesta voluptate et valetudine ("On Right Pleasure and Good Health") first appeared in 1474. Compiled by Bartolomeo Platina (ITA), the healthy-living guide contains recipes such as "Red Chickpea Broth" and "Date Torte with Almonds and Other Things".

First TV cookery show
Cook's Night Out debuted on British screens on 21 Jan 1937. Broadcast by the BBC, the live 15-min show was presented by the French chef Marcel Boulestin, who demonstrated how to prepare an omelette. A five-course meal was made across the five-part series.

Most Michelin-starred restaurants in a country
France remains a bastion of *haute cuisine*, with 630 eateries listed in the 2023 *MICHELIN Guide*, the prestigious restaurant reference. Japan was second, with 414; of these, 200 were in the capital Tokyo alone – the **most Michelin-starred restaurants in a city**.

Most Michelin stars awarded to a living chef
The restaurants of Alain Ducasse (FRA) have received 21 Michelin stars. As of 2023, he presided over the kitchens of 34 fine-dining establishments, including the three-starred Le Louis XV in Monaco.

Anne-Sophie Pic (FRA, inset) holds the women's record with 10. This includes her three-starred Maison Pic in Valence, France.

Most Michelin-starred restaurants visited in 24 hours
On 25–26 May 2023, gallivanting gourmet Joshua Fyksen (USA) ate at 22 of the finest dining establishments in New York City, USA. Joshua allowed himself only 15 min per restaurant (including travel) and chose dishes only from à la carte menus. He visited 16 eateries on the evening of 25 May before resting and returning for six helpings of lunch. His favourite dish of the gastro tour? Roasted octopus with shrimp and Ibérico pork at Le Pavillon.

Largest beef wellington
On 11 May 2023, Nick DiGiovanni (USA, *inset left; see also p.111.*) teamed up with Gordon Ramsay (UK, *inset right*) to produce a supersized pastry-encrusted steak weighing 25.76 kg (56 lb 12 oz). Five cuts of beef sirloin were bonded with meat glue, cooked in a sous-vide machine for 10 hr and then blowtorched.

NICK'S XL GASTRONOMY

Largest...	Record	Date
Cake pop*	44.24 kg (97 lb 8 oz)	23 Nov 2021
Chicken nugget*	20.96 kg (46 lb 3 oz)	25 May 2022
Doughnut cake*	102.50 kg (225 lb 15 oz)	3 Apr 2023
Fortune cookie†	1.47 kg (3 lb 3 oz)	12 Nov 2022
Sushi roll (width)*	2.16 m (7 ft 1 in)	7 Oct 2022

*with Lynn Davis (JPN); †with Uncle Roger (MYS)

Most TikTok followers for a chef
CZN Burak (TUR, b. Burak Özdemir) had 74.6 million fans as of 17 Jan 2024, making him the eighth-top TikToker overall. Burak, who specializes in mouthwatering Anatolian cuisine, rose to foodie fame after first appearing in a friend's video.

Lata Tondon (IND) – 87 hr 45 min;
Rewa, India, 3–7 Sep 2019

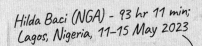

Hilda Baci (NGA) – 93 hr 11 min;
Lagos, Nigeria, 11–15 May 2023

Rob Smink (NLD) – 36 hr 58 min;
Nieuwleusen, Netherlands,
29–30 Sep 2012

Since 2010, the GWR title for endurance cooking has been held by 16 different chefs from all around the world (three examples above). In May 2023, Hilda Baci's (centre) record-breaking effort caused a sensation in her home country of Nigeria, inspiring others to attempt their own marathon world records.

Longest cooking marathon

On 28 Sep 2023, Alan Fisher (IRL) embarked on a gruelling shift that lasted 119 hr 57 min 16 sec. He was cooking at the Kyojin Stewhouse, his own restaurant dedicated to promoting Irish cuisine in the Japanese city of Matsue, Shimane. Over the five days, Alan produced a variety of soups, stews and other Gaelic recipes, peeling around 300 kg (660 lb) of potatoes. Despite battling fatigue and even hallucinations, he served up his last dish – the 3,360th portion! – on 3 Oct.

Unbelievably, Alan began the cookathon just a day after having completed the **longest baking marathon:** 47 hr 21 min 21 sec (inset). He produced 487 loaves of soda bread over the course of three days (25–27 Sep).

Cheese

Largest cheese sculpture
The Cheese Lady, aka Sarah Kaufmann (USA), chiselled a single block of Wisconsin Cheddar into the likeness of an alligator in a chef's hat frying a turkey. The sculpture was commissioned by Erik Acquistapace for his family's deli in Covington, Louisiana, USA, in Nov 2018 and weighed 1,415.6 kg (3,121 lb) – about five times heavier than the average alligator. Master cheese-maker Kerry Henning provided the Cheddar. Sarah, the "Michelangelo of Cheese", has been sculpting everything from guitars to cows since 1981.

Sarah has chiselled so many things from cheese that she's lost count. "It's well over 4,000 sculptures," she reckons.

Oldest cheese
Cheese is the solid or semi-solid result of the coagulation of milk protein, which is then typically ripened to enhance the flavour. The oldest residue of solid cheese dates from the 13th-century-BCE tomb of Ptahmes, the mayor of Memphis in Egypt. Found in a broken jar, it was described as a "solidified whitish mass". A few milligrams of the 3,200-year-old sample were analysed by mass spectrometry, helping chemists to determine that it was a solid dairy product obtained by mixing the milk of cows with that of sheep or goats.

Largest cheese (cow's milk)
Agropur (CAN) made a single Cheddar weighing 26.09 tonnes (57,518 lb) for Loblaws supermarket at Granby in Quebec, Canada, on 7 Sep 1995. Weighing the same as 17 family saloon cars, the cheese required c. 245 tonnes (540,000 lb) of milk – the equivalent output of 5,000 cows working non-stop for a day.

The **largest goat's cheese** was a Petroto weighing 939 kg (2,070 lb) that was made by Ioannis Stathoris (GRC) at Ierissos, Halkidiki, Greece, on 29 Dec 2010.

The **largest cheese slice** was equal in size to the typical bath towel – albeit 15 cm (5.9 in) thick – and weighed 135.5 kg (298 lb 11 oz). It was created by Halayeb Katilo Co (EGY) in Cairo, Egypt, on 13 Jul 2012.

Smelliest cheese
According to research by Cranfield University (UK) in Nov 2004, Vieux Boulogne – a soft French cow's cheese matured for nine weeks – proved more pungent than 14 rivals when reviewed by a panel of 19 human noses and one electronic; the latter tested for the release of gaseous molecules.

Largest cheese slicer
To celebrate the life and work of Thor Bjørklund (1889–1975) – inventor of the cheese slicer – this enormous 7.79-m-long (25-ft 6.6-in) utensil was erected at the Kvitfjell ski resort in Norway on 7 Mar 2015. The project was coordinated by Kristen Gunstad for Gudbrandsdal Industrier (NOR), the company that continues to make slicers to Bjørklund's original design.

Dear GWR...
I would like to apply for a new world record to be the fastest cheese grater... My friends/family have noticed how quick i am at grating cheese... it can be put on live video as entertainment for the public. I hope this can be considered as a new record. I look forward to your response. ████████, UK

Most varieties of cheese on a pizza
One record that will take some topping is the cheesiest pizza. On 8 Oct 2023, Fabien Montellanico, Sophie Hatat Richart-Luna, Florian OnAir and Benoît Bruel (all FRA) piled a pizza high with 1,001 different types of cheese from all over the world. The record was staged at Déliss' Pizza in Lyon, France, and required a minimum of 2 g (0.07 oz) per cheese and a maximum pizza diameter of 12 in (30.5 cm).

Most expensive sandwich
The "Quintessential Grilled Cheese" went on sale for $214 (£132.64) at Serendipity 3 in New York City, USA, on 29 Oct 2014. Among its many luxury ingredients is a very rare Caciocavallo Podolico cheese.

The **largest grilled cheese sandwich** was a 3.32-m-long (10-ft 10.7-in) toastie made in Milwaukee, Wisconsin, USA, on 21 Oct 2023 by YouTubers Exodus and Iggy Chaudhry (both USA). Bigger than a king-sized bed, it weighed 189 kg (418 lb) – equal to about 900 regular sandwiches!

The cheeses have been supplied by the local, award-winning Smart's Farm since the 1980s.

Cheese Rolling on Cooper's Hill, Gloucestershire, Charles March Gere (1869–1957). There are categories for men, women and children, and this 1948 painting depicts the latter. The aim for all groups is the same: catch (and win) the 3.6-kg (8-lb) cheese as it hurtles down the 1:2 incline of Cooper's Hill, or at least be the first to the bottom of the slope.

LONGEST-RUNNING CHEESE-ROLLING RACE

The tradition of chasing a Double Gloucester cheese down the 180-m-long (590-ft) Cooper's Hill in Brockworth, Gloucestershire, UK, can be traced back at least to a written account from 1826, although historians believe that the ceremony stretches back for hundreds of years. It may even have its roots in pagan fertility rituals predating the Roman era.

The **most victorious cheese chaser** since the advent of written records is Chris Anderson (UK, *above*), whose 23rd win came in the first race of the 2022 event, after which he announced his retirement.

The **most wins of the women's race** is four, shared by Ilse Koeppler (UK; 1941–44) and Florence "Flo" Early (UK, *above left*; 2008, 2016, 2018–19). She also announced her retirement, after her last race left her with a sprained ankle.

Hardcore Hobbies

Farthest backwards basketball shot
On 11 Jan 2024, Joshua Walker (USA) found the hoop from 26.21 m (86 ft) – while facing the other way! It was one of five trick-shot GWR titles that Joshua set on the same day in Monroe, Louisiana, USA. They included the **farthest blindfolded hook shot** of 18.28 m (60 ft) and the **farthest behind-the-back shot** of 17.22 m (56 ft 6 in).

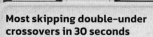

Most skipping double-under crossovers in 30 seconds
Dunsin Dubem (*centre*) completed 78 criss-crosses on 18 Aug 2023 in Akure, Nigeria. Dunsin is one of a trio of talented teenage Nigerian skippers, alongside Gbenga Ezekiel (*left*) – **most double-under skips on one leg in one minute** (144) – and Philip Solomon (*right*) – **most rope crossovers while skipping on one leg in 30 seconds** (69).

Most skips in one minute
Zhou Qi (CHN) completed 374 skips in 60 sec on 30 Apr 2023 in Ningbo, Zhejiang, China. The hot-stepping teen beat Daisuke Mimura's record of 348, which had stood since 2013.

Fastest marathon dribbling a basketball (female)
Elementary school teacher Maria Babineau (CAN) ran the TCS Toronto Waterfront Marathon in 3 hr 57 min 40 sec on 15 Oct 2023. It was Maria's first-ever marathon, which she attempted after just seven weeks of training.

Greatest vertical distance rock climbing in one hour
Justin Valli (USA) scaled 390 m (1,279 ft) of cliff-face on 8 Oct 2022 in Red Rock Canyon, Nevada, USA. He completed 100 reps of a 1.65-m (5-ft) climb and 225 reps of a 1-m (3-ft) climb. On the same day, Justin also achieved the **three-minute** record of 37.95 m (124 ft).

Most kips in 30 seconds (II2)
On 8 Dec 2023, US gymnast Chelsea Werner performed 10 full-body outward extensions from a bar in Dublin, California, USA. Chelsea, who has Down syndrome, earned three 30-second titles in GWR's Intellectual Impairment category, including the **most backwards walkovers** – 14 – and the **most backwards handsprings** – 16. On 31 Jan 2024, she added the **most pull-ups in 30 seconds** – 11. Chelsea is a double world champion and has featured on the cover of *Teen Vogue* and *Dazed*.

Most consecutive flying bar jumps (male)
On 21 Feb 2023, *Ninja Warrior* champion Joel Mattli (CHE) executed 27 athletic leaps in a row. Dead-hanging from a metal bar 2.4 m (7 ft 10 in) above the ground, he used his strength to propel both himself and the bar between platforms that were 1.2 m (3 ft 11 in) apart.

Most fingertip push-ups carrying an 80-lb pack in one hour (male)
Serial record breaker Alejandro Soler Tarí (ESP) pushed himself up using just his fingers 175 times in 60 min in La Marina, Alicante, Spain, on 21 Mar 2024. He also recently set the **most L-sit chin-ups from a flying helicopter in one minute**: 26, on 19 Nov 2023.

Most 360° SUP rotations in one minute
On 3 Sep 2023, Vincenzo Manobianco (ITA) span his stand-up paddleboard around 20 times in a pool in Bari, Italy. Vincenzo is a national SUP athlete who has competed at the International Canoe Federation's Stand Up Paddling World Championships.

Most bicycle backflips in three minutes
On 8 Dec 2023, Ben Gilbertson (NOR) went head over heels on his bike 15 times in 180 sec in Vanse, Agder, Norway.

Most full-extension punches in one minute (female)
Atefeh Safaei (IRN) struck a boxing pad 385 times in Tehran, Iran, on 5 Aug 2023. She threw an average of more than six punches every second.

The equivalent record **while wearing boxing gloves** – 298 – was also set in 2023, by amateur boxer Ioan Croft (UK) in Cardigan, UK, on 8 Dec. He went head to head with his twin, Garan, for the title.

MOST BACKSIDE 540 SKATEBOARD TRICKS IN ONE MINUTE

On 13 Feb 2024, Ema Kawakami (JPN) nailed eight jumps inside a halfpipe on TV talent show *Lo Show dei Record* in Milan, Italy. Each jump had to last one-and-a-half rotations, while Ema gripped the board with one hand behind his back. The nine-year-old took up skating at the age of just five. In 2022, Ema went viral when he was filmed landing a two-and-a-half-rotation 900 jump – first performed by skateboard legend Tony Hawk in 1999. For more precocious talent following in Tony Hawk's wheel tracks, check out p.187.

GWR talks to...

Who are your biggest skateboarding inspirations and why?
Tony Hawk, Shaun White, Gui Khury [*see p.243*] and Pierre-Luc Gagnon. They all have difficult tricks that they've created, and have executed world firsts; I want to do the sort of things they've achieved.

How does it feel to know that Tony Hawk follows you on Instagram?
When my dad told me, I was thrilled! Tony Hawk is someone I look up to, and I was speechless when he shared my video because I realized he'd seen me skateboarding.

What was it like to win first place at the 2023 WINGRAM CUP?
It was the first time that I'd entered a vertical contest, so I didn't expect to win. As I knew that Gui Khury would be there, I put the 900 in my routine so I could perform it in front of him. I was very happy [that it worked out].

Tell us about your experience on *Lo Show dei Record*.
Everything was fun because I'd never been overseas before. Although I felt nervous in front of the camera, everyone was kind and I made some new skateboarding friends.

What challenges did you face during training?
When I was continuously performing 540s on the vertical ramp, it was less about how much I could spin and more about not getting too dizzy!

How often do you go skateboarding?
I practise four or five times a week, and each session lasts about three to four hours.

What other hobbies do you have?
I like watching skateboarding videos and rap battles online. Me and my younger brother sometimes challenge each other to rap battles.

Ema competed in his first tournament aged five, just six months after taking up skateboarding.

Brainteasers

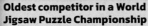

Fastest time to complete a 200-piece jigsaw (II)
On 20 Jun 2023, Noura Hassan Al Aidarous (UAE) set a new record in GWR's Intellectual Impairment category when she finished a jigsaw in 2 hr 16 min in Abu Dhabi, UAE. She started puzzling in 2011, using nine-piece jigsaws. Noura was supported by the UAE's Zayed Higher Organization for People of Determination.

Oldest competitor in a World Jigsaw Puzzle Championship
Antonia María García de Soria (ESP, b. 26 Jan 1930) was 92 years 149 days old when she took on the world's best dissectologists in Valladolid, Spain, on 24 Jun 2022. Participating in the pairs category alongside Juan Antonio Ávarez-Ossorio, Antonia had 1 hr 30 min to assemble a 500-piece scene of a puppy in a basket. The duo managed 401 pieces in the time frame, finishing 73rd out of 87.

Most wins of the American Crossword Puzzle Tournament
Inaugurated in 1978, the ACPT is the USA's largest and longest-running crossword contest. On 2 Apr 2023, Dan Feyer (USA) secured his ninth title, overcoming a record field of 774 in-person competitors at the Stamford Marriott Hotel in Connecticut, USA.

The **most wins of *The Times* Crossword Championships** is 12, by Mark Goodliffe (UK) in 1999, 2008–17 and 2019. He has also won the newspaper's sudoku championship twice.

Most wins of the World Sudoku Championship
Kota Morinishi (JPN) is a four-time winner of the global number-puzzle tournament, triumphing in 2014–15 and 2017–18. Staged under the auspices of the World Puzzle Federation, the competition has been held annually since 2006.

Fastest time to solve a 4x4 Klotski puzzle
On 26 Jan 2023, Lim Kai Yi (MYS) unscrambled this classic sliding-block puzzle in 5.18 sec in Butterworth, Malaysia. Lim is a Klotski master, also acing the following configurations in record time:
- **4x4, one-handed**: 8.27 sec
- **4x5**: 5.20 sec
- **4x5, blindfolded**: 6.35 sec
- **4x5, one-handed**: 9.24 sec
- **4x5, using feet**: 14.20 sec.

Fastest time to mentally add 50 five-digit numbers
On the set of *Lo Show dei Record* in Milan, Italy, mental mathlete Aaryan Shukla (IND) totted up 50 numbers to reach a total of 2,676,355 in 25.19 sec on 29 Feb 2024.

Longest binary-number sequence memorized in one minute
On 20 Jun 2023, Mustafa Alam (PAK) recalled a 342-digit string of 0s and 1s in Karachi, Sindh, Pakistan. He had only 60 sec to commit the numbers to memory – an average of five every second.

Most three-digit flash numbers memorized
On 28 Mar 2023, Syed Nabeel Hasan Rizvi (PAK) recalled 40 sets of randomly generated triple digits – having looked at each one for just one second – in Karachi, Pakistan. Syed, the 2019 UK Junior Memory Champion, is a regular mind-sports competitor.

Most animals identified by scientific name in one minute
Sudarsanam Sivakumar (IND) recognized the Latin names of 48 creatures in 60 sec on 7 Jan 2023 in Chennai, Tamil Nadu, India.

Fastest time to mentally count letters in 10 sentences
On 4 Oct 2023, Mohammad Sayaheen (JOR) took just 35.5 sec to calculate the 267 characters in 10 randomly generated Arabic phrases. The former *Arabs Got Talent* contestant is nicknamed Abo AlHorof ("Father of Letters").

Largest spelling bee
On 18 Jun 2023, a total of 2,000 students took part in a supersized spell-off in Al Basra, Iraq. The event was organized by Al Bushra for Education and Sciences and Basra International Schools (both IRQ).

Let's get quizzical!
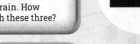
Put your grey cells to the test with this compilation of picture-based challenges. Will you be able to emulate the success of the quick-fire quizzers below? *Find the answers on p.253*.

Fastest time to identify every national flag
On 5 Aug 2023, vexillologist Adam Saeed (BHR) named all 197 national flags in 2 min 55 sec in Manama, Bahrain. How will you fare with these three?

Most *Star Wars* characters identified in one minute
The Force was strong with Adhav Rajaprabhu (IND) on 10 Jan 2021 when he recognized 34 sci-fi stalwarts in Tamil Nadu, India. Name these, can you?

Most soccer teams identified by club badge in one minute
On 3 Oct 2023, Alexandre Mairano (BRA) was on target with 95 iconic football club logos in Esteio, Rio Grande do Sul, Brazil. How will you score with this trio?

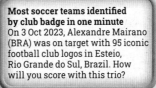

Most rotating puzzle cubes solved while running a marathon

Kei Suga (JPN) cracked 420 cubes during the Kashiwanoha Campus Marathon in Chiba, Japan, on 15 Oct 2022. He finished the 26.2-mi (42-km) course in 4 hr 34 min 23 sec, averaging one solve every 100 m (328 ft) and beating the previous best by 166. Kei said that his astonishing feat had taken 10 years of training.

Dear GWR...

My name is ████████████ and I am 14 years old. I am attempting to break the world record for fastest time to solve a Rubik's Cube with a broken wrist. I decided to do this because I felt it would be a fun and challenging experience for people who have broken their wrist and want to break a record. I would appreciate if you can get this done as soon as possible because a broken wrist doesn't last forever. Thank you very much.

Fastest time to solve a rotating puzzle cube while in freefall

On 22 Apr 2023, Sam Sieracki (AUS) calmly completed a Rubik's Cube in 28.25 sec, all the while hurtling through the sky over Jurien Bay in Western Australia at around 200 km/h (124 mph)! The 17-year-old – a licensed skydiver and competitive cuber – needed just five attempts to break the previous record of 30.14 sec.

Most rotating puzzle tetrahedrons solved underwater

Singapore's Daryl Tan Hong An unscrambled 15 pyramid-shaped puzzles on a single breath on 18 Apr 2021. It was one of four records that Daryl set on the same day, all for subaquatic solves: the **most 2x2x2 cubes** (26), **3x3x3 cubes** (16) and **3x3x3 cubes one-handed** (eight). He had spent two months breath training in preparation.

OFFICIAL SPEEDCUBING RECORDS

Puzzle type		Time	Name	Date
3x3x3	single	3.13 sec	Max Park (USA, see p.85)	11 Jun 2023
	average	4.48 sec	Yiheng Wang (CHN, see p.85)	20 Jun 2023
2x2x2	single	0.43 sec	Teodor Zajder (POL)	5 Nov 2023
	average	0.92 sec	Zayn Khanani (USA)	9 Mar 2024
4x4x4	single	16.79 sec	Max Park	3 Apr 2022
	average	19.38 sec	Max Park	19 Mar 2023
5x5x5	single	32.52 sec	Max Park	16 Dec 2023
	average	35.94 sec	Max Park	16 Dec 2023
6x6x6	single	59.74 sec	Max Park	31 Jul 2022
	average	1 min 6.46 sec	Nahm Seung-hyuk (KOR)	4 Feb 2024
7x7x7	single	1 min 35.68 sec	Max Park	24 Sep 2022
	average	1 min 41.78 sec	Max Park	27 Jan 2024
Clock	single	2.54 sec	Neil Gour (IND)	6 Jan 2024
Megaminx	single	23.18 sec	Leandro Martín López (ARG)	13 Apr 2024
Pyraminx	single	0.73 sec	Simon Kellum (USA)	21 Dec 2023
Square-1	single	3.41 sec	Ryan Pilat (USA)	2 Mar 2024

*All ratified by the World Cube Association; correct as of 16 Apr 2024

Most rotating puzzle cubes solved one-handed while hula hooping

On 20 Feb 2021, Josiah Plett (CAN) resolved 531 cubes with his left hand in Victoria, British Columbia, Canada. He destroyed the previous record, which he had seen on TV, by 501 solves. Josiah also holds the **two-handed** version of this record – which at 1,015, is 815 more than the former mark.

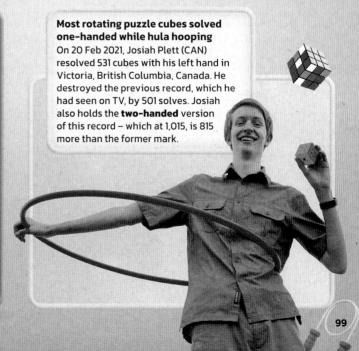

Most people dressed as vampires

To mark the 125th anniversary of Bram Stoker's iconic gothic novel *Dracula* (1897), English Heritage (UK) assembled 1,369 fan(g)s kitted out as the book's undead count at Whitby Abbey on 26 May 2022. The seaside town in North Yorkshire, UK, with its evocative church and cemetery, left a lasting impression on Stoker after a visit in 1890. *See more ghoulish gatherings in the table below.*

Largest broomstick

"Kreteam 2006" (NLD) crafted a 32.65-m-long (107-ft 1-in) witch's broomstick – complete with rider – in Sint-Annaland, Zeeland, Netherlands, on 12 Sep 2006. The broom was longer than three US school buses.

COVENS, HORDES AND HAUNTINGS

Most...	People	Organizer / year
Catrinas/ Catrines	865	Instituto de la Juventud Guanajuatense (MEX), 2016
Ghosts	1,024	Fischer's and fans (JPN), 2023
Witches	1,607	La Bruixa d'Or (ESP), 2013
Skeletons	2,018	Jokers' Masquerade (UK, *right*), 2011
Zombies	15,458	Zombie Pub Crawl (USA), 2014

Largest ouija board

Overseen by Blair Murphy (USA), a giant 121-m² (1,302.4-sq-ft) version of the spiritual communication device was created on the roof of the Grand Midway Hotel in Windber, Pennsylvania, USA, on 28 Oct 2016. The former coal-mining town guesthouse has a long history of ghostly sightings, including ladies of the night and the apparition of a child.

Largest collection of *Casper the Friendly Ghost* memorabilia

Vanessa Irino (USA) owns 1,153 items related to the spookless spectre, as verified in San Antonio, Texas, USA, on 25 Oct 2023. She hopes her record will promote the positivity and inclusivity that Casper "embodies", while inspiring others to celebrate their passions.

Tallest Calavera Catrina

Día de los Muertos ("Day of the Dead"), a holiday celebrating departed loved ones, traditionally takes place in the days just after Halloween. On 2 Nov 2023, Puerto Vallarta in Jalisco, Mexico, took the festival to new heights with a 28.15-m-tall (92-ft 4-in) female skeleton sculpture. Artist José Guadalupe Posada first conceived the elegant poised figure of "La Catrina" in the early 20th century, as a reminder that, despite our class or position in society, we're all mortal.

Highest-grossing horror movie

It (USA, 2017) – adapted from Stephen King's 1986 novel about Pennywise, a shape-shifting trans-dimensional entity that preys on children's deepest fears – had grossed $701,012,746 (£577.4 m) worldwide by 27 Feb 2024, according to The Numbers. The **highest-grossing horror-movie series** is *The Conjuring Universe* (USA). Its eight releases – the most recent being *The Nun II* (2023) – had taken a spine-tingling $2,250,924,388 (£1.77 bn) as of the same date.

2022

2020

Both Maverick and Tiger King were carved by Mike Rudolph (USA)

2023

HEAVIEST JACK O'LANTERN

Experienced carver Eric Jones (USA) transformed a 2,749-lb (1,246.9-kg) squash into a jumbo jack o'lantern (*inset left, with Eric on right*) on 9 Nov 2023 – a month after the very same gourd had been validated as the **heaviest pumpkin** (*see p.110*). Jones took Veterans Day as his inspiration, with motifs featuring several service people and a dog. At a whopping 642.6 cm (21 ft 1 in) around, it is also the **largest jack o'lantern by circumference**. Both this and the two previous record-setting jack o'lanterns (*Maverick, main; and Tiger King, inset above*), which took a more traditional Halloween animal theme, were carved from prodigious pumpkins grown by Travis Gienger (USA, *shown left*).

Largest squash mosaic

For the Nelson family (UK; *Tom Nelson pictured*), it has become a Halloween custom to create a *spook*-tacular artwork out of pumpkins and other gourds (*Cucurbita*) at Sunnyfields Farm near Southampton in Hampshire, UK. Their latest effort – spanning 193.35 m² (2,081 sq ft) on 18 Oct 2023 – paid homage to Tim Burton's animation *The Nightmare Before Christmas* (USA, 1993), three decades after the film's release.

Collections

Avatar: The Last Airbender
Jessica Carey (USA) owns 2,026 items of merch – including plush toys, clothing and trading cards – from this Nickelodeon cartoon, as verified in Owasso, Oklahoma, USA, on 13 Feb 2023. She told GWR: "One of the best feelings as I walk into my office is feeling so inspired by the items around me. It encourages me to work on my own art and storytelling."

Crayon Shin-chan
As of 12 May 2022, Japanese TikToker Nonohara Sayane (aka Sayaka Suzuki) had amassed 2,854 collectables related to this best-selling manga. A fan since the age of 13, her favourite piece is a set of pin badges that commemorated the series' 30th anniversary in 2020.

Hairclips
Nine-year-old Alina Gupta (IND) has stockpiled 1,124 hairpins, as confirmed in Delhi, India, on 3 Aug 2023. She started her collection aged just four. Alina said: "Seeing them in my wardrobe feels like one of my dreams has come true... I will definitely continue to collect more and more unique clips!"

Soccer shirts
As of 17 Mar 2023, Santiago Hank Guerreiro (MEX) owned 1,077 football tops, which he stores in Mexico City. He began collecting after his father bought him some national team shirts from the 2018 World Cup. One of his most prized possessions is a jersey signed by the soccer legend Pelé.

COLOSSAL COLLECTIONS

Pencils
69,255, by Aaron Bartholmey in Colfax, Iowa, USA

House bricks
8,882, by Clem Reinkemeyer in Tulsa, Oklahoma, USA

Mobile phones
3,456, by Andrei Bilbie Argentis of Cluj, Romania

Christmas baubles
3,101, by Karen Torp in Østfold, Norway

Nativity sets
2,324, by Michael Zahs in Washington, Iowa, USA

Guinness World Records
As verified on 1 Feb 2024, Martyn Tovey (UK) owns 3,089 unique *GWR*-related items, including toys, games, spin-off publications, novelty items and promotional material. Martyn has also built up the **largest collection of *Guinness World Records* annuals**, with 816 unique editions. He's most proud of a book from 1960, with handwritten corrections by Norris McWhirter, *GWR*'s then co-editor.

Rabbit-related items
Candace Frazee and Steve Lubanski (both USA) have accumulated 40,550 leporine objects, which they display at their Bunny Museum in Altadena, California, USA. The couple first achieved this record back in 1999 with 8,437 items and were happy to have it updated in 2023 – which aptly was the Year of the Rabbit in the Chinese zodiac calendar.

The couple's love for bunnies began when Steve gave Candace a stuffed rabbit toy for Valentine's Day in 1993.

Handmade sock monkeys
2,098, by Arlene Okun in Illinois, USA

Jigsaws
2,022, by John Walczak (USA) in Carmel, Indiana, USA

Axes
1,023, by Kadri Prekaj of Pejë, Kosovo

Pringles tubes
629, by Salacnib "Sonny" Molina (USA, b. PHL) in Illinois, USA

Dart flights
501, by Patrick Hopkins in Clacton-on-Sea, Essex, UK

Fantastic Feats

Oldest man to fly in a wingsuit

Vidar Sie (NOR, b. 13 Jul 1961) was 62 years 55 days old when he jumped from a plane at an altitude of 12,500 ft (3,810 m) and flew in a wingsuit for more than 2 min. At 4,000 ft (1,219 m), he opened his parachute. Vidar's skydive took place above Jarlsberg Airport in Vestfold, Norway, on 6 Sep 2023.

Most stairs descended in a wheelchair in 12 hours

On 24 Sep 2023, Haki Doku (ITA) rode down 12,000 stairs in Frankfurt, Germany, breaking his own record by 500 steps. He spread his attempt across three sites – the Deutsche Bank headquarters, the Westend Gate Tower and the 63-storey Messeturm – making ten, four and one descents respectively.

Farthest axe throw

Simone Freddi (ITA) hurled an axe a distance of 40.1 m (131 ft 6 in) to strike a 3-ft-wide (91-cm) target in Gradisca d'Isonzo, Gorizia, Italy, on 10 Jun 2023. This was almost 13 m (42 ft 7 in) farther than the previous record. He used a replica "francisca" – a throwing axe used by the Franks in the early Middle Ages.

Most aerial hoop somersaults in one minute (female)

On 8 Feb 2023, Mexico's Yammel Rodriguez flipped through a suspended hoop 47 times in just 60 sec. The attempt took place in Las Vegas, Nevada, USA. Yammel learned the basics of her art from YouTube tutorials before enrolling at Canada's famed École de Cirque de Québec.

Longest time to spin a burning log on the shoulders

Circus strongman Battulga Battogtokh (MNG) kept a flaming wooden beam revolving around his shoulders for 1 min 19.11 sec on the set of *Lo Show dei Record* in Monza, Italy, on 13 Dec 2023.

On the same day, Battulga broke his own record for the **longest time to spin a burning log held in the teeth**, with a time of 38.27 sec.

Longest duration full-body ice contact

Ice swimmer Krzysztof Gajewski (POL; *right, and see p.134*) submerged his entire body (excluding his head) in ice cubes for 3 hr 11 min 27 sec in Inowrocław, Poland, on 29 Jul 2023. This was shattered by compatriot Łukasz Szpunar with a time of 4 hr 2 min in Tarnobrzeg, Poland, on 4 Nov 2023.

The ◐ **women's** record of 3 hr 6 min 45 sec was set by fellow Pole Katarzyna Jakubowska (*above*) in Międzyzdroje, Poland, on 30 Dec 2023. Katarzyna is also a competitive ice swimmer.

Farthest walk *en pointe*

With her feet clad in ballet shoes, Yoana Tsekova (BGR) tip-toed for 400 m (1,312 ft) at the National Sports Academy in Sofia, Bulgaria, on 23 Sep 2023. It took the dance teacher just over 21 min to cover the distance.

Most Carolina reaper chillies eaten in one minute

Fredy Rubio (USA) wolfed down 122 g (4.3 oz) of these super-hot chillies at the Portland Hot Sauce Expo in Oregon, USA, on 13 Aug 2023. Formerly the **hottest chilli pepper**, that title now goes to "Pepper X", grown by Ed Currie of the PuckerButt Pepper Company (USA), at an average of 2,693,000 Scoville Heat Units (SHU). Regular tabasco sauce measures around 400 SHU.

Heaviest weight sustained on the body

On 15 Jul 2023, Kosovo's Muli Bujar supported cement bags weighing 1,531 kg (3,375 lb 4 oz) on his chest in his home town of Vushtrri. That's about the same as a Mini Cooper car.

▶ Longest motorcycle jump with passenger

Daredevil husband–and–wife team Jake Bennett and Mel Eckert (both AUS) completed a 37.1-m (121-ft 8-in) jump on a Honda CRF450 in Picton, New South Wales, Australia, on 16 Jul 2023. The duo surpassed the previous record – which had stood for nearly 23 years – by more than 7 m (22 ft). Both Jake and Mel work as movie stunt performers.

MOST OVERHEAD CANNONBALL TWISTS IN 30 SECONDS

Daniel Teplitski (UK) span a pair of aluminium cannonballs above his head 26 times in Birmingham, UK, on 6 Dec 2023. Linked by a chain, each ball weighed around 20 kg (44 lb) – about three times heavier than a standard bowling ball. Now in his late teens, Daniel started training aged seven. He went on to perform with his parents' acrobatic academy, Elite, and by the age of 10 had become the UK's only child "strong juggler". "I'm passionate about being the best I can be," he told GWR. "And what better way to do this than by achieving a record?"

Daniel is a fourth-generation juggler. His father performed strongman juggling in the Moscow State Circus.

Wacky World Championships

Longest-running annual swamp soccer tournament

The first Swamp Soccer World Championships were held in 2000 in Hyrynsalmi, Finland. This muddy version of the beautiful game grew out of cross-country skiers' summer training. Teams of six play on a 30 x 60-m (98 x 196-ft) quagmire.

Most wins of the World Gurning Championships

Face-pulling competitions have been held annually at Egremont Crab Fair in Cumbria, UK, for more than 150 years. In 2023, Tommy Mattinson (UK) claimed his 18th **men's** title. He attributes his success to his ability to transform into "The Wolf", his snarling alter-ego.

The **women's** record is 28, by gurning legend Anne Woods (UK, 1947–2015; *inset*) between 1977 and 2014.

Longest-running chess-boxing championship

Combatants in this hybrid sport compete in alternating rounds of blitz chess and boxing. The first World Chess Boxing Organisation championship match was held on 14 Nov 2003. It was won by the sport's founder, Iepe "The Joker" Rubingh (NLD, 1974–2020), who beat Jean-Louis "The Lawyer" Veenstra.

Most wins of the World Gravy Wrestling Championships

Joel Hicks (UK, *right*) is a six-time **men's** champion at this saucy sporting tournament, held annually outside the Rose 'n' Bowl pub in Stacksteads, Lancashire, UK. The **women's** record of two is shared by Emma Slater and The Oxo Fox, aka Roxy Afzal (*below*, both UK). Competitors in the two-minute bouts are judged on their look and entertainment value as much as their combative skills.

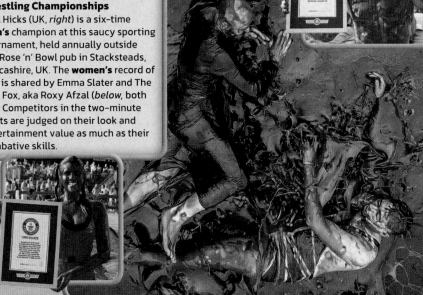

Largest hobbyhorse championship

On 18 Jun 2022, a total of 2,000 competitors saddled up for a contest at Seinäjoki Areena organized by the Finnish Hobbyhorse Association. The **highest hobbyhorse jump** – 1.41 m (4 ft 7 in) – was logged by Marie Kärkkäinen (FIN) at the event on 15 Jun 2019.

Swimming strokes such as front crawl are banned; naturally, "boggy paddle" is the choice for many.

LONGEST-RUNNING BOG-SNORKELLING WORLD CHAMPIONSHIPS

Since 1985, the Waen Rhydd peat bog in the Welsh town of Llanwrtyd Wells has hosted a mucky yearly challenge for those brave enough to take the plunge. Competitors swim two lengths of a 60-yard (180-ft; 55-m) waterlogged trench cut into the marshland. Snorkels, flippers and masks are required; fancy dress is optional – although in 2023, even Barbie tried out a bogwear look (*below*). To date, the **most entrants** for this event is 200, set in 2009.

The water-filled trenches are 55 m (180 ft) long and about 1 m (3 ft) deep

Fastest time at the World Bog Snorkelling Championships
On 27 Aug 2023, Neil Rutter (UK) snorkelled to victory in 1 min 12.35 sec. Extending his record for the **most wins** (five, all in succession), this also broke his own record time from 2018. According to Neil, a summer of rain had created "perfect bog conditions".

The **women's** record is 1 min 22.56 sec, by Kirsty Johnson (UK) on 24 Aug 2014.

Ball Control

Most steps climbed on a ladder while balancing a football on the head

On 10 Aug 2023, Tonye Solomon (NGA) proved his head for heights when he ascended 150 rungs up a radio mast in Yenagoa, Nigeria. It took him a little over 12 min to scale the 76-m (249-ft) structure, keeping the ball glued to his head. Tonye is a member of the Chukwuebuka Freestyle Academy, which has produced a number of record-breaking freestyle-football stars.

Most soccer-ball touches with alternating feet in one hour

This GWR title was broken twice in 2023 – by two Chinese freestylers with quite an age gap. On 26 Feb, 10-year-old Tang Jinfan (*above*) juggled the ball 8,147 times in 60 min in Shenzhen, Guangdong. His record stood for just 14 weeks before it fell to 60-year-old retired lecturer Zhou Daohua (*inset*), who managed 8,407 keepie-uppies in Xuzhou, Jiangsu, on 4 Jun.

Fastest 100 m juggling a football

Abraham Muñoz (MEX) sprinted 100 m with a ball in 17.53 sec around York College's running track in Queens, New York City, USA, on 9 Aug 2009. The "keep-up king" also holds the equivalent records for the **mile** – 8 min 17.28 sec – and the **marathon** – 5 hr 41 min 52 sec.

Greatest distance moving backwards while juggling a football on the head in one hour

On 11 Jun 2022, Dariusz Kołodziejczyk (POL) reversed his way 2.4 km (1.5 mi) around an athletics track in Chorzów, Poland, while heading a ball. The Polish freestyle pro used his feat to promote healthy living.

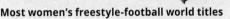

Longest time controlling a football (female)

On 2 Jul 2023, Raquel Tateishi Benetti (BRA) kept a ball off the ground for 10 hr 22 min 8 sec in São Paulo, Brazil. The 33-year-old freestyler and model was inspired at the age of six by previous record holder Cláudia Martini, whom she watched set the former mark of 7 hr 5 min 25 sec on TV.

Most men's freestyle-football world titles

Erlend Fagerli (NOR) is a 10-time world champion, according to the World Freestyle Football Association. He won his first title in 2016, aged 19, and claimed his 10th in Nairobi, Kenya, in Nov 2023, before retiring from the sport. Erlend has earned a number of GWR titles, including one-minute trick records too for the **most hop-the-worlds** – 92 – and **most side-head stalls** – 131.

Most women's freestyle-football world titles

Mélody Donchet (FRA) and Aguśka Mnich (POL) are both six-time world champions. Mélody is a four-time winner of the Red Bull Street Style and also has one Super Ball and one World Tour victory to her name. Aguśka has placed first in four Super Balls and one Red Bull Street Style, and claimed the 2023 World Freestyle Football Championship in Nairobi, Kenya.

Longest time controlling a football with the feet (male)

Saeid Momivand (IRN) did keep-ups for exactly 12 hr on 2 Dec 2022 in Parand, Iran. He beat the previous record by almost two hours.

Most football touches with the feet on a treadmill in one minute (female)

On 13 Mar 2023, Mohadeseh Goudasiaei (IRN) completed 178 keep-ups in 60 sec while also running on a treadmill in Tehran, Iran. Mohadeseh – who has played for the Iranian women's U19 team – beat the previous record, set by freestyle legend Laura Biondo, by eight.

Most football arm rolls in one minute

On 14 Jul 2023, Konok Karmakar (BGD) executed 147 arm rolls in 60 sec in Chittagong, Bangladesh. Konok's cousin Antar also got in on the action, completing the **most football rolls across the forehead in 30 seconds** – 52.

Most football neck-catch passes in 30 seconds

Daniel Ali (PAK) and Ammar Alkhudhairi (YEM) teamed up to flick a ball back and forth 27 times using only their necks on 9 Aug 2023. The duo performed the trick in Dubai, UAE.

The **one-minute** record is 52, set by brothers Erlend (*see left*) and Brynjar Fagerli (both NOR) in Stavanger, Norway, on 12 Nov 2022.

Most consecutive football touches with alternating feet while skipping

On 14 Aug 2023, Yi Bingsheng (CHN) juggled a ball 125 times in Beijing, China. He started practising in 2020, at the age of eight, and rose to fame showing off his skipping/ freestyle mash-up on the Chinese social-media app Douyin.

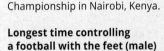

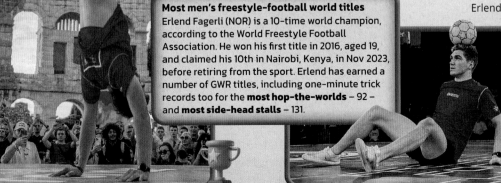

▶ YOUNGEST FREESTYLE-FOOTBALL WORLD CHAMPION

Isabel Wilkins (UK, b. 29 Aug 2007) was aged just 15 years 347 days when she blazed to glory at the 2023 Super Ball in Prague, Czechia, on 11 Aug. She saw off world champion Caitlyn Schrepfer in the final. Isabel took up freestyle during the COVID-19 lockdown and practises for a couple of hours a day after school; in the winter, she trains in her family's converted garage.

On 8 Jan 2024, GWR travelled to Isabel's home to watch her ace four trick records: **most hop-the-worlds in 30 seconds** (47), **most clippers in one minute – female** (46), **most half-beck around-the-worlds in one minute** (12) and the **most Abbas around-the-worlds in 30 seconds** (18).

Even at the age of two, the future freestyle champion was never too far away from a ball!

Isabel was one of 211 freestylers to descend on Prague's Gutovka Park for the 2023 Super Ball World Open. Competitors took part in head-to-head "battles", showing off their best routines before receiving scores out of 10 from judges. In the semi-finals, the 15-year-old overcame Aguśka Mnich (*pictured below in background*), who is one of the world's most successful competitive freestylers (*see opposite*).

Superlative Skills

Largest pumpkin by circumference

There was a bumper crop of giant vegetable records in 2023. On 9 Oct, Travis Gienger (USA) presented a pumpkin measuring 6.42 m (21 ft 1 in) from stem to blossom at the World Championship Pumpkin Weigh-Off in Half Moon Bay, California, USA. At 2,749 lb (1,246.9 kg), it is also the **heaviest pumpkin**. After the weigh-off, it was transformed into a record-setting jack o'lantern (*see p.101*).

Gareth Griffin (UK) grew the **heaviest onion,** weighing 8.97 kg (19 lb 12 oz). He presented it at the Harrogate Autumn Flower Show in North Yorkshire, UK, on 15 Sep 2023.

Tallest stilts

On 17 Oct 2023, performer Doug the Great (aka Doug Hunt, CAN) went for a walk on a pair of 16.76-m (55-ft) stilts in Brantford, Ontario, Canada. The 67-year-old defied strong winds to take 14 steps on his sky-high supports – four more than the minimum required. He reclaimed pole position after last holding this title back in 2002.

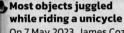

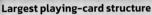

Most objects juggled while riding a unicycle

On 7 May 2023, James Cozens (UK) kept seven balls aloft for 10 sec at Selwyn College in Cambridge, UK. He equalled the mark set by Jasper Moens (BEL) on 30 Apr 2022. James, a Cambridge University student, developed his own software program to analyse his juggling patterns and improve his technique.

Largest playing-card structure

India's Arnav Daga used around 143,000 playing cards to recreate four iconic buildings from his home city of Kolkata: the Writers' Building, the Shaheed Minar, Salt Lake Stadium and St Paul's Cathedral. The 15-year-old spent six weeks on his project, which covered a total area of 62 m² (667 sq ft) and rose to 3.47 m (11 ft 4 in) at its highest point when verified on 23 Jan 2023. Once his record was confirmed, Arnav celebrated by rolling over his labour of love.

Longest time juggling three flaming torches

On 14 Jul 2023, Aidan Webster (USA) kept a trio of torches in the air for 5 min 2.31 sec on a beach in St Petersburg, Florida, USA. It was one of three records the student oceanographer earned that day, along with the **most one-up back somersaults in one minute** – 11 – and the **most juggling catches in one minute with one hand while in the dead-hang position (two objects)** – 162.

This giant java was created to celebrate Nick's team-up with Dunkin' on the forthcoming "Chef Nick" drink.

The Mighty Mercurios

Multiple GWR title holder Rocco Mercurio (ITA) can now share two more records – with his sons! He teamed up with Christian (*left*) on 10 Feb 2023 to achieve the **fastest time to flip six water bottles (team of two)** in 3.78 sec. And Michael (*right*) equalled his dad's record for the **most tennis balls held in the hand (palm down)** – eight – on 15 May 2023.

Largest iced latte

Nick DiGiovanni and Dunkin' (both USA) served up a 260-gal (1,044.9-litre) thirst-quencher in Canton, Massachusetts, USA, on 20 Mar 2024. The ingredients followed those found in Dunkin's own latte recipe. It took 20 people more than 24 hours to create the scaled-up drink, which contained 25 gal (94.6 litres) of espresso and 100 gal (378 litres) of milk. *For more of Nick's outsized gastronomic delights, see p.92.*

Pyro Stunts

Most fire-eating extinguishes in one minute (two rods)
On 22 Apr 2023, Japanese circus performer Hero (aka Hirokuni Miyagi) snuffed out 94 flaming torches with his mouth in Niigata, Japan. This was Hero's second GWR title – the previous year, on 11 Jun, he had broken the equivalent **30 seconds** title with 57 torches extinguished – almost two every second.

Most catches of a fire sword in one minute
Serial record holder David Rush (USA) threw and caught a blazing blade 136 times in 60 sec on 27 Feb 2023. This wasn't the first time playing with fire for Rush, who holds more than 100 GWR titles – in Oct 2022, he accommodated the **most lit candles in the mouth**: an eyebrow-scorching 150.

Fastest 4 x 25 m relay on fire
On 29 Jan 2022, Italian stuntmen Ivan Forlani and Marco Lascari teamed up with Raffael Armbruster (DEU) and GWR veteran Josef Tödtling (*see opposite*) to cover 100 m in 1 min 8.74 sec as a four-man flaming relay. The attempt required each burning runner to use his body to ignite the next teammate.

Dear GWR...

Hi, my name's ▇▇▇▇▇▇▇ and I'm writing from the ▇▇▇ & ▇▇▇ *Show* on ▇▇▇▇ ▇▇▇ FM Radio in ▇▇▇▇▇▇, New York. We are going to light a 510-lb man's fart on fire and we are interested in knowing if there is a record to be broken on the distance that the flame will go. Could we have an official adjudicator come and take measurements?

Fastest 20-m tightrope crossing
On a freezing cold winter's evening in Feb 2022, Italian funambulist Maurizio Zavatta employed a novel tactic for keeping warm. He traversed a 20-m (65-ft 6-in) tightrope in just 14.34 sec while both himself and his balance pole were fully engulfed in flames.

⚠️ The activities on these pages are strictly for experts only – **don't try them at home!**

Longest duration juggling three fire balls
Michael Francis (CAN) donned a pair of heatproof gloves to juggle three oil-soaked balls of fire in Kitchener, Ontario, on 5 Jun 2021. The multiple record holder (*see also p.181*) kept them in the air for 2 min 25.2 sec. He needed to be extra careful with his hands as his speciality is prestidigitation (sleight-of-hand) records, including **most consecutive coin rolls** (353).

Highest bungee jump while on fire
On 14 Sep 2012, French daredevil Yoni Roch was set on fire before leaping from the 65-m-high (213-ft) Viaduc de la Souleuvre in Normandy, France. Roch's burning overalls were quickly extinguished when he plunged into the chilly Souleuvre River at the limit of his bungee-rope's travel.

Highest flame blown
For more than a decade, this record has been held by Antonio Restivo (USA), who scorched the 8.05-m-high (26-ft 5-in) ceiling of a warehouse in Las Vegas, Nevada, with the burning fumes from a mouthful of flaming paraffin in Jan 2011.

Farthest run on fire without oxygen
On 10 Sep 2022, firefighter Jonathan Vero (FRA) covered 272.2 m (893 ft) while fully aflame. The record attempt, which took place at a running track in Haubourdin, France, required helpers positioned around the track to spray more fuel on Vero to make sure that his flames did not go out!

First person to surf a wave while on fire
Pro surfer Jamie O'Brien (USA) was challenged to ride a breaker ablaze in an Instagram comment from a stranger, and thought it sounded like fun. After taking some classes in stunt performance, he headed to Tahiti in French Polynesia. He successfully surfed one of the world's most gnarly waves as a human torch on 22 Jul 2015.

Longest quadbike ride through a tunnel of fire
Daredevils Enrico Schoeman and André de Kock (both ZAF) sped through a 36.5-m (120-ft) gauntlet of fire in Meyerton, Guateng, South Africa, on 14 Sep 2019. Schoeman, who was driving, had to rely on muscle memory as his view was almost completely obscured by smoke and flames.

BURNING MAN: JOSEF TÖDTLING
Since blazing into the record books in 2013, Austrian stunt performer Josef Tödtling has become GWR's most prolific pyromaniac. He debuted with the **longest full-body burn without oxygen**, which involved him carefully fanning flames away from his face for 5 min 41 sec. As if that wasn't perilous enough, he went on to add a little more danger with the **farthest distance pulled by a vehicle while on fire**, covering an agonizing 582 m (1,909 ft).

His more recent flaming feats include the human-torch variations on **fastest 200 m on a bicycle** (which he managed in 49.5 sec on the set of *Lo Show dei Record* in Jan 2022) and **farthest distance on a zip wire** – an impressive 61.45 m (201 ft 7 in) during the Black Rose stunt show in Jeddah, Saudi Arabia, in May 2023.

To reduce risk, human torches use fuel that burns at a low temperature, fireproof clothes and cooling gel.

Core Strength

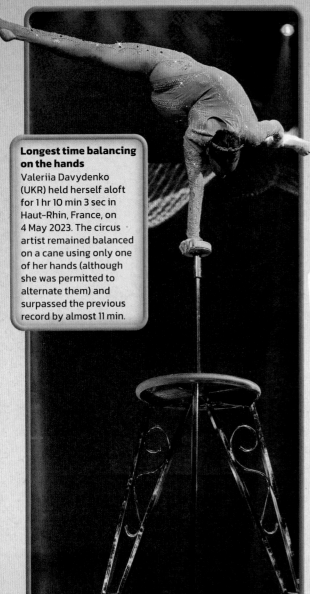

Longest time balancing on the hands

Valeriia Davydenko (UKR) held herself aloft for 1 hr 10 min 3 sec in Haut-Rhin, France, on 4 May 2023. The circus artist remained balanced on a cane using only one of her hands (although she was permitted to alternate them) and surpassed the previous record by almost 11 min.

Most consecutive pull-ups on a bar between two moving trucks

On 23 Jun 2023, Grigor Manukyan (ARM) completed 44 pull-ups while sandwiched between two moving HGVs in Talin, Armenia. Grigor broke this record just weeks after his 18th birthday. The previous year, the extreme athlete had achieved the **most chin-ups from a flying helicopter in one minute** – 36.

Most consecutive yoga positions underwater

India's Kamal Kaloi executed 21 *asanas* while submerged in a pool in Nam Định City, Vietnam, on 3 Jul 2020. In an exhibition of phenomenal lung power and limber limbs, the yogi completed the routine on just one breath. The display lasted for nearly 4 min, with each pose held for at least 5 sec.

Largest paddleboard yoga class

On 11 Sep 2022, a group of 305 people enjoyed an unconventional yoga session on Lake Constance in Überlingen, Baden-Württemberg, Germany. The class was led by Raphaela Schäufele (DEU, *pictured upright in pink top*), who runs a local yoga festival.

TOP 10 LONGEST YOGA POSES (*all IND, unless indicated*)

1
Womb
8 hr 34 min 11 sec
Yash Moradiya
25 Oct 2022

2
Tortoise
7 hr 55 min 45 sec
Yash Moradiya
23 Oct 2022

3
Tree
7 hr 53 min
Yash Moradiya
24 Oct 2022

4
Centre split
3 hr 10 min 12 sec
Smita Kumari
17 Dec 2022

5
Downward dog
1 hr 30 min 38 sec
Sedhu Ram
Kumar Kumar
25 Jun 2023

Youngest yoga instructor

Praanvi Gupta (IND, b. 15 Jun 2015) was aged 7 years 165 days when she was certified to teach yoga on 27 Nov 2022, as verified in Dubai, UAE. She had completed a 200-hr Yoga Alliance–approved training course.

The **male** record is held by Dubai-based Reyansh Surani (IND, b. 20 Dec 2011), aged 9 years 219 days on 27 Jul 2021.

Longest time to maintain a human flag (female)

Miki Nakamasu (JPN) sustained a demanding "horizontal handstand" for 36.80 sec in Nakagami, Okinawa, Japan, on 15 May 2021. Miki is the sole woman in the performance team Street Workout Okinawa.

She later set the female title for **most consecutive ring muscle-ups** (11) on 9 Apr 2023, and with compatriot Tomoki Wakinaguni completed the **most consecutive tandem push-ups (mixed)** – 34 – on 26 Aug 2023.

Most pull-ups in a wheelchair in one minute

Wheelchair user Adnan Almousa Alfermli (SYR) pulled himself up 10 times in 60 sec in Tenerife, Spain, on 23 Nov 2023.

Not content with one GWR title, the following day Adnan achieved the **heaviest single repetition weighted pull-up in a wheelchair** – 32.6 kg (71 lb 12 oz) – by lifting his chair and a set of weights. His sights are now set on qualifying for the Paralympics as a handcyclist, while also fundraising for children who, like himself, became disabled while living in a war zone.

Longest time in the abdominal-plank position

Josef Šálek (CZE) held a plank pose for an *abs*-tonishing 9 hr 38 min 47 sec in Plzeň, Czechia, on 20 May 2023. When he's not breaking GWR titles (*see also p.142*), Josef is a therapist and personal-development coach.

Dana Glowacka (CAN) achieved the **women's** title – planking for 4 hr 19 min 55 sec in Naperville, Illinois, USA, on 18 May 2019. Her son suggested she try for the record after reading about it in a past edition of the *Guinness World Records* book.

6 Mermaid
1 hr 15 min 5 sec
Rooba Ganesan
1 Jan 2023

7 Wheel
55 min 16 sec
Yash Moradiya
21 Jun 2022

8 Eagle
33 min 12 sec
Monika Kumawat
13 Dec 2021

9 Peacock
30 min 53 sec
Yash Moradiya
21 Jun 2022

10 Dimbasana
30 min 3 sec
Stefanie Millinger (AUT)
14 Jul 2022

Papercraft

Largest display of quilled flowers

Quilling involves rolling, shaping and gluing thin strips of paper into intricate forms, which are then typically combined to create larger artworks. Named for the feathers once used to manipulate the paper, it was popularized in religious art in the 15th century.

Brid Mc Cann (IRL) has found a way to fold a passion for quilling into breaking records, presenting 14,072 paper blooms (*examples above*) in Gort, Galway, Ireland, on 30 Jun 2019. Brid has since produced record quilled displays of **angels** (3,239, on 14 Nov 2019; *left*) and **snowflakes** (1,736, on 23 Dec 2021).

Largest display of quilled dolls

Thirty-nine members of the Facebook group Doll Making Enthusiasts showed off 3,441 paper figurines in Chennai, Tamil Nadu, India, on 18 Sep 2022. This surpassed the previous record by more than 1,200.

Largest origami rhinoceros

Artist Liu Tong (CHN) takes papercraft to a whole new scale. His first record came in the form of a 7.83-m-long, 4-m-tall (25-ft 8-in x 13-ft 1-in) rhino. Tong and his team spent over three hours shaping the 100-kg (220-lb) paper pachyderm, which was displayed at a shopping mall in Zhengzhou, Henan, China, on 19 Apr 2017.

Later that year, on 19 Dec, Tong added to his mega menagerie with three more supersized origami beasts: a 4.64-m-tall (15-ft 2-in) **dove**, a 5.15-m-long (16-ft 10-in) **whale** and a 3.7-m-long (12-ft 1-in) **leopard**.

Largest origami snail

Origamist Pei Haozheng (CHN) and his team unveiled a 4.1-m-long, 1.3-m-tall (13-ft 5-in x 4-ft 3-in) gastropod in Nanjing, Jiangsu, China, on 11 Mar 2023. It was made from a 9.2-m-long (30-ft 2-in) sheet of gold foil paper weighing *c*. 50 kg (110 lb). Haozheng had previously created the **most origami flowers from a single sheet of paper** – 100 – on 9 Sep 2022.

Fastest time to make 1,000 origami cranes

As a way to raise funds for British health workers, Evelyne Chia of Colchester, Essex, UK, folded 1,000 of these classic paper birds in 9 hr 31 min 13 sec on 22 Jun 2021. Cranes, aka *tancho*, symbolize peace, fidelity and luck, and in Japanese folklore are said to live 1,000 years, hence why this number is significant.

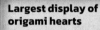

Largest display of origami hearts

With a 10,000-strong army of volunteers, Cambodia's Union of Youth Federations created a multicoloured sea of 3,917,805 paper hearts at Angkor Wat (the world's **largest religious structure**) in Siem Reap, Cambodia, on 11 Apr 2023. It was their way of showing support for the 32nd Southeast Asian Games and 12th ASEAN Para Games being hosted by the country.

Largest origami swan

Paul Frasco and Ryan Dong (both USA) turned an 18 x 18-ft (5.5 x 5.5-m) sheet into a 4.69-m-long (15-ft 4-in) bird at the OrigamiUSA Convention in New York City, USA, on 23 Jun 2023.

This wasn't Frasco's first foray into superlative paper art. Along with fellow origami designer Shrikant Iyer (USA), he spent two days creating the **largest origami dragon**, a hatchling that measured 3.87 m (12 ft 8 in) long and 1.99 m (6 ft 6 in) tall on 9 Aug 2020.

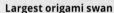

Largest origami heart

To mark the UAE's 50th National Day on 29 Jan 2022, Arshia Shahriari (IRN) and Amra Mahmood (PHL) folded a 4.01-m (13-ft 1-in) symbol of love in Dubai, UAE.

ORIGANIMALS: TOP 10 BIGGEST BEASTLY DISPLAYS

1 **Cranes**: 2,331,631, by GP43 Ltd (CHN) on 31 Jul 2022

2 **Doves**: 33,206, by Shindori Tsubasa School (JPN) on 3 Nov 2021

3 **Butterflies**: 29,416, by Juanne-Pierre De Abreu (ZAF) on 5 Dec 2019

4 **Horses**: 22,500, by Bridle Up Hope Foundation (USA) on 26 Jul 2022

5  **Giraffes**: 18,490, by Tiergarten Schönbrunn (AUT) on 6 May 2015

Arranged end to end, the strips of paper used in this vast Van Gogh work would cover a distance of 58 km (36 mi)!

LARGEST QUILLING MOSAIC (IMAGE)

On 8 Apr 2022, greeting-card manufacturer Quilling Card (VNM) unveiled a 26.73-m² (287.72-sq-ft) recreation of Vincent van Gogh's famous artwork *The Starry Night* in Ho Chi Minh City, Vietnam. The labour of love, created to celebrate the company's 10-year anniversary, took 3,399 hr to make, using almost 12 kg (26 lb) of glue and 191,948 paper strips. The final work is 39 times the size of the original oil painting. The mobile art installation is now available to be exhibited worldwide.

On the same day, the company brought together 300 of its artisans (*above*) to produce quilled birthday cards – setting another record for the **most people quilling simultaneously**.

6 Fish: 18,303, by Miyagi Prefecture (JPN) on 25 Feb 2021

7 Swans: 10,593, by Jamila Navagharwala (IND) on 15 Jan 2023

8 Whales: 9,210, by Seirin Elementary School (JPN) on 10 Jun 2023

9 Bats: 6,239, by the Conner Prairie museum (USA) on 3 Nov 2015

10 Rabbits: 3,988, by Murata Manufacturing Co (JPN) on 4 Apr 2023

Round-Up

Most blankets arm-knitted in 24 hours

Dan Soar (UK) knitted 19 blankets using his arms as needles in Alfreton, Derbyshire, UK, on 5 Apr 2024. The event raised £2,300 ($2,910) for a mental-health charity and hospice. Dan learned the craft in late 2021, since when his "Tattooed Knitter" TikTok videos have won him more than 300,000 followers.

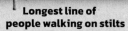

Longest line of people walking on stilts

On 21 Jan 2024, a group of 721 people on bamboo stilts – a local tradition known as Kang Dong Dang – formed a 2.4-km-long (1.2-mi) line in Karbi Anglong, Assam, India. The event was part of the 50th Karbi Youth Festival, overseen by Karbi Anglong Autonomous Council (IND).

Fastest time to visit every location on the London Monopoly® board by bicycle

Barclay Bram (UK) took only 1 hr 12 min 43 sec to cycle to every real-life site in Monopoly's London game on 20 Aug 2023. The ride began at Old Kent Road and ended at Angel Islington.

Fastest time to complete the GWR Ravensburger panorama jigsaw (team)

Eight finalists at the World Jigsaw Puzzle Championship assembled this 2,000-piece puzzle in just 1 hr 24 min 4 sec on 24 Sep 2023 in Valladolid, Spain. The image comprises the connected covers of the *2021, 2022* and *2023 Guinness World Records* books, and was created by artist Rod Hunt.

Largest soccer boot

On 1 Oct 2022, Muhammed D (IND) unveiled a football boot measuring 5.35 m (17 ft 6 in) long, 2.05 m (6 ft 8 in) tall and 1.70 m (5 ft 6 in) wide in Doha, Qatar. It was made for an art contest in the build-up to the 2022 FIFA World Cup.

Longest water skis

Julian Macias Lizaola (MEX) and Erick Julian Macias-Sedano (USA) made a 6.07-m-long (19-ft 10-in) pair of wooden skis, as verified in Rancho Avándaro, Mexico, on 18 Mar 2023.

Largest bobblehead

US bargain chain Ollie's erected a 5.04-m (16-ft 6-in) figurine outside its flagship store in Harrisburg, Pennsylvania, USA, as verified on 28 Sep 2022. Four months in the making, the XXL toy was created to mark the brand's 40th birthday. It's based on the Ollie's mascot, which itself nods to company co-founder Oliver E "Ollie" Rosenberg.

Longest string of worry beads

Over a four-year period, Angelos Iosif (CYP) hand-made a 317.9-m-long (1,042-ft 11-in) set of *komboloi*, or prayer beads, from clay and fruit seeds. It was measured in Strovolos, Nicosia District, Cyprus, on 17 May 2023.

Most wasabi eaten in one minute

Takamasa Suzuki (JPN) wolfed down 391 g (13.79 oz) of sinus-stinging wasabi on the set of *Lo Show dei Record* in Milan, Italy, on 29 Feb 2024.

Alaina Ballantyne (CAN) hit the sweet spot with the **most honey eaten in one minute** – 238 g (8.39 oz) – in Mississauga, Ontario, Canada, on 29 Apr 2023.

Longest tug-of-war rope

Two sides pulled on a rope stretched 516.85 m (1,695 ft 8 in) between them at Cefn Sidan Beach, Carmarthenshire, UK, on 1 Mar 2024. The contest, which lasted 1 min 15 sec, featured 100 participants and was arranged by Coleg Sir Gâr, Pembrey Country Park and Wales YFC (all UK).

Most people to jump through the same hula hoop

On 16 Aug 2023, four performers from Hoops Désolé Circus leapt through a hoop thrown backwards by the first person in the line. The Québécois quartet are (*left to right*): Theddy Nardin, Augustin Thériault, Jacob Grégoire (all CAN) and Santiago Esviza (ARG). The self-styled "crazy circus company" formed in 2017.

Largest electric toothbrush
YouTubers Ruth Amos and Shawn Brown (both UK) created a 2-m (6-ft 7-in) powered toothbrush, as verified in Sheffield, South Yorkshire, UK, on 22 Nov 2023. The idea for the attempt was suggested by eight-year-old George, one of the subscribers to the duo's channel "Kids Invent Stuff".

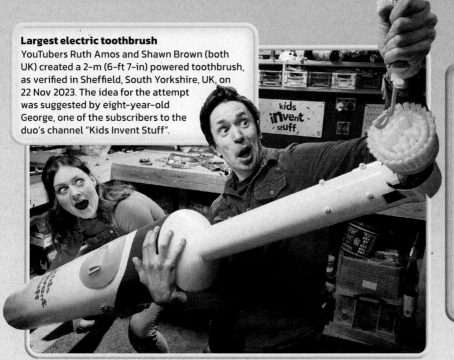

Largest chocolate sculpture of a balloon animal
On 18 Jan 2024, Amaury Guichon (FRA) unveiled a polished pink canine confection standing 1.60 m (5 ft 3 in) tall and 1.62 m (5 ft 4 in) wide at his kitchen in Las Vegas, Nevada, USA. A pastry chef and chocolatier par excellence, Amaury has amassed more than 24 million followers on TikTok.

Longest group hug
Raising funds for charity, Stephen Rattigan, Brian Cawley, Nicky Kearney and Robert Tuomey (all IRL) embraced for 30 hr 1 min in Castlebar, County Mayo, Ireland, on 4–5 May 2019.

Longest marathon by a quiz master
On 1–2 Apr 2023, Zsolt Kovács (ROM) posed trivia brainteasers for 34 hr 35 min 45 sec in Satu Mare, Romania. Zsolt asked a total of 2,000 questions to two teams. Zsolt is a veteran quiz master and host of the Transylvanian Quiz Championship.

MOST...
Cannon rolls in a car
US stuntman Logan Holladay controlled a Jeep Grand Cherokee through eight-and-a-half rolls in Sydney, New South Wales, Australia, on 1 Dec 2022. Staged during filming for *The Fall Guy* (2024), the event was organized by Universal Pictures and 87North Productions (both USA).

Spoons balanced on the body
On 17 Nov 2023, Abolfazl Saber Mokhtari (IRN) held 88 stainless-steel spoons on his body for the required time of 5 sec in Karaj, Iran. He improved on his own record, set in 2021, by a count of three.

Participants in a pickleball exhibition match
Kicking off the week-long 2023 USA Pickleball National Championships, 264 people played a showcase game in Farmers Branch, Texas, USA, on 5 Nov 2023. The fast-rising sport is a hybrid of tennis, table tennis and badminton.

Consecutive pogo-stick jumps
James Roumeliotis (USA) bounced 115,170 times on his pogo stick over a period of 11 hr 38 min on 9 Sep 2023. The marathon took place at Pogopalooza in Boston, Massachusetts, USA. He attempted this record to promote his charity Hopping for Heroes, which raises funds for veterans.

Longest handstand on a skateboard (LA3)
Kanya Sesser (USA) supported herself on her hands for 19.65 sec atop her board in Los Angeles, California, USA, on 9 Dec 2023. She was born without legs and abandoned in Thailand as a baby, but Kanya's maxim of "This is me and I'm going to go for it" has seen her triumph in multiple fields. A talented skate- and snowboarder, she's also worked as a TV and movie actress, and has modelled for brands such as Adidas and Abercrombie & Fitch.

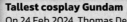

Tallest cosplay Gundam
On 24 Feb 2024, Thomas DePetrillo (USA) presented a 3.12-m-tall (10-ft 3-in) model of mech RX-78-2 Gundam in Rhode Island, USA. The manned robot appears in the Japanese sci-fi anime *Mobile Suit Gundam*, which premiered in 1979. It's pictured here alongside cosplayer Halie Pfefferkorn – who assisted Thomas with the build – dressed as villainous ace pilot Char Aznable, a key character in the franchise.

FASTEST HIGH-ALTITUDE MILE RUN (LA4)
On 1 Apr 2022, Andrea Lanfri (ITA) ran a mile around Everest Base Camp in Nepal, situated at 5,364 m (17,598 ft) above sea level, in 9 min 48 sec. This is the fastest time recorded by an LA4 athlete – GWR's classification for bilateral below-knee amputees.

In 2015, at the age of 29, Andrea contracted meningitis; he awoke from a month-long coma to find that he had lost seven fingers and both lower legs. Undaunted, he set his sights on returning to his great passion: mountain climbing. After a spell as a para athlete, Andrea crowdfunded a specialized climbing prosthesis and began to tackle higher and higher peaks.

On 13 May 2022, six weeks after his record-breaking run at base camp, Andrea went on to scale the world's **highest mountain**, fulfilling his desire to "touch the sky with three fingers".

To date, Andrea has topped four of the Seven Summits – the highest mountain on each continent.

Andrea carried two sets of prostheses with him on his Everest adventure – one designed for trekking (*left*) and another for climbing (*above*).

Highest Human

Here we present the progressive history of the absolute human altitude record – the story of humankind's ambition to escape the pull of gravity and take to the skies... and beyond!

The highest altitude that people can live long-term is around 5,000 m (16,400 ft) above sea level. Ancient human settlements have been found on the Tibetan Plateau and in the Andes Mountains at around this height. The present-day town of La Rinconada in Peru – the **highest permanent human settlement** – is at 5,100 m (16,730 ft).

While it is certain that intrepid souls have been climbing higher since prehistory, most left no trace of their adventures. The highest altitude confirmed to have been reached by humans before the invention of flying machines (see p.130) is 6,739 m (22,109 ft). That's the height of the summit of Volcán Llullaillaco on the Argentina–Chile border, where a team working at the **highest archaeological site** uncovered an Incan ceremonial altar dating to around 1500 CE.

Once flight was possible, not even the sky was the limit. Here we chart 220 years of humanity's ascent into the heavens.

1931 Physicist Auguste Piccard and his assistant Paul Kipfer (both CHE) soared to 15,781 m (51,775 ft) in the balloon *FNRS* ("Fonds National de la Recherche Scientifique"), which had a pressurized gondola. It was followed by a series of similar balloons that combined Piccard's revolutionary gondola design with ever-larger envelopes, culminating in the gigantic 100,000-m³ (3.5-million-cu-ft) *Explorer II* balloon (see 1935).

1951 Douglas Aircraft Company test pilot Bill Bridgeman (USA) flew the D-558-2 Skyrocket to 24,230 m (79,494 ft) from Edwards Air Force Base in California, USA. This was the first of many speed and altitude records broken by experimental rocket planes over the Mojave Desert.

1923 Test pilot Joseph Sadi-Lecointe (FRA) became the **first aeroplane pilot to break the altitude record**, flying to 11,145 m (36,564 ft) in an extensively modified Nieuport-Delage NiD.29 biplane fighter.

1804 Joseph-Louis Gay-Lussac (FRA) rose 7,016 m (23,018 ft) above Paris in a 160-m³ (5,650-cu-ft) hydrogen balloon. Similar gas balloons with open wicker baskets would be used for every record-breaking flight for more than a century.

1953 Marion Carl (USA) in the Douglas Skyrocket: 25,370 m (83,235 ft)

1935 Albert Stevens and Orvil Anderson (both USA) in *Explorer II*: 22,066 m (72,395 ft)

1933 Georgy Prokofiev, Konstantin Godunov and Ernst Birnbaum (all USSR) in *CCCP-1*: 19,000 m (62,335 ft)

1932 Auguste Piccard and Max Cosyns (BEL) in *FNRS*: 16,201 m (53,150 ft)

1927 Hawthorne Gray (USA): 12,874 m (42,240 ft)

1954 Kit Murray (USA) in the Bell X-1A: 27,566 m (90,440 ft)

1901 Arthur Berson and Reinhard Süring (both DEU) in *Preussen*: 10,800 m (35,430 ft)

1862 Henry Coxwell and James Glaisher (both UK) in *Mammoth*: 9,144 m (30,000 ft)

1956 Iven Kincheloe (USA) in the Bell X-2: 38,465 m (126,200 ft)

1838 Charles Green and George Rush (both UK) in *Nassau*: 8,274 m (27,146 ft)

The Gemini missions involved spacecraft docking with a rocket booster in orbit, then flying to higher altitudes.

1968 The crew of *Apollo 8* – Frank Borman, Jim Lovell and William Anders (all USA) – became the **first humans to leave Earth orbit** during a mission that flew around the far side of the Moon. At their most distant point, they were 377,349 km (234,474 mi) from Earth.

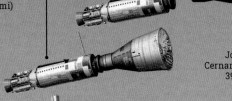

Sep 1966 Pete Conrad and Richard Gordon (both USA) in *Gemini XI*: 1,368.9 km (850.6 mi)

Jul 1966 John Young and Michael Collins (both USA) in *Gemini X*: 763.4 km (474.3 mi)

Apr 1961 Soviet cosmonaut Yuri Gagarin became the **first human in space** on 12 Apr, smashing the altitude record in the process. Riding on top of a modified R-7 intercontinental ballistic missile, Gagarin's *Vostok* capsule was launched into an orbit with an apogee – farthest point from Earth – of 327 km (203 mi).

1969 Tom Stafford, John Young and Eugene Cernan (all USA) in *Apollo 10*: 399,820 km (248,436 mi)

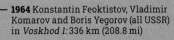

1964 Konstantin Feoktistov, Vladimir Komarov and Boris Yegorov (all USSR) in *Voskhod 1*: 336 km (208.8 mi)

1965 During the second mission of the Voskhod programme, cosmonaut Alexei Leonov carried out the **first spacewalk**, supported by his crewmate Pavel Belayev (both USSR). Despite its historic success, the mission was plagued with technical problems. Its booster rocket burned for too long, sending the spacecraft to an orbit with an apogee of 475 km (295 mi) – around 100 km (62 mi) higher than planned.

1960 Robert White (USA) in the North American X-15: 41,605 m (136,500 ft)

Mar 1961 Joe Walker (USA) flew an upgraded version of the X-15, now fitted with the much more powerful XLR99 rocket engine, to 51,694 m (169,600 ft) on 30 Mar. He increased the record by more than 10,000 m (32,800 ft), but only had two weeks to enjoy the limelight before Yuri Gagarin ushered in the Space Age. The X-15 still has the record for the **fastest speed achieved in Earth's atmosphere** – 7,270 km/h (4,520 mph), or Mach 6.7, set with Pete Knight (USA) at the controls in 1967.

Highest altitude reached by humans

Apollo 13, which launched on 11 Apr 1970, was supposed to make humanity's third landing on the surface of the Moon. Two days into the mission, however, an explosion in its oxygen tanks left the spacecraft barely able to support its crew. Astronauts Fred Haise, Jim Lovell and Jack Swigert (all USA, *left to right*) steered the ship on a "free return" trajectory that saw them swing around the far side of the Moon at a higher altitude than any previous mission. At their most distant point, *Apollo 13* was 400,041 km (248,573 mi) from Earth. Against the odds, the crew made it back safely, touching down on 17 Apr, and have held the record for more than 50 years.

Everest

First ascent by a woman
Junko Tabei (JPN) climbed Everest on 16 May 1975 – despite being knocked unconscious by an avalanche during her ascent.

On 28 Jul 1992, Tabei became the **first woman to climb the Seven Summits** (the highest peak on each continent) when she topped Elbrus. In all, she scaled 70 of the highest mountains before her death in 2016.

Most climbs without supplementary oxygen
Between 7 May 1983 and 23 May 1996, Ang Rita Sherpa (NPL) scaled Everest 10 times without bottled oxygen. On 22 Dec 1987, he made the **first** (and to date, only) **winter climb without supplementary oxygen**. He has also topped Kangchenjunga – the third-highest peak, at 8,586 m (28,169 ft), and widely considered a tougher climb than Everest – in winter, without bottled oxygen.

FIRST ASCENT...
In winter
Krzysztof Wielicki and Leszek Cichy (both POL) scaled Everest on 17 Feb 1980, with the use of bottled oxygen. Winter ascents present mountaineers with additional challenges. Conditions are more treacherous in the extreme cold, and the air is less rich in oxygen (owing to lower barometric pressure), making climbs more exhausting.

Solo
Reinhold Messner (ITA) completed the first single-handed ascent of Everest on 20 Aug 1980. It took him three days to reach the summit from his base camp at 6,500 m (21,325 ft). The climb was made all the more difficult by the fact that he did not use bottled oxygen.

Oldest woman to complete an ascent
Tamae Watanabe (JPN, b. 21 Nov 1938) topped Everest on 19 May 2012, aged 73 years 180 days. In doing so, she reclaimed the record she had first set 10 years previously.

Yuichiro Miura (JPN, b. 12 Oct 1932) holds the **men's** – and overall – record, summitting on 23 May 2013, aged 80 years 223 days.*

From sea level
On 11 May 1990, Tim Macartney-Snape (AUS) reached the world's highest point after trekking 1,200 km (745 mi) from Ganga Sagar on the Indian coast. He summitted unaided by sherpas or bottled oxygen.

By an amputee
Tom Whittaker (UK) scaled Everest on 27 May 1998. His right foot had to be removed following a car accident in 1979.

The **women's** record is held by Arunima Sinha (IND), who summitted on 21 May 2013. Her left leg was amputated in 2011, owing to injuries sustained during a robbery.

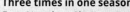

By a blind person
On 25 May 2001, Erik Weihenmayer (USA) reached Everest's peak. He was born with retinoschisis, an eye condition that left him blind by the age of 13.

He went on to become the **first blind person to climb the Seven Summits** – the continental extremes – on 26 Aug 2008.

Three times in one season
Four Nepalese Sherpas reached the top of Everest three times in spring 2007, on each occasion climbing from the advanced base camp up the north side. All four completed their first climb on 30 Apr and their last on 14 Jun: Phurba Tashi (who made his second ascent on 15 May), Son Dorje and Lhakpa Nuru (both 21 May), and Dorje Sonam Gyalzen (22 May).

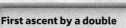

The youngest person to have climbed Everest was 13-year-old Jordan Romero in 2010, although GWR does not condone ascents by climbers under the age of 16.

First ascent by a double above-knee amputee
Hari Budha Magar (NPL) topped Everest on 19 May 2023. He took on this challenge as an inspiration to others, and to help change common assumptions about disability. A former Gurkha soldier, Magar lost his legs when he stepped on an explosive device while serving in Afghanistan in 2010.

In absolute terms, the **first double amputee to climb Everest** was Mark Inglis (NZ) on 15 May 2006. In 1982, he had to have his legs amputated below the knees as a result of frostbite.

Most ascents
At 9:20 a.m. on 23 May 2023, while leading clients for Seven Summit Treks, mountain guide Kami Rita Sherpa (NPL) topped Everest for the 28th time. His record for the **most ascents of the 8,000ers** – the 14 peaks over 8,000 m (26,246 ft) – now stands at 39.

The **women's** record is held by Lhakpa Sherpa (NPL), who reached the top of Everest for the 10th time on 12 May 2022.

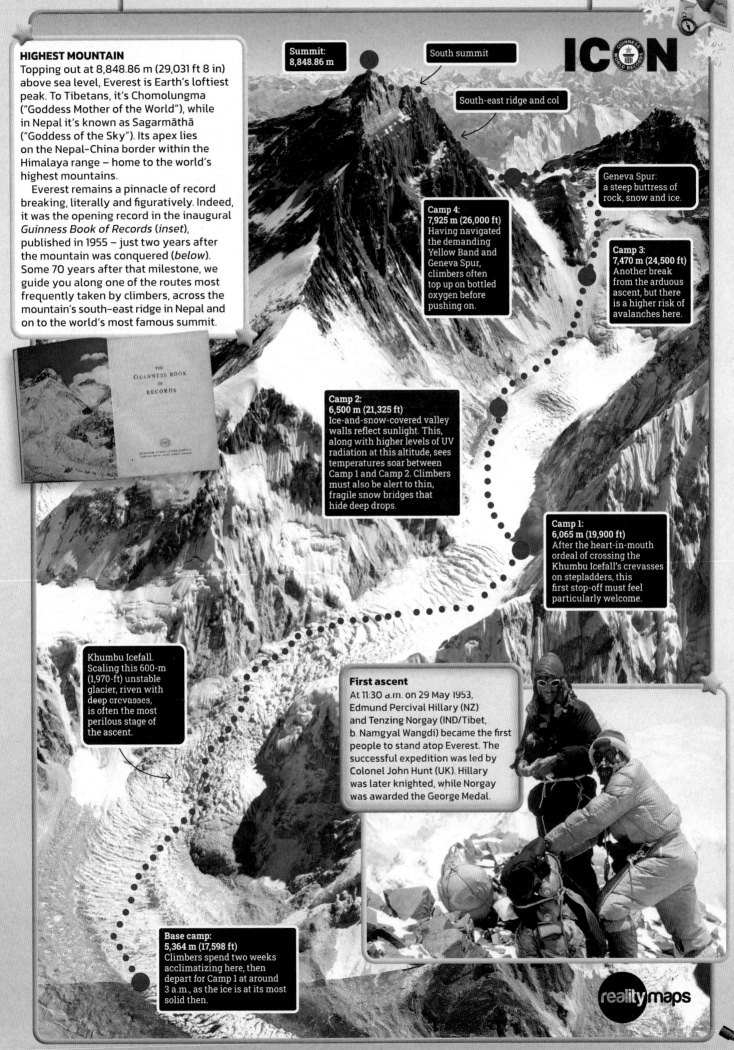

HIGHEST MOUNTAIN

Topping out at 8,848.86 m (29,031 ft 8 in) above sea level, Everest is Earth's loftiest peak. To Tibetans, it's Chomolungma ("Goddess Mother of the World"), while in Nepal it's known as Sagarmāthā ("Goddess of the Sky"). Its apex lies on the Nepal–China border within the Himalaya range – home to the world's highest mountains.

Everest remains a pinnacle of record breaking, literally and figuratively. Indeed, it was the opening record in the inaugural *Guinness Book of Records* (*inset*), published in 1955 – just two years after the mountain was conquered (*below*). Some 70 years after that milestone, we guide you along one of the routes most frequently taken by climbers, across the mountain's south–east ridge in Nepal and on to the world's most famous summit.

THE GUINNESS BOOK OF RECORDS

Summit:
8,848.86 m

South summit

South-east ridge and col

Geneva Spur: a steep buttress of rock, snow and ice.

Camp 4:
7,925 m (26,000 ft)
Having navigated the demanding Yellow Band and Geneva Spur, climbers often top up on bottled oxygen before pushing on.

Camp 3:
7,470 m (24,500 ft)
Another break from the arduous ascent, but there is a higher risk of avalanches here.

Camp 2:
6,500 m (21,325 ft)
Ice-and-snow-covered valley walls reflect sunlight. This, along with higher levels of UV radiation at this altitude, sees temperatures soar between Camp 1 and Camp 2. Climbers must also be alert to thin, fragile snow bridges that hide deep drops.

Camp 1:
6,065 m (19,900 ft)
After the heart-in-mouth ordeal of crossing the Khumbu Icefall's crevasses on stepladders, this first stop-off must feel particularly welcome.

Khumbu Icefall. Scaling this 600-m (1,970-ft) unstable glacier, riven with deep crevasses, is often the most perilous stage of the ascent.

First ascent
At 11:30 a.m. on 29 May 1953, Edmund Percival Hillary (NZ) and Tenzing Norgay (IND/Tibet, b. Namgyal Wangdi) became the first people to stand atop Everest. The successful expedition was led by Colonel John Hunt (UK). Hillary was later knighted, while Norgay was awarded the George Medal.

Base camp:
5,364 m (17,598 ft)
Climbers spend two weeks acclimatizing here, then depart for Camp 1 at around 3 a.m., as the ice is at its most solid then.

reality maps

Ballooning

Longest time flying a balloon

Brian Jones (UK) and Bertrand Piccard (CHE) spent 19 days 21 hr 47 min airborne in the *Breitling Orbiter 3* between 1 and 21 Mar 1999. Setting out from Château-d'Œx in Switzerland, they completed the **first circumnavigation by balloon**, travelling 40,814 km (25,361 mi) before landing in Cairo, Egypt. Their aerial odyssey remains the **farthest flight in a balloon**.

First crewed flight

On 15 Oct 1783, science educator Jean-François Pilâtre de Rozier (FRA; *see right*) rose 25 m (82 ft) into the sky above Paris in a lighter-than-air balloon that was tethered to the ground. He remained aloft for four minutes, controlling his altitude by stoking a fire in the gondola. The flight took place a month after a test that saw the **first animal passengers** (a duck, sheep and rooster) take to the air and land unharmed.

First Atlantic crossing by hot-air balloon

Adventurer Richard Branson (UK) and pilot Per Lindstrand (SWE) flew from Sugarloaf in Maine, USA, to Limavady in Northern Ireland, UK,

on 2–3 Jul 1987. The epic journey in the *Virgin Atlantic Flyer* lasted 31 hr 41 min and covered 4,947 km (3,074 mi).

The same duo went on to complete the **first Pacific crossing by hot-air balloon**, on 15–17 Jan 1991. They flew 10,880 km (6,761 mi) from Japan to Canada's Northwest Territories in the *Virgin Otsuka Pacific Flyer*.

Highest flight by a hot-air balloon

At the age of 67, Dr Vijaypat Singhania (IND) soared to an altitude of 21,027 m (68,986 ft) over Mumbai, India, on 26 Nov 2005.

The altitude record for a **lifting-gas balloon** is still held by Malcolm Ross and Victor Prather (both USA), who flew the helium-filled *Strato Lab V* to 34,668 m (113,740 ft) on 4 May 1960.

Most wins of the Gordon Bennett Cup

First held in 1906, the Gordon Bennett Cup is the **oldest aviation race**. Pilots compete to guide their 1,000-m³ (35,314-cu-ft) gas balloons the farthest from the launch site. Vincent Leÿs (FRA) won the race nine times between 1997 (his debut) and 2017.

First untethered crewed flight

On 21 Nov 1783, Jean-François Pilâtre de Rozier and the Marquis d'Arlandes (both FRA) took a flight into the unknown above Paris, France. They launched from the Bois de Boulogne before crossing the Seine and gliding over the rooftops of the city centre. The balloon came down south-east of Paris 25 min later.

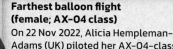

Farthest balloon flight (female; AX-04 class)

On 22 Nov 2022, Alicia Hempleman-Adams (UK) piloted her AX-04-class balloon 301.9 km (187.1 mi) across Canada. She also set a record for the **longest-duration flight** in her category: 7 hr 39 min 30 sec. The FAI's AX-04 class is for relatively small balloons – c. 13 m (42 ft) in diameter – operated by a single pilot in a 1-m-wide (3-ft 3-in) basket.

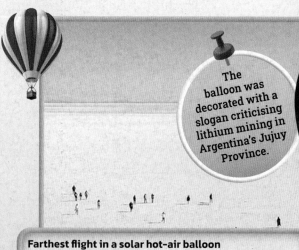

The balloon was decorated with a slogan criticising lithium mining in Argentina's Jujuy Province.

Farthest flight in a solar hot-air balloon

On 25 Jan 2020, aeronaut Leticia Noemi Marques (ARG) soared for 667.85 m (2,191 ft) across the Salinas Grandes salt flats in Argentina in the sun-powered *Aerocene Pacha*. The eco-friendly flight was the brainchild of the Aerocene Project, led by Argentine artist Tomás Saraceno, which aims to create a new generation of non-fossil-fuel-powered aircraft. The balloon envelope was made from a fabric called Skytex, a matt black material that is very efficient at absorbing energy from sunlight.

The *Aerocene Pacha* is a type of hopper balloon – rather than standing in a basket, pilot Leticia Noemi Marques was suspended by a harness beneath the envelope. She guided the balloon to an altitude of 272.1 m (892 ft) above ground.

GREATEST MASS HOT-AIR BALLOON ASCENT
On 6 Oct 2019, a total of 524 hot-air balloons filled the skies above New Mexico, USA, during morning mass ascension at the 48th Albuquerque International Balloon Fiesta. The annual festival attracts balloon enthusiasts from the USA and across the world, lured by its promise of "an enchanted world of special-shaped balloon rodeos, twilight balloon glows, and vibrant balloon-filled skies".

Aerobatics

Heaviest aircraft to perform an aerobatic loop

A 36.74-tonne (40.05-ton) Lockheed Martin LM-100J (*left*) performed a loop at the Farnborough International Airshow in Hampshire, UK, on 18 Jul 2018. The aircraft was flown by Wayne Roberts and co-pilot Steve Knoblock (both USA).

The **heaviest aircraft flown inverted** is the 41.78-tonne (46.06-ton) Boeing 367-80. During a public demonstration on 7 Aug 1955, Alvin "Tex" Johnston (USA) barrel-rolled the prototype airliner over Lake Washington near Seattle, Washington, USA.

First loop-the-loop in a helicopter

On 9 May 1949, test pilot Harold E "Tommy" Thompson (USA) guided his Sikorsky S-52 through a series of loops over Bridgeport, Connecticut, USA. Earlier that year, a US Navy pilot had accidentally flown inverted while pulling out of a dive in a Piasecki helicopter, but it's not clear if this was a full loop.

Longest inverted flight

On 24 Jul 1991, Joann Osterud (USA, b. CAN; 1945–2017) flew her Ultimate 10-300S biplane upside down for 4 hr 38 min 10 sec between Vancouver and Vanderhoof in Canada. She trained by attaching a pilot's seat to her garage ceiling and hanging there in 20-min stretches.

Osterud, a stunt pilot and Alaska Airlines' first female commercial pilot, also holds the record for the **most outside loops**. She guided her Supernova Hiperbipe through 208 in a 2-hr display over Oregon, USA, on 13 Jul 1989.

Most wins of the Red Bull Air Race Championship

Paul Bonhomme (UK; *inset below*) won the airborne obstacle course championship three times, in 2009, 2010 and 2015. Bonhomme – one of several pilots in his family – gained his pilot's licence aged 18 and also flew commercial airliners. He announced his retirement from air-racing after winning his third Red Bull title in 2015. Bonhomme had taken part in all 65 races since the championship's inception in 2003, winning 19.

Most aircraft in inverted aerobatic flight

Popularly known as the "Smoke Squadron", Esquadrão de Demonstração Aérea is the Brazilian Air Force's display team. During a performance at Campo Fontenelle aerodrome in Pirassununga on 29 Oct 2006, the team's pilots flew 12 T-27 Tucanos in formation upside down for more than 30 sec.

Most wins of the World Glider Aerobatic Championships

Jerzy Makula (POL) won seven titles at the FAI's premier gliding competition between 1985 and 2011. He also contributed to Poland's record for the **most team titles**, winning nine times.

Most aircraft in an aerobatic loop

On 4 Sep 1958, the British Royal Air Force "Black Arrows" display team performed a loop with 22 planes arranged in a chevron formation at the Farnborough Airshow in Hampshire, UK. Drawn from the ranks of the RAF's 111 Squadron, the Black Arrows were one of a number of display teams superseded by the Red Arrows in 1965.

Most jet aircraft in a military aerobatic display team

Formed in 1961, the Frecce Tricolori are the aerobatic demonstration team of the Italian Air Force. They perform using 10 Aermacchi MB–339 jet trainers; during displays, nine planes fly in close formation, with one soloist. Each pilot's call–sign is "Pony" and a number signifying their position in formation.

Longest tunnel flown through in an aeroplane

Stunt pilot Dario Costa (ITA) flew his racing plane along a 1.73-km (1.07-mi) stretch of the Çatalca Tunnels in Türkiye on 4 Sep 2021. Despite a gap of only 4 m (13 ft) between the wingtips and the walls, Costa navigated the course in 44 sec at an average speed of 245 km/h (152 mph). Upon emerging from the tunnels, he executed a celebratory mid–air loop.

The 2023 Reno Air Races were the last to be held at Stead Airport. A new venue is being sought.

LONGEST-RUNNING AIR-RACE TOURNAMENT

The National Championship Air Races (also known as the Reno Air Races) have been held annually at Stead Airport in Reno, Nevada, USA, since 1964. Founded by World War II pilot Bill Stead, the event sees various single-seat aircraft race at high speed and low altitude around an 8-mi (12.8-km) oval course marked out by pylons. There are several classes, including races for modern aerobatics planes and small jets, but the most prestigious event is the "unlimited" class. The planes that compete in this category are almost all heavily modified WWII fighter aircraft.

Steven Hinton Jr (USA) has racked up the **most unlimited-class wins at the National Championship Air Races** – eight – between 2009 and 2023. Hinton also holds the record for the **fastest speed in a piston-engined aircraft** – an average of 855.59 km/h (531.64 mph), in the modified P-51 Mustang *Voodoo* on 2 Sep 2017.

Race Across the World

Fastest circumnavigation by scheduled flights

From 14 to 15 Jun 2022, Tomas Reisinger (CZE) flew round the world in 41 hr 18 min – more than 5 hr faster than the previous record. He did so in just two hops, taking Singapore Airlines flight SQ 22 from Singapore Changi Airport to Newark Liberty International Airport in New Jersey, USA, and then boarding return flight SQ 21 via the same airline. (SQ 21 also currently represents the **longest duration non-stop scheduled flight**, at 18 hr 30 min.)

As Reisinger's feat cannot be meaningfully improved on using current technology, Guinness World Records is resting the record. Aspiring globetrotters are invited to apply for a related category: **fastest circumnavigation by scheduled surface transport**.

Fastest circumnavigation by bicycle

Mark Beaumont (UK) cycled the globe in 78 days 14 hr 40 min between 2 Jul and 18 Sep 2017, beginning and ending near the Arc de Triomphe in Paris, France. He passed through 16 countries during his record-breaking ride.

Fellow Brit Jenny Graham holds the **women's** record – 124 days 11 hr – in a round trip from Berlin, Germany, from 16 Jun to 18 Oct 2018.

Fastest circumnavigation by car

The record for the first and fastest man and woman to have circumnavigated the Earth by car covering six continents under the rules applicable in 1989 and 1991 embracing more than an equator's length of driving (24,901 road miles; 40,075 km), is held by Saloo Choudhury and his wife Neena Choudhury (both India). The journey took 69 days 19 hours 5 minutes from 9 September to 17 November 1989. The couple drove a 1989 Hindustan "Contessa Classic" starting and finishing in Delhi, India.

Fastest crossing of the USA by skateboard

Chad Caruso (USA) took only 57 days 6 hr 56 min to travel from Venice Beach, California, to Virginia Beach, Virginia, between 24 Mar and 19 May 2023. To build up stamina, Caruso made a string of long-distance skates in the six months leading up to his attempt. He used his feat to promote awareness about the causes of addiction and poor mental health.

Fastest sail around Antarctica

From 21 Feb to 25 May 2022, Lisa Blair (AUS) circled Antarctica in 92 days 18 hr 21 min 22 sec in her 50-ft (15.2-m) monohull *Climate Action Now*. She is only the third adventurer to complete this journey. The feat – a round trip from Albany in Western Australia – won her the 25,920-km (14,000-nautical-mi) Antarctica Cup Ocean Race.

Fastest crossing of New Zealand by foot (female)

It took Emma Timmis only 20 days 17 hr 15 min 57 sec to traverse her home country between 18 Dec 2021 and 7 Jan 2022. She averaged more than 100 km (62 mi) per day on her run from Cape Reinga in North Island to the town of Bluff at the bottom of South Island.

Fastest bicycle circumnavigation by a married couple

Caroline Soubayroux (FRA) and David Ferguson (UK) cycled around the world in 204 days 17 hr 25 min between 25 Sep 2021 and 16 Apr 2022. Their rapid ride raised money for Barts Health NHS Trust. The journey started and finished at the Royal London Hospital, UK.

Fastest west-to-east crossing of India by bicycle (female)

Preeti Maske (IND) rode between the states of Gujarat and Arunachal Pradesh in 13 days 18 hr 38 min, ending on 15 Nov 2022. She used her 3,954-km (2,457-mi) trek to raise awareness of the ReBirth Foundation, which promotes organ donation.

Maske also holds the **north-to-south** record – 11 days 22 hr 23 min – achieved on 24 Feb 2023 when she arrived in Tamil Nadu, at the southernmost tip of the country.

Fastest Atlantic crossing in a Mini-class sailboat

Jay Thompson (USA) set off from New York City in *Speedy Gonzales* at 6:35 p.m. on 3 Aug 2023. After just 17 days 9 hr 51 min 9 sec, and despite bad weather and equipment failures, he passed Lizard Point in Cornwall, UK, at 4:26 a.m. on 21 Aug. Thompson then continued, ending his journey at Port du Château in Brest, France. Mini-class vessels are 6.5 m (21 ft 3 in) long, 3 m (9 ft 10 in) wide and designed to be operated single-handed.

Charlesworth's paddleboard was loaded with waterproof bags for his clothes, food and camping equipment.

LONGEST JOURNEY BY STAND-UP PADDLEBOARD

From 4 Mar to 11 Jun 2023, Peter Charlesworth (AUS) rowed 2,677.34 km (1,663.62 mi) standing on a paddleboard. Travelling solo and unsupported, he navigated the length of Australia's longest river (the Murray) while executing a full lap of lakes Hume, Mulwala, Albert and Alexandrina along the way. Charlesworth embarked on the challenge, which was 18 months in the planning, to advocate for greater heart-health awareness following his triple-bypass surgery in 2020.

Extreme Swimming

Fastest time to complete an open-water 10-km swim on six continents
Brothers Joe and John Zemaitis (both USA) took just 4 days 23 hr 43 min to wrap up a whistlestop tour of long-distance swims around the globe. They started in Cartagena, Colombia, on 6 Jun 2023, and finished on 11 Jun in Sydney, Australia. They went by way of the USA and Morocco, and completed two swims in Türkiye – one in Europe and one in Asia.

Farthest swim with a monofin
On 15 Apr 2023, Estonia's Merle Liivand completed a 50-km (31-mi) "mermaid swim" in Biscayne Bay, off Miami, Florida, USA. Liivand swam for 14 hr 15 min without using her arms, propelling herself using only a monofin. The champion swimmer uses publicity from her record attempts to call for an end to ocean pollution; this was her fifth time extending the distance in this category.

Youngest person to complete the Oceans Seven
Prabhat Koli (IND, b. 27 Jul 1999) was aged 23 years 217 days when he finished the open-water marathon challenge (*see opposite*) on 1 Mar 2023.
The **women's** record was also set in 2023, by Croatia's Dina Levačić (b. 14 Mar 1996). Her final swim was executed on her 27th birthday.

Fastest relay swim crossing of the North Channel (LA)
British team "Bits Missing" – David Burke, Mary Clewlow, Andrew Smith, Kate Sunley and Jonty Warneken – took turns to swim from Northern Ireland to Scotland, UK, in 15 hr 8 min 35 sec on 22 Jun 2022. All leg amputees, they are the first para team to swim this 35-km (21.5-mi) route.
On 8 Sep 2023, Warneken returned to the North Channel to set the **solo LA2** record: 15 hr 22 min 41 sec. Both swims were ratified by the Irish Long Distance Swimming Association.

Longest distance ice swim
On 19 Apr 2023, Krzysztof Gajewski (POL, *see also pp.104–05*) swam for 6 km (3.7 mi) in a lake near Sienna, Poland. His epic effort lasted 1 hr 46 min 16 sec. As per International Ice Swimming Association (IISA) rules, Krzysztof wore only a standard swimsuit, cap and goggles, and the water temperature was below 5°C (41°F).

Oldest person to swim Lake Malawi
Pat Gallant-Charette (USA, b. 2 Feb 1951) was aged 72 years 109 days when she traversed the 23.5-km (14.6-mi) distance from Cape Ngombo to Senga Bay on 22 May 2023. Her feat was verified by the Marathon Swimmers Federation.

Fastest Ice Mile swim
On 12 Mar 2023, Marcin Szarpak (POL) covered 1 mi (1.6 km) in 19 min 27 sec in an outdoor pool in Świętochłowice, Poland.
The **oldest Ice Mile swimmer** is Jerrie Roberts (UK, b. 26 Jun 1950). On 1 Dec 2023, she braved the frigid waters of Loch Morlich in the Scottish Highlands, UK, at the age of 73 years 158 days. She completed the mile in 54 min 43 sec. Both records were confirmed by IISA.

Longest continuous swim in a counter-current pool
On 28–30 Dec 2023, in honour of a close friend who died from cancer aged 45, Maarten van der Weijden (NLD) powered against a constant flow of water for 45 hr straight in Vught, Netherlands. Van der Weijden himself overcame leukaemia in his early 20s and came back to win Olympic gold for open-water swimming in 2008. He reclaimed a GWR title that he had formerly set in 2021, with a time of 32 hr 20 min 50 sec.

Fastest stage swim from Land's End to John o' Groats (female)
Multi-discipline adventurer Jasmine Harrison (UK) took 109 days 55 min to swim the length of Great Britain from 1 Jul to 18 Oct 2022. She swam along the west coast for up to 12 hr a day, resting in between on board her support crew's yacht. Jasmine's epic 1,040-km (646-mi) journey was verified by the World Open Water Swimming Association.

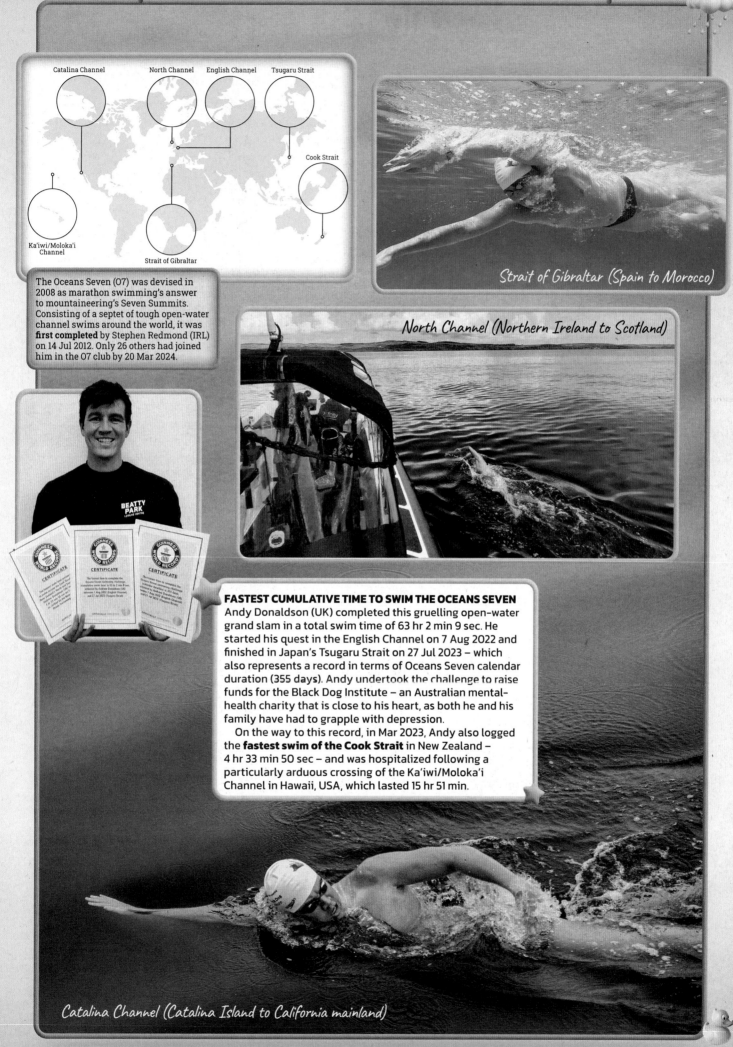

Catalina Channel   North Channel   English Channel   Tsugaru Strait

Cook Strait

Ka'iwi/Moloka'i Channel

Strait of Gibraltar

The Oceans Seven (O7) was devised in 2008 as marathon swimming's answer to mountaineering's Seven Summits. Consisting of a septet of tough open-water channel swims around the world, it was **first completed** by Stephen Redmond (IRL) on 14 Jul 2012. Only 26 others had joined him in the O7 club by 20 Mar 2024.

Strait of Gibraltar (Spain to Morocco)

North Channel (Northern Ireland to Scotland)

FASTEST CUMULATIVE TIME TO SWIM THE OCEANS SEVEN

Andy Donaldson (UK) completed this gruelling open-water grand slam in a total swim time of 63 hr 2 min 9 sec. He started his quest in the English Channel on 7 Aug 2022 and finished in Japan's Tsugaru Strait on 27 Jul 2023 – which also represents a record in terms of Oceans Seven calendar duration (355 days). Andy undertook the challenge to raise funds for the Black Dog Institute – an Australian mental-health charity that is close to his heart, as both he and his family have had to grapple with depression.

On the way to this record, in Mar 2023, Andy also logged the **fastest swim of the Cook Strait** in New Zealand – 4 hr 33 min 50 sec – and was hospitalized following a particularly arduous crossing of the Ka'iwi/Moloka'i Channel in Hawaii, USA, which lasted 15 hr 51 min.

Catalina Channel (Catalina Island to California mainland)

All at Sea

Fastest English Channel crossing by prone paddleboard

Mark Walton (IRL, *above*) arrived in Tardinghen, France, on 2 Oct 2023, 3 hr 54 min 50 sec after departing the UK. During the journey, he had to briefly exit the water to be ferried across a shipping lane in a support boat.

The **fastest continuous crossing**, meanwhile, is 5 hr 9 min, by Michael O'Shaughnessy (USA) on 18 Jul 2006. The keen surfer from Florida has also paddleboarded across Loch Ness and the Irish Sea.

Fastest time to sail across the Irish Sea in a two-person catamaran

Partners Anna Burnet and John Gimson (both UK) took just 1 hr 30 min 41 sec to cross from Bangor in Northern Ireland to the Scottish village of Portpatrick, UK, on 26 Sep 2023. The pair, who won silver at Tokyo 2020 and were also selected to compete for Team GB at the Paris Olympics in 2024, rode on a Nacra 17 catamaran. They attempted the record to promote zero-emissions marine technology.

First person to kayak across the South Atlantic (east to west)

Richard Kohler (ZAF) paddled from Cape Town, South Africa, to Salvador, Brazil, between 18 Dec 2022 and 19 Feb 2023. He made the trip solo and unsupported in his vessel *Osiyeza* ("The Crossing"). Kohler covered 3,332 nautical mi (6,170 km; 3,834 mi) in just under 63 days 7 hr, but had to swim the last few metres to shore as there was nowhere to dock!

FIRST...

Person to achieve the Ocean Explorers Grand Slam

By 2019, Fiann Paul (ISL) had rowed across all five oceans, with various crews. He began by traversing the Atlantic, east to west, in 2011, and finished by crossing the Southern Ocean in 2019. The latter was the **first row on the Southern Ocean**, when Paul served as captain of a six-person team. They rowed from Cape Horn, Chile, to Charles Point on mainland Antarctica between 13 and 25 Dec 2019, on board *Ohana*.

Woman to row on the Southern Ocean

From 11 to 17 Jan 2023, Lisa Farthofer (AUT) rowed from King George Island to Laurie Island in the seas around Antarctica, as part of a five-strong crew. This also made her the **first woman to row on polar open waters**. Remarkably, the crew set eight other GWR titles on the trip, including the **longest distance rowed on the Southern Ocean** – 407 nautical mi (753 km; 468 mi).

Person to kayak the Mid-Pacific unsupported

Cyril Derreumaux (FRA) paddled his kayak *Valentine* across 2,013 nautical mi (3,728 km; 2,316 mi) between 21 Jun and 20 Sep 2022. The voyage took 90 days 9 hr, beginning in Monterey, California, and ending in Hilo, Hawaii, USA. He described the trip as "a magnificent adventure".

Person to row the Indian Ocean from mainland Australia to mainland Africa

Between 25 Apr and 20 Jul 2023, Robert Barton (AUS) voyaged singlehandedly from Carnarvon, Western Australia, to Tanga, Tanzania. He covered 4,829 nautical mi (8,943 km; 5,557 mi) in 85 days 12 hr 9 min in his open-class boat *Hope*.

MOST...

Days at sea by an ocean rower

During a series of trips between Nov 2005 and Mar 2022, Turkish-American engineer Erden Eruç spent 1,167 days on the high seas, either rowing solo or as part of a crew of two.

Eruç has also accumulated the **greatest aggregate distance by a solo ocean rower** – a total of 26,705 nautical mi (49,457 km; 30,731 mi) – in his vessel *Around-n-Over*.

Solo ocean rows

Between 2001 and 2019, Emmanuel Coindre (FRA) completed seven unaccompanied ocean crossings. He traversed the Atlantic five times and the Pacific and Indian oceans once each.

Consecutive completions of the Sydney Hobart Yacht Race

Lindsay May (AUS) has finished this race 50 times, most recently on 31 Dec 2023. Competitors sail c. 628 nautical mi (1,163 km; 722 mi) from New South Wales, Australia, to the Tasmanian capital Hobart, crossing the treacherous Bass Strait.

The **most completions** of the race overall is 54, by Tony Ellis (AUS) between 1963 and 2023.

Greatest distance by kayak on open water in 24 hours (female)

On 12–13 Sep 2022, Bonnie Hancock (AUS) paddled her surfski kayak 127 nautical mi (235 km; 146 mi) off the coast of Queensland, Australia.

Hancock set this record just two weeks after completing the **fastest circumnavigation of Australia by kayak (female)**, returning to her start point on 28 Aug, 254 days 6 hr after departing.

OLDEST PERSON TO ROW ACROSS ANY OCEAN SOLO

Frank Rothwell (UK, b. 9 Jul 1950) was aged 73 years 157 days when he set out from San Sebastián, La Gomera, in Spain's Canary Islands, on 13 Dec 2023. The owner and chairman of Oldham Athletic football club completed his row across the Atlantic 64 days later, aged 73 years 221 days, when he arrived at English Harbour in Antigua on 15 Feb 2024. Aptly enough, Rothwell named his vessel *Never Too Old*.

GWR talks to...

You first rowed across the Atlantic in 2020–21. Why did you return for a second crossing?

On my first Atlantic row I raised over £1 m [$1.3 m] for Alzheimer's Research UK. In 2023, my best mate Phil Wiggett died aged 62 with early-onset Alzheimer's. Seeing Phil deteriorate made me think, "What can I do to help?" At 73, I felt I was still strong enough to row and raise more awareness and funds.

Can you share a few favourite memories from your time at sea?

At about the halfway stage I saw an 8-m [26-ft] whale cross my path about 10 m [33 ft] from the rear of the boat. Also, opening the homemade cards from my grandchildren on Christmas Day was very, very special.

How did you train for the row?

Quickly! I trained in all weathers, rowing up to 30 mi [48 km] a day on the Firth of Clyde in Scotland, and in the North Sea between Scarborough and Whitby in North Yorkshire.

What were the hardest challenges during your recent row?

The doldrums [windless waters that occur around the Equator] and adverse trade winds made the 2023–24 row far harder than my 2020–21 attempt. I'm experienced, and I had a much lighter boat, so I expected to reduce my time. [But this latest crossing] took me an *additional* week.

What advice would you give to people of your age who are considering taking on extreme adventure records?

Only do something that you're 100% sure you can complete safely, without endangering the lives of anyone else, or expecting them to come and rescue you.

Will you attempt to break more records in the future?

I'd love to row across the Pacific in 2025, when I will turn 75. But my family aren't too keen on me going again – *at all!*

Rothwell had his share of high drama on the high seas. He capsized four times, but a tether kept him secured to his vessel.

Trailblazers

First paraplegic ascent of El Capitan (female)

Karen Darke (UK) topped El Capitan in California, USA, on 5 Oct 2007, after a four-day climb. Led by then partner Andy Kirkpatrick, she hauled herself up the 914-m-tall (3,000-ft) granite monolith in Yosemite National Park by performing the equivalent of around 4,000 pull-ups. Since becoming paralysed from the chest down when she was 21, Darke has sea-kayaked from Canada to Alaska, won a gold medal at the Paralympics in handcycling and embarked on an epic expedition in Antarctica (see p.140).

Mark Wellman (USA) made the first paraplegic ascent of El Capitan on 26 Jul 1989, led by friend Mike Corbett.

Deepest underground balloon flight

Ivan Trifonov (AUT) piloted a hot-air balloon 206 m (675 ft) down into the Mamet Cave in Obrovac, Croatia, on 18 Sep 2014. It took him 25 min to descend to the bottom and then re-emerge. Trifonov undertook the subterranean sojourn in honour of the adventure writer Jules Verne and his novel *Journey to the Centre of the Earth*, which was marking its 150-year anniversary.

The pioneering balloonist can also lay claim to the **first solo balloon flight over the North Pole** – on 21 Apr 1996 – and **South Pole** – on 8 Jan 2000.

First aerial loop with a jet-propelled wing

Former fighter pilot Yves Rossy (CHE) loop-the-looped his way into history with a jet-powered wing on 5 Nov 2010. The aviation milestone took place 2,400 m (7,870 ft) above Bercher, Switzerland, after Rossy had launched himself from the *Esprit Breitling Orbiter* balloon. After a few minutes of flying to stabilize the wing, he executed a full loop before parachuting back to terra firma.

First person to explore the Darvaza Crater

In Nov 2013, explorer and storm-chaser George Kourounis (CAN) entered the "Door to Hell" – the blazing Darvaza Crater, in a gas field in Turkmenistan. Using an insulated aluminium suit and Kevlar climbing harness, he descended to the base and collected rock samples, which were later found to host bacteria, in spite of the 1,000°C (1,832°F) environment. Ignited in 1971, the **longest-burning methane crater** was still alight as of Mar 2024.

Highest wakeBASE jump

On 29 Nov 2023, Brian Grubb (USA) took on a daredevil world first nearly a decade in the planning. After being towed on a board by a custom-built drone (i.e., "wakeskating") across a rooftop pool, he proceeded to leap off the edge from 294 m (964 ft) up. "I wanted to be the first person to do a combination wakeskating switch into BASE jump," he explained. "Then we found this awesome location [the Address Beach Resort hotel in Dubai, UAE] and I just pulled off the sickest thing I've ever done on a wakeskate." Although already a leading wakeskater, Grubb dedicated a year to honing his BASE-jumping skills with pro Miles Daisher in preparation for the freefall element, enabling him to safely parachute down to the streets below.

The epic stunt saw Grubb wakeskate across the highest outdoor infinity pool, located on the 77th storey of the hotel.

Tallest waterfall descent by kayak (female)

Nouria Newman (FRA, *below*) kayaked 31.69 m (104 ft) down Don Wilo's Falls, on the Río Pucuno in Orellana, Ecuador, on 18 Feb 2021. She is the first woman to run a waterfall taller than 100 ft (30.4 m).

The **male** record of 57.6 m (189 ft) was achieved by Tyler Bradt (USA), on the Palouse Falls in Washington, USA, on 21 Apr 2009. Compatriots Knox Hammack and James Shimizu have since also successfully run Palouse Falls.

First ice climb of Niagara Falls

On 27 Jan 2015, veteran climber Will Gadd (CAN) scaled Niagara's semi-frozen Horseshoe Falls, on the border between the USA and Canada.

Gadd's partner, Sarah Hueniken (CAN) – who grew up near Niagara – followed later that day, becoming the **first woman** to perform the feat. She was forced to shelter in a hollow during her ascent to avoid falling chunks of ice.

Fastest crossing of Salar de Uyuni on foot

Valmor "Pepe" Fiamoncini (BRA) traversed Bolivia's Salar de Uyuni – the world's **largest salt flat** – in 33 hr 4 min 10 sec. He set off from Llica and arrived at the city of Uyuni on 11 May 2023. The trek covered c. 170 km (105 mi) – the equivalent of four marathons – through the harsh habitat, where temperatures can hit 40°C (104°F) during the day and plummet to –10°C (14°F) at night. Fiamoncini, who spent three years preparing for this trip, was supported by a team in a car carrying essential supplies.

Polar Exploits

On 2 May 1986, Ann Bancroft (USA) became the **first woman to reach the North Pole**. She travelled with the eight-person Steger International Polar Expedition, led by Will Steger (USA), which made the **first unsupported expedition to the North Pole**, using dog sleds.

First solo expedition to the South Pole
Norway's Erling Kagge reached the South Pole after an unsupported surface trek on 7 Jan 1993. His 1,400-km (870-mi) journey from Berkner Island took 50 days.

Naomi Uemura (JPN) set the equivalent **North Pole** record on 29 Apr 1978. He began his 770-km (478-mi) adventure over the Arctic sea-ice on 5 Mar, travelling from Canada's Ellesmere Island and carrying supplies on a dog sled.

Longest unsupported ski expedition on the Greenland Ice Sheet
From 25 Mar to 16 Jul 2008, Alex Hibbert and George Bullard (both UK) skied 2,211 km (1,374 mi) across the world's second-largest ice sheet. It took them 113 days to traverse the **largest island** from Tasiilaq on the east coast to the west coast and back again.

First people to reach the South Pole
A Norwegian party of five men led by Roald Amundsen arrived at the South Pole on 14 Dec 1911, after a 53-day journey with dog sleds from the Bay of Whales.

On 17 Jan 1989, Shirley Metz and Victoria "Tori" Murden (both USA) became the **first women to reach the South Pole overland**. They were part of an 11-person expedition that used skis, snowmobiles and resupplies. It was more than 50 years after the **first women in Antarctica** – Ingrid Christensen, Augusta Sofie Christensen, Ingebjørg Lillemor Rachlew and Solveig Widerøe (all NOR) – stepped foot on the continent's mainland on 30 Jan 1937.

First person to reach the North Pole
This record remains a matter of debate. Robert Peary, travelling with Matt Henson, declared that he had reached the pole on 6 Apr 1909; however, Frederick Cook (all USA) stated that he had done so on 21 Apr 1908. Neither claim has been unquestionably proven to date.

Longest polar ultramarathon on foot
Donna Urquhart (AUS) ran 1,402.21 km (871.29 mi) on Antarctica's Union Glacier between 15 Dec 2023 and 14 Jan 2024, averaging 50 km (31 mi) per day. To help prepare for the savage conditions, Urquhart trained in a wind tunnel and an ArcticStore cold-storage container (*inset*). "I believe sport has such incredible power to make a difference," she told GWR. "I wanted to use the record attempt as a platform to raise awareness and support for young girls in sports and provide them with the opportunity to find out what's possible."

Longest sit-ski journey in Antarctica
British Paralympian Karen Darke sit-skied 309.7 km (192.4 mi) across Antarctica from 22 Dec 2022 to 5 Jan 2023, with Mike Webster and Mike Christie on skis. During the trip, the team reached 79° latitude and longitude – a previously uncharted point on the Ronne Ice Shelf that they dubbed the "Pole of Possibility". (*For another of Darke's trailblazing records, see p.138.*)

First solo unsupported crossing of Antarctica
On 17 Jan 1997, Børge Ousland (NOR) completed a 2,999-km (1,863-mi) snowkite trip from Berkner Island in the Weddell Sea to McMurdo Sound. He crossed both the Ronne and Ross ice shelves on the 63-day traverse, which remains the **fastest solo unsupported crossing of Antarctica**.

Fastest solo unsupported ski journey to the South Pole
Vincent Colliard (FRA) skied to the South Pole from the Hercules Inlet in 22 days 6 hr 8 min. Setting out on 20 Dec 2023, he covered some 1,130 km (700 mi) – c. 51 km (32 mi) per day – arriving on 11 Jan 2024. *For the **women's** record, set in Dec 2023, venture to pp.144–45.*

Most ski expeditions to the South Pole
Hannah McKeand (UK) skied to the South Pole from a coastline six times between 4 Nov 2004 and 9 Jan 2013. This record was equalled by polar guide Devon McDiarmid (CAN) between Nov 2002 and Jan 2023.

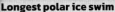

Longest polar ice swim
On 5 Feb 2023, "Ice Mermaid" Bárbara Hernández Huerta (CHL) swam 2.5 km (1.5 mi) in Chile Bay, aka Discovery Bay, off Greenwich Island, South Shetland Islands. The average water temperature was 2.23°C (36°F) and Huerta was in the sea for 45 min 30 sec.

The **men's** record is 1.85 km (1.15 mi), set by Łukasz Tkacz (POL) off Spitsbergen, Svalbard, Norway, on 22 Jun 2017, in waters that averaged 4.5°C (40.1°F).

Legend

- ○ Station/Base/Runway
- ● Outer coast
- ◎ Inner coast
- ▢ Ice shelf
- Queen Maud Land
- Support Force Glacier
- Berkner Island
- Messner Start
- Hercules Inlet
- Kansas Glacier
- Leverett Glacier/SPoT Road
- Axel Heiberg Glacier
- Shackleton Glacier

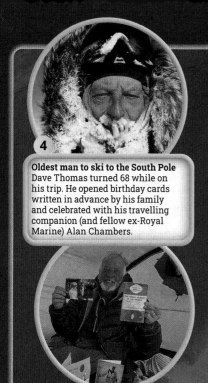

4 Oldest man to ski to the South Pole
Dave Thomas turned 68 while on his trip. He opened birthday cards written in advance by his family and celebrated with his travelling companion (and fellow ex-Royal Marine) Alan Chambers.

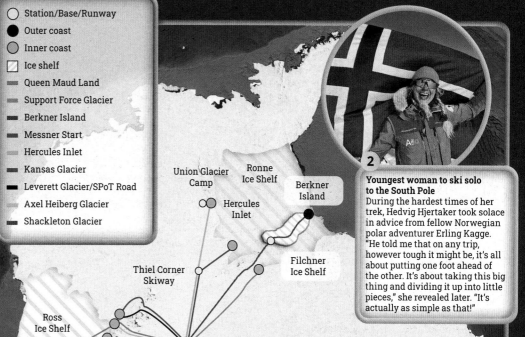

2 Youngest woman to ski solo to the South Pole
During the hardest times of her trek, Hedvig Hjertaker took solace in advice from fellow Norwegian polar adventurer Erling Kagge. "He told me that on any trip, however tough it might be, it's all about putting one foot ahead of the other. It's about taking this big thing and dividing it up into little pieces," she revealed later. "It's actually as simple as that!"

Map labels

- Union Glacier Camp
- Ronne Ice Shelf
- Berkner Island
- Hercules Inlet
- Filchner Ice Shelf
- Thiel Corner Skiway
- Ross Ice Shelf
- South Pole Station (USA)
- Troll Station (NOR)
- McMurdo Station (USA)

3 Oldest man to ski solo and unsupported to the South Pole
As part of the preparation for his demanding trip, James Baxter pulled car tyres for some 5 km (3 mi) along a beach. He also hiked up and down hills near his Edinburgh home carrying a 30-kg (66-lb) rucksack packed with bags of bird seed.

1 Youngest man to ski solo and unsupported to the South Pole
The unpredictable weather in Antarctica proved hugely challenging for Pierre Hedan. "There were weeks when it was constantly white out, with no visibility," he told GWR. "The minimum temperature was below -40°C (-40°F) with the wind. Sometimes it snowed really hard and the fresh snow was like sand – a nightmare to walk on."

YOUNGEST/OLDEST ANTARCTIC ADVENTURERS

YOUNGEST		Name	Age	Year	
Solo full unsupported South Pole ski expedition	F	Anja Blacha (DEU, b. 18 Jun 1990)	29 y 205 d	2020	
	M	Erling Kagge (NOR, b. 15 Jan 1963)	29 y 358 d	1993	
Full unsupported South Pole ski expedition	F	Anja Blacha	29 y 205 d	2020	
	M	Erling Kagge	29 y 358 d	1993	
Solo unsupported South Pole ski expedition	M	Pierre Hedan (FRA, b. 24 Oct 1997)	26 y 75 d	2024	1
	F	Anja Blacha	29 y 205 d	2020	
Unsupported South Pole ski expedition	F	Jade Hameister (AUS, b. 5 Jun 2001) †	16 y 219 d	2018	
	M	Pierre Hedan	26 y 75 d	2024	
Solo South Pole ski expedition	M	Pierre Hedan	26 y 75 d	2024	
	F	Hedvig Hjertaker (NOR, b. 4 Apr 1994)	28 y 285 d	2023	2
South Pole ski expedition	M	Lewis Clarke (UK, b. 18 Nov 1997) †	16 y 61 d	2014	
	F	Jade Hameister †	16 y 219 d	2018	
Full ski crossing of Antarctica		*A full crossing between the outer coasts of Antarctica – solo, team, supported or unsupported – has never been completed*			
Solo ski crossing of Antarctica	M	Colin O'Brady (USA, b. 16 Mar 1985)	33 y 285 d	2018	
	F	Felicity Aston (UK, b. 7 Oct 1977)	34 y 108 d	2012	
Unsupported ski crossing of Antarctica	F	Cecilie Skog (NOR, b. 9 Aug 1974)	35 y 165 d	2010	
	M	Ryan Waters (USA, b. 27 Aug 1973)	36 y 147 d	2010	
Ski crossing of Antarctica	M	Alex Brazier (UK, b. 18 Jul 1990)	26 y 187 d	2017	
	F	Jenni Stephenson (UK, b. 29 Apr 1989)	28 y 266 d	2018	
Full unsupported snowkite crossing of Antarctica	M	Børge Ousland (NOR, b. 31 May 1962)	34 y 231 d	1997	
	F	–	–	–	
Unsupported snowkite crossing of Antarctica	M	Rolf Bae (NOR, 9 Jan 1975–1 Aug 2008)	26 y 27 d	2001	
	F	–	–	–	
Snowkite crossing of Antarctica	M	Teodor Johansen (NOR, b. 14 Aug 1991) †	20 y 151 d	2012	
	F	Gøril Hustad (NOR, b. 23 Aug 1982) †	29 y 142 d	2012	
OLDEST		**Name**	**Age**	**Year**	
Solo unsupported South Pole ski expedition	M	James Baxter (UK, b. 11 Oct 1959)	64 y 100 d	2024	3
	F	Małgorzata Wojtaczka (POL, b. 12 Dec 1965)	51 y 44 d	2017	
Solo South Pole ski expedition	M	Dave Thomas (UK, b. 10 Dec 1955)	68 y 40 d	2024	4
	F	Merete Spilling Gjertsen (NOR, b. 8 Oct 1947)	60 y 96 d	2008	
Unsupported South Pole ski expedition	M	James Baxter	64 y 100 d	2024	
	F	Alexandra Guryeva (AUT, b. 30 Dec 1968) †	54 y 12 d	2023	
South Pole ski expedition	M	Dave Thomas	68 y 40 d	2024	
	F	Merete Spilling Gjertsen †	60 y 96 d	2008	

All records confirmed by the Polar Expeditions Classification Scheme (PECS);
† Expedition included a guide
- **Full South Pole expedition**: starts or ends at an outer coastline
- **Full crossing of Antarctica**: starts and ends on an opposing outer coast
- **Unsupported**: explorers must carry their own supplies and they should not use any road, vehicle track or marked route, or have a supporting vehicle

Round-Up

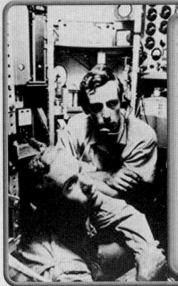

First dive to the Challenger Deep by a crewed vessel
Pioneering explorer and oceanographer Don Walsh (USA, *below left*) passed away on 12 Nov 2023, aged 92. Alongside Swiss engineer Jacques Piccard (who died in 2008), Walsh piloted the US Navy bathyscaphe *Trieste* to a depth of 10,911 m (35,797 ft) in the Pacific Ocean on 23 Jan 1960. They were the first people ever to reach the Challenger Deep – the **deepest point in the sea**.

Fastest completion of the Manali–Leh highway on foot
Sufiya Sufi (IND) took just 4 days 2 hr 27 min to traverse this iconic 430-km (267-mi) road in northern India on 27–31 Aug 2023. It runs between the state of Himachal Pradesh and the Himalayan region of Ladakh. Low oxygen levels (owing to the high altitude) and below-zero temperatures are both factors that add to the challenge.
The **men's** record stands at 4 days 21 hr 13 min, set by Mahendra Mahajan (IND) on 7 Jul 2022.

First bungee jump
On 1 Apr 1979, David Kirke (UK) tied himself to an elasticated rope and leapt off the 76-m-high (250-ft) Clifton Suspension Bridge in Bristol, UK. Kirke (d. 2023) was a founder of Oxford University's Dangerous Sports Club. He was inspired by a land-diving ritual from the South Pacific nation of Vanuatu, where local men plunge from wooden towers, with tree vines wrapped around their ankles, in a brave act said to ensure a successful yam harvest.

Highest altitude wingsuit jump
On 1 Jul 2023, Aaron Smith (USA) glided back to Earth from 13,183.7 m (43,253 ft) above Whiteville, Tennessee, USA. This is approximately 2 km (1.2 mi) higher than an airliner's cruising altitude.

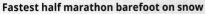

Oldest person to cross the Grand Canyon
Alfredo Aliaga Burdío (ESP, b. 28 Aug 1931) was aged 92 years 48 days when he traversed this famous gorge in Arizona, USA, on 15 Oct 2023. Burdío, who is a geologist, hiked the Grand Canyon on many occasions when he was younger and has compared this iconic natural wonder to a "geology textbook".

Fastest half marathon barefoot on snow
Josef Šálek (CZE) completed a 21-km (13.1-mi) run in 1 hr 50 min 42 sec in Pec pod Sněžkou, Czechia, on 18 Feb 2024. Only wearing shorts, he ran on an open circuit in a valley near Sněžka, the highest mountain in the country. Fitness fanatic Šálek also holds the **abdominal plank** endurance record (*see p.115*).

Fastest time to visit the New Seven Wonders of the World
On 6–12 Mar 2023, Jamie "Adventureman" McDonald (UK), aided by Travelport, visited the Great Wall of China, the Taj Mahal in India, Petra in Jordan, the Colosseum in Italy, Christ the Redeemer in Brazil, Machu Picchu in Peru and Chichén Itzá in Mexico all within 6 days 16 hr 14 min.

Fastest English Channel swim
German Olympian Andreas Waschburger took only 6 hr 45 min 25 sec to swim from Kent, UK, to Cap Gris-Nez, France, on 8 Sep 2023. The year 2025 marks the 150th anniversary of the first universally recognized swim crossing of the English Channel. You'll find it below, along with several other notable swims across this world-famous waterway.

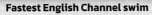

ENGLISH CHANNEL SWIMMING MILESTONES

First...	Name	Date
Single crossing*	Matthew Webb (UK)	24–25 Aug 1875
Single crossing (f)	Gertrude C Ederle (USA)	6 Aug 1926
Double crossing	Antonio Abertondo (ARG)	20–22 Sep 1961
Double crossing (f)	Cindy Nicholas (CAN)	7–8 Sep 1977
Triple crossing	Jon Erikson (USA)	11–12 Aug 1981
Triple crossing (f)	Alison Streeter (UK)	2–3 Aug 1990
Lengthwise swim	Lewis Pugh (UK)	12 Jul–29 Aug 2018
Quadruple crossing	Sarah Thomas (USA)	15–17 Sep 2019

*Paul Boyton (USA) swum from Cap Gris-Nez to South Foreland, Kent, UK, aided by an inflatable suit on 28–29 May 1875. Napoleonic soldier Giovan Maria Salati (ITA) may have escaped from a prison barge off Dover and swum to Boulogne c. Jul/Aug 1815, but that is contested.

Longest journey by pumpkin boat
Steve Kueny (USA) paddled 63.04 km (39.17 mi) along the Missouri River from Kansas City to Napoleon, Missouri, USA, on 8 Oct 2023. He had grown the hollowed-out vegetable vessel himself. Members of the "Paddle KC Paddling Club" accompanied him to witness his attempt and to ensure that – in Kueny's words – "We're doing something very silly very safely."

Fastest time to row the Thames by double kayak

TV presenter and naturalist Steve Backshall (*inset*) and Tom McGibbon (both UK) rowed the UK's second-longest river from start to finish in 20 hr 29 min. The duo began in Lechlade, Gloucestershire, on 8 Aug 2023 and arrived in Teddington Lock, London, the following day. "Tom and I trained for the race by paddling each section of the river in turn, getting to grips with its twists and turns, especially the bits we would be doing in the dark," Backshall explained. "This didn't stop us from getting lost several times at night, and very nearly paddling over a weir!"

Fastest speed volcano surfing

Using a variation on a snowboard, Chase Boehringer (USA) hit 45.06 km/h (27.99 mph) on the ash-covered slopes of Parícutin, a cinder-cone volcano near Uruapan, Michoacán, Mexico, on 24 Jan 2021. "There was no area to slow down," he recalled. "There was just a steep volcano and then a large rock wall at the end. I had to come to terms with the fact that the only way to stop myself was to crash!"

Longest journey in a single country by electric skateboard

On 14 Jun 2023, Italy's Stefano Rotella completed a 1,260-km (782-mi) trip through his home nation on a self-made e-skate when he arrived in Avetrana, Taranto. He had set out on 27 May from Brenner, near the Austrian border. Rotella, who works as a technical designer, converted an ordinary skateboard by adding batteries and motors.

This isn't Rotella's first record-setting electric-powered voyage: on 10–25 Aug 2021, he rode through Italy, Austria, Germany, Czechia, Slovakia and Hungary – the **most countries visited by electric skateboard (single journey)**.

Fastest time to cross all 10 Australian deserts by motorcycle

Nicholas Arley (AUS) rode his 2021 Suzuki DR650 through every desert in Australia in 14 days 2 hr 12 min, from 25 Jul to 7 Aug 2023 – two weeks faster than the previous holder. He began in South Australia and ended in Northern Territory.

Greatest vertical descent on a mountain bike in 24 hours

On 15–16 Mar 2023, Annie Ford (NZ) rode the trail down Coronet Peak 100 times in Queenstown, New Zealand. Over the course of the day, she travelled a total downhill distance of 41,900 m (137,467 ft).

Fastest time to climb El Capitan solo

Nick Ehman (USA) took just 4 hr 39 min to scale this 914-m-tall (3,000-ft) granite cliff in Yosemite National Park, California, USA, on 10 Oct 2023. Ehman was more than an hour faster than the former holder, rock-climbing legend Alex Honnold (USA), who was also the **first person to free solo climb El Capitan**, on 3 Jun 2017.

Longest barefoot journey

On 19 Jul 2023, a shoeless Paweł Durakiewicz (POL) put his best foot forward to explore 3,409.7 km (2,118.7 mi) of the Iberian Peninsula. He called time in San José, Andalusia, Spain, on 9 Jan 2024.

Most swim crossings from Robben Island

On 2 Aug 2023, Howard Warrington (ZAF) completed his 155th swim from Robben Island to Blouberg beach in Cape Town, South Africa. The 7.5-km (4.6-mi) route is challenging even for experienced ocean swimmers, not least because of the cold water and the area's sizeable population of great white sharks!

Most countries visited by recumbent bicycle in 24 hours

Laidback cyclist Mohamed Elewa (EGY) passed through five European nations on 24–25 Jun 2023. Starting in Vaals, Netherlands, he rode via Germany, Belgium and Luxembourg before ending in Évrange, France. In all, he covered some 240 km (150 mi) on the trip.

Fastest true-summit ascent of the 8,000ers

The fastest time to climb the 14 mountains that stand more than 8,000 m (24,247 ft) above sea level is 92 days, by Kristin Harila (NOR) and Tenjen Lama Sherpa (NPL) on 27 Jul 2023, as the pair topped K2. This obliterated Harila's previous record – only set on 3 May 2023 – by 278 days. Sadly, Tenjen died during an avalanche on Shisha Pangma later that year on 7 Oct.

Largest GPS drawing by kayak

Claudia Santori (AUS) paddled a 10.38-km (6.44-mi) route in the shape of a weedy seadragon (*inset*) in Sydney Harbour, New South Wales, Australia, on 12 Nov 2023. An ecologist and diver, Santori began to plot animal shapes on her GPS tracker while kayaking during the COVID-19 lockdowns. Her subject matter seeks to celebrate Australia's remarkable marine wildlife, while also highlighting that much of it is endangered.

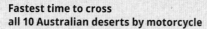

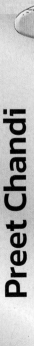

ICON

Preet Chandi

Explorer and British Army captain Preet Chandi has spent her life seeking out new challenges. And in the icy wastes of Antarctica, the challenges don't come much more extreme. From an early age, Preet has sought to defy any traditional expectations that people might have of her. "I don't want to just break the glass ceiling," she says. "I want to smash it into a million pieces." As a teenager, she spent time at a Czech tennis academy before returning to the UK and taking up ultramarathon running. She joined the British Army and served in Nepal, Kenya and South Sudan as a physiotherapist. But Preet was still looking to push boundaries – and so, in 2019, she resolved to ski to the South Pole.

She spent two years planning her first expedition, including training sessions in Norway and Greenland. Upon arriving in Antarctica, she set out from Hercules Inlet on 21 Nov 2021, skiing for up to 13 hr a day through temperatures as low as –50°C (–58°F). On 3 Jan 2022, "Polar Preet" reached her goal, becoming the **first Asian woman to ski solo to the South Pole**. She has since returned twice to the frozen continent, setting new records each time (see below) and continuing to push her powers of physical and mental endurance to the limit.

Name	Captain Harpreet Chandi
Birthplace	Derby, UK
Birth date	7 Feb 1989
Current GWR titles	Four, including the fastest solo, unsupported ski journey to the **South Pole (female)** and the longest solo, unsupported one-way polar ski journey
Honours	Member of the British Empire (MBE)

Preet and her elder brothers Pardeep and Jagdeep were raised by their grandfather, Baba Ji. She credits Baba Ji's support in helping her challenge traditional views of Sikh women and has credited him as one of the key inspirations behind her polar adventures.

On 21 Feb 2023, Preet was presented with an MBE at Windsor Castle, in honour of her record-breaking polar exploits. "If I can do something like this," she said afterwards, "anyone can achieve anything."

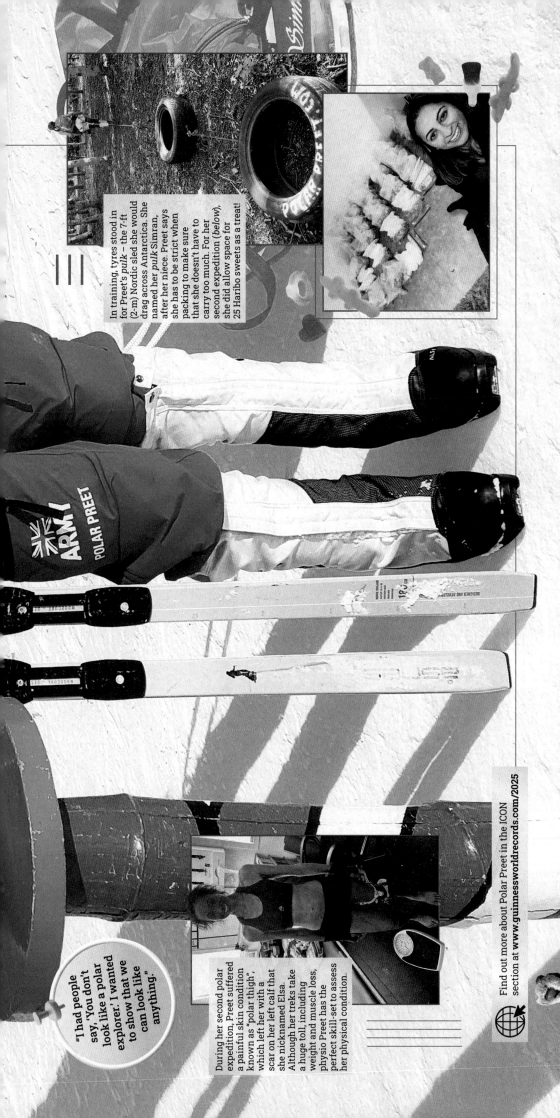

In training, tyres stood in for Preet's *pulk* – the 7-ft (2-m) Nordic sled she would drag across Antarctica. She named her *pulk* Simran, after her niece. Preet says she has to be strict when packing to make sure that she doesn't have to carry too much. For her second expedition (*below*), she did allow space for 25 Haribo sweets as a treat!

"I had people say, 'You don't look like a polar explorer.' I wanted to show that we can look like anything."

During her second polar expedition, Preet suffered a painful skin condition known as "polar thigh", which left her with a scar on her left calf that she nicknamed Elsa. Although her treks take a huge toll, including weight and muscle loss, physio Preet has the perfect skill-set to assess her physical condition.

Find out more about Polar Preet in the ICON section at www.guinnessworldrecords.com/2025

2023

On trip #3, Preet achieved the **fastest solo, unsupported ski journey to the South Pole (female)**. Without resupplies, she covered the roughly 1,130 km (700 mi) from Hercules Inlet in 31 days 13 hr 19 min, between 26 Nov and 28 Dec.

2022–23

Bad weather dashed Preet's ambition of becoming the first solo woman to ski unsupported coast-to-coast across the Antarctic continent. But she did complete the **longest solo, unsupported one-way polar ski journey** – 1,484.53 km (922.44 mi).

2021–22

Preet's debut polar expedition saw her become the **first Asian woman to ski solo to the South Pole**, on 3 Jan 2022. She completed her icebound odyssey in just 40 days 7 hr 3 min, the third-fastest time recorded by a female solo skier.

LARGEST ROCKET

The SpaceX Starship is 121 m (397 ft) tall, 9 m (29 ft 6 in) wide and has a fuelled mass of some 5,000 tonnes (5,510 tons). That's 10 m (32 ft) taller and more than 2,000 tonnes heavier than the previous record holder, the Saturn V Moon rocket, which held the title for 56 years.

Starship made its first full-power take-off on 18 Nov 2023. The launch was part of SpaceX's "hardware-rich" development process, which involves building and testing dozens of prototypes (this was No.25). The first stage performed as planned, but failed during landing manoeuvres, while the second stage reached an altitude of 150 km (93 mi) – above the boundary of space – before self-destructing.

The 69-m-tall (226-ft) "Super Heavy" first stage is powered by three concentric rings of Raptor engines – 33 in all – that burn liquid methane and oxygen. Each engine generates 2,300 kN (520,000 lbf) at sea level, also making the SpaceX Starship the **most powerful rocket**. It is hoped that once operational, Starship will be able to lift a payload of 150 tonnes (165 tons) or a habitable space larger than the pressurized volume of the *International Space Station*.

The metal structure in the foreground is *Starhopper*, a vertical landing test vehicle that flew in 2019.

CONTENTS

Starship is one-third taller than the Statue of Liberty, from the pedestal base to the tip of the torch.

121 m

93 m

Tallest Structures

Ever since the construction of the first permanent settlements, the limit of how high we can build has been a constant battle between imagination and physics. Here we present the history of the **tallest freestanding structure**, which stretches from the earliest temples of prehistory, through the towering spires of Gothic cathedrals and finally the glass-and-steel skyscrapers that dominate modern cities.

1. "Enclosure D" (*c.* 9600–8000 BCE)
5.5 m (18 ft)
This round structure once stood in the neolithic complex of Göbekli Tepe in present-day Türkiye. Archaeologists are unsure what it was used for. Its two carved central pillars were about three times taller than an adult man. Eleven smaller carved pillars are set into the outer walls.

2. Tower of Jericho (8000–4000 BCE)
8.5 m (27 ft 10 in)
Made from dry-stone masonry, this roughly circular stone tower is located in the ancient settlement of Jericho in the Jordan River valley, in what is now the West Bank. It was discovered in 1956 by archaeologist Kathleen Kenyon, who has dated the site to the late Stone Age – an assessment confirmed by more recent investigations. Its purpose remains a mystery.

3. White Temple of Uruk (4000–2670 BCE)
12 m (40 ft)
Raised in honour of the Mesopotamian sun god Anu, this was a later addition to a ziggurat (a pyramid-like structure with a flat top) created *c.* 4000 BCE on the plain of Uruk, in what today is Iraq. The walls were plastered in gypsum, which would have reflected the sunlight, making the temple visible from far away.

4. Pyramid of Djoser (2670–2600 BCE)
62.5 m (205 ft; 119 royal cubits)
This limestone step pyramid was built for the pharaoh Djoser. Located in the Saqqara necropolis in Egypt, it began as a *mastaba* – a subterranean vault covered by a flat-roofed structure. This was usually made of mud brick, but by using stone instead, the architect Imhotep bolstered its strength, enabling the tomb to be built much larger. His work also displays a firm grasp of engineering principles: the angled walls create an inward-acting force to resist the outward force exerted by the pyramid's mass.

5. Meidum Pyramid (*c.* 2600 BCE)
70 m (230 ft; 133 royal cubits)
Thought to have been built under the pharaohs Huni and Sneferu, it's likely that this pyramid collapsed during construction. Only a 70-m-tall limestone core was left, which weathered down to 65 m (213 ft). It stands on a rocky plateau on the west bank of the Nile, some 72 km (45 mi) south of the Egyptian capital, Cairo.

6/7. Bent Pyramid and Red Pyramid (*c.* 2600–2580 BCE)
104.7 m (344 ft; 200 royal cubits)
These limestone pyramids were of equal height and were built during the reign of the pharaoh Sneferu. They stand in the Dahshur necropolis in Egypt. The Bent Pyramid was built first, but the project was beset by structural problems and had multiple redesigns. The Red Pyramid was the follow-up design, using lessons learned from its predecessor and probably also from the partial collapse of the Meidum Pyramid (*see above*).

8. Great Pyramid of Khufu (*c.* 2580 BCE–1311 CE)
146.7 m (481 ft 4 in; 280 royal cubits)
This monumental tomb was the world's **tallest structure** for 3,890 years, and to this day remains the **tallest pyramid**. It stands at Giza (al-Jizah), an area of high ground that overlooks the Nile valley near present-day Cairo. The pyramid utilizes three types of masonry: giant blocks of granite for the burial chambers; rough-cut limestone blocks that form the main walls; and smoother white limestone on the surface.

9. Lincoln Cathedral (1311–1548)
c. 152.4 m (500 ft)
The spire of this Gothic cathedral in Lincolnshire, UK, may possibly have reached 160 m (525 ft). But even at the minimum probable height of 147.04 m (482 ft 4 in), it would have been the first structure to surpass the Great Pyramid of Khufu in almost 4,000 years. Work on the tower commenced in 1240, and construction of the spire began *c.* 1306, supervised by master mason Richard of Stow. The spire was completed by 1311 but collapsed in 1548, during a storm.

10. St Mary's Church, Stralsund (1548–1647)
151 m (495 ft)
St Mary's was a parish church expanded to the scale of a cathedral to reflect the prosperity of Stralsund, a Hanseatic League port city in Germany. Between 1416 and 1647, it was topped by a tower and spire, but the latter was destroyed by a fire from a lightning strike in 1647.

11. Notre-Dame-de-Strasbourg (1647–1874)
142 m (465 ft)
Located in Strasbourg, France, Notre-Dame is a huge Gothic cathedral built *c.* 1200–1439. It became the **tallest structure** after the spire of St Mary's Church was wrecked. It was intended to resemble the twin-towered western facades of cathedrals such as Notre-Dame-de-Paris, but due to funding issues only the north tower was ever made. The upper part of the tower and its spire were the handiwork of master masons Ulrich von Ensingen and Johannes Hültz.

12. St Nicholas Church, Hamburg (1874–76)
147.8 m (484 ft 10 in)
Designed by British architect George Gilbert Scott in the Gothic Revival style, St Nicholas' was part of a wave of huge churches raised in the second half of the 19th century. Improved engineering knowledge enabled engineers to calculate loads and stresses more accurately and so build higher than the master masons of the medieval period, while new machinery greatly reduced build time and cost.

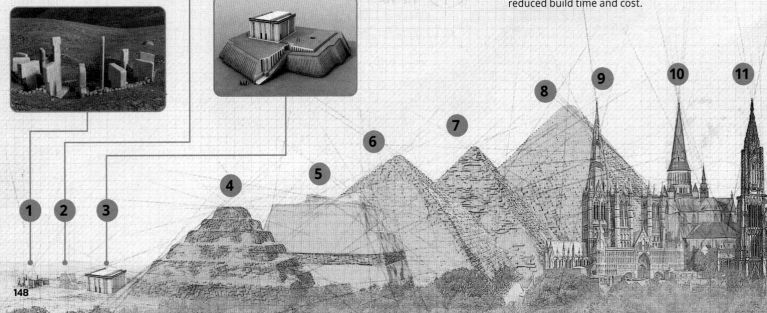

ICON

21

13. Rouen Cathedral (1876–80)
151 m (495 ft)
Following a fire in 1822, this medieval building was fitted with a spire made from cast iron (then a fairly novel structural material), designed by Jean-Antoine Alavoine. Owing to economic and political turmoil, however, it took more than 50 years to finish it. Local master ironworker Ferdinand Marrou added the final details.

14. Cologne Cathedral (1880–85)
157.2 m (515 ft 8 in)
The foundation stone of this twin-towered cathedral in Germany was laid in 1248. Progress was slow, however, and work ceased altogether in the wake of the Protestant Reformation. It resumed in the 1820s, after the rediscovery of the original architectural plans by Gerhard of Reil, and was finally topped out 632 years after construction began.

15. Washington Monument (1885–89)
169 m (554 ft 7 in)
Plans for a memorial in Washington, DC, to the first US president date back to 1791. It was not until 1845, however, that a design was chosen. The work stalled – not least because of the American Civil War – resuming in 1876. The finished edifice is a hollow obelisk with an internal iron frame and granite walls that taper to just a few inches thick at the top.

16. Eiffel Tower (1889–1930)
300 m (984 ft 3 in)
Built for the 1889 Exposition Universelle, this landmark still dominates the skyline of Paris, France. Its radical design, favouring minimalism over ornate decoration, was opposed by many influential Parisians. It was intended as a temporary feature, but the populace campaigned to keep it. The tower now stands 330 m (1,083 ft) tall, if broadcast aerials are included, and remains the **tallest iron structure**.

17. Chrysler Building
(1930–31)
318.9 m (1,046 ft 3 in)
This stunning Art Deco edifice in New York City, USA, was designed by William Van Alen. The exterior decoration utilizes polished aluminium and stainless steel; the steel eagle-head gargoyles and arches nod to Chrysler car-hood ornaments and hubcaps, respectively. This was the first time that the **tallest building** (defined as having occupiable floors for more than half its height) was also the **tallest structure** of any kind.

As built, the top floors of the Chrysler Building included a penthouse with what was then the world's highest toilet.

18. Empire State Building (1931–67)
443.2 m (1,454 ft)
Architect William Lamb originally envisaged a flat roof for what became New York City's most iconic skyscraper. But after a surprise extension to the Chrysler Building's spire in 1930, the Empire State's financial backer John Raskob ordered changes that would secure its status as the **tallest building**. In response, Lamb added observation decks and a spire – ostensibly an airship mooring mast – that enabled it to hold on to the record until the completion of the World Trade Center in 1971.

19. Ostankino Tower (1967–76)
537.4 m (1,763 ft 3 in)
This TV and radio tower in Moscow, Russia, was overseen by Nikolai Nikitin, chief designer of the Mosproekt-2 bureau, which oversaw the city's Soviet-era public works. Construction started in 1960, but problems with the foundation caused lengthy delays. Made from pre-stressed reinforced concrete, the tower is highly flexible; in high winds, the upper levels are designed to sway by several metres.

20. CN Tower (1976–2010)
553.3 m (1,815 ft 5 in)
Named after Canadian National, the rail company that built it, this broadcast tower is a symbol of Toronto. Its construction utilized "slip-forming", in which concrete is poured into a mould that continuously raises itself on hydraulic jacks, resulting in a seamless and strong structure. Although never used on such a large-scale project before, this is now the standard technique for creating the cores of tall buildings.

❯ 21. Burj Khalifa (2010–present)
828 m (2,716 ft 6 in)
Construction of this mixed-use skyscraper in Dubai, UAE, began in 2004, with the exterior completed on 1 Oct 2009. It was developed by Emaar Properties and designed by architects Skidmore, Owings & Merrill. The Burj Khalifa is history's **tallest building** and **structure**. It boasts the **most floors in a building** –163 – and the **highest residential apartments** – at 385 m (1,263 ft).

This timeline presents history's tallest free-standing structures. Some were towers or monuments larger than the highest buildings of their day.

149

Artificial Intelligence

First artificial neural network

On 7 Jul 1958, Frank Rosenblatt (USA) unveiled the Perceptron – a computer that learned from experience. After being shown training images, it could identify the location of a black dot on a white card. It worked by sending each pixel to a "neuron", which applied some simple tests before writing a value to memory. Another layer of neurons then examined these values to produce the answer.

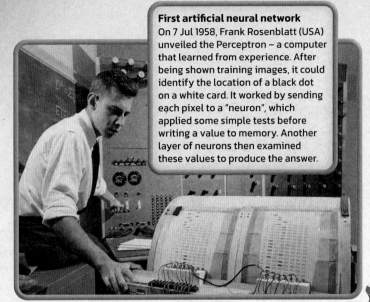

Most expensive AI-generated artwork sold at auction

Edmond de Belamy fetched $432,500 (£334,531) on 25 Oct 2018. The brainchild of French art collective Obvious, the portrait was created by a type of artificial intelligence (AI) called a generative adversarial network, which produced a new image based on analysis of 15,000 portraits. It was signed with part of the algorithm that created it.

First chatbot

Developed by Joseph Weizenbaum (USA, b. DEU) at the Massachusetts Institute of Technology in 1964–66, ELIZA simulated human conversation. Users typed what they wanted to say; ELIZA scanned the text for keywords and generated a response based on rules associated with those words.

The entire program only contained around 200 lines of code but its persona – an imitation of a psychoanalyst who asked only vague questions – convinced many study participants, who shared personal worries and deep secrets with the machine.

First neural network to identify handwritten characters

Converting handwriting into digital text was one of the key challenges that 1960s AI researchers set out to tackle. It was not until the 1980s, however, that new neural-network designs – so-called "deep learning" systems with extra layers of neurons between the input and output – finally made this possible. In 1989, a neural network designed by Yann LeCun (FRA) and his colleagues at AT&T Bell Labs (USA) recognized 95% of the letters in a set of 2,007 handwritten zip codes provided by the US Postal Service.

Largest expert system

Although they dominate today, neural networks are not the only approach to engineering artificial intelligence. Expert systems are a type of AI designed to mimic the reasoning of specialists using complex sets of logical rules. The largest is Cyc, which makes decisions based on more than 30 million rules. It is maintained by Cycorp (USA).

Fastest autonomous car

On 27 Apr 2022, a Dallara AV-21 achieved a two-way average speed of 309.3 km/h (192.2 mph) over a flying kilometre at the Kennedy Space Center in Florida, USA. The AV-21 was under the control of onboard computers programmed by the PoliMOVE Autonomous Racing Team (ITA).

Highest AI score in the US Bar Exam

The recent mainstream rise of AI has been driven by systems called large language models (LLMs), which are trained by trawling through billions of words of text. LLMs excel at writing and reading comprehension.

First robot battle-rapper

In Feb 2020, a robot named Shimon faced off in a lyrical duel with rapper Dash Smith. Using a neural network and voice synthesis software, Shimon used Dash's lyrics as a seed to develop real-time counter rhymes. The battle-rapping robot was developed by Gil Weinberg (ISR/USA).

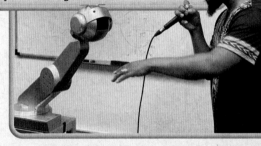

The basis for the popular ChatGPT service – an LLM called GPT-4 – scored 298 out of 400 when it sat the United States Uniform Bar Exam in Mar 2023. The score puts GPT-4 ahead of 90% of the humans to have taken the test, and would – in theory – have qualified it to practise law. GPT-4 has also achieved the **highest AI score in the SAT exam** – earning 1,410 out of 1,600 in the US college admission test, also in Mar 2023.

Greatest aggregate distance driven by an autonomous vehicle fleet

Two US self-driving car companies – Cruise (*left*) and Waymo (*right*) – operate fleets that had each logged *c.* 5 million mi (8 million km) as of Sep 2023. Their cars have "Level 4 Autonomy", meaning they have no onboard driver, but occasionally need remote human input. They use cameras and LiDAR (light detection and ranging) to gather data about their environment, which they interpret using deep-learning neural networks.

The team worked with animators Speech Graphics to make an avatar that spoke with a reconstruction of Ann's old voice.

The neural network used in this project was trained by monitoring Ann's brain activity while she consciously tried to read sets of characters and words. Through repetition, the neural network learned to associate these patterns with the intended parts of speech.

FASTEST COMMUNICATION SPEED USING A BRAIN-COMPUTER INTERFACE

A team at the University of California San Francisco (UCSF) led by Dr Edward Chang (USA) has produced an AI-powered interface capable of translating neural signals into text at a rate of 78 words per minute.

This "neuroprosthesis" enables paralysed people to communicate, even though they cannot speak. The volunteer who tested the UCSF prototype was a woman identified only as "Ann" (*above*), who suffered a debilitating stroke when she was 30 years old. The system uses a brain implant combined with deep-learning networks to transcribe attempted speech into written language, which can then be displayed. For Ann, who has spent 18 years using an eye-tracking pointer system to write things out, it offers hope that she can one day begin a new career as a counsellor.

The implant used in this trial is called a "surface electrocorticogram" – this is a dense array of electrical sensors printed on to a thin film of plastic. The film is laid across the surface of the brain, inside the skull, allowing the team to pick up activity in detail without having to put implants into Ann's brain.

Horology

First hourglass

The consistent flow of sand between two chambers has been used to keep time since the 11th century. Medieval navigators used these devices to calculate their progress, but their use went mostly unrecorded until 1338. This is when painter Ambrogio Lorenzetti depicted one to symbolize "temperance" in his fresco *Allegory of Good Government* in Siena, Italy.

The first timekeeping devices were ancient sundials and water clocks that worked like hourglasses.

The numbers only appeared when a button was pressed

First electronic digital watch

The Pulsar Time Computer was released to much fanfare on 4 Apr 1972. This high-tech luxury item was available in gold or silver, though its quartz–crystal circuitry and LED display accounted for most of the watch's $2,100 price tag – equal to around $15,500 (£12,500) today! A version graced the wrist of James Bond in 1973's *Live and Let Die*.

Dear GWR...

I watched time go by today. I stared at a standard clock for approximately two hours. The clock had a radius of six inches, and contained a second, minute and hour hand. I did blink, but I never disengaged from the clock for two hours. Nor did I turn my head in any direction. I was firmly locked on the clock.

There was a witness who eventually broke my concentration. His name is ▇▇▇▇▇▇▇▇▇▇▇.

First pendulum clock

Once set in motion, a pendulum will swing at a consistent frequency. In 1656, Dutch scientist Christiaan Huygens devised a clock that used this principle to regulate its mechanism. His innovation enabled timekeeping that was accurate to a few seconds a day, a huge improvement on earlier mechanical clocks.

Huygens recognized the practical uses of his invention and licensed the design to clockmaker Salomon Coster (NLD). The **oldest pendulum clock**, now in the collection of the Rijksmuseum Boerhaave in Leiden, Netherlands, is one of Coster's creations. It dates from 1657, and has an inscription which mentions that it was made with Huygens' approval.

Most accurate free-air pendulum clock

Although they are no longer at the horological cutting edge, clockmakers are still tinkering with pendulum designs. The current record holder (for a clock that is not kept in a vacuum) is "Clock B", designed by Martin Burgess (UK), based on the ideas of master clockmaker John Harrison (*see opposite*). During a trial at the Royal Observatory Greenwich in 2014, it drifted by only 0.125 sec over 100 days.

First quartz clock

Due to a phenomenon called the piezoelectric effect, quartz crystals generate a consistent pulse when exposed to an electrical current. In the mid-1920s, Bell Labs engineers Warren Marrison and J W Horton (both USA) came up with a circuit that sustained this signal and converted it into a timekeeping reference. They revealed their new clock in Oct 1927. Tiny and cheap quartz-crystal oscillators are now found in almost every electronic device.

First atomic clock

In 1948, scientist Harold Lyons (USA) developed an ammonia-based atomic clock at the US National Bureau of Standards. Lyons's clock was a proof-of-concept that wasn't very accurate, but the idea was refined into a form that is still used to define international time standards.

At the heart of these clocks is a stream of caesium atoms. They pass through a microwave beam and then their energy state is measured. The frequency of the microwave emitter is adjusted up and down by tiny increments until it is at exactly the resonant frequency of the atoms, which pushes them into a higher energy state in a predictable way. Once stabilized, this frequency provides a clock reference, with a second defined as 9,192,631,770 oscillations of the microwave beam. These clocks would take 100 million years to lose a single second.

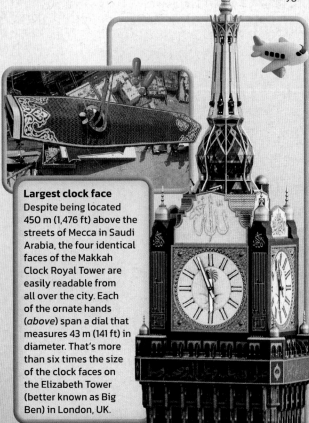

Largest clock face

Despite being located 450 m (1,476 ft) above the streets of Mecca in Saudi Arabia, the four identical faces of the Makkah Clock Royal Tower are easily readable from all over the city. Each of the ornate hands (*above*) span a dial that measures 43 m (141 ft) in diameter. That's more than six times the size of the clock faces on the Elizabeth Tower (better known as Big Ben) in London, UK.

Most precise clock

The Optical Lattice Clock is a type of atomic clock (*see above*) developed by Jun Ye (USA, b. CHN) at the University of Colorado, USA. As of 2022, the clock is so precise that it would lose less than a second in 15 billion years. Its clock reference – derived from the resonant frequency of strontium atoms contained in a vacuum by a lattice of lasers – "ticks" 429 trillion times a second.

MOST EXPENSIVE POCKET WATCH

On 11 Nov 2014, the hammer came down at Sotheby's in Geneva, Switzerland, ending the highly competitive auction for a pocket watch called the Henry Graves Supercomplication. The anonymous winner paid a record 23,237,000 Swiss Francs ($24 m; £15.1 m) for this remarkable timepiece, which is named for the extraordinary number of special functions (what horologists call "complications") that were incorporated into its design.

Crown
For setting the time and winding the mechanism

Night sky
The rear face of the watch has yet more unusual complications. What's visible in this panel shifts with the seasons, showing the section of the night sky that would – in theory at least – be visible above Graves's luxurious apartment on Fifth Avenue in New York City.

Moon-phase dial
Tracks the changing phases of the Moon every month

Stopwatch
Start/stop button

Sunrise/sunset
Time of dawn and dusk shown on inset dials

24-hour face
Showing sidereal time (calculated from the motion of distant stars)

Inset dial 1
The outer dial allows the stopwatch to run for up to 12 hours while the inner dial shows the winding power level for the chimes.

Equation of time
Some of the watch's features involve extremely obscure bits of horological trivia. This dial shows the difference between mean solar time (what is shown on the front clock face) and apparent solar time (what would be displayed on a sundial).

Main clock face
The front face of the watch has five hands. In addition to the hour and minute hands, there is also a hand showing the alarm time and the second and split-second hands for the stopwatch.

Alarm
On/off switch

Internal workings
The watch is entirely mechanical, and these complex functions are all derived from the movements of painstakingly machined gears, springs and cams. This was all planned before computers or electronic calculators – the staggeringly complex mathematics involved in the design had to be worked out on paper between 1925 and 1928. Patek Philippe had to sub-contract this work to dozens of master watchmakers across Switzerland, costing Graves $15,000 – equal to $322,000 (£259,000) today.

Mute switch
Silences the various chimes and bells

Chime mode
Cycles between different sounds

Outer case
Made from gold and 37 mm (1.5 in) thick

The watch was made by Patek Philippe for American banker Henry Graves Jr between 1928 and 1932.

Calendar
The outer face of this dial shows the date, while the inset indicators on the sides of the main clock face show the day and month. The calendar adjusts for leap years and will be correct until the year 2100. The inner face is the second hand for the main clock.

Minute repeater
On the press of this button, the watch expresses the time as a series of chimes with different tones for hours and minutes.

Inset dial 2
The outer dial records minutes for the stopwatch while the inner dial shows the mainspring winding power level.

First marine chronometer

Developed by clockmaker John Harrison (UK) in 1730–35, H1 was the first mechanical timepiece that could maintain accuracy at sea. When tested on a voyage from London to Lisbon in 1736, its two connected balances kept time in conditions that would have made a pendulum clock useless. Harrison spent the rest of his life refining his designs, culminating in the large pocket-watch-style H4, which could keep time on long ocean crossings.

By comparing local solar time to a reference clock, navigators can find out how far east or west they have travelled.

Most expensive wrist watch

On 9 Nov 2019, a modern descendant of the Supercomplication (*above*) went up for auction at Christie's in Geneva, Switzerland, and sold for 31 million Swiss francs (£24.3 m; $33.6 m). The Patek Philippe Grandmaster Chime can be turned over to show two independent dials, displaying 20 complications in a 1.6-cm-thick (0.6-in) case.

In the Lab

Longest mantle rock core sample

In May 2023, the crew of the research vessel *JOIDES Resolution* drilled a 1,268-m-long (4,160-ft) rock sample from deep beneath the Atlantic Ocean. The core includes a 1,000-m (3,280-ft) section of mantle rock that was recently pushed up by geological processes. The mantle makes up 86% of Earth's volume, but is usually too deep below the surface to study. This sample was taken from the Mid Atlantic Ridge, where our planet's crust is extremely thin.

Most powerful X-ray laser

The Linac Coherent Light Source II (LCLS–II) uses a superconducting particle accelerator to propel electrons to near light speed. Their energy is then converted into extremely bright X-rays that can be directed on to a target at a rate of 1 million flashes per second. Among its potential applications, LCLS–II will enable scientists to examine fleeting chemical reactions, with implications for advances in medicine and cleaner energy technologies. It is operated by the US Department of Energy.

Fastest DNA sequencing technique

On 16 Mar 2021, Euan Ashley (USA/UK) and a team from the USA's Stanford University sequenced a human genome in 5 hr 2 min using an Oxford Nanopore PromethION-48 machine. Sequencing involves determining the precise order of bases or nucleotides – the most basic level of genetic information – in a DNA molecule. It can help with the diagnosis and treatment of diseases and genetic disorders.

Most efficient solar cell

Commercially available solar cells typically achieve 20–25% efficiency. In Jul 2023, however, researchers at Helmholtz-Zentrum Berlin (DEU) demonstrated a tandem-layer silicon-perovskite solar cell that can convert 32.5% of the energy from sunlight into electricity.

The **plastic solar cell** record also changed hands in 2023. A team at Hong Kong Polytechnic University in China achieved an efficiency of 19.31% by using engineered polymers. Plastic solar cells are particularly notable because they are lighter and can be semi-transparent – opening up the potential for tinted windows that generate electricity.

Most qubits for a quantum computer

On 24 Oct 2023, a prototype 1,180-qubit quantum computer was unveiled by Atom Computing (USA). Each qubit is a supercooled ytterbium atom held in an optical lattice (the same technique used for the **most precise clock** – *see p.152*). The machine operates by using the infinitely variable quantum states of these atoms instead of traditional binary ones and zeros.

Lowest temperature to charge a lithium-ion battery

The USA's Vilas Pol Energy Research group powered up a lithium-ion battery at -100°C (-148°F). This implies that such cells could be used in the vacuum of space, among other places. The test was staged at Purdue University in West Lafayette, Indiana, USA, on 21 Dec 2022.

Fastest satellite datalink

On 28 Apr 2023, the TeraByte InfraRed Delivery (TBIRD) transmitter sent 4.8 terabytes of error-free data in under 5 min using a 200-gigabit-per-second laser communications link. TBIRD, which is around the size of a tissue box, was placed into orbit as part of NASA's *Pathfinder 3* mission. It relays data about 1,000 times faster than the radio connections typically used by satellites.

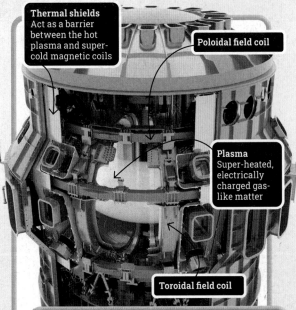

Thermal shields
Act as a barrier between the hot plasma and super-cold magnetic coils

Poloidal field coil

Plasma
Super-heated, electrically charged gas-like matter

Toroidal field coil

Largest tokamak

On 1 Dec 2023, the JT–60SA (*above*) was operated for the first time in Naka, Ibaraki, Japan. The JT–60SA is a tokamak – an experimental device that uses powerful magnetic fields to contain plasma in a toroidal (doughnut-shaped) chamber at temperatures and pressures that trigger nuclear fusion. When atoms fuse together, they release energy that it is hoped could one day be used to generate abundant clean electricity.

The JT–60SA can hold 135 m³ (4,767 cu ft) of plasma, and will be used for research in support of the International Thermonuclear Experimental Reactor (ITER), under construction in Cadarache, France. The ITER megaproject achieved a record of its own in Mar 2024 with the completion of the **largest superconducting magnets**. Known as Poloidal Field Coils 3 and 4 (PF4 *pictured left*), they are 24 m (78 ft) in diameter and weigh 350 tonnes (385 tons). The reactor will be six times the size of the JT–60SA.

The laser creates a path of ionized air, drawing the lightning down an invisible "filament" of conductive plasma.

FIRST LASER-GUIDED LIGHTNING

At just after 4 p.m. on 24 Jul 2021, a laser diverted the path of a lightning strike in the skies above Säntis, a mountain in Switzerland. A research team led by Aurélien Houard (FRA) and Jean-Pierre Wolf (CHE) had set up a terawatt near-infrared laser to intercept the lightning that routinely strikes the broadcast tower near the summit. The bolt of lightning followed the path of the laser for 50 m (164 ft) before turning back towards its original target. Details of the experiment appeared in *Nature Photonics* on 16 Jan 2023. It is hoped that similar high-power lasers could one day be used to divert lightning strikes away from vulnerable sites such as airports, which are too large to effectively protect with conventional lightning towers.

Wacky Wheels

Fastest monowheel motorcycle

Mark Foster of the UK Monowheel Team hit 129.890 km/h (80.710 mph) in *Trojan* at Elvington airfield in North Yorkshire, UK, on 25 Sep 2022. The team comprises four engineers, with Mark as the rider, and has been building progressively faster monowheels since 2010. Mark achieved the previous record – 117.346 km/h (72.915 mph) – on the same machine in 2019, but he was eager to try again as *Trojan* had been designed to reach 80 mph (128.7 km/h).

Most LED lights on a van

A total of 65,759 LED lights – which can switch colours – adorned the body of a 12-seater Toyota van for an event organized by Carnival Magic Theme Park (THA). This record attempt was part of the celebrations to mark the opening of the park in Phuket, Thailand, on 19 Jul 2022.

Fastest wheelie bin

On 24 May 2023, Michael Wallhead (UK) drove a heavily adapted trash can at 88.344 km/h (54.894 mph) at Elvington airfield in North Yorkshire, UK. He spent around £700 ($870) modding it, adding the two-stroke engine from a Suzuki GP125, a five-speed gearbox and a steering damper to improve the stability of this ultra-short-wheelbase vehicle.

Fastest electric mobility vehicles

Jason Liversidge (UK), who passed away in Aug 2023 aged 47, suffered from motor neurone disease and was mostly paralysed from the neck down. But that didn't stop him achieving a brace of GWR titles. In 2020, after making attempts with a go-kart-based design (*below*), Jason drove his specially adapted wheelchair to 107.546 km/h (66.826 mph) – the **fastest electric mobility vehicle** (*right*). Two years later, this vehicle was adapted for his worsening condition so he could set another speed record for a **head-operated electric mobility vehicle** – 77.92 km/h (48.42 mph).

Jason also wheeled up Mount Snowdon (aka Yr Wyddfa) – Wales's highest peak – and abseiled off the Humber Bridge.

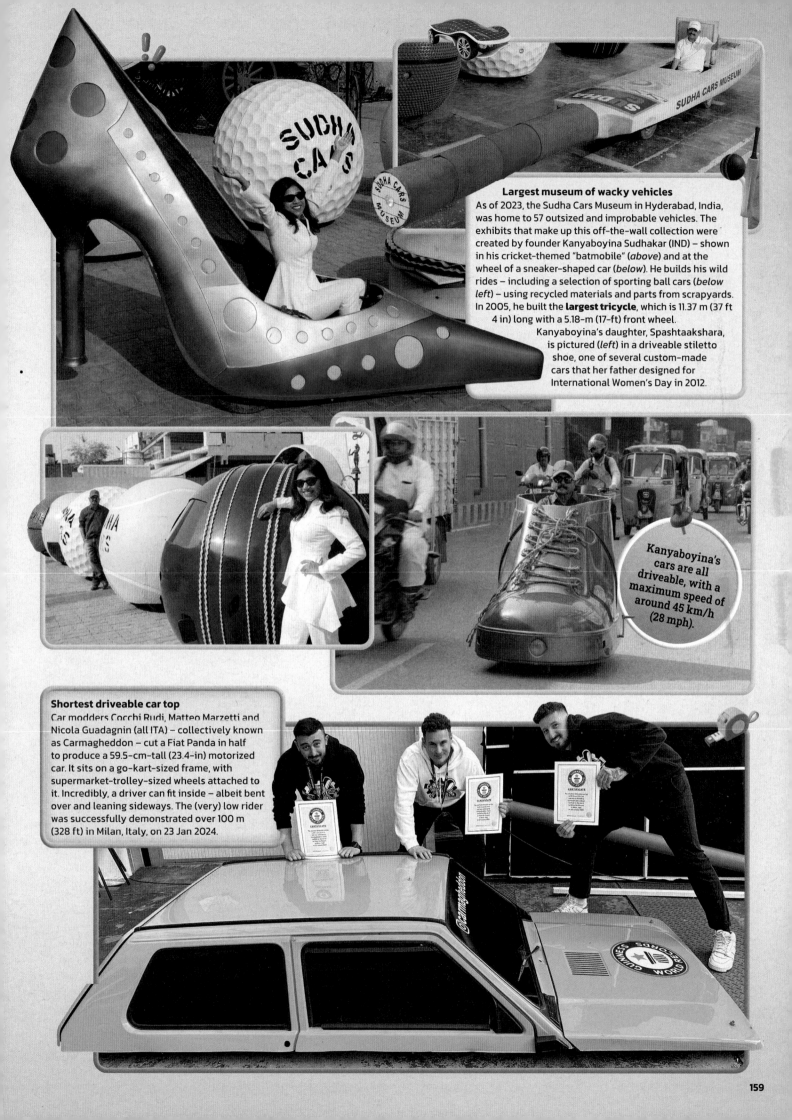

Largest museum of wacky vehicles

As of 2023, the Sudha Cars Museum in Hyderabad, India, was home to 57 outsized and improbable vehicles. The exhibits that make up this off-the-wall collection were created by founder Kanyaboyina Sudhakar (IND) – shown in his cricket-themed "batmobile" (*above*) and at the wheel of a sneaker-shaped car (*below*). He builds his wild rides – including a selection of sporting ball cars (*below left*) – using recycled materials and parts from scrapyards. In 2005, he built the **largest tricycle**, which is 11.37 m (37 ft 4 in) long with a 5.18-m (17-ft) front wheel.

Kanyaboyina's daughter, Spashtaakshara, is pictured (*left*) in a driveable stiletto shoe, one of several custom-made cars that her father designed for International Women's Day in 2012.

Kanyaboyina's cars are all driveable, with a maximum speed of around 45 km/h (28 mph).

Shortest driveable car top

Car modders Cocchi Rudi, Matteo Marzetti and Nicola Guadagnin (all ITA) – collectively known as Carmagheddon – cut a Fiat Panda in half to produce a 59.5-cm-tall (23.4-in) motorized car. It sits on a go-kart-sized frame, with supermarket-trolley-sized wheels attached to it. Incredibly, a driver can fit inside – albeit bent over and leaning sideways. The (very) low rider was successfully demonstrated over 100 m (328 ft) in Milan, Italy, on 23 Jan 2024.

Railways

Highest-capacity metro line

The Al Mashaaer Al Mugaddassah Line in Mecca, Saudi Arabia, can transport 72,000 passengers per hour each way. It opened in Nov 2010 and runs for just 10 days a year during the Hajj pilgrimage, shuttling the Muslim faithful between three key sites: Mina, Muzdalifah and Arafat. The 18.1-km-long (11.2-mi) route employs 12-car trains, each capable of taking around 3,000 people, and runs 24 trains per hour.

Longest railway spiral

The Dulishan Spiral is part of the Alishan Forest Railway, built in 1912 to serve the logging industry in Chiayi County, Taiwan, China. The spiral's start and end are only 570 m (1,870 ft) apart, but separated by an elevation of 233 m (764 ft). As a result, trains going between the neighbouring villages of Zhangnaoliao and Liyuanliao have to cover 5.1 km (3.1 mi) of twisting track.

First steam-powered passenger train

The year 2025 marks the 200th anniversary of George Stephenson's Stockton and Darlington Railway. Covering the 40 km (25 mi) between the two eponymous UK towns, it first carried passengers on 27 Sep 1825. There were earlier passenger railways – the **first** was the Oystermouth Railway, which opened in Swansea, UK, in 1807 – but these used horse-drawn trains.

First public electric railway service

On 16 May 1881, the Gross Lichterfelde Tramway electrified rail service began at Lichterfelde in Berlin, Germany. It was 2.5 km (1.5 mi) long and carried 26 passengers. Each tram was powered by a 180-V direct-current electric motor.

Most frequent travellers by train

As of 2022, Swiss citizens covered an average of 2,113.35 km (1,313.17 mi) by rail per year. The figure represents the kilometres travelled by passengers, divided by the population.

On 29 Oct 2022, Switzerland marked the 175th anniversary of its rail system by running the **longest narrow-gauge train** – which was 1,906 m (6,254 ft) long – through the winding mountain routes in the Rhaetian Alps.

Longest rail network

The USA had 148,533 km (92,306 mi) of actively maintained track as of 2023, according to the International Union of Railways (UIC).

China has the **longest high-speed rail network** – routes with an average speed of 200 km/h (124 mph) or higher – with a total of 42,233 km (26,242 mi) of electrified high-speed track.

Busiest...

• **Metro system**: The Shanghai Subway in China averaged a daily ridership of 7,363,500 people in 2022 and carried 2,287,917,700 passengers over the year. This puts it narrowly ahead of the Beijing Subway, which has been slower to bounce back from pandemic restrictions.

• **Rail network (country)**: Japan boasted some 6,565,700,000 passengers in 2023. The East Japan Railway Company, the largest single operator, is second only to Indian Railways in terms of passenger numbers.

• **Rail network for freight (country)**: China's railways carried 2.57 trillion tonnes (2.83 trillion tons) of goods and materials in 2023.

Steepest railway grade

The Calçada de São Francisco, a street in Lisbon, Portugal, has a section with a grade of 1 in 7.2 (13.8%; or around 7.9°). The route is part of Line 28 of the Lisbon tramway system. Because of the extreme inclines that the trams have to negotiate here, Line 28 utilizes single-unit streetcars, rather than larger articulated vehicles.

Busiest station

Shinjuku Station in Tokyo, Japan, received an average of 2.7 million commuters every day in 2022. By comparison, both the Gare de Lyon in Paris and Grand Central Station in New York City are used by "only" around 700,000 people daily. Passenger numbers at Shinjuku are dramatically down on their pre-pandemic peak, however, which was around 3.7 million commuters per day in 2019.

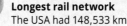

"Big Boy" locomotives were capable of pulling 4,200-ton (3,810-tonne) freight trains.

MOST POWERFUL STEAM LOCOMOTIVE

The Union Pacific "Big Boy" 4014 is capable of a tractive effort (pulling force) of 135,375 lbf (602,178 kN) – equal to around 100 semi-trucks – at 10 mph (16 km/h). In all, 25 "Big Boys" were built between 1941 and 1944; they could reach speeds of 70 mph (112 km/h). No.4014 was constructed in Nov 1941 for the Union Pacific Railroad and remained in service until Jul 1959. It was put on display at the RailGiants Train Museum in Los Angeles, California, USA, in 1962. In 2012, however, No.4014 was transferred back to Union Pacific, who restored it to working order on 4 May 2019 and returned it to service pulling excursion trains.

Sea Rescue

Longest career as a lifeguard

Chris Lewis (UK) has been helping to keep swimmers safe for more than 58 years. He became a volunteer lifeguard as a 15-year-old schoolboy in 1965. Aged 72 in Mar 2024, Lewis was still patrolling beaches in Bournemouth, Dorset, UK, on behalf of the RNLI (*see opposite*). He has also received an MBE for his services to maritime safety.

First helicopter hoist rescue

On 29 Nov 1945, Captain Joseph Pawlik and crewman Steven Penninger became stranded on an oil barge off Fairfield, Connecticut, USA, in a raging storm. High waves made it impossible for a rescue vessel to reach them. Instead, the men made history as the first people to be lifted to safety by helicopter. Piloting the Sikorsky R-5 was Jimmy Viner, aided by Jack Beighle (both USA).

Most people rescued at sea by a horse

On 1 Jun 1773, the Dutch ship *De Jonge Thomas* foundered on a sandbar in Table Bay off Cape Town, South Africa. Farmer Wolraad Woltemade (ZAF) rode his horse Vonk ("Spark") to the site, but they were unable to quite reach the wreck, so he ordered two crew to jump and grab the tail of the horse, which then towed them back to shore; 14 men were saved in this way. Tragically, on the final run, six desperate men jumped and swamped Woltemade and his exhausted steed, leading them all to perish.

First purpose-built lifeboat

In 1790, British shipbuilder Henry Francis Greathead created the *Original* in Tyne and Wear, UK. It measured 9 m (29 ft 6 in) long and could hold 20 people, including a crew of 12. To boost buoyancy, its interior was lined with cork – one

Oldest surviving lifeboat

Built by Henry Francis Greathead in 1802, the *Zetland* now resides at its own dedicated museum in Redcar, North Yorkshire, UK. The timber vessel was in service for 78 years, during which it helped to rescue at least 502 people in distress. The *Zetland* was based on the same design as the **first lifeboat** (*see left*).

of several features that distinguished its design from more general vessels such as fishing boats. The *Original* first saw action on 30 Jan 1790, rescuing the stranded survivors of a shipwreck on Herd Sand in South Tyneside, UK.

Largest helicopter sea rescue

On the night of 31 Jan 1953, a storm surge brought catastrophic flooding to England, Scotland, Belgium and the Netherlands. When Dutch sea defences gave way, an international rescue mission was launched involving American helicopters sent from Germany and British Dragonfly helicopters from the 705 Naval Air Squadron unit based in Gosport, Hampshire, UK. During the first two weeks of Feb 1953, at least 810 people were air-lifted from flooded coastal areas in the UK and on the continent.

Fastest lifeboat

The SAR 60 is rated to reach a speed of up to 60 knots (69 mph; 111.1 km/h). It was designed by the late Italian powerboat builder and racer Fabio Buzzi. On 12 Jul 2016, the vessel travelled from Monte Carlo, Monaco, to Venice, Italy – a distance of 1,120 nautical mi (2,074 km; 1,289 mi) – in just 22 hr 5 min 42 sec, clocking an average speed of 52.3 knots (60.2 mph; 96.9 km/h).

Largest coastguard ships

Tasked with scientific research, escort duties, law enforcement and maritime rescue, the 128-m-long (420-ft) icebreaker USCGC *Healy* has a displacement of 16,000 tons (14,515 tonnes).

By length, the biggest examples are the China Coast Guard's Zhaotou-class patrol cutters, at 165 m (541 ft) from bow to stern.

Most people saved at sea in one rescue

On 13 Jan 2012, the cruise ship *Costa Concordia* struck a reef near Isola del Giglio, off the coast of Tuscany, Italy. The impact tore two huge strips of steel from the hull and water poured into the engine rooms. A joint operation between the Italian Navy, Coast Guard and Air Force rescued 4,196 passengers and crew in lifeboats, motorboats and helicopters; sadly, it's believed that 33 people lost their lives.

OLDEST NATIONAL LIFESAVING ORGANIZATION
On 4 Mar 1824, the National Institution for the Preservation of Life from Shipwreck was formed. Renamed the Royal National Lifeboat Institution (RNLI) in 1854, it has been responsible for saving more than 144,000 lives in the waters surrounding the UK, the Republic of Ireland, the Channel Islands and the Isle of Man. The RNLI is a charity, staffed mostly by volunteers and funded largely by donations. Its 200-year history is studded with remarkable individuals and astonishing feats of bravery (*a few highlighted below*).

The busiest RNLI station is the Tower on the River Thames. It opened in 2002 and responded to its 10,000th callout in 2023.

1. The UK's Sir William Hillary vigorously petitioned the British parliament for the creation of an organization devoted to saving lives at sea, and is regarded as the "Father of the Institution".
2. On 7 Sep 1838, Grace Darling and her father, William – a lighthouse keeper – risked their lives to save survivors of the wrecked steamship *Forfarshire*, off Northumberland. Grace became a national heroine and the first female recipient of an RNLI Medal for Gallantry.
3. Henry Blogg retired in 1947 as the RNLI's most decorated lifeboatman, with three gold and four silver medals for bravery. For 53 years, he was stationed at Cromer in Norfolk, taking part in 387 rescues and helping to save 873 lives.
4. On 17 Mar 1907, in dense fog and bad weather, the White Star Line ship SS *Suevic* struck the Maenheere Reef off the Lizard Point in Cornwall. During a 16-hr operation led by the RNLI, some 60 volunteer lifeboatmen retrieved all passengers and crew in what remains the **largest sea rescue by lifeboats**. A total of 456 people were saved, including 70 babies.

Round-Up

Largest glass-floor observation platform

Henan Baoquan Tourism (CHN) have erected a 716.09-m² (7,707.92-sq-ft) glass-bottomed viewing station in Xinxiang, Henan, China, as ratified on 24 Apr 2023. It is part of Cliff World, a major park in the Baoquan tourist resort. The same day saw confirmation of the **tallest elevator within a mountain** – a 336-m (1,102-ft) construction installed in Xinxiang by the same organization.

Fastest 100 m by a quadrupedal robot

From a standing start, HOUND dashed 100 m in 19.87 sec on 26 Oct 2023. The attempt took place at an athletics track at the Korea Advanced Institute of Science and Technology in Daejeon, South Korea. The fleet-footed 'bot was built by KAIST Dynamic Robot Control and Design Laboratory (KOR).

Fastest electro-jet dual-propulsion car

The Sapheria Bluebird reached 75.53 km/h (46.93 mph) at Elvington airfield in North Yorkshire, UK, on 21 May 2023. The hybrid electric/jet turbine-powered three-wheeler was built by Formula Gravity – Sapheria Bluebird Project (UK). The team's long-term aim is to attract more students into the fields of engineering, science and technology.

Most southerly lunar lander

The uncrewed probe *Vikram* (*below*) touched down at a lunar latitude of 69.37° S on 23 Aug 2023, breaking a record set by NASA's *Surveyor 7* in 1968. *Vikram* was the lander segment of the Indian Space Research Organization's *Chandrayaan-3* spacecraft, making that country only the fourth to have successfully landed on the Moon. Its record did not stand for long, however – on 21 Feb 2024, the *Odysseus* lander from Intuitive Machines (USA) descended near the Malapert A crater at 80.13° S.

Most launches in a year (single rocket model)

The Falcon 9, made by SpaceX (USA), achieved 91 successful launches in 2023, an average of one every four days. This surpassed the previous record of 60 – also by SpaceX, in 2022.

On 13 Apr 2024, Falcon 9 core B1062 achieved the milestone of 20 orbital launches – the **most missions flown by a rocket first stage**. The launch – carrying 23 Starlink satellites from Cape Canaveral Space Force Station in Florida, USA – surpassed the previous record of 19, which had been set on the final flight of core B1058 on 23 Dec 2023. This veteran booster had long been the series leader, but was destroyed in a storm during its landing barge's return to base.

First ham radio station on the Moon

JS1YMG was registered by the JAXA Ham Radio Club (JPN) on 2 Feb 2024. Its transmitter is fitted to the tiny LEV-1 "hopper" rover, which was released on to the Moon's surface by Japan's Smart Lander for Investigating Moon on 19 Jan 2024. The rover's telemetry (performance data) was transmitted using a ham (amateur) radio band at a frequency of 437.41 MHz. Ham enthusiasts around the world scrambled to devise a means of picking up its signal, which – given its distance and low power (1 Watt) – could not be received with standard equipment.

Tightest knotted structure

The Au6 knot is a loop of 54 atoms – principally gold, phosphorus and oxygen – bonded into a chain that is entwined in a two-nanometre-wide trefoil knot. This is the simplest "non-trivial" knot, with three points at which the chain crosses over itself – equivalent to a conventional overhand knot with the ends of the string bonded together.

The Au6 knot was made by Zhiwen Li, Jingjing Zhang and Gao Li (all CHN) at the Dalian Institute of Chemical Physics in China, working with remote collaborator Richard Puddephatt (CAN, b. UK) at the University of Western Ontario, Canada.

Largest drystone wall built by robot

A robotic excavator named HEAP (Hydraulic Excavator for an Autonomous Purpose) constructed a freestanding mortar-free wall that was 10 m (32 ft 9 in) long, 1.7 m (5 ft 7 in) wide and 4 m (13 ft 1 in) high in Zurich, Switzerland. The project was executed by Gramazio Kohler Research and the Robotics Systems Lab at ETH Zurich (both CHE). The details were made public on 22 Nov 2023.

After its successful trial, HEAP built a 65-m-long (213-ft) retaining wall in a park in Oberglatt, Switzerland.

Largest K'NEX tunnel-boring machine

Using the construction toy K'NEX, Sarah Jolliffe (UK) built a replica tunnel-boring machine measuring 3.13 m (10 ft 3 in) long, with a 1.65-m (5-ft 4-in) diameter. The structure weighed some 163 kg (359 lb), comprised 92,364 pieces and took around 1,000 hr to complete, as verified in Downham Market, Norfolk, UK, on 30 Apr 2021. *For the largest tunnel-boring machine, see p.167.*

Heaviest commercial satellite

Jupiter-3, which was built by Maxar Technologies for Hughes Network Systems (both USA), has a mass of 9,200 kg (20,282 lb). The body of this telecommunications satellite is about the size of a school bus, with solar panels that unfold to span 38.7 m (127 ft). *Jupiter-3* launched atop a SpaceX Falcon Heavy rocket from the Kennedy Space Center in Florida, USA, on 29 Jul 2023. There may be larger military reconnaissance satellites in orbit, but details such as their mass are top secret and cannot be verified by GWR.

Greatest distance driven in a hydrogen-powered vehicle

Eco-Runner XIII travelled 2,488 km (1,546 ml) on just 45 litres (1.5 cu ft) of pressurized hydrogen between 23 and 26 Jun 2023. The vehicle was developed by Eco-Runner Team Delft (NLD) and tested at the Mercedes-Benz proving ground in Immendingen, Germany.

First electric hydrofoil ferry

On 16 Nov 2023, Swedish shipbuilder Candela Technology completed sea trials for its prototype P-12 electric hydrofoil. This 30-seat passenger vessel is designed to replace diesel ferries on urban waterways, using electric motors and a set of lifting hydrofoil fins to achieve high speeds with little noise or wake.

Largest cruise ship

Icon of the Seas was commissioned into the fleet of Royal Caribbean International (USA) on 27 Nov 2023. Built at the Meyer Turku shipyard in Finland, the ocean liner has a gross tonnage of 250,800 and measures 364.75 m (1,196 ft 8 in) from bow to stern.

Smallest humanoid robot

A 141-mm-tall (5.55-in) automaton was engineered and built by members of the DBS Robotics team (CHN) at the Diocesan Boys' School in Hong Kong, China, as verified on 6 Jan 2024. The students used computer-aided design to create the robot, making most of the components with a laser cutter and 3D printer. It is rechargeable and programmable.

The acrylic body panels were created with an UltiMaker 3D printer and Lasertec laser cutter

DBS Robotics plans to open-source the robot's design and programming code to promote STEAM education.

A set of eight servo motors enable leg movement

As well as walking, the robot can dance and even kick a ball!

100%

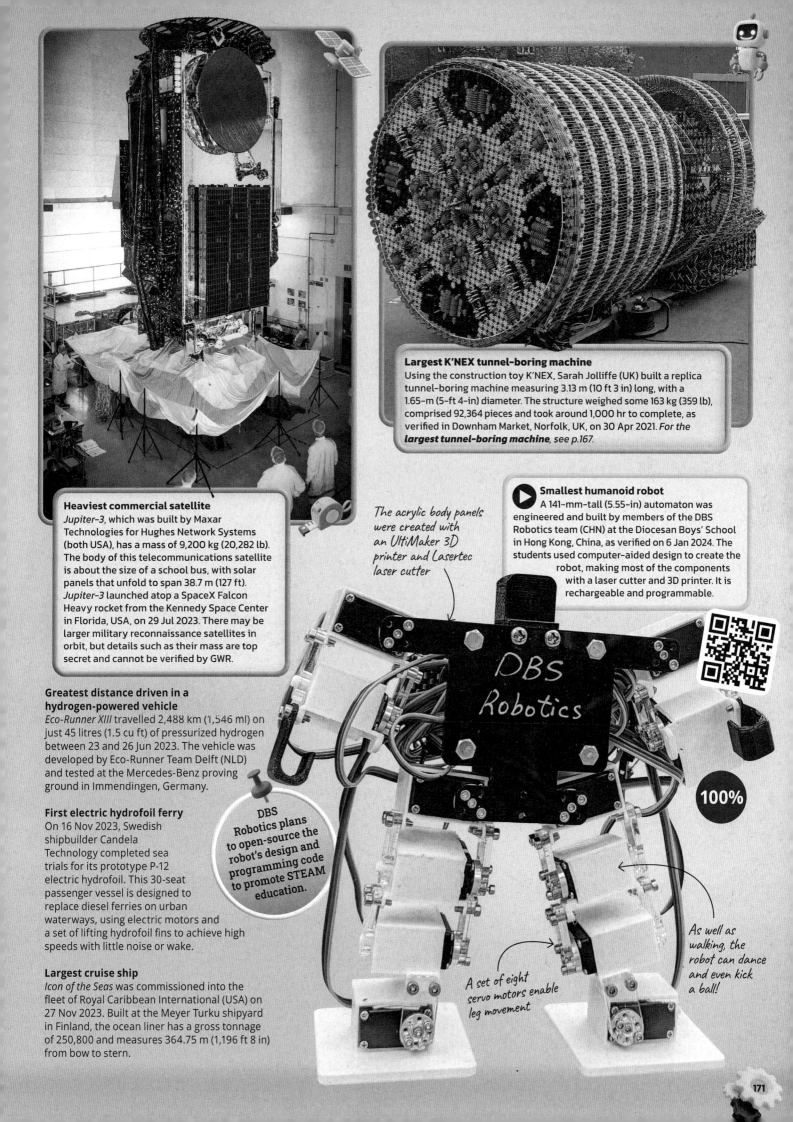

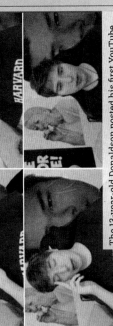

ICON

MrBeast

Meet Jimmy "MrBeast" Donaldson (USA) – social-media sensation, innovative entrepreneur and high-stakes philanthropist. But let's face it: there's a good chance you already knew this.

After all, Donaldson is YouTube's **most subscribed** and **highest-earning individual** – *Forbes* estimated that he raked in $54 m (£42.4 m) in 2023. That year, *TIME* magazine also bestowed him a spot in its prestigious 100 Most Influential People list. He first posted on YouTube aged 13, and spent years studying the platform's algorithms, analysing how to craft eye-catching, fan-pleasing videos. His meteoric success was built on a multi-pronged attack of off-the-wall clickbait: stunts (microwaving a microwave, anyone?), "junklord" videos (such as "I ate $100,000 golden ice cream") and spectacular prizes or cash gifts. The MrBeast business model gradually became established: rising viewer revenue enabled ever-more-astonishing giveaways (usually via sponsorship or Google's AdSense programme) and an expanding viewership – further increasing revenue.

That burgeoning income has already been put to good use: his channel Beast Philanthropy has already organized food drives, donations of prosthetic limbs and paid for 1,000 cataract operations, to name just a few worthy deeds.

In Sep 2022, the MrBeast team found time to cook up the **largest vegetarian burger** – 2,092.4 kg (4,612 lb 15 oz) – in Greenville, North Carolina, USA, which required more than 40 people to prepare.

The 13-year-old Donaldson posted his first YouTube video in 2012, but his breakthrough as MrBeast came in 2017 as he filmed himself counting to 100,000 in real time (*above*), a feat that took more than 40 hr. Despite his weary demeanour, the video secured him millions of views and a considerable following.

VITAL STATISTICS

Name	Jimmy Stephen Donaldson
Birthplace	Wichita, Kansas, USA
Birth date	7 May 1998
Current GWR titles	Several, including **most subscribers for an individual on YouTube** – 250 million, as of 21 Apr 2024
Honours include	Streamy Awards (11), Nickelodeon Kids' Choice Awards (2), Shorty Awards (2), People's Choice Award (1)

Donaldson has won two Nickelodeon Kids' Choice Awards for Favorite Male Creator, in 2022 and 2023. His 2022 appearance was also record-worthy: he was one of 1,000 people to be splattered with Nickelodeon's trademark shower of green goo – the **most people slimed at an awards show.**

In 2022, Donaldson launched the food brand Feastables. To promote his MrBeast Bars, he dressed as the Roald Dahl character Willy Wonka and built a replica of Wonka's chocolate factory. He then offered 10 competitors the chance to win the deeds to the factory, or a cash prize of $500,000 (£411,150). For the final challenge, contestants had to bake a chocolate dessert to impress the TV chef Gordon Ramsay (*above*); the winner opted to take home the cash prize!

A dedicated crew helps to create MrBeast's viral content. Shown left to right are Kris Tyson, Chandler Hallow, Nolan Hansen, Tareq Salameh, Jimmy, and Karl Jacobs. Here, the team shows off the new branding and new formula for Feastables chocolate bars.

In Nov 2021, Donaldson recruited 456 super-keen survivalists for the video "$456,000 *Squid Game* in Real Life!" Based on the smash Netflix series, it saw competitors battle it out for that lucrative cash prize (£340,764). It was a characteristically big-budget affair, with Donaldson splashing out more than $3 m (£2.25 m) on production costs, including sets that mirrored some of those in the original show. As of Jan 2024, it had garnered more than 559 million views, becoming his most-watched video.

When Donaldson hit 20 million subscribers in 2019, he marked the milestone by planting 20 million trees. And so, project #TEAMTREES was born. Working with the Arbor Day Foundation and fellow green-minded YouTuber Mark Rober, Donaldson and his team planted one tree for every dollar pledged by the public. #TEAMSEAS followed swiftly: a pound (0.45 kg) of ocean rubbish salvaged for the same donation. The result, as of Jan 2024, was more than 24 million new trees planted and 33.65 million lb (15.26 million kg) of garbage cleared.

 Find out more about MrBeast in the ICON section at www.guinnessworldrecords.com/2025

Kids' Zone

Here at GWR, we don't see why grown-ups should get to have all the fun. That's why we've been putting a lot of effort into upping our game when it comes to GWR's younger audience. The most exciting part of this initiative is the ever-expanding collection of records we've ring-fenced in the "Under-16" category. So hands off, old-timers! Whether it's identifying Pokémon, scoring goals in *FIFA* or speed-packing a schoolbag, there's a challenge to suit everyone (*turn the page for more*).

If you think you've got what it takes to join the growing ranks of junior record breakers, then find out how in our step-by-step guide below. If you need some inspiration, you'll hear from our latest squad of talented Young Achievers (*pp.182–89*). And if you *still* need proof that age is only a number, check out **kids.guinnessworldrecords.com** and our "GWR Kids" YouTube channel. Long-time GWR nerds, meanwhile, can pit their record trivia against our devilishly difficult quiz (*pp.190–91*), which features several precocious record stars. Only one question remains: which record will *you* take on first?!

Some records may require a venue to be hired, expert witnesses recruited or specialist gear sourced.

1

CHOOSE IT!
So you want to be a record breaker – but what record are you going to break? You could take on one of the thousands of existing GWR titles or dream up a new challenge. Either way, you'll need to set up an account with us beforehand. Head to **guinnessworldrecords.com** and click on "Register" at the top of the screen. Don't worry, it'll only take a few minutes!

Start

The most seasoned record setters know to allow plenty of time to train for an attempt!

Do your homework before submitting a new category idea. Find out the kind of things we like in the *GWR* books and website.

Have you got all the equipment you need for your record attempt? Check the guidelines!

PRACTISE IT!
Once you've chosen a record, submit an initial application via your GWR account. If the title already exists – or we like your new idea – we'll send over a specific set of guidelines. Read these very carefully as they must be followed to the letter. Now you know the rules, the all-important training can begin! Regardless of age, preparation is always vital to success.

2

CONTENTS

DO IT!

The day of reckoning has arrived. You've honed your skills, everything set out in the guidelines is in place, and you've tested key kit such as stopwatches and cameras to ensure they're working properly. You're ready! Remember, nerves are natural and things won't always go to plan, so don't put pressure on yourself if things don't work out on the first go. Take your time, restock and try again – don't forget to ENJOY IT too!

3

GWR talks to...

Dave Wilson is one of Guinness World Records' official Adjudicators, who are stationed all around the globe. We persuaded him to put down his clipboard long enough to answer some of your burning record-related questions...

What advice do you have to help me become a record holder?
Use the search function on our website as much as possible! Whatever your hobby or skill, it's very possible that there's already a record in our system that you could apply for. The best thing about Guinness World Records is that there really is something for everyone.

Can I suggest a brand-new record title?
We'd love to hear if you've got an idea for a record, but we do have some rules. New records have to be achievable, breakable, measurable and – most importantly – open to everyone. Do your homework and make sure you know your stuff before proposing your idea.

Which record would you like to try?
Sadly, GWR staff aren't allowed to attempt records. But if I could, I'd love to try **most Cadbury Creme Eggs eaten in one minute**. It would definitely be one of the eating ones!

What's the best part of being an official GWR Adjudicator?
Getting a record means so much to people – I feel so lucky to be a part of that. We all do! Putting on that famous suit is an honour.

Record breaking is tough, however old you are! If one record doesn't work out, consider another.

PROVE IT!

Now it's time to send us the evidence. Depending on the record, this might include videos, photos and witness statements. Be sure not to miss anything! We'll need a few weeks to review the proof. If successful, you'll receive email confirmation and later your authentic GWR certificate, ratifying that you are now part of the Officially Amazing GWR family!

4

Finish

5

Follow the steps like I did, and you could also be Officially Amazing! Now, where shall I hang this...?

Under-16 Records

Most records (bar the most dangerous ones!) are open to all ages. But in 2021, GWR decided it was high time that our younger fans had some just for them. Here, we present a few of the major under-16 themes, each with an example record yet to be broken. Could YOU be their first holder? If so, you'll join the super-kids who have already made GWR history (*see bottom panel*).

TOYS

Fastest time to disassemble and assemble a Mr. Potato Head

You'll need speedy fingers to add all the parts on to this classic toy in record time.
- Start with a fully assembled Mr. Potato Head. Each attachment must be inserted correctly.
- Keep your hands flat on a surface until the timer starts on a "3, 2, 1, GO!"
- Disassemble the toy, laying the parts out separately in front of you.
- Put Mr. Potato Head back together again.
- The timer stops as soon as Mr. Potato Head is fully built and stood upright, and you raise your hands in the air to signal that you've finished.
- **Minimum requirement**: 15 sec

Get in touch!
Applying to set, or break, a GWR title is simple! Scan the QR code below, which will take you to the "Set a Record" page on the GWR Kids website. There, you'll find a range of Under-16 records to try. You can also see our step-by-step guide on the previous page. Remember: the titles here aren't the only options; if you have an idea for a new record, please let us know!

SEASONAL

Fastest Christmas-cracker relay (team of four)

Feeling festive? If you and your Christmas buddies really pull together, you could receive the best-ever present: a GWR title!
- Mark two lines on the ground 5 m (16 ft 5 in) apart, with two people standing on either line, each holding one shop-bought Christmas cracker.
- When the timer starts, the first person should run to one of their friends standing by the other line, pull their cracker and put on their hat. Only then can the next person run.
- The timer stops when everyone has travelled 5 m, all the crackers have been pulled and everyone is wearing a paper hat.
- **Minimum requirement**: 31 sec

Be sure to recycle all the spent crackers, but check if any parts are non-recyclable. And hang on to the novelties and jokes!

Fastest time to sort two bags of recyclable materials (team of two): 34.78 sec, by Dhakshana and Sana Kaarthick (both USA) in Morrisville, North Carolina, USA, on 16 Oct 2023.

Fastest time to stack a 20-level right-angle LEGO®-brick tower: 13.33 sec, by Ryoma Arakawa (JPN) in Nagoya, Aichi, Japan, on 23 Mar 2023.

Most dominoes set up and toppled in 30 seconds (team of two): 20, by Tyler Tai and Reid Kwok Barrington-Foote (both CAN) in London, UK, on 12 Jul 2023.

FOOD

Fastest time to make a cupcake pyramid

Arranging teatime treats could earn you a tasty record – not to mention a well-earned snack once you're done!

• Set out six cupcakes, either home-made or bought.
• Before the timer starts, each cupcake must be placed separately and flat on a surface.
• Build the pyramid in the following order using only one hand: three cupcakes at the base, followed by a layer of two, and the final cupcake placed on top.
• Only pick up one cupcake at a time without sliding them across the table.
• The pyramid has to stand for at least five seconds. If it falls, try again.
• **Minimum requirement**: 10 sec

GAMING

Fastest taming of a parrot in _Minecraft_ with touch controls

How quickly could you train a rare mob in the **best-selling videogame**?

• From the menu, select Play, then Create New, followed by Create New World.
• Pick Survival mode and Normal difficulty.
• Set the world seed to the Jungle world template and then place your gameplay device down on a flat surface and put your hands behind your back.
• Film the attempt so both you and your device are visible.
• After the countdown, start the challenge. As soon as the wild mob is tamed, shout "Stop!"
• Right after the stopwatch ends, show that the parrot has been tamed by either sitting it on the floor or on your shoulders.
• **Minimum requirement**: 30 sec

SPORT

Most basketball chest passes in one minute (team of two)

Could you and a pal propel yourselves into the record books?

• You will need a regular-sized basketball.
• Stand at least 3 m (9 ft 10 in) apart from each other. You can mark this distance on the ground with two lines.
• After a countdown, start chest passing the ball between the two of you. You must throw it with both hands.
• Both of you should catch and control the ball without it hitting the ground.
• If you drop the ball, that pass won't count, but you can pick up the ball and continue.
• **Minimum requirement**: 30

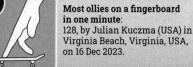

Most ollies on a fingerboard in one minute:
128, by Julian Kuczma (USA) in Virginia Beach, Virginia, USA, on 16 Dec 2023.

Most socks put on one foot in 30 seconds:
26, by Landon Williamson (USA) in Lebanon, Ohio, USA, on 1 Jul 2023.

Most soft toys caught blindfolded in one minute (team of two):
20, by Jivika Bang and Preksha Lathi (both IND) in Jalgaon, Maharashtra, India, on 24 Sep 2023.

Family Feats

Had enough of board games and movie night? Looking for a new family challenge? How about breaking a world record together? Whether you team up with a sibling, parent, grandparent, cousin or your best buddy, who could be better placed to join you on this journey to becoming Officially Amazing? For some inspiration, check out a few record-breaking relatives who've already gone the distance...

Just like his dad Silvio, young Cristian Sabba (both ITA) has become a multiple GWR title holder. On 7 Jan 2021, the duo combined to achieve the **fastest time to stack a set of dominoes (team of two)** in 10.31 sec in Milan, Italy. Cristian has some way to go to catch up to his father though... Silvio currently boasts around 200 records to his name, making him one of the world's most prolific record setters!

Australia's Nunan sisters – Lara (*left*) and Ashley – are the queens of rapid recall! Their mega memory power has secured them several records based around identifying famous faces, both fictional and real as shown in the table (Lara's titles in *blue* and Ashley's in *red*).

MEMORABLE SISTER ACT		
Marvel characters (one minute)*	88	5 Sep 2021
Cartoon characters (one minute)	102	6 Jan 2022
US presidents (30 seconds)	40	22 May 2022
Company logos (one minute)	102	14 Sep 2022
Harry Potter character quotes (one minute)	44	23 Dec 2022

*Marvel characters record since broken by Shreyas M (IND), with 98 characters on 17 Jun 2023.

Frédéric is dad to four daughters, and plans to take each of them on an adventure for their 16th birthday!

Mathilde de Lanouvelle celebrated turning 16 by going on an epic journey with her father, Frédéric (both FRA). The pair cycled 2,162 km (1,343 mi) on a tandem around France to create the **largest GPS drawing by bicycle (team)** from 16 to 31 Aug 2023. What's more, their big-hearted feat raised €26,000 ($28,331; £22,348) for charity.

On 1 Mar 2023, Serbian siblings Luka and Ilija Pejovski enlisted their father, Dragan, to help build the **tallest GEOMAG tower** – on national TV! They used the magnetic toy to make a 3.46-m-tall (11-ft 4-in) skyscraper in Belgrade, Serbia.

The Rashed AlMheiri siblings are a trio of talented wordsmiths from the UAE who each have earned literary-themed record titles:
• AlDhabi (b. 13 Jul 2014, **1**) is the **youngest person to publish a bilingual book series (female)** – *I Had an Idea* and *Here was the Beginning* – aged 8 years 239 days on 9 Mar 2023.
• Saeed (b. 30 Aug 2018, **2**) was aged 4 years 218 days when he became the **youngest person to publish a book (male)** – *The Elephant Saeed and the Bear* – on 9 Mar 2023.
• AlMaha (b. 22 Feb 2020, **3**) became the **youngest person to publish a book series (female)** – *The Flower* and *Honey Bee* – on 7 Jan 2024, aged just 3 years 319 days.

Full-time bubble artist Eran Backler (aka The Highland Joker, UK) has passed on the secrets of bubbleology to his children. On 25 Nov 2018, he teamed up with son Lucian to set the **longest bubble rally**, bouncing a bubble between two bubble rackets 17 times without any of them popping! When this record was broken, Eran enlisted his daughter Paikea to reclaim it (*above*), achieving 27 on 13 Nov 2022 in Newport, Isle of Wight, UK. Eran also spent the **longest time inside a bubble** – 1 min 2.92 sec – with his wife, Lauren, on 22 Dec 2018.

Talk about *running* in the family... On 29 Jul 2023, Chad Kempel (USA, *top*) took to the track with his children Savannah, Avery, Noelle, Grayson and Preston. Father-of-seven Chad managed the **fastest men's 1 km pushing a quintuple pram** – 5 min 34 sec – in Eagle, Idaho, USA.
   Another on-the-go parent is Rachael Rozhdestvenskaya (UK, *above*). On 1 May 2022, club runner Rachael completed the **fastest women's 10 km pushing a pram** with her daughter, Eva – who slept through most of it! – in a lightning-quick 39 min 24 sec in Manchester, UK.

Mason Gonzales and his grandfather Tim Trevitt, assisted by Glen Chase (all USA), used a fireman's ladder to achieve the **most loop-the-loops in a supported Hot Wheels track** – 28 – on 2 Sep 2023 in Susanville, California, USA.

Playtime!

A toy box is not just a toy box – it's a portal to a limitless world of record breaking! Here are some inspirational ideas to take *your* playtime to a superlative new level...

Longest time to spin a fidget spinner on...
- **One finger**: 25 min 43.21 sec, by William Lee (SGP) on 1 May 2019
- **One toe**: 6 min 52.28 sec, by Brendan Kelbie (AUS) on 2 Jul 2020

Largest toy wagon
On 20 Dec 2016, to mark the upcoming centenary of Radio Flyer Inc. (USA), CEO Robert Pasin (*front*) rolled out a supersized version of their iconic cart at the firm's headquarters in Chicago, Illinois. It measured 8.05 m long and 3.55 m tall (26 ft 5 in x 11 ft 8 in).

Most juggling catches in one minute
All set by Simeon Graham (UK)
- **Five balls**: 423 on 25 Oct 2022
- **Six balls**: 396 on 25 Oct 2022
- **Seven balls**: 378 on 4 Feb 2023

Most JENGA blocks removed in one minute
- **Individual**: 33, by Lim Kai Yi (MYS) on 20 Oct 2023
- **Pair**: 22, by Lim Kai Yi (MYS) and Zheng Haoran (CHN) on 18 Jan 2023

Tallest K'NEX tower
30.87 m (101 ft 3.4 in), by K'NEX Manufacturing (UK) on 5–6 Jun 1999, using 50,342 pieces!

- **Largest collection of teddy bears**
20,367, by Istvánné Arnóczki (HUN), as counted on 27 Apr 2019
- **Longest line of teddies**
15,534, by Finlay Church (UK) on 3 May 2015

Fastest time to build Mr. Potato Head
- **Individual**: 5.43 sec, by Lim Kai Yi (MYS) on 9 Aug 2022
- **Pair**: 9.5 sec, by Lim Kai Yi and Ang Boon Hong (both MYS) on 26 Jul 2023
- **Blindfolded**: 10.88 sec, by Lim Kai Yi on 8 Apr 2023 and equalled by Brendan Kelbie (AUS) on 30 Nov 2023

For an under-16 Mr. Potato Head record, see p.176

Longest time to spin a spinning top
- **Single spin**: 1 hr 37 min 42 sec, by Inosuke Mori (JPN) on 24 Oct 1999
- **Sustained**: 7 hr 1 min 14 sec, by Ashrita Furman (USA) on 18 Nov 2006

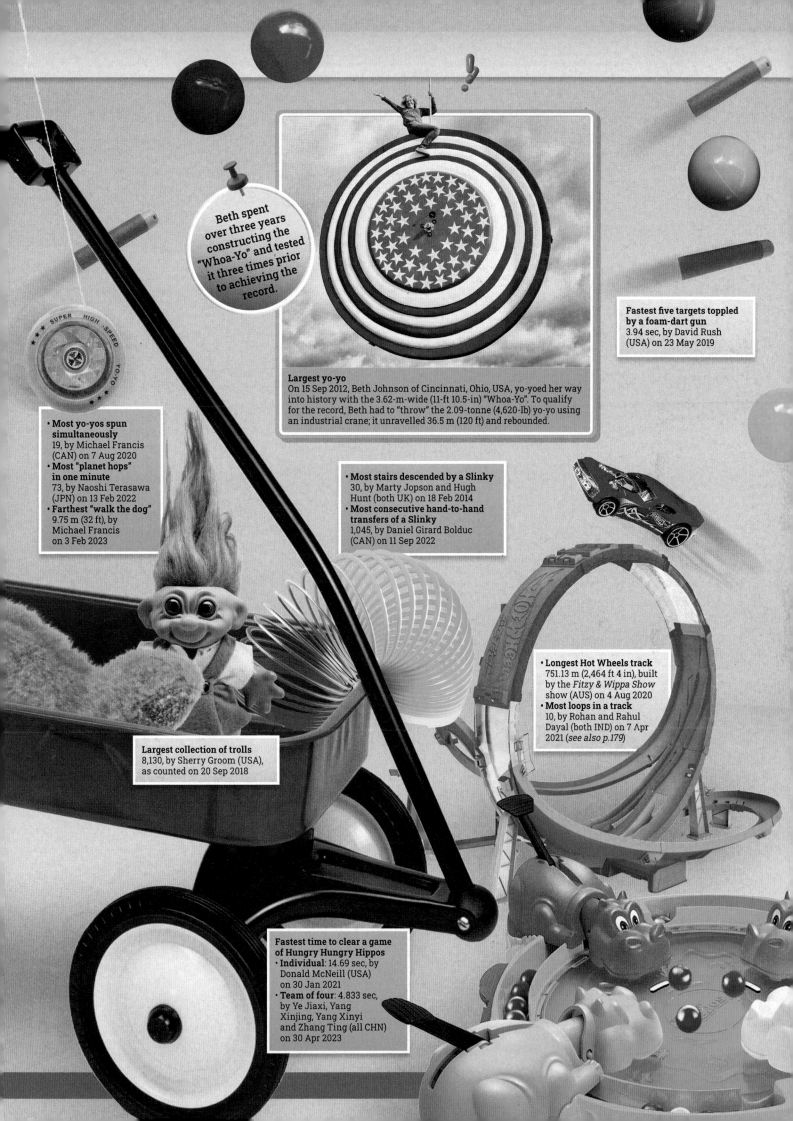

Beth spent over three years constructing the "Whoa-Yo" and tested it three times prior to achieving the record.

Fastest five targets toppled by a foam-dart gun
3.94 sec, by David Rush (USA) on 23 May 2019

Largest yo-yo
On 15 Sep 2012, Beth Johnson of Cincinnati, Ohio, USA, yo-yoed her way into history with the 3.62-m-wide (11-ft 10.5-in) "Whoa-Yo". To qualify for the record, Beth had to "throw" the 2.09-tonne (4,620-lb) yo-yo using an industrial crane; it unravelled 36.5 m (120 ft) and rebounded.

- **Most yo-yos spun simultaneously**
  19, by Michael Francis (CAN) on 7 Aug 2020
- **Most "planet hops" in one minute**
  73, by Naoshi Terasawa (JPN) on 13 Feb 2022
- **Farthest "walk the dog"**
  9.75 m (32 ft), by Michael Francis on 3 Feb 2023

- **Most stairs descended by a Slinky**
  30, by Marty Jopson and Hugh Hunt (both UK) on 18 Feb 2014
- **Most consecutive hand-to-hand transfers of a Slinky**
  1,045, by Daniel Girard Bolduc (CAN) on 11 Sep 2022

- **Longest Hot Wheels track**
  751.13 m (2,464 ft 4 in), built by the *Fitzy & Wippa Show* show (AUS) on 4 Aug 2020
- **Most loops in a track**
  10, by Rohan and Rahul Dayal (both IND) on 7 Apr 2021 (*see also p.179*)

Largest collection of trolls
8,130, by Sherry Groom (USA), as counted on 20 Sep 2018

Fastest time to clear a game of Hungry Hungry Hippos
- **Individual:** 14.69 sec, by Donald McNeill (USA) on 30 Jan 2021
- **Team of four:** 4.833 sec, by Ye Jiaxi, Yang Xinjing, Yang Xinyi and Zhang Ting (all CHN) on 30 Apr 2023

Chennai Hoopers

A hula hoop might seem like just a fun toy, but for a dedicated group of youngsters in India it has become an intrinsic part of their identity – and their secret to making GWR history.

The Chennai Hoopers school was established in 2018 by Vijayalakshmi Saravana – a teacher and avid hooper herself. It has since grown from a handful of students being taught in a small room into a full-blown academy that has now trained more than 500 children.

The school registered its first GWR title in 2019, when Tharun R S achieved the **most times to spin a hoop around the knees in one minute** (194). Six years on, the troupe's record tally has exceeded 30.

Keen to see this talent in person, GWR invited three of the star spinners to its London HQ in Jan 2023. While there, Balasaranitha Balaji, Janani Saravana (Vijayalakshmi's daughter) and Mamathi Vinoth (*pictured left to right*) rose to the occasion, smashing an incredible nine titles. These included the **most rotations around the shoulders in 30 seconds** (53, by Bala), the **most elbow passes in one minute** (46, by Janani) and the **most hops while spinning a hoop on the ankle in one minute** (110, by Mamathi). All we can say is *hoop hoop* hooray for the Chennai Hoopers!

*All record holders IND

There are currently about 75 students who regularly meet to exercise and have fun with hoops, both in person and online.

Ten-year-old Shashwath S claimed the **most hula-hoop rotations around the elbow in one minute** – 218 – on 22 Apr 2023. He bettered the previous mark by 20 spins. He told us: "I felt so proud of myself when I broke my first record. It was a confidence boost and will push me to achieve more."

Why is hooping such a great hobby?
Mamathi: It's a great sport that brings out energy in you. Hooping is a journey of self-improvement that enables you to set personal goals and witness progress over time.

Do you have any hooping heroes?
Janani: My mother [Vijayalakshmi] is my hooping hero. She runs Chennai Hoopers and was my inspiration to start.
Bala: Yes, my friend Manognya is my hero. She's good at hula hooping, and watching her sparked my curiosity about hooping and inspired me to become professional.

How did it feel when you set a record?
Mamathi: I felt an overwhelming sense of elation. It's a moment of pure happiness when you realize all the hard work has paid off.

What are the benefits of being part of a community who share your passion?
Janani: At Chennai Hoopers, the students not only learn but teach. When you're qualified as a "senior", you're given the chance to teach the younger kids. Being someone who has always been shy, I feel like this is a really advantageous practice, as it not only helps in developing my teaching skills but also gets me out of my comfort zone.

Any advice for newcomers to hooping?
Janani: One thing I've noticed while teaching beginners is that they get frustrated after trying for just a few minutes. So, in my opinion the most useful tip is to have patience.

Will you always be a hooper?
Bala: Definitely. I love hula hooping! It brings me so much joy and fun that I don't see myself giving up on it anytime soon.

CHENNAI HOOPERS

Instructor Vijayalakshmi Saravana (*seated farthest right*) is the driving force behind the Chennai Hoopers.

The talented hoopers are amassing quite a haul of GWR certificates... As of Sep 2023, they had achieved more than 30 records.

Ollie & Harry Ferguson

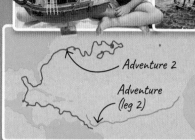

Many of us have a bucket list, but few will have 500 goals. Fewer still could imagine ticking off so many before leaving school. But Ollie and Harry Ferguson (UK) aren't your average bucket-listers. For several years, these Aberdeenshire-based brothers – supported by parents Mac and Vicki – have been on a mission to complete 500 challenges before they turn 18. These vary from panning for gold and eating *surströmming* (fermented herring) to hunting for fossils and starting their own country!

But it was a Playmobil pirate ship that secured Ollie and Harry a place in the record books. In 2017, they launched *Adventure* (**1**) on to the high seas – their take on a "message in a bottle". From Scotland, the boat made its way first to Sweden and – after hitching a lift from a passing sailship – on to west Africa, where it then rode the Atlantic currents to the Caribbean. After logging 6,072.5 km (3,773.3 mi), it became the **most travelled toy ship**.

Of course, this daring duo weren't content to leave it there... They've not only gone on to break their own record, collaborating with another family (*see* **2**), but they've recently embarked on a third even *more* ambitious voyage (**3**).

1 **Adventure**: Ollie (*left*) and Harry building a Playmobil ship with a few tweaks, such as polystyrene to bolster buoyancy and a GPS tracker. Its ultimate journey would play out over two legs: the first from Scotland to Scandinavia, and the second (*see map*) from near the Canary Islands to Barbados.

Adventure 2
Adventure (leg 2)

2 **Adventure 2**: With help from the Fergusons, a second ship was built by brothers Jax, Kai (*both above*) and Fynn Lewis in Trinidad. It was released off Guyana by their dad, Keith, in Sep 2020 and reached the Gulf of Mexico, after surviving two hurricanes! It then moved up the US east coast before vanishing in the Atlantic in Nov 2021, setting a new distance record of 15,439 km (9,593.3 mi). This may well be bettered yet, though...

3 ***Erebus* and *Terror***: The newest expedition, with models based on the HMS *Erebus* and HMS *Terror*, launched in summer 2023 with the aim of circling Antarctica. The journey could take up to two years and cover *c.* 22,000 km (13,670 mi).

Did you make any changes between the *Adventure* and *Adventure 2* voyages?
Harry: The first *Adventure* went really well and we didn't want to change anything, so we did *Adventure 2* in exactly the same way. We used the same type of boat and prepared it in a similar way, though this time we were working with Jax, Kai and Fynn Lewis, who live in Trinidad.

When you launch a toy boat into the sea, do you know which route it will take?
Ollie: We rely completely on the direction of the current. Because we know where most ocean currents are, we can choose where to put the boat. That helps us navigate a path by drifting the boats in the direction that we want to travel. But some currents are not very straight and that can cause problems when the boats end up going in circles and wasting battery life.

How will your new expedition to the Antarctic be different?
Harry: It took two years to build the boats and we tried to make them as-close-as-possible replicas of *Erebus* and *Terror*. The hulls are made of 200-year-old elm and are coated in copper.
Ollie: Being as faithful as possible to the original design may mean that the boats don't survive as long, but it was important to us not to use plastic. They'll travel around the circumpolar current in a similar way to the original vessels in 1839. And also like the Ross Expedition, we'll be collecting scientific data such as air and water temperature, and ocean pH levels.

Tell us about some of your other "mini adventures".
Ollie: We have a list of 500 and so far we've done 456 [as of Sep 2023]. Probably the hardest were sending LEGO® Minifigures into space and the boats. The most difficult adventure that we're working on just now is driving 30 forms of transport!

 Find out more about GWR's amazing younger record breakers and under-16 titles at **kids.guinnessworldrecords.com**

Simar Khurana

It's not unusual for kids to spend their free time playing videogames. But Simar Khurana from Ontario, Canada, likes to create them too. Encouraged by her parents, Manpreet and Paras, she decided to learn coding at the age of six. "Finding a coding class wasn't easy," her dad Paras told GWR. "Game development requires advanced reading and writing, and most coding institutes couldn't believe that Simar could do both at such a high level for her age." Soon, however, a teacher was found, and her coding journey began.

As Paras saw how quickly Simar was progressing, he realized that she could break the record for **youngest videogame developer**. The only problem? She had four months to do it to be within the age limit. Paras said: "Simar was willing to work hard. Imagine a six-year-old balancing school, evening classes, homework and coding projects. That's challenging even for a grown-up!" But Simar did it: aged 6 years 364 days, her first-ever game – *Healthy Food Challenge* – was released online for fellow young gamers to play.

"I'm amazed by the way coding lets me instruct computers and make them communicate with others."

When she's not busy coding, sport-loving Simar takes dance, gymnastics and karate classes.

What appealed to you about coding?
Maths is my favourite school subject and I'm really good at it. I could do grade two maths when I was in kindergarten. When I was very little, I learned maths on my own by watching YouTube videos. Plus, I like to make things, like crafts and games. So, my daddy told me I should try coding.

How did you come up with the concept behind *Healthy Food Challenge*?
I don't like eating lots of foods, but the doctor told my sister and me that we need to eat healthily. She showed us what good food looks like. By then, I was already having four coding lessons a week, and needed to choose a topic for my game.

Did you face any difficulties when developing the game?
Making the game took a really long time. It's hard to be patient, and sometimes I wished that I could play outside! But in the end, breaking a world record made me feel really happy and my family were so proud of me.

What else do you like to do for fun?
I love playing *Roblox* the most. I also like arts and crafts and have a YouTube channel called "Simars World".

With her educational videogame, Simar wanted to help kids like her learn the difference between healthy and unhealthy food. She was also keen to highlight the negative effects of eating too much junk food.

What's your No.1 tip for someone who wants to give coding a try?
If you want to start coding, just do it! It's fun. And if it's hard, don't worry... It's like riding a bike: once you learn, you never forget it.

What are your plans for the future?
I want to be a developer of games and apps. And if I get another Guinness World Records title, that would be really cool!

Find out more about GWR's amazing younger record breakers and under-16 titles at **kids.guinnessworldrecords.com**

Naemi & Alena Stump

Scrapes and bruises are inevitable when learning to skate, and such knocks can be a turn-off for many, but not for Swiss sisters Naemi and Alena Stump.

The twins began inline skating when they were eight years old, and despite many crash landings along the way, their passion was undinted. What's more, the pair also demonstrated an uncanny ability to coordinate their routines. Proving this, on 14 Oct 2023, they set two records together on a 3.9-m (12-ft 9-in) vert ramp: **most synchronized tricks on inline skates in 30 seconds** (11) and **one minute** (21).

The sisters became inspired to attempt a record after reading about Fabiola da Silva, a Brazilian inline skater who earned the **most Summer X Games gold medals (female)** – seven – in an edition of the *GWR* book. Yet they thought holding a record of their own was impossible – when Alena was just two years old, a brain tumour left her with frequent headaches and memory issues. The now 14-year-old refused to let this get in the way of her goals, which she happily achieves with her sibling right by her side.

The twins began synchronized inline skating because they wanted a hobby they could do together.

When the Stump sisters took to the vert ramp, they already had plenty of experience on skates. At just five years of age, they joined a local ice-hockey club and went on to play in national and international tournaments.

What is the secret to synchronized inline skating?
You should know each other so well that you know what the other person is doing without having to communicate. The one who is better at the trick adapts to the other.

What are your favourite skate tricks?
I [Naemi] enjoy doing barani flips and aerials; Alena prefers doing handplants and backflips.

Tell us about the training that went into your record.
We put together a sequence of tricks and practised doing them at exactly the same height and skating at exactly the same speed.

What was the biggest challenge that you faced during training?
Alena has suffered from memory problems since her brain tumour and kept forgetting the order of the tricks. So, we practised the line together for several weeks so that she could memorize the movements.

How did you feel on the day of your record attempt?
We were very nervous because we were afraid that we wouldn't make it. At the same time, we were overjoyed that we'd been given the opportunity to set a world record.

How did you celebrate becoming record breakers?
We cooked dinner for everyone who helped us with the record attempt. That way we could thank them and celebrate together.

What advice would you give to other young people hoping to achieve a Guinness World Records title?
Dare to do something that you think is impossible. Never give up and always try to better yourself.

Aside from skating, what else do you enjoy doing?
In winter, we love freestyle skiing. We're also fascinated by anything with wheels, such as skateboards, free skates and roller skates.

DJ RINOKA

DJ RINOKA captivates 100-plus clubbers on the way to achieving her first GWR title in 2023. She conducted her set using a twin-deck XDJ-Rx3 controller.

Skateboarding is another of RINOKA's passions. She's also taking hip-hop and jazz dance lessons, and enjoys drawing.

Browsing videos on YouTube doesn't tend to trigger life-changing moments. But for a four-year-old music fan from Japan, it proved to be a significant turning point...

After watching a female DJ beat-mixing online, RINOKA (b. 4 Feb 2017) set her heart on becoming a mixmaster maestro herself. One of her Christmas presents in 2022 was a DJ controller – two decks joined by a mixer – and before long her natural talent shone through. Putting those skills to the test on 9 Jul 2023, DJ RINOKA staged a solo gig at a venue in her home city of Tokyo, aged just 6 years 155 days. Unfazed by the demands of playing for more than an hour to a crowded dancefloor, her show went on to earn her acclaim as the world's **youngest female club DJ**!

DJ RINOKA now wants to go on tour and play festivals around the globe. That ambition got underway on 21 Jan 2024 when she appeared at Neon Oasis '24 in Taipei City, Taiwan, China, aged 6 years 351 days, making her the **youngest female DJ to perform at a music festival**.

Why did you start DJing?
Ever since I can remember, I've loved dancing and listening to different genres of music. One day, when I was four years old, I saw a live video of a female DJ on YouTube and decided I wanted to try DJing for myself. I was five years old when I began. I'd been asking Santa for a DDJ-200 all year long, and I received one as a gift for Christmas in Dec 2022!

How did you prepare the set for your record attempt at the club?
I searched for songs I like on my computer, made a set list and practised.

Would you like to become a professional DJ when you grow up?
I want to be a cool artist who can also DJ.

Who are your biggest inspirations in the DJ world?
I think Amelie Lens and Nina Kraviz are great.

Finally, what advice would you give to other young people who are thinking of challenging this world record?
I think they should give it a go, not only for the record, but also to entertain everyone.

The **youngest club DJ** overall is DJ Archie (UK, b. 20 Nov 2014), who was just 4 years 130 days old when he set his record in 2019. Archie now plays club gigs worldwide with his dad.

Japan is also home to the **oldest club DJ**. First recognized by GWR in 2018, Sumiko Iwamuro – aka DJ Sumirock (b. 27 Jan 1935) – was still spinning the decks at clubs in Tokyo in 2023, aged 88!

Find out more about GWR's amazing younger record breakers and under-16 titles at **kids.guinnessworldrecords.com**

Arisa Trew

The 720 – two full mid-air rotations – is one of skateboarding's rarest feats. But it's become something of a signature trick for Arisa Trew (AUS). On 24 Jun 2023, this bodacious boarder performed the **first 720 in competition (female)** in Salt Lake City, Utah, USA. She was competing at Tony Hawk's Vert Alert, a warm-up event for the Summer X Games. (Aptly, boarding legend Hawk debuted this trick back in 1985 – a quarter of a century before Arisa was born!). The following month, she pulled off another 720 in the women's vert contest at X Games in California, USA – a feat that earned her a gold medal. Aged 13 years 108 days, she is the youngest person ever to successfully execute this manoeuvre at X Games in the contest's near-30-year history (*see also below*).

Arisa says she might try the 900 (two-and-a-half rotations) one day, although right now she's focused on qualifying for the Paris 2024 Olympic Games, following the sport's debut at Tokyo 2020. Whatever the future holds, this skateboarding prodigy has already left her wheel marks on the sport.

What drew you to boarding?
I began when I was eight years old, after it became too cold for surfing one winter.

How do you fit in practice with school?
I go to the LVLUP AUS skate school. We devote three hours to education in the morning and four hours to skating in the afternoon.

How confident were you that you could nail the 720 again when it came to the X Games?
I knew that if I wanted to win I'd have to land it. In that run, I did the sketchiest body variable 540 I've ever done – my foot almost didn't come on to the board, and I nearly fell. As I came up to the trick, I just had to land it... and I did! I could hear my friends cheering and it was one of the most amazing experiences ever.

How does it feel to be a double-gold X Games winner?
It's astonishing for me, because after I won first place in vert I didn't really care how I did in park, I just wanted to get on the podium. When I won park as well, I couldn't have been happier.

What do your family and friends think of you being a record setter?
I think everyone's very shocked as well as proud of me.

Any tips for other boarders attempting ramp tricks such as the 720?
It definitely helps to be coached. I would've never been able to land it without my coach, Trevor Ward.

Tell us what you need to become a successful competitive skateboarder.
Determination, a passion for skating and – always – to get a lot of fun out of it!

A day after winning the women's vert at X Games 2023, Arisa (b. 5 Apr 2010) also nailed the park competition. At 13 years 109 days, she is the **youngest X Games double-gold medallist**.

Away from the ramp, Arisa swaps her skateboard for a surfboard when the breakers are good.

Cillian O'Connor

The world of magic is renowned for its intrigue and mystery – but if there's one thing far from secret: Cillian O'Connor (IRL) has truly got talent!

Neither young age nor autism were going to stand in the way of this determined 15-year-old conjurer. He has appeared on national and international TV, such as *Ireland AM*, *Blue Peter* and *Britain's Got Talent* (*BGT*), hosted his own TEDx talk and is an ambassador for the toy brand Marvin's Magic. Achieving his first GWR title on 26 Aug 2023 – the **most magic tricks in one minute (Under 16s)**, nailing 28 tricks – almost one every two seconds! – is just the latest feather in his cap.

In 2023, Cillian spent his summer holidays embarking on his first live tour, *My World of Magic*. He visited 14 cities and towns across the UK and Ireland, and was joined by fellow magician Ryland Petty, who starred on *BGT* in 2022.

With designs on a worldwide tour and more records, Cillian is also keen to visit schools to share his journey with autism and magic so it might inspire others.

Cillian, pictured with his sister Casey, won the hearts of the nation during his time on *Britain's Got Talent* in 2023. After his audition he received a standing ovation from the judges and the crowd. Cillian remained in the competition all the way to the final, where he came in third.

In Oct 2023, Cillian won the Marvin's Magic Rising Star Award. He accepted the trophy in Los Angeles, California, USA, while on set for *America's Got Talent: Fantasy League*.

Cillian was inspired by young magician and Britain's Got Talent 2017 runner-up, Issy Simpson.

When were you introduced to magic?
I was seven years old when I started doing magic, and the first trick I ever saw was by my Uncle Dessie. He took his thumb and appeared to split it in half and then put it back together. That scared me a lot and I ran a mile in fear that my thumb would fall off too!

How has learning magic impacted your life?
My autism was one of the main reasons why I began magic; it has allowed me to improve my social skills and be able to interact with people. When I was younger, I knew what to say, but I didn't know how to say it. Now, magic does the talking for me.

What are the biggest challenges of being a magician?
Some tricks with difficult sleight of hand are challenging for me due to my dyspraxia [a disorder that affects physical coordination]. It used to be hard for me to use my hands in general, but one Christmas, Santa got me a GANCUBE and a deck of cards, which really helped improve my condition.

What is your favourite type of magic?
My favourites are mental magic and card magic, because I prefer performing close-up tricks.

Do you have any other hobbies?
I like collecting decks of cards. I have a shelf just for that. I also enjoy chess and photography, and I'm a big fan of wrestling and football.

What advice would you give to other kids dreaming of GWR glory?
DOG, which stands for: **D**on't give up on your dreams. **O**nly you can create your story. **G**o the distance.

Find out more about GWR's amazing younger record breakers and under-16 titles at kids.guinnessworldrecords.com

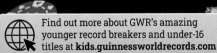

Auldin Maxwell

Auldin Maxwell's extraordinary knack for stacking Jenga blocks earned him his first record title when he was just 12. Now his story has inspired a movie! The Canadian teen, who is on the autism spectrum, says he doesn't see Jenga as just a game, but rather a tool for building all sorts of structures: "It's an engineering challenge that allows endless creativity," he enthused. Auldin currently holds two record titles, both set in Jan 2023: **most Jenga blocks stacked on one vertical Jenga block** (1,840, *inset below*), and **most Jenga GIANT blocks stacked on one vertical Jenga GIANT block** (900, *inset bottom*).

The festive Hallmark movie *A World Record Christmas* (USA, 2023) tells the story of a young autistic boy who dreams of breaking a record. His ambition brings his family and the whole town together as they turn his record attempt into a community fundraiser. "I never thought I would have been picked for a movie," Auldin told GWR. "Sometimes it feels like it's still not real!"

Beyond Jenga stacking, Auldin also loves basketball, unicycling, bowling, cubing and playing strategy crib games. In the future, he aspires to be a basketball player or an actor.

Did you take part in the movie?
I was given a cameo role – it was fantastic! The cast and crew were incredibly kind and treated me like a celebrity. A speech was given about me being the reason they were all there and everyone clapped for me. I will never forget that.

What gave you the idea of attempting a record using Jenga bricks?
I've always wanted to break a record. I had some Jenga sets, and started building different designs. I came up with stacking ideas and discovered that it was easy for me. Then I saw the record on YouTube and was determined to attempt it.

How do you train?
First, I clear my head by riding my unicycle or playing basketball with my stepdad. During the attempts, I always listen to music – it helps me concentrate. When a tower topples over or I feel like it's about to collapse, I take a break. I reset my mind and pretend that I never built that tower. It helps me to find a fresh perspective.

Was there any point during the attempts at which you felt like giving up?
When I read the official rules, I realized I had been practising the wrong way. I was stacking with three blocks in each hand, so once we applied and saw that you had to stack one block at a time, I wanted to give up. Luckily, my mum encouraged me to try the new way and I mastered it within a few weeks.

Any more records on the horizon?
I've considered trying for the **most puzzle cubes solved on a unicycle**, the **most behind-the-backboard basketball shots in one minute**, the **largest stack of bowling balls**, and of course, defending my titles to the best of my capabilities.

What is your No.1 tip for people who want to break a record?
Find an activity that suits your abilities, practise and be patient with yourself. Don't give up because dreams can come true!

A WORLD RECORD CHRISTMAS

The Big GWR Quiz

Are you a grade-A Guinness World Records geek? Put your knowledge of superlatives to the test with these 25 fiendish brainteasers!

For the latest record news, videos, games and more pop quizzes, head to the GWR Kids website via this QR!

There are more ways to arrange a deck of playing cards than there are atoms on Earth.

1. The **most magic tricks performed underwater in three minutes** is 38, by 13-year-old Avery Emerson Fisher (USA). And she couldn't even say "Abracadabra!" Dating back nearly 2,000 years, what was this Hebrew term's original purpose? **a)** To cure illness **b)** As a battle cry **c)** To welcome guests

2. The **highest-ranking penguin** is Major General Nils Olav III (*see p.57*). At just below 1 m (3 ft 3 in) tall, king penguins such as Nils are the second-largest species of this bird, but which is the largest? **a)** Gentoo **b)** Pharaoh **c)** Emperor

3. Using some 143,000 cards, 15-year-old Arnav Daga (IND) painstakingly built the **largest playing-card structure** (*see p.110*). What did Arnav do with his city of cards afterwards? **a)** He donated it to a museum **b)** He rolled over it and destroyed it **c)** He glued it all together

4. Blindfolded, Tommy Cherry (USA) solved a 3x3x3 puzzle cube in 12 sec flat in Feb 2024. Which of these Rubik's Cube facts is TRUE? **a)** After Ernő Rubik invented the puzzle in 1974, it took him a month to solve it **b)** Only geniuses with an IQ of above 150 can unscramble it **c)** There is only one method to solve the cube

5. Viswajith V from India really knows his dinosaurs: aged five, he claimed the record for the **most dinosaurs identified in one minute** – 41. Which of these is *not* a real dinosaur? **a)** *Gasosaurus* **b)** *Pukisaurus* **c)** *Bambiraptor*

6. The **fastest time to make and eat three cakes in *Minecraft*** is 27.29 sec, by Kenneth Cullen (USA). *Minecraft* is the **best-selling videogame**, but how many copies (in round numbers) had it sold as of early 2024? **a)** 100 million **b)** 300 million **c)** 500 million

7. A pooch called Daiquiri and his owner, Jennifer Fraser (*below*), love breaking records together, including a one-minute title for the **most socks removed by a dog** – 21. What breed is Daiquiri? **a)** Australian shepherd **b)** Dachshund **c)** Husky

8. Eleven-year-old McCauley Hoover (USA) holds the female one-minute records for **most skateboard backside grinds** – 34 – and **frontside grinds** – 33. In which US state did skateboarding originate? **a)** New York **b)** Florida **c)** California

9. The **most piano keys hit in 30 seconds** is 495, by teenager Keita Hattori (JPN). How many keys did Keita strike per second, on average? (No calculators allowed!) **a)** 16.5 **b)** 25 **c)** 33.5

10. Kimberly Winter (USA) let rip the **loudest burp by a woman** in Apr 2023 (*see p.78*). What is the formal name for this release of excess gas? **a)** Eructation **b)** Degassification **c)** Belchosis

11. YouTuber Airrack (USA) and fast-food favourite Pizza Hut cooked up the **largest pizza** – at 1,296.72 m² (13,957.77 sq ft), it's the size of five tennis courts! When does the earliest reference to pizza date from? **a)** 812 BCE **b)** 997 CE **c)** 1788

12. The **most goals scored in *FIFA 23* on "Legendary" difficulty** is 11, achieved by Simeone De Cesare (UK). Which country boasts the most wins of the real FIFA World Cup? **a)** Brazil **b)** Argentina **c)** England

13. Siblings Mack and Zara Rutherford (both UK/BEL) are the **youngest people to circumnavigate the world by aircraft solo**, aged 17 years 64 days and 19 years 199 days respectively. Which siblings performed the **first powered flight** in 1903? The **a)** Wrong brothers **b)** Kardashian sisters **c)** Wright brothers

14. Murata Manufacturing (JPN) created the **largest display of origami rabbits** (*see p.117*). Which of the following is FALSE? **a)** The term derives from the Japanese words *ori* ("folded") and *kami* ("paper") **b)** It was invented 30 years ago **c)** Neither scissors nor glue are allowed

15. The **largest soccer boot** (*see p.118*) was created by Muhammed D of India. What was its purpose? **a)** To be worn by the world's **tallest man** (*see pp.64–65*) **b)** As an entry in an art contest **c)** To be sold at auction

16. As of Jan 2024, MrBeast (USA) has the **most subscribers for an individual on YouTube** (*see pp.172–73*). What game was he playing in the first video he uploaded? **a)** *Minecraft* **b)** *FIFA* **c)** *Fortnite*

17. The **most Big Macs eaten in a lifetime** is 34,128, by McDonald's superfan Donald Gorske (USA). Which of these facts is FALSE? **a)** It was first named "The Aristocrat" **b)** There's a Big Mac Museum **c)** It's the company's best-seller

18. *Barbie* was 2023's **highest-grossing movie**. The iconic doll's slogan is "You Can Be Anything" – indeed, Barbie (*see pp.192–93*) has had just about every career you could imagine – but not (yet)... **a)** Flight attendant **b)** Chef **c)** Janitor

19. The **fastest time to assemble three LEGO® characters** is 13.28 sec, by Thoren Zumstein (USA). Some 340 million LEGO Minifigures are made each year, which is comparable to the population of... **a)** China **b)** New Zealand **c)** USA

20. Deb Hoffmann (USA) has the **largest collection of Winnie the Pooh memorabilia** – 23,623 items. Which animal does *not* feature in the Pooh stories? **a)** Badger **b)** Tiger **c)** Donkey

21. The **most expensive worn sneakers sold at auction** are a pair of Nike Air Jordan XIIIs owned by basketball legend Michael Jordan; they fetched $2.2 m (£1.7 m) in Apr 2023. With which NBA team did he play for most of his career? **a)** LA Lakers **b)** Boston Celtics **c)** Chicago Bulls

22. Taylor Swift (*see pp.216–17*) dominated pop in 2023. Her record-breaking 2023–24 tour was titled... **a)** *Eons* **b)** *Eras* **c)** *Speak Now*

23. As of Mar 2024, K-pop sensations BLACKPINK had the **most YouTube subscribers for a band** (93.1 million). What are their fans known as? **a)** Pinks **b)** Blinks **c)** Blanks

24. The **most goals by a footballer in a 38-game English Premier League season** is 36, scored by Erling Haaland in 2022/23. Where was he born? **a)** Oslo, Norway **b)** Dortmund, Germany **c)** Leeds, UK

25. Simone Biles (USA) has racked up the **most medals at the World Artistic Gymnastics Championships** (*see p.242*). She's a big advocate of healthy eating, but confesses to a weakness for... **a)** Cinnamon rolls **b)** Easter eggs **c)** Fortune cookies

Find the answers on p.253... Good luck!

Minecraft's Steve character is so famous that he has cameoed in other games, such as Borderlands 2.

ICON

Barbie

When a blonde-haired doll debuted at the American International Toy Fair on 9 Mar 1959, few could have guessed that they were witnessing the birth of a cultural icon.

Barbie was the creation of Ruth Handler (USA), a co-founder of toy manufacturer Mattel. Ruth noticed that the dolls her daughter Barbara played with were all infants, and that there was a gap in the market for a grown-up female doll that could be dressed in different outfits. Her vision connected with girls across America, with more than 350,000 Barbies selling in the first year alone. It is estimated that a staggering 1 billion dolls have since been purchased, at the current rate of three every second.

Over the decades, Barbie has reflected changing times and attitudes. She has had 250 careers, from Air Force pilot to baseball player. In 2016, three new body shapes were introduced – petite, tall and curvy – which led to Barbie gracing the cover of *TIME* magazine. And as the success of 2023's *Barbie* movie proves, Ruth Handler's 65-year-old doll has lost none of her ability to capture the public imagination.

1959: The very first Barbie came with a striking black-and-white bathing costume and sunshades to ensure that she stood out from other child-like dolls.

1965: Launched in a silver spacesuit, Miss Astronaut Barbie reflected women's rising aspirations and the opening up of previously male-dominated professions during the 1960s.

1961: Barbie's beau, Ken, was introduced two years after her. He was named after Ruth Handler's son. His hair was originally made of felt, which often fell off when wet.

1970: Model #1116 – Dramatic New Living Barbie – could swivel at the waist and bend at the knees and elbows. She was the first fully poseable Barbie.

VITAL STATISTICS

Full name	Barbara Millicent Roberts
Birthplace	Willows, Wisconsin, USA (but not the real Wisconsin town of Willow!)
Birth date	9 Mar 1959
Height	11.5 in (29.2 cm)
Signature colour	Barbie Pink
Current GWR title	**Best-selling doll:** 86 million dolls were shipped in 2021; estimated lifetime sales of more than 1 billion as of 2023

Ruth Handler created Barbie with the aim of empowering the dreams of young women. "My whole philosophy... was that through the doll, the little girl could be anything she wanted to be," she said.

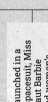

Barbie was inspired in part by Bild Lilli, a West German polystyrene doll based on a comic-strip character in the newspaper *Bild*. Handler bought several models while in Europe; Mattel would go on to buy the rights to Lilli in 1964.

Superfan Bettina Dorfmann (DEU) has held the GWR title for **the largest collection of Barbie dolls** since 2005. She received her first figurine – Barbie's friend Midge – in 1966. By Dec 2022, Bettina's collection had grown to an amazing 18,500 dolls, all of them unique.

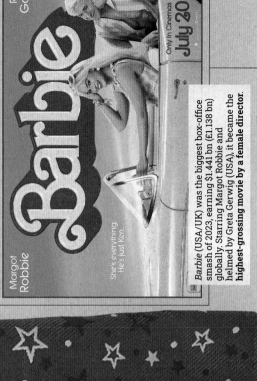

Margot Robbie

Ryan Gosling

Barbie

She's everything. He's just Ken.

Only In Cinemas
July 20

Barbie (USA/UK) was the biggest box-office smash of 2023, earning $1.441 bn (£1.138 bn) globally. Starring Margot Robbie and helmed by Greta Gerwig (USA), it became the **highest-grossing movie by a female director.**

1992: Totally Hair Barbie sold more than 10 million, making her the **best-selling Barbie doll.** She was re-released in 2017, her 25th birthday.

2017: Modelled on US Olympic fencer Ibtihaj Muhammad, this was the first doll in the range to wear a hijat. She was part of Mattel's "Shero" line.

2023: Mattel worked with the National Down Syndrome Society to release the first Barbie with Down syndrome. Her necklace has three chevrons, representing the three copies of the 21st chromosome that cause the condition.

1980: Barbie's Black friend Christie appeared in the range in 1968. But Barbie herself wasn't available as a Black doll until 12 years later. She was created by Kitty Black Perkins, Mattel's first Black designer.

2004: Barbie first ran for high office in 1992. By the 2004 US election, her Presidential doll had ditched a red-white-and-blue dress for a more modern pantsuit.

2019: The first wheelchair-using Barbie-range doll was Becky in 1997. By 2019, the Fashionistas line included Wheelchair Barbie (*left*) as well as a friend with a prosthetic leg.

 Find out more about Barbie in the ICON section at www.guinnessworldrecords.com/2025

Arts & Entertainment

CONTENTS

Charles Martinet – who voices Mario in the videogames – makes two cameo appearances in the film.

HIGHEST-GROSSING MOVIE BASED ON A VIDEOGAME

Global takings for *The Super Mario Bros. Movie* (USA, 2023) had mushroomed to $1,363,377,030 (£1.08 bn) by 17 Jan 2024, according to The Numbers. The animated fantasy, inspired by the Nintendo gaming franchise, sees the titular plumbers transported via a Warp Pipe from New York City to Mushroom World, but not all goes to plan... Once there, Mario (voiced by Chris Pratt) teams up with Princess Peach (Anya Taylor-Joy) and Toad (Keegan-Michael Key) to save the Mushroom Kingdom – as well as his brother Luigi (Charlie Day) – from the evil clutches of Bowser (Jack Black).

Despite mixed critical reviews, *The Super Mario Bros. Movie* was a smash hit with audiences, overtaking *Pokémon Detective Pikachu* (USA/JPN, 2019) just a week after its release to become the most successful videogame-inspired film in history – as well as the first of its genre to surpass the $1-bn box-office milestone.

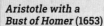

Aristotle with a Bust of Homer (1653)
- Rembrandt van Rijn (NLD)
- $2.3 m (1961)

New York's Metropolitan Museum of Art ("The Met") shelled out the unprecedented sum at auction for this oil on canvas by the Dutch master. The **most expensive painting by Rembrandt** is currently *The Standard Bearer* (1636), which was bought by the Dutch government in 2022 – *see No.7 below*.

Irises (1889)
- Vincent van Gogh (NLD)
- $53.9 m (1987)

The dramatic cropping and highly patterned textures of *Irises* are informed by the artist's interest in Japanese woodblock prints.

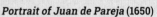

Portrait of Juan de Pareja (1650)
- Diego Velázquez (ESP)
- £2.31 m (1970)

This 17th-century work was the first painting to command more than £1 m. The buyer was, once again, the Met museum in New York.

FLASHBACK: ARTS & ENTERTAINMENT
Most Expensive Paintings

Welcome to the GWR Gallery, where we've curated a whistlestop tour of history's priciest artworks. Each of the famous masterpieces displayed here has been the **most expensive painting** in the world at one point. During the 20th century, fine art increasingly came to be seen as a lucrative investment. But trace these sales over time and you'll see that prices markedly skyrocketed from the 1980s onwards – driven partly by a global economic boom but also by more sophisticated marketing by auction houses. We've focused here on paintings that were sold in the 70 years post–1955 (when the first *GWR* book was published), largely because sales data prior to that becomes increasingly patchy.*

Below, we present the Top 20 known most expensive paintings in history, in order of increasing value.
During the 19th century, art dealers and collectors prioritized Old Masters over contemporary artworks. As this list attests, however, paintings made after 1900 now dominate the market for fine art.

- ● Old Master
- ○ Post-Impressionism
- ○ Symbolism
- ○ Expressionism
- ○ Cubism
- ○ Abstract Expressionism
- ○ 20th-century Figuration
- ● Pop Art
- ○ Xieyi

Portrait of Adele Bloch-Bauer I (1907)
- Gustav Klimt (AUT)
- $135 m (2006)

Adele Bloch-Bauer was a wealthy Viennese socialite, one of Klimt's leading patrons and, reputedly, the only model that he painted twice (*see also No.16 below*). Incorporating gold and silver leaf, this richly decorative painting typifies the artist's "Golden Phase" (1901–09).

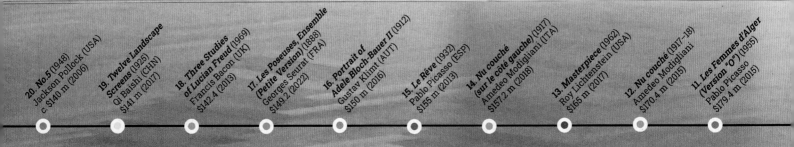

20. *No.5* (1948)
Jackson Pollock (USA)
c. $140 m (2006)

19. *Twelve Landscape Screens* (1925)
Qi Baishi (CHN)
$141 m (2017)

18. *Three Studies of Lucian Freud* (1969)
Francis Bacon (UK)
$142.4 (2013)

17. *Les Poseuses, Ensemble (Petite Version)* (1888)
Georges Seurat (FRA)
$149.2 (2022)

16. *Portrait of Adele Bloch-Bauer II* (1912)
Gustav Klimt (AUT)
$150 m (2016)

15. *Le Rêve* (1932)
Pablo Picasso (ESP)
$155 m (2013)

14. *Nu couché (sur le côté gauche)* (1917)
Amedeo Modigliani (ITA)
$157.2 m (2018)

13. *Masterpiece* (1962)
Roy Lichtenstein (USA)
$165 m (2017)

12. *Nu couché* (1917–18)
Amedeo Modigliani
$170.4 m (2015)

11. *Les Femmes d'Alger (Version "O")* (1955)
Pablo Picasso
$179.4 m (2015)

Bal du moulin de la Galette (1876)
· **Pierre-Auguste Renoir (FRA)**
· **$78.1 m (1990)**
Renoir's iconic Impressionist work depicts a dance garden in Montmartre, Paris. It was purchased by high-end art collector Ryoei Saito.

Portrait of Dr Gachet (1890)
· **Vincent van Gogh**
· **$82.5 m (1990)**
This is the first of two portraits that van Gogh painted of Dr Paul Gachet, who cared for him in his final months. The troubled artist made little money from his work during his life. But posthumously – and thanks largely to the industrious efforts of his brother's widow – his canvases became highly prized. The **most expensive painting by van Gogh** is now *Orchard with Cypresses* (1888), which sold for $117.1 m in 2022.

Boy with a Pipe (1905)
· **Pablo Picasso (ESP)**
· **$104.1 m (2004)**
The artist created this artwork during his "Rose" period. The term refers to his choice of warm colours, such as oranges and pinks. The **most expensive Picasso painting** (*see No.11 below*) sold in 2015.

The Card Players (1890–95)
· **Paul Cézanne (FRA)**
· *c.* **$250 m (2011)**
This remains the **most expensive painting by Cézanne**. The artist's *Curtain, Jug and Fruit Bowl* (1894), which realized $60.5 m at auction in 1999, is the **most expensive still-life painting**.

Interchanged (1955)
· **Willem de Kooning (USA, b. NLD)**
· *c.* **$300 m (2015)**
Not long after finishing this piece, Abstract Expressionist de Kooning sold the work for the modest sum of $4,000. Today, it is the **most expensive 20th-century painting**.

Salvator Mundi (*c.* 1500)
· **Leonardo da Vinci (ITA)**
· **$450.3 m (2017)**
Depicting Christ making the sign of the cross, history's **most expensive painting** was deemed lost for many years. Even after its rediscovery, it was first thought to be a copy. Extensive cleaning and restoration were required before the piece was offered for sale by Christie's in 2017. It is reported to have been purchased by the Saudi royal family. Prior to this sale, it was sold at an online auction for a far more modest $1,175!

* Paintings not to scale. All prices, including those from auctions or private sales, based on the most recent available public data, as of publication

10. Water Serpents II (1907)
Gustav Klimt
$183.8 m (2012)

9. No.6 (Violet, Green and Red) (1951)
Mark Rothko (USA)
$186 m (2014)

8. Shot Sage Blue Marilyn (1964)
Andy Warhol (USA)
$195 m (2022)

7. The Standard Bearer (1636)
Rembrandt van Rijn (NLD)
$198 m (2022)

6. No.17A (1948)
Jackson Pollock
$200 m (2015)

5. When Will You Marry? (1892)
Paul Gauguin (FRA)
$210 m (2015)

4. Marilyn Monroe (Orange) (1964)
Andy Warhol
$200–$250 m (2018)

3. The Card Players (1890–95)
Paul Cézanne (FRA)
c. $250 m (2011)

2. Interchanged (1955)
Willem de Kooning (USA, b. NLD)
c. $300 m (2015)

1. Salvator Mundi (*c.* 1500)
Leonardo da Vinci (ITA)
$450.3 m (2017)

Influencers

Most Instagram followers

Portuguese soccer star Cristiano Ronaldo has an Insta fanbase of 621,979,902 – almost twice the population of the USA. Ronaldo currently has 120 million followers more than the site's next-most-popular user – his great on-field rival, Lionel Messi (ARG). Messi can, however, boast the **most liked Instagram image** – a photo of him holding aloft the FIFA World Cup in 2022 (*below*), which received 75,504,160 hearts.

Most YouTube subscribers for an individual female

Diana Kidisyuk (USA, b. UKR) has amassed 118 million subscribers for her channel, "Kids Diana Show". The 10-year-old, who is often joined by her brother Roma, specializes in unboxing, roleplaying and children's songs. She has also starred in the series *Love, Diana*, alongside a host of animated characters. *For YouTube's **most subscribed contributor overall**, see pp.172–73.*

In Aug 2023, Khaby Lame appeared as an "Icon series" skin in *Fortnite Battle Royale*.

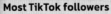

Most TikTok followers

Italian influencer Khabane "Khaby" Lame (*right*) has 161.5 million fans on the short-form video platform. The Senegalese-born performer – famed for his wordless lampoons of life-hack videos – became TikTok's most popular creator on 22 Jun 2022, overtaking US dancer and influencer Charli D'Amelio (*left*). Charli retains the **female** record, with 152 million followers. She is also the **most liked TikTok user**, having received 11.5 billion hearts for her posts.

All figures correct as of 4 Mar 2024

Most X followers

Elon Musk (USA, b. ZAF) has a total of 173,149,588 followers on the platform formerly known as Twitter – the site he bought on 27 Oct 2022. The tech billionaire boasts 40 million more fans than the second-most-popular figure, former US president Barack Obama. More than 40% of Musk's following were accrued in the wake of his purchase of X. His activity on the network frequently ignites controversy, but he continues to maintain the account himself and posts up to 30 times a day.

Most followed woman on X

Rihanna (BRB, b. Robyn Rihanna Fenty) has found love on the social-media site X, earning herself a following of 108,167,892. The Barbadian singer and entrepreneur overtook Katy Perry in Apr 2023 to take the women's No.1 spot. It was the first time this record had changed hands since Perry claimed it in 2013. Rihanna hit the headlines in 2023 with her dazzling half-time performance at Super Bowl LVII, while pregnant with her second son, Riot. More than 120 million viewers tuned in to watch her.

Highest concurrent peak viewership on Twitch

On 1 Jul 2023, a total of 3,442,725 simultaneous viewers watched *La Velada del Año 3*, a live boxing event streamed by esports personality Ibai Llanos (ESP; *left*). Ibai, who began his career commentating on *League of Legends* matches, has become a highly influential streamer, attracting interviews with music superstars such as Bad Bunny (*see p.203*) and Ed Sheeran.

The **most followed woman on Twitch** is Canada's Pokimane (b. Imane Anys, *right*), with 9,332,274 fans. In Jan 2024, she made the shock announcement that she was leaving Twitch for YouTube, but her old account and its archived streams remains active and popular.

Gaming

First player to reach the *Tetris* killscreen
On 21 Dec 2023, Blue Scuti (aka Willis Gibson, USA) reached Level 157 of the classic NES puzzler – triggering a "killscreen" (i.e., the point at which the game crashes). The 13-year-old played for 38 min, racking up 6,850,560 points before the game froze. Skills such as hypertapping and rolling have allowed gamers to go far beyond Level 29, long thought to be *Tetris*'s upper limit.

Best-selling FPS series
The *Call of Duty* franchise has sold more than 400 million copies, according to its publisher Activision–Blizzard (USA). There have been 20 main titles in the series since the release of the original *Call of Duty* in 2003, expanding beyond its World War II setting to include Cold War spycraft and sci-fi battlefields. The most recent title, 2023's *Call of Duty: Modern Warfare III*, sees Task Force 141 trying to stop World War III from breaking out.

Largest Game Boy Color
In 2022, YouTuber Nick Carlini (USA) created a working version of the classic Nintendo handheld fit for a giant, measuring 7 ft 4 in tall, 4 ft 1 in wide and 2 ft deep (2.23 x 1.24 x 0.6 m). Carlini ran Game Boy emulators on a PC inside the wooden cabinet and used an Xbox adaptive controller to link to the plus-size buttons.

GWR Gamer's Edition 2025
The *GWR Gamer's Edition* is BACK! We've rebooted our chronicle of videogaming superlatives and now it's bigger and brighter than ever. Join us for a countdown of the 100 most significant GWR record categories in gaming – the biggest-selling and most critically acclaimed titles, the highest scores and the fastest speedruns. We profile decorated esports champions, dedicated collectors and cosplayers. From Activision to *Zelda*, we've got it covered. Which gaming record do YOU think will come in at No.1?

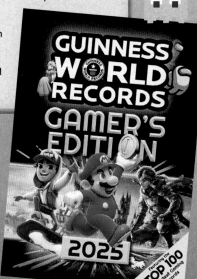

Largest user-generated content platform

Released in 2006, *Roblox* is a videogame environment that provides players with tools that allow them to create their own games (referred to as "Experiences"). These completed games can then be made available to all players. On 13 Aug 2023, *Roblox* reported an average of 70.2 million daily active users.

Fastest-selling *Legend of Zelda* videogame

Following its release on 12 May 2023, Nintendo's *The Legend of Zelda: Tears of the Kingdom* shifted 10 million copies in three days – about 40 every second! The epic open-world adventure across the lands and skies of Hyrule had sold more than 30 million units by the end of the year, making it one of the five best-selling titles in the history of the Nintendo Switch.

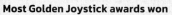

Best-selling videogame

Sales of *Minecraft* have surpassed 300 million, as confirmed by publisher Microsoft on 15 Oct 2023. Originally coded by Markus "Notch" Persson, who released an "alpha" build on 17 May 2009, the sandbox game has built up a devoted following. In 2023, *Minecraft* fans celebrated the release of a *Trails & Tales* update and action-strategy spin-off *Minecraft Legends* (*left*).

First dog to complete a videogame speedrun

On 13 Jul 2023, gamer "JSR_" uploaded a video of his Shiba Inu, Peanut Butter, speedrunning the 1985 NES platformer *Gyromite*. Using his paws to press oversize buttons on a custom controller, Peanut Butter guided the sleepwalking Professor Hector to the end of the game in 25 min 29 sec. He repeated the feat for charity at Awesome Games Done Quick 2024.

Most Golden Joystick awards won

Baldur's Gate 3 (Larian Studios, 2023) triumphed in seven categories – including Ultimate Game of the Year – at the 2023 UK videogame awards. The RPG, set in the world of tabletop fantasy *Dungeons & Dragons*, has been a critical and commercial smash. In Dec 2023, just four months after its release, Larian revealed that gamers had spent 452,556,984 hr – or 51,662 years – inside the Forgotten Realms.

Music

Most No.1s on The Official MENA chart

BTS's Jung Kook (KOR) has scored three solo No.1 hits on the Middle East and North Africa (MENA) listings, which launched in Nov 2022. Each track topped the chart for two weeks, the most recent being "Standing Next to You" in Nov 2023.

Most Best Metal Performance Grammys

On 4 Feb 2024, Metallica (USA) secured their seventh gong in this category at the 66th Grammy Awards, for "72 Seasons", the title track of their 11th studio set. Founded in 1981 by Lars Ulrich (drummer) and James Hetfield (singer/guitarist), the heavy-metal band have sold 125 million-plus albums.

Longest span of UK No.1 singles

"Now and Then" – dubbed "the last song" by The Beatles (UK) – became their 18th UK chart-topper on 16 Nov 2023, a full 60 years 198 days after their first No.1, "From Me to You", on 2 May 1963.

Prior to "Now and Then", the band had last hit the top on 25 Jun 1969 with "The Ballad of John and Yoko" – the **longest gap between UK No.1 singles**, at 54 years 144 days.

Longest *Billboard* Hot 100 entry

Clocking in at 12 min 20 sec, "I Swear, I Really Wanted to Make a 'Rap' Album but This Is Literally the Way the Wind Blew Me This Time" hit No.90 on the US singles chart on 2 Dec 2023. It was the first single from OutKast star André 3000's (USA, b. André Benjamin) ambient jazz flute album *New Blue Sun*.

Most consecutive years with a Japanese No.1 single

Between 1997 and 2024, the J-pop duo KinKi Kids (Koichi and Tsuyoshi Domoto) scored at least one No.1 hit per year. Their latest chart-topper was "Schrödinger" on 8 Jan 2024.

Most simultaneous new entries on the *Billboard* Hot 100

Country superstar Morgan Wallen (USA) had no less than 27 new entries (plus three re-entries) on the Hot 100 on 18 Mar 2023. His highest debut came with "Thinkin' Bout Me" (No.9). On the same date, Wallen's hit-packed third studio album – *One Thing at a Time* – debuted at No.1 on the *Billboard* 200.

Most "seismic" music concert

Taylor Swift's (USA, *see pp.216–17*) unprecedented *Eras Tour* has generated shockwaves – literally. Her two shows at Lumen Field in Seattle, Washington, USA, on 22–23 Jul 2023 produced the equivalent of a 2.3-magnitude earthquake. In all, 144,000 "Swifties" attended the double-header, with seismologists attributing the activity to crowd noise and the sound system.

Most wins of the Eurovision Song Contest by a performer

Loreen (SWE, b. Lorine Talhaoui) triumphed at Eurovision for a second time on 13 May 2023, with her dance-pop song "Tattoo". She had previously won with "Euphoria" in 2012. The only other two-time winner to date is Ireland's Johnny Logan (b. Seán Sherrard, AUS) with "What's Another Year" (1980) and "Hold Me Now" (1987).

Oldest Best New Artist Grammy

Aged 34 years 279 days, Victoria Monét (USA, b. 1 May 1989) was named Best New Artist at the 66th Grammys in 2024. Her debut studio set *Jaguar II* (2023) also picked up trophies for Best R&B Album and Best Engineered Album, Non-Classical.

On 10 Nov 2023, Monét's daughter, Hazel, became the **youngest Grammy nominee** – at just 2 years 262 days – for contributing to her song "Hollywood".

Most BRIT awards won in a single year

Multi-genre artist RAYE (b. Rachel Keen, UK) took home six trophies at the 2024 BRIT Awards in London on 2 Mar. The singer-songwriter won British Album of the Year (*My 21st Century Blues*), Song of the Year ("Escapism.", feat. 070 Shake), Artist of the Year, Best R&B Act, Best New Artist and Songwriter of the Year. Prior to the event, RAYE had racked up the **most BRIT Awards nominations in a single year** – seven: her track "Prada", feat. cassö & D-Block Europe, had also received a nod for Song of the Year.

Bad Bunny's stage name was inspired by a photo of him as a boy, scowling in a rabbit outfit that he was forced to wear to school.

SPOTIFY'S STREAMING LEADERBOARD

Record	Streams	Name
Track (male)	4.08 bn	"Blinding Lights", The Weeknd (CAN)
Track (female)	2.99 bn	"Dance Monkey", Tones and I (AUS)
Track (group/duo)	2.96 bn	"STAY", The Kid LAROI (AUS) and Justin Bieber (CAN)
Album (male)	15.73 bn	*Un Verano Sin Ti*, Bad Bunny (PRI)
Album (female)	11.95 bn	*Dua Lipa*, Dua Lipa (UK/ALB)
Album (group/duo)	8.73 bn	*AM*, Arctic Monkeys (UK)
Act (male)	94.50 bn	Drake (CAN)
Act (female)	73.07 bn	Taylor Swift (USA)
Act (group/duo)	38.08 bn	BTS (KOR)

Total cumulative streams, correct as of 24 Feb 2024

MOST STREAMED ALBUM ON SPOTIFY

The all-time most listened-to album on Spotify is 2022's *Un Verano Sin Ti* ("A Summer Without You") by Puerto Rican rapper Bad Bunny (b. Benito Ocasio), which had amassed 15,738,250,533 plays by 24 Feb 2024. Six of its tracks have individually topped the 1-billion mark.

Un Verano Sin Ti was Spotify's **most streamed album** for two years in a row (2022–23), amassing 4.5 billion plays in 2023 alone. It has also collected many awards and nominations, including the **first Album of the Year Grammy nomination for a Spanish-language album**, and at the 65th Grammy Awards in 2023 it was named Best Música Urbana Album (*below, with R&B star SZA*).

Also known as the "King of Latin Trap", Bad Bunny was Spotify's **most streamed annual act** for three years running (2020–22). And he went one better at the 2023 Billboard Latin Music Awards, extending his record for the **most consecutive Artist of the Year wins** to four.

A lifelong aficionado of pro wrestling, Bad Bunny has hopped from fan to fighter in recent years. In 2021, he formed a tag team with superstar wrestler Damian Priest, winning the World Wrestling Entertainment (WWE) 24/7 Championship. The two allies turned rivals at 2023's WWE Backlash (*above*), however, in a frenetic street fight that spilled over from ring to ringside – with the chart-topping singer eventually defeating Priest thanks to his signature move, the "Bunny Destroyer".

Breaking

Together with DJing, MCing and graffiti, breaking is one of the founding elements of hip-hop culture. It originated in the 1970s in the Bronx borough of New York City, USA, where dancers would improvise routines during instrumental sections of tracks known as "breaks". Using two turntables, pioneering DJs such as Kool Herc began mixing songs to extend the breaks, allowing the artform to flourish. Now breaking is firmly part of mainstream culture and has found acceptance as a competitive dancesport. In 2024, breaking made its debut as an Olympic sport in Paris.

Most B-Boy titles at Red Bull BC One

On 21 Oct 2023, Hong 10 (aka Kim Hong-yul, KOR) claimed his third overall victory at the global one-on-one breaking contest. The veteran B-Boy, who was aged 39, took the honours at Stade Roland Garros in Paris, France, having notched up previous wins in 2006 and 2013. Hong 10 matched the feat of Menno (NLD, b. Menno van Gorp) in 2014, 2017 and 2019.

The record for the **B-Girl** competition, first held in 2018, is two – by Kastet (aka Natasha Kiliachikhina, RUS) in 2019–20, and Ami (JPN, *see opposite*) in 2018 and 2023.

Longest head slide

Breaking champion Michele Gagno (ITA) slid 2.6 m (8 ft 6 in) across the floor on his head for the *La Notte dei Record* TV show in Rome, Italy, on 24 Nov 2018.

Most windmills in 30 seconds

Originally credited to Crazy Legs of hip-hop trailblazers the Rock Steady Crew, the windmill is an iconic move that sees dancers roll across the floor on their back and upper torso while twirling their legs in the air. On 10 Oct 2010, B-Boy Cico (aka Mauro Peruzzi, ITA) performed 50 windmills in half a minute at the World Finals of the UK B-Boy Championships in London.

The next day, Cico pulled off the **most consecutive aerials** – six acrobatic spins.

Most consecutive elbow hops

Ashitaka (aka Takahiro Igarashi, JPN) thrust himself into the air off his elbow 187 times on 24 Nov 2016 in Tokyo, Japan. He almost trebled the previous highest total. The Japanese B-Boy set two records in one day, along with the **most consecutive one-hand jumps** – 139.

Most jackhammer hops in 30 seconds (female)

On 24 Feb 2024, B-Girl Solid (aka Giovanna Fontana, ITA) completed 25 jackhammer hops – pushing herself into the air on one hand while rotating her body – in London, UK. B-Girl Solid practises for up to six days a week. "We train as athletes but we dance as artists," she says.

Most kip-ups in 30 seconds

On 6 Mar 2023, Noman Mehsood (PAK) flipped himself up from a supine position to his feet 32 times in half a minute in Dera Ismail Khan, Pakistan. Noman also holds the **one-minute** record of 52, which he set on 12 Dec 2020.

The **most no-handed kip-ups in one minute** is 43, by Daniyal Mehsood (PAK), also in Dera Ismail Khan, on 2 Jul 2021.

Youngest winner of Red Bull BC One

Logistx (aka Logan Edra, USA, b. 8 May 2003) was 18 years 182 days old when she won the B-Girl title on 6 Nov 2021 in Gdańsk, Poland. She defeated Vavi in the final, aged 80 days younger than 2020's B-Boy champion, Shigekix. Logistx was given her B-Girl moniker by her father. She won competitions in Philadelphia, USA, and Singapore before becoming the third Red Bull BC One B-Girl champion.

Most crew wins of the Battle of the Year

First held in 1990, the Battle of the Year (BOTY) is an international breaking competition. Crews take part in a showcase round before four are selected for a head-to-head battle play-off. A trio of crews have won three times: Vagabonds (FRA) in 2006 and 2011–12; The Floorriorz (JPN) in 2015–17; and Jinjo Crew (KOR, *right*) in 2010, 2018 and 2021.

Victor's signature moves include a backflip flare and the "Super Montalvo", a one-handed spin.

MOST B-BOY TITLES AT THE WDSF WORLD BREAKING CHAMPIONSHIP

On 24 Sep 2023, Victor (aka Victor Montalvo, USA) became the first two-time B-Boy champion at the World DanceSport Federation event. A previous winner in 2021, he defeated defending champion Phil Wizard (aka Philip Kim) 2–1 in the final battle in Leuven, Belgium. This also earned Victor a place on Team USA for breaking's Olympic debut at Paris 2024. He was introduced to breaking aged six by his father and uncle – Mexican breaking pioneers Victor and Hector Bermudez. He is also a two-time winner of Red Bull BC One (*see opposite*), taking home the trophy in 2015 and 2022.

Most B-Girl titles at the WDSF World Breaking Championship

Ami (aka Ami Yuasa, JPN) has won this global dancesport competition twice. She earned her second title at the 2022 tournament in Seoul, South Korea, defeating China's B-Girl 671 (aka Qingyi Liu) in the final battle on 22 Oct. Famed for her smooth flow and power moves, Ami became Red Bull BC One's first-ever B-Girl champion in 2018. Her elder sister, Ayu, is also a B-Girl.

Movie Costumes

Most expensive wardrobe for a movie
A reported $10 m (£6.9 m) was spent on lavish designer wardrobes for the stars of *Sex and the City 2* (USA, 2010). Each of its four main characters routinely appears dressed in the latest couture. Journalists counted 41 costume changes for Carrie Bradshaw (played by Sarah Jessica Parker, *second from right*) alone, with one outfit costing around $230,000 (£160,000).

Most costumes used in a movie
The historical epic *Quo Vadis* (USA, 1951) featured 32,000 costumes, many made for its 30,000 extras. They included 15,000 hand-sewn sandals and 12,000 pieces of bespoke jewellery. Subsequently, some 15,000 outfits were sent to studio MGM's costume warehouse, and were reused for decades in movies set in the ancient world.

First credited movie costume designer
Helen Gardner (USA) and a creative known as "Madame Stippange" both appear in the opening credits of *Cleopatra* (USA, 1912). Actor/producer Gardner designed her own outfits for the title role, while Stippange made costumes for the rest of the cast. It's not clear who Madame Stippange was, as the name is unique to the credits of this film, which was one of the first feature-length movies made in the USA.

First fashion movie
Released on 10 Feb 1910, *Fifty Years of Paris Fashions 1859–1909* was a silent short film by Gaumont (UK) that presented a series of tableaux featuring stylish designs from the past. The film ran for approximately 7 min. Such output proved popular with female audiences and soon newsreel companies were producing their own versions, usually showcasing the latest trends in Paris or London.

Most fabric used in a movie costume (including multiples)
Eight copies, known as "multiples", were made of the ball gown worn by Lily James in Disney's live-action remake of *Cinderella* (USA, 2015). Each one incorporated 273 yards (250 m) of fabric, for a total of 2,184 yards (1,997 m) – enough to cover half a soccer pitch! The multiples were needed for the large amount of screen time that featured the dress, and included a subtly shortened version for when Cinderella runs from the ball at midnight.

24 Dec 2023. Her work has appeared in a string of blockbusters including *Harry Potter and the Philosopher's Stone* (UK/USA, 2001), *The Hunger Games* (USA, 2012) and *Avengers: Endgame* (USA, 2019).

Heaviest movie costume
Adrian Greenburg (usually credited under the mononym "Adrian") designed a dress that weighed 110 lb (49.9 kg) for the wedding scene in the period drama *Marie Antoinette* (USA, 1938). Modelled on those worn at the court of France's King Louis XVI, it consisted of steel-frame crinoline, 10 petticoats and 500 yards (457 m) of white silk satin fabric – hand-embroidered with silver-thread fleurs-de-lis and edged with seed-pearl beads. Lead actress Norma Shearer reportedly weighed less than her clothes when she filmed this scene.

Highest-grossing costume designer at the global box office
According to The Numbers, the 24 movies in which Judianna Makovsky (USA) served as costume designer had generated $12,175,907,030 (£9.57 bn) as of

Oldest costume house
Angels Costumes (UK) first opened its doors in 1840. The company supplies costumes for movie, television and theatrical productions, and has more than 5 million pieces stored in a facility in north-west London, UK. It is now run by the seventh-generation descendants of Angels founder Daniel Angel, a tailor who arrived in London from Frankfurt, Germany, in 1813.

Most costume changes in a movie by one character
Robert De Niro underwent 102 wardrobe changes for his role as Frank Sheeran in the epic gangster film *The Irishman* (USA, 2019). The costumes were designed by Sandy Powell and Christopher Peterson. Powell described the film as a "challenging project on every level". The story spans a period from the 1950s to 2003 and required painstakingly researched attire for not only the lead, but also numerous supporting characters and extras.

MOST CREDITED COSTUME DESIGNER

Edith Head (USA) oversaw the wardrobe departments on 432 Hollywood productions between 1925 and 1982, in addition to her 111 earlier credits as a costumer and assistant. During her long career, she designed for almost every leading actress and amassed the **most Oscar nominations (female)** and **wins (female)** – 35 and eight, respectively. Head's sleek hairstyle and glasses made the designer as visually distinctive as many of the stars she dressed (*see below*), and she is thought to have inspired the character of *The Incredibles'* Edna "E" Mode (*far right*).

Edith Head (1897–1981)

For Grace Kelly's stylish character in <u>Rear Window</u> (1954), Head created chic designs including a "New Look" style fitted black bodice and a chiffon-tulle skirt.

Head designed a parrot-green outfit for Tippi Hedren in Alfred Hitchcock's thriller <u>The Birds</u> (1963). Hedren wore the same costume for much of the film, and recalled that Head opted for a muted colour choice "so people would not be sick of looking at me in it".

Head's costumes for Audrey Hepburn in <u>Roman Holiday</u> (1953), which ranged from chic streetwear to high-glamour ball gowns, are credited with propelling the young actress into superstardom. The film earned an Oscar for both Head and Audrey.

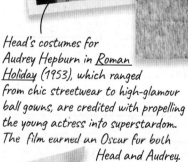

Most costly movie costume
Several famous outfits have been described as the "most expensive ever made", but the most credible candidate is a fur-trimmed sequinned showgirl ensemble created by Edith Head for Ginger Rogers in <u>Lady in the Dark</u> (1944). Two versions of this dress were made – a "hero costume", for static close-ups, and a lighter "multiple" for dancing – at a total cost of $35,000 (£8,660). This sum is equivalent to $620,000 (£491,400) in 2023 when adjusted for inflation.

Her work on <u>The Sting</u> (1973) – which included standout period suits for Robert Redford (*pictured*) and Paul Newman – won Head her eighth and final Oscar.

213

Round-Up

Longest dance marathon

Srushti Sudhir Jagtap (IND) danced for 127 hr at Dayanand College in Latur, Maharashtra, India, from 29 May to 3 Jun 2023. The 16-year-old student performed mostly Kathak, one of the eight major forms of classical Indian dance. Srushti, who was allowed 5 min of rest for every hour of activity, utilized "yogic sleep" to help keep her going across the five days.

Largest gathering of people dressed as Dolly Parton

On 24 Jun 2023, the town of Listowel in County Kerry, Ireland, held a charity fundraiser that saw 959 people imitate the iconic "9 to 5" country singer. Blond wigs and high heels were de rigueur for "Dollyday", and there was line-dancing through the town's streets, which were decked in American flags.

Highest annual earnings for a film actor (current year)

Adam Sandler (USA) made an estimated $73 m (£57.3 m) in 2023, according to *Forbes*. The actor and stand-up comedian had an exclusive deal with Netflix, for whom he produced four movies in 2023, including *The Out-Laws*, *Murder Mystery 2* and the animated *Leo*.

The **highest-earning actress** of 2023 was Margot Robbie (AUS), whose $59 m (£46.3 m) placed her second on the list behind Sandler. At 33, the *Barbie* star (*see pp.192–93*) was the youngest actor on *Forbes*'s Top 10 by a decade.

Most films seen at the cinema in one year

Between 5 Jul 2022 and 30 Jun 2023, Zachariah Swope (USA) watched 777 movies in Harrisburg, Pennsylvania, USA. He patronized a total of five theatres and did not eat or drink during any of the screenings, as stipulated in the guidelines. Zachariah's favourite during his filmathon was *Spider-Man: Across the Spider-Verse* (USA, 2023).

Deepest underwater model photoshoot

On 5 Dec 2023, model Kim Bruneau (CAN) posed for a series of shots at a depth of 40.2 m (131 ft) off Nassau in The Bahamas. Kim, a trained freediver, used scuba gear to descend to the shipwreck of the *Sea Trader*. She then removed her mask for each shot, with a weight belt hidden beneath her ballerina dress. The photographer was Pia Oyarzún (CHL).

Fastest music track to reach 1 billion streams on Spotify

The "explicit version" of "Seven" by Jung Kook (KOR) feat. Latto (USA, b. Alyssa Stephens) was streamed for the billionth time on Spotify on its 109th day of availability, 30 Oct 2023.

Most Nickelodeon Kids' Choice Awards blimps won by a cartoon

Marking its 25th year in 2024, *SpongeBob SquarePants* (Nickelodeon, USA) was voted Favorite Cartoon/Animated Series by viewers on 20 occasions between 2003 and 2023.

Largest collection of...

• **Ariana Grande memorabilia**: 1,609 items, by Lucien Musolino (CHE) as of 9 Jul 2023.
• **Elvis Presley memorabilia**: 1,848 items, by Constante Firme (USA) as of 17 May 2023.
• **KISS memorabilia**: 3,799 items, by LaVern Simon (USA) as of 8 Apr 2023.

Smallest bookshop

Sowa Delight (JPN) has a floor space of just 1.246 m² (13.41 sq ft), as verified on 23 Dec 2023. Located in Maebashi, Gunma, Japan, the children's book store was intentionally scaled for younger readers, in order to discourage grown-ups from interrupting them while they browse.

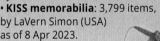

Most northerly concert

On 20 Jun 2023, Louis Jarto (DNK) staged a surprise gig at Station Nord in Greenland – a military facility some 1,700 km (1,060 mi) north of the Arctic Circle, at 81.60°N. His audience numbered five (the station's entire staff). Louis specializes in "random concerts", and aims one day to make the bill at the legendary Roskilde music festival.

Most expensive *Spider-Man* comic

On 11 Jan 2024, a near-mint copy of *The Amazing Spider-Man* #1 was sold by Heritage Auctions (USA) for $1.38 m (£1.08 m). First published in Mar 1963 – for a cover price of just 12 cents – it marked the launch of the superhero in his own title, and included a team-up with the Fantastic Four.

Best-selling PlayStation 5-exclusive videogame

Marvel's *Spider-Man 2* (Insomniac Games, 2023) sold 2.5 million copies within its first 24 hr of release on 20 Oct 2023. The third instalment in the *Spider-Man* series sees webbed wonders Peter Parker and Miles Morales take on a panoply of villains, including Venom and The Flame. It has since gone on to top sales of 10 million.

Youngest female artist to chart on the *Billboard* Hot 100

Rumi Carter (USA, b. 13 Jun 2017) was 6 years 305 days old on 13 Apr 2024, when she debuted at No.42 on the Hot 100 – alongside her mother Beyoncé – with "Protector" from *Cowboy Carter*.

Fastest-selling non-fiction book

Prince Harry's (UK) memoir *Spare* shifted 1,430,000 copies on 10 Jan 2023, its first day of release. The headline-grabbing autobiography smashed the previous record of 887,000, for Barack Obama's *A Promised Land* (2020).

Longest videogame marathon playing...

• **An MMORPG**: 59 hr 20 min 12 sec, by Barñabás Vujity-Zsolnay (HUN) on *World of Warcraft* in Budapest, Hungary, on 26–28 Sep 2022.
• **A racing game**: 90 hr, by GrassHopper (aka Szabolcs Csépe, HUN) on *Gran Turismo 7* in Kecskemét, Hungary, on 29 Jun–3 Jul 2023.
• **A virtual-reality game**: 50 hr, by Robin Schmidt (NLD) of the "Based AF" channel, playing *Minecraft* in Voorschoten, Netherlands, on 18–20 Oct 2023.

Youngest double Oscar winner

Billie Eilish (USA, b. 18 Dec 2001) claimed her second Academy Award at the age of 22 years 83 days on 10 Mar 2024. She won Best Original Song as the co-composer (with her brother FINNEAS) of *Barbie*'s "What Was I Made For?"

Most people doing the baby shark dance

On 5 May 2023, the Sugarloaf School in Florida, USA, celebrated the opening of their new elementary wing by performing the online dance craze with 887 participants. Students, teachers and even local law enforcement joined in the fun, organized by Ajax Building Company (USA).

Longest underwater video livestream

On 16 Oct 2023, a subaquatic broadcast lasting 5 hr 44 min 30 sec took place at Ripley's Aquarium of Canada in Toronto. It featured segments led by divers on the attraction's animal residents and interactive quizzes with viewers.

Largest chalk street art by one artist

On 3 Oct 2023, Preeti Gundapwar (USA, *circled above*) completed a 226.50-m² (2,438-sq-ft) artwork in a cul-de-sac in South Windsor, Connecticut, USA. The depiction of the Northern Lights took three days to draw and required 500 sticks of chalk and three pairs of gloves. Preeti said that her picture reflects her love for the natural world.

Youngest radio broadcast presenter

Amatullah Hamid (PAK, b. 4 Feb 2018) hosts *The Amatullah Show* weekly on VOK FM 105.8 in Rawalakot, Pakistan. She was aged 4 years 69 days when the segment launched on 14 Apr 2022. Her career began at the age of two, when she was invited on-air by Hassan Hamid (PAK, b. 8 Apr 2015), who holds the **male** record at 4 years 70 days. Amatullah covers science, social education, stories and poems on her show.

ICON

Some lyrics and melodies come to Swift in her dreams, including those for 1989's "All You Had To Do Was Stay".

Taylor Swift

She's been described as the "biggest pop star in the world" – and when it comes to her superlative "reputation", it's not hard to see why. Since her debut, Taylor has amassed 114 million album sales, dominated at awards ceremonies and embarked on six global concert tours, including the ongoing *Eras*, which became the **highest-grossing music tour of all time** in late 2023, with unprecedented takings already in excess of $1 bn (£840 m).

From an early age, Taylor's passion for music shone through. Her own icons were country stars such as Loretta Lynn and Dolly Parton and, fittingly, her career started in Nashville. Since the release of *Fearless* in 2008, all 14 of her albums have entered at the top – the **most debuts at No.1 on the US albums chart** – a title now shared only with US rapper Jay-Z and a testament to the devotion of her "Swiftie" fans. She was also the **first act to debut at 1–10 simultaneously on the US Hot 100**, with a full sweep of 10 tracks from *Midnights* on 5 Nov 2022; this was matched by her latest release, *The Tortured Poets Department*, on 4 May 2024.

With a trophy collection numbering in the hundreds, Taylor has clearly captured the hearts of critics as much as those of her vast fanbase. To date, her haul includes gongs from the Grammys (14), American Music Awards (40, *see below left*), MTV Video Music Awards (23) and the Teen Choice Awards (26, the **most won by an individual**).

Taylor is known for her often fanfare-free philanthropy, lending her support (in the form of both finance and influence) to a range of charities, as well as everyday people whose stories have touched her. As her career continues to evolve, be that in music style or more varied, off-stage roles (such as directing), it's clear to see that the world's "love story" with Miss Americana is far from over.

Find out more about Taylor in the ICON section at www.guinnessworldrecords.com/2025

VITAL STATISTICS

Name	Taylor Alison Swift
Birthplace	West Reading, Pennsylvania, USA
Birth date	13 Dec 1989
Current GWR titles	Multiple, including: • **Most Album of the Year Grammys (vocalist)** (4) • **Most entries on the US Hot 100** (263) • **Highest-grossing music tour in a year** ($1,039,263,762; £840.2 m)
No.1 albums	14 (USA) / 12 (UK)

Above as of 1 May 2024

Taylor's rise to fame began when she sang the American national anthem at a Philadelphia 76ers basketball game in 2002, aged 12. Two years later, she signed a record deal with Sony/ATV, becoming the youngest artist ever in the company's history.

Taylor received an honorary doctorate in fine arts from New York University in 2022. Sporting a purple robe and student cap, she delivered a commencement speech at the ceremony, held at the Yankee Stadium.

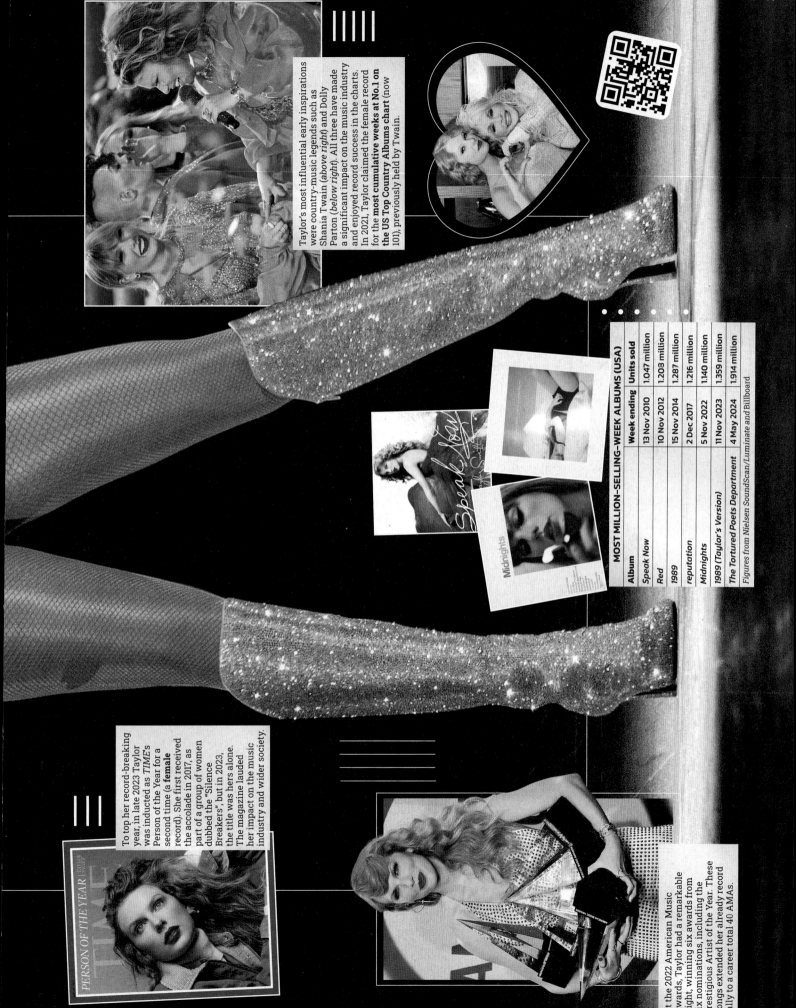

Taylor's most influential early inspirations were country-music legends such as Shania Twain (*above right*) and Dolly Parton (*below right*). All three have made a significant impact on the music industry and enjoyed record success in the charts. In 2021, Taylor claimed the female record for the **most cumulative weeks at No.1 on the US Top Country Albums chart** (now 101), previously held by Twain.

MOST MILLION-SELLING-WEEK ALBUMS (USA)

Album	Week ending	Units sold
Speak Now	13 Nov 2010	1.047 million
Red	10 Nov 2012	1.203 million
1989	15 Nov 2014	1.287 million
reputation	2 Dec 2017	1.216 million
Midnights	5 Nov 2022	1.140 million
1989 (Taylor's Version)	11 Nov 2023	1.359 million
The Tortured Poets Department	4 May 2024	1.914 million

Figures from Nielsen SoundScan/Luminate and Billboard

Midnights

To top her record-breaking year, in late 2023 Taylor was inducted as *TIME's* Person of the Year for a second time (a **female record**). She first received the accolade in 2017, as part of a group of women dubbed the "Silence Breakers", but in 2023, the title was hers alone. The magazine lauded her impact on the music industry and wider society.

PERSON OF THE YEAR

t the 2022 American Music wards, Taylor had a remarkable ight, winning six awards from x nominations, including the restigious Artist of the Year. These ongs extended her already record nly to a career total 40 AMAs.

HIGHEST ATTENDANCE AT A WOMEN'S VOLLEYBALL MATCH
On 30 Aug 2023, a total of 92,003 spectators crammed into Memorial Stadium in Lincoln, Nebraska, USA, to watch a college volleyball game between the Nebraska Cornhuskers and the Omaha Mavericks. Nebraska, five-time NCAA champions, saw off their in-state rivals in straight sets, winning 25-14, 25-14, 25-13. The "Volleyball Day" double-header, which also featured an exhibition match between the Nebraska–Kearney Lopers and the Wayne State Wildcats, had been organized in the hope of breaking the all-time attendance record in women's sport. However, the resulting media coverage helped shine a light on the *actual* record: a previously little-known soccer tournament that had played out to even larger crowds (*see opposite*).

Highest attendance at a women's sporting event
On 5 Sep 1971, an estimated crowd of 110,000 watched the final of the Women's World Cup (II Campeonato Mundial de Fútbol Femenil) at Mexico City's Azteca Stadium. The soccer tournament, which took place 20 years before the first FIFA Women's World Cup in 1991, was contested by six teams and drew huge crowds. The final – between home nation Mexico and Denmark – was won 3–0 by the Europeans, courtesy of a hat-trick by 15-year-old Susanne Augustesen.

Nicknamed "The Sea of Red", Memorial Stadium has sold out every Huskers football game since 1962.

Most Expensive Soccer Player

Since the advent of professional soccer in 1885, big-money transfers have caused excitement and controversy in equal measure. The players on our list of bank-busting signings – some of the game's greatest – did everything they could to live up to their fee.

When striker Alf Common moved from Sunderland to Middlesbrough for £1,000 ($1,265) in 1905, an outraged newspaper article described it as "a new type of... slave trade". Yet over the next century, as the game continued to grow in popularity and clubs transformed into huge businesses, transfer fees did not just rise – they rocketed into the stratosphere.

Throughout the first half of the 20th century, it was largely English players who commanded the highest sums – with the notable exception of the powerful Argentine striker Bernabé Ferreyra, whose move from Tigre to River Plate for 35,000 pesos (£23,000; $20,500) in 1932 remained the record for 17 years. By the time GWR started monitoring the category in 1955, it was the Italian clubs flexing their financial muscles; in 1992, AC Milan and Juventus shelled out unprecedented fees three times in just two months.

In the 2000s, Real Madrid embarked on a policy of dazzling marquee signings – known as *galácticos* – that saw them break the transfer record five times in a row. But in 2017, Qatari-backed Paris Saint-Germain bought Neymar from Barcelona for €222 m (£198 m; $262 m), doubling the previous highest fee. No transfer has come close since – has soccer's superlative spending finally ended?

RUUD GULLIT
AC Milan (1987–94)
£6,000,000
Shirt No. 4

Games **125**
Goals **38**
League titles **3**
European Cups **2**
Career caps **66**

Gullit won the Ballon d'Or in the same year that he signed for AC Milan – 1987. Together with Dutch teammates Frank Rijkaard and Marco van Basten, the stylish midfielder propelled Milan to league and European Cup glory.

ROBERTO BAGGIO
Juventus (1990–95)
£8,000,000
Shirt No. 10

Games **141**
Goals **78**
League titles **1**
UEFA Cups **1**
Career caps **56**

Baggio's transfer from Fiorentina caused riots from heartbroken fans in Florence. "The Divine Ponytail" proved equally popular at Juve, leading their successful UEFA Cup run in 1992/93 and winning the Ballon d'Or.

DIEGO MARADONA
Napoli (1984–91)
£5,000,000
Shirt No. 10

Games **188**
Goals **81**
League titles **2**
UEFA Cups **1**
Career caps **91**

The Argentine maestro transformed Napoli, leading them from the lower reaches of the Serie A table to their first-ever title, in 1986/87. After Maradona's death in 2020, Napoli's stadium was renamed in his honour.

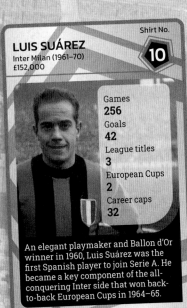

LUIS SUÁREZ
Inter Milan (1961–70)
£152,000
Shirt No. 10

Games **256**
Goals **42**
League titles **3**
European Cups **2**
Career caps **32**

An elegant playmaker and Ballon d'Or winner in 1960, Luis Suárez was the first Spanish player to join Serie A. He became a key component of the all-conquering Inter side that won back-to-back European Cups in 1964–65.

JOHANN CRUYFF
Barcelona (1973–78)
£922,000
Shirt No. 9

Games **143**
Goals **48**
League titles **1**
Copas del Rey **1**
Career caps **48**

The Dutch master guided Barca to their first La Liga title in 14 years in his first season at the club, winning the Ballon d'Or in 1973 and 1974. Cruyff returned to Barcelona as manager in 1988 and won four league titles.

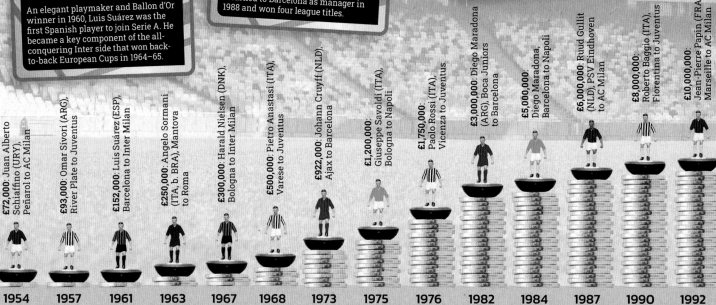

£72,000: Juan Alberto Schiaffino (URY), Peñarol to AC Milan — 1954

£93,000: Omar Sivori (ARG), River Plate to Juventus — 1957

£152,000: Luis Suárez (ESP), Barcelona to Inter Milan — 1961

£250,000: Angelo Sormani (ITA, b. BRA), Mantova to Roma — 1963

£300,000: Harald Nielsen (DNK), Bologna to Inter Milan — 1967

£500,000: Pietro Anastasi (ITA), Varese to Juventus — 1968

£922,000: Johann Cruyff (NLD), Ajax to Barcelona — 1973

£1,200,000: Giuseppe Savoldi (ITA), Bologna to Napoli — 1975

£1,750,000: Paolo Rossi (ITA), Vicenza to Juventus — 1976

£3,000,000: Diego Maradona (ARG), Boca Juniors to Barcelona — 1982

£5,000,000: Diego Maradona, Barcelona to Napoli — 1984

£6,000,000: Ruud Gullit (NLD), PSV Eindhoven to AC Milan — 1987

£8,000,000: Roberto Baggio (ITA), Fiorentina to Juventus — 1990

£10,000,000: Jean-Pierre Papin (FRA), Marseille to AC Milan — 1992

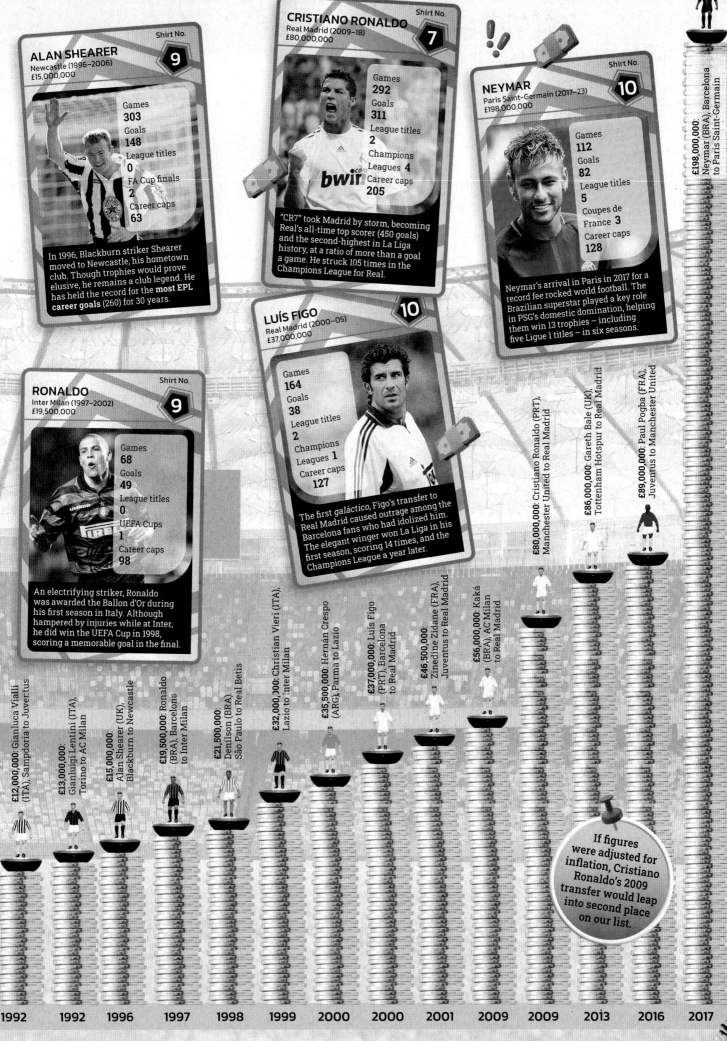

ALAN SHEARER
Newcastle (1996–2006)
£15,000,000

Shirt No. **9**

Games **303**
Goals **148**
League titles **0**
FA Cup finals **2**
Career caps **63**

In 1996, Blackburn striker Shearer moved to Newcastle, his hometown club. Though trophies would prove elusive, he remains a club legend. He has held the record for the **most EPL career goals** (260) for 30 years.

CRISTIANO RONALDO
Real Madrid (2009–18)
£80,000,000

Shirt No. **7**

Games **292**
Goals **311**
League titles **2**
Champions Leagues **4**
Career caps **205**

"CR7" took Madrid by storm, becoming Real's all-time top scorer (450 goals) and the second-highest in La Liga history, at a ratio of more than a goal a game. He struck 105 times in the Champions League for Real.

NEYMAR
Paris Saint-Germain (2017–23)
£198,000,000

Shirt No. **10**

Games **112**
Goals **82**
League titles **5**
Coupes de France **3**
Career caps **128**

Neymar's arrival in Paris in 2017 for a record fee rocked world football. The Brazilian superstar played a key role in PSG's domestic domination, helping them win 13 trophies – including five Ligue 1 titles – in six seasons.

RONALDO
Inter Milan (1997–2002)
£19,500,000

Shirt No. **9**

Games **68**
Goals **49**
League titles **0**
UEFA Cups **1**
Career caps **98**

An electrifying striker, Ronaldo was awarded the Ballon d'Or during his first season in Italy. Although hampered by injuries while at Inter, he did win the UEFA Cup in 1998, scoring a memorable goal in the final.

LUÍS FIGO
Real Madrid (2000–05)
£37,000,000

Shirt No. **10**

Games **164**
Goals **38**
League titles **2**
Champions Leagues **1**
Career caps **127**

The first *galáctico*, Figo's transfer to Real Madrid caused outrage among the Barcelona fans who had idolized him. The elegant winger won La Liga in his first season, scoring 14 times, and the Champions League a year later.

£198,000,000: Neymar (BRA), Barcelona to Paris Saint-Germain

£80,000,000: Cristiano Ronaldo (PRT), Manchester United to Real Madrid

£86,000,000: Gareth Bale (UK), Tottenham Hotspur to Real Madrid

£89,000,000: Paul Pogba (FRA), Juventus to Manchester United

£56,000,000: Kaká (BRA), AC Milan to Real Madrid

£46,500,000: Zinedine Zidane (FRA), Juventus to Real Madrid

£37,000,000: Luis Figo (PRT), Barcelona to Real Madrid

£35,500,000: Hernán Crespo (ARG), Parma to Lazio

£32,000,000: Christian Vieri (ITA), Lazio to Inter Milan

£21,500,000: Denilson (BRA), São Paulo to Real Betis

£19,500,000: Ronaldo (BRA), Barcelona to Inter Milan

£15,000,000: Alan Shearer (UK), Blackburn to Newcastle

£13,000,000: Gianluigi Lentini (ITA), Torino to AC Milan

£12,000,000: Gianluca Vialli (ITA), Sampdoria to Juventus

If figures were adjusted for inflation, Cristiano Ronaldo's 2009 transfer would leap into second place on our list.

1992   1992   1996   1997   1998   1999   2000   2000   2001   2009   2009   2013   2016   2017

US Sports

Youngest NBA player to record 20 points and 20 rebounds in a game

Victor Wembanyama (FRA, b. 4 Jan 2004) was aged 19 years 338 days when he registered 21 points and 20 rebounds for the San Antonio Spurs against the Chicago Bulls on 8 Dec 2023. The 2.24-m-tall (7-ft 4-in) phenom is regarded as one of the hottest prospects in basketball.

Most consecutive NFL games to score a touchdown

Christian McCaffrey found the end zone 17 games in a row from 4 Dec 2022 to 29 Oct 2023. The San Francisco 49ers running back equalled the record set by the Baltimore Colts' Lenny Moore in 1963–64. McCaffrey scored a total of 23 TDs during his prolific streak – 15 rushing and eight receiving.

Youngest quarterback to win an NFL postseason game

C J Stroud (b. 3 Oct 2001) was just 22 years 102 days old when he led the Houston Texans to a 45–14 victory over the Cleveland Browns on 13 Jan 2024. The rookie threw for 274 yards and three touchdowns.

Another record-breaking QB in 2023 was the Buffalo Bills' Josh Allen, who achieved the **most games passing and running for touchdowns in a season** – 11. The previous best was nine, by the Arizona Cardinals' Kyler Murray in 2020.

Most interceptions returned for a touchdown in an NFL season

DaRon Bland of the Dallas Cowboys recorded five "pick-sixes" in 2023. He returned an interception for 63 yards against the Washington Commanders on 23 Nov 2023 to claim his fifth, and the single-season record.

Most home runs by a team in an MLB season

The Atlanta Braves hit 307 dingers in 2023, equalling the mark set by the 2019 Minnesota Twins. Matt Olson led the way with a franchise record of 54 homers.

Most points in Game 7 of an NBA playoff series

On 14 May 2023, Jayson Tatum posted 51 points during the deciding game of the Eastern Conference semi-final between his Boston Celtics and the Philadelphia 76ers. The Celtics won 112–88.

Tatum also holds the record for the **most points in an NBA All-Star Game** – 55, playing for Team Giannis on 19 Feb 2023.

Most wins of the NHL's Selke Trophy

Patrice Bergeron (CAN) of the Boston Bruins claimed his sixth award for defensive play by a forward in the 2022/23 season.

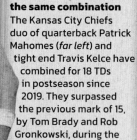

Most NFL postseason touchdown passes by the same combination

The Kansas City Chiefs duo of quarterback Patrick Mahomes (*far left*) and tight end Travis Kelce have combined for 18 TDs in postseason since 2019. They surpassed the previous mark of 15, by Tom Brady and Rob Gronkowski, during the Chiefs' 27–24 win over the Buffalo Bills on 21 Jan 2024. Mahomes and Kelce each earned their third championship ring at Super Bowl LVIII, as the Chiefs edged the San Francisco 49ers 25–22.

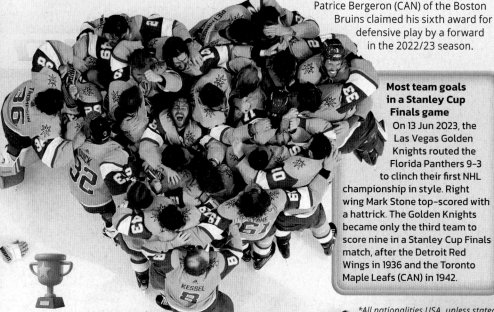

Most team goals in a Stanley Cup Finals game

On 13 Jun 2023, the Las Vegas Golden Knights routed the Florida Panthers 9–3 to clinch their first NHL championship in style. Right wing Mark Stone top-scored with a hattrick. The Golden Knights became only the third team to score nine in a Stanley Cup Finals match, after the Detroit Red Wings in 1936 and the Toronto Maple Leafs (CAN) in 1942.

Most WNBA points

Diana Taurasi has scored 10,108 points for the Phoenix Mercury since 2004. She became the first WNBA player to hit the 10,000-point milestone on 3 Aug 2023, when she dropped 42 points against the Atlanta Dream.

On 22 Aug 2023, A'ja Wilson of the Las Vegas Aces equalled Liz Cambage's (AUS) **single-game** record of 53 points, set on 17 Jul 2018.

All nationalities USA, unless stated

Standing 6 ft 4 in (1.93 m) tall and capable of throwing a 102-mph (164-km/h) fastball, Ohtani is a fearsome presence on the mound. He had struck out 608 MLB batters by the end of the 2023 season, at an earned run average of 3.01. However, he is not expected to pitch again until 2025, following elbow surgery.

LARGEST MLB CONTRACT

Baseball player Shohei Ohtani (JPN) signed a 10-year deal worth $700 m (£557 m) with the Los Angeles Dodgers, as reported on 9 Dec 2023. His remarkable two-way talents as both a pitcher and a designated hitter have led to comparisons with the legendary Babe Ruth. Ohtani joined the MLB in 2018 and was named American League Rookie of the Year. He left the Los Angeles Angels five years later as a free agent, having become the first player to be unanimously voted MVP twice, in 2021 and 2023.

Before choosing baseball, Ohtani was touted as a potential Olympic prospect at swimming.

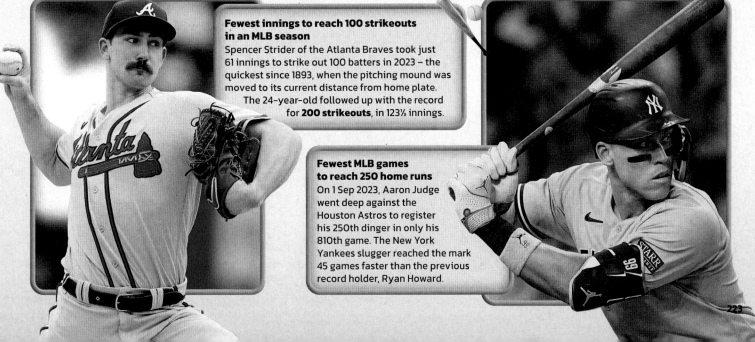

Fewest innings to reach 100 strikeouts in an MLB season

Spencer Strider of the Atlanta Braves took just 61 innings to strike out 100 batters in 2023 – the quickest since 1893, when the pitching mound was moved to its current distance from home plate. The 24-year-old followed up with the record for **200 strikeouts**, in 123⅓ innings.

Fewest MLB games to reach 250 home runs

On 1 Sep 2023, Aaron Judge went deep against the Houston Astros to register his 250th dinger in only his 810th game. The New York Yankees slugger reached the mark 45 games faster than the previous record holder, Ryan Howard.

Ball Sports

Most Men's Wheelchair Basketball World Championships

On 20 Jun 2023, the USA earned their seventh title since 1979 – and their first in 20 years – when they downed holders Great Britain 67–66 in the final in Dubai, UAE. Brian Bell top-scored for Team USA with 18 points; teammates Trévon Jenifer and Steve Serio (*right*) each added 16.

Most wins of the Netball World Cup

Australia have won netball's premier international competition 12 times. The Diamonds recorded their latest victory at the 2023 edition in South Africa, defeating England 61–45 in the final on 6 Aug. New Zealand and Trinidad and Tobago are the only other teams to have won the event, which was known as the World Netball Championship from 1963 to 2011.

Most appearances in Netball World Cup tournaments

Three players took to the court for their sixth World Cup in 2023: England's Jade Clarke and Geva Mentor (consecutively, from 2003 to 2023) and Latonia Blackman of Barbados (1999–2003 and 2011–23). They matched the feat of Trinidad and Tobago's Rhonda John-Davis (1999–2019).

Most World Lacrosse Men's Championships

The USA have won this quadrennial tournament 11 times since 1967. Their latest victory came on 1 Jul 2023, when they defeated Canada 10–7 in the final at Snapdragon Stadium in San Diego, California, USA. Canada are the only other nation to have won the event – three times, in 1978, 2006 and 2014.

Most Women's World Floorball Championships

A form of indoor hockey that uses a plastic ball with holes in it, floorball was invented in Sweden in the 1960s. In 2023, Sweden's women continued their domination of the sport with their 11th overall – and ninth consecutive – world championship. They defeated Finland 6–4 in the final, held on 10 Dec in Singapore.

Most World Croquet Championships

Robert Fulford (UK) claimed his sixth title in 2023. He came from two games down to beat the USA's Matthew Essick 3–2 in a 7-hr final thriller.

Most consecutive wins of the All-Ireland Hurling Final

Limerick chalked up their fourth successive hurling championship on 23 Jul 2023, defeating Kilkenny by 0–30 to 2–15 in the final at Croke Park in Dublin. This equalled the feat of Cork in 1941–44 and Kilkenny in 2006–09. The fast-moving sport, one of Ireland's Gaelic games, sees teams of 15 wield their hurley sticks to battle for control of the ball, known as a *sliotar*.

Most goals in the Women's EHF Handball Champions League

Jovanka Radičević (MNE) scored 1,069 times in European handball's blue-riband club competition from 2005 to 2023. The right winger overtook Anita Görbicz's mark of 1,016 in the course of her final season, playing for Slovenian outfit Krim.

Most wins of the FIBA men's 3x3 World Cup

This form of basketball is played on a half-court with one basket. The winners are the first team to reach 21 points, or the highest scorers at the end of the 10-min game. Serbia secured their sixth World Cup with a 21–19 win over the USA on 4 Jun 2023 in Vienna, Austria.

The **women's** record is three, by the USA in 2012, 2014 and 2023.

Most international rugby union tests refereed

At the 2023 Rugby World Cup final, Wayne Barnes (UK) blew the whistle on an international career that had spanned 111 games. He made his debut on 24 Jun 2006, overseeing Fiji's 23–20 win over Samoa at the Pacific 5 Nations tournament. Barnes officiated 27 games at five World Cups, and his final game proved to be one of his most eventful (*see opposite*).

MOST WINS OF THE RUGBY WORLD CUP

On 28 Oct 2023, South Africa lifted the Webb Ellis Cup for a fourth time, defeating New Zealand 12–11 in the final at the Stade de France in Paris. The Springboks – winners in 1995, 2007 and 2019 – have only entered eight of the 10 tournaments held since the first edition in 1987. They overcame three-time winners New Zealand despite conceding a try in the final for the first time. The game was also notable for the **first red card in a Rugby World Cup final**, shown to All Blacks skipper Sam Cane.

All Black Sam Whitelock won his first 18 Rugby World Cup games, lifting the trophy in 2011 and 2015.

Most tries at a Rugby World Cup

Will Jordan (NZ) touched down eight times for the All Blacks at the 2023 World Cup. The flying winger scored a hat-trick in the semi-final against Argentina to match the single-tournament total of Jonah Lomu (NZ) in 1999, Bryan Habana (ZAF) in 2007 and Julian Savea (NZ) in 2015. Following New Zealand's defeat in the final, Jordan's international record stood at a remarkable 31 tries in 31 games.

RUGBY WORLD CUP PLAYER RECORDS

Most...	Total	Player	Nation	Tournaments
Points	277	Jonny Wilkinson	England	1999–2011
Tries	15	Jonah Lomu	New Zealand	1995–99
		Bryan Habana	South Africa	2007–15
Penalties	58	Jonny Wilkinson	England	1999–2011
Conversions	58	Dan Carter	New Zealand	2003–15
Drop goals	14	Jonny Wilkinson	England	1999–2011
Games	26	Sam Whitelock (*above*)	New Zealand	2011–23
Tournaments	5	Brian Lima	Samoa	1991–2007
		Mauro Bergamasco	Italy	1999–2015
		Sergio Parisse	Italy	2003–19

Racket Sports

Most wins of the Women's Racquetball World Championships

Five-time singles world champion Paola Longoria (MEX) claimed her latest title in her home city of San Luis Potosí on 25 Aug 2022. She lost just one game across seven matches. At the same championship, Longoria extended her **women's doubles** record to five, alongside partner Samantha Salas (MEX).

Most consecutive wins of the Women's World Squash Championships

On 11 May 2023, Nour El Sherbini (EGY) won her fifth world title in a row, equalling the feat of Nicol David (MYS) in 2008–12. Sherbini defeated No.1 seed Nouran Gohar in the final in Chicago, Illinois, USA. She has won seven world championships overall – just one behind David's **outright** record of eight.

Longest women's squash match

On 25 Jun 2023, Nouran Gohar and Hania El Hammamy (both EGY) played out a titanic tussle that lasted for 130 min in Cairo, Egypt. It was Gohar who emerged victorious, winning her second Women's PSA World Tour Finals title 10–11, 11–9, 9–11, 11–6, 12–10. The same two players had also recorded 105-min and 107-min encounters in the previous three months.

The **longest men's squash match** clocked in at 170 min and took place at the 2015 Holtrand Gas City Pro-Am. Hong Kong's Leo Au (CHN) downed Shawn Delierre (CAN) 11–6, 4–11, 11–6, 7–11, 16–14 in Medicine Hat, Alberta, Canada.

Most wins of the World Badminton Championships women's doubles

Chen Qingchen and Jia Yifan (both CHN) claimed their fourth world title at the 2023 edition in Copenhagen, Denmark. They took just 41 min to despatch their final opponents on 27 Aug.

Fastest badminton hit

On 14 Apr 2023, Satwiksairaj Rankireddy (IND) unleashed a 565–km/h (351.07–mph) shuttlecock smash at the Yonex Tokyo Factory in Sōka, Saitama, Japan. That's around 200 km/h (124 mph) faster than a Formula One car's top speed. Tan Pearly (MYS) broke the **women's** record at the same event, with a 438-km/h (272.16-mph) hit.

Most wins of badminton's Sudirman Cup

China claimed its 13th world mixed team championship on 21 May 2023, sweeping South Korea 3–0 in the final in Suzhou, China. The mixed doubles pairing of Huang Yaqiong and Zheng Siwei (*below*) led the way with an opening win, before victories for singles players Shi Yuqi and Chen Yufei sealed the tie.

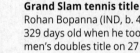

Oldest winner of a men's Grand Slam tennis title

Rohan Bopanna (IND, b. 4 Mar 1980) was 43 years 329 days old when he took the Australian Open men's doubles title on 27 Jan 2024. Playing alongside Matthew Ebden, Bopanna won his first Grand Slam at the 61st attempt – 16 years after making his debut at Melbourne Park.

Oldest winners of a women's Grand Slam tennis doubles title (combined age)

Barbora Strýcová (CZE, b. 28 Mar 1986) and Taiwan's Su-Wei Hsieh (CHN, b. 4 Jan 1986) had a combined age of 74 years 303 days when they teamed up to win on the grass at Wimbledon on 16 Jul 2023.

Most consecutive women's Grand Slam tennis wheelchair singles titles

At the Australian Open on 27 Jan 2024, Diede de Groot (NLD) captured her 13th Grand Slam singles title in a row. Her winning streak – which began at the 2021 Australian Open – formed part of a 135-match unbeaten run in singles competition for the Dutch champion.

Youngest winner of a men's Grand Slam singles tennis title

On 10 Jun 2023, Tokito Oda (JPN, b. 8 May 2006) won the French Open in Paris aged 17 years 33 days. He beat top seed Alfie Hewett 6–1, 6–4 in the wheelchair final, surpassing the previous youngest men's Grand Slam champion – Michael Chang, at the 1989 French Open – by 76 days. Two days after his victory, Oda became the **youngest wheelchair tennis player to be ranked world No.1**.

Oda began playing wheelchair tennis aged 10 – and was world junior No.1 just four years later!

MOST GRAND SLAM SINGLES TENNIS TITLES

On 10 Sep 2023, Novak Djokovic (SRB) defeated Daniil Medvedev 6–3, 7–6, 6–3 in the final of the US Open to claim his 24th Grand Slam title. This equalled the record of Margaret Court (AUS) between 1960 and 1973. Djokovic's total comprises three French Opens, four US Opens, seven Wimbledons and the **most wins of the Australian Open men's singles** – 10.

Additionally in 2023, Djokovic extended his records for the **most ATP Masters 1000 singles titles** – 40 – and the **most weeks ranked No.1 in men's singles** – 405, by the year's end. He also claimed sole ownership of the **most singles wins at the ATP Finals**, completing his seventh victory.

Novak Djokovic's victory at the 2023 US Open took his career prize money to an incredible $175,281,484 (£140 m) – the **highest earnings in men's tennis**. He had won over $40 m (£32 m) more than his nearest rival, Spain's Rafael Nadal.

Vondroušová and her coach got matching tattoos to celebrate her Wimbledon triumph.

FIRST UNSEEDED WIMBLEDON LADIES CHAMPION

In 2023, Markéta Vondroušová (CZE) enjoyed a fairytale run at the world's **oldest tennis tournament** (established in 1877). Having missed six months of the 2022 season with a wrist injury, Vondroušová had been ranked No.42 heading into Wimbledon, and she had won just four matches on grass in her entire career. Yet the 24-year-old defied expectations to march through the draw and defeat Ons Jabeur 6–4, 6–4 in the final on 15 Jul. Vondroušová's victory earned her a cool £2.35 m ($3.08 m) and a rise to No.10 in the WTA rankings.

Motor Sports

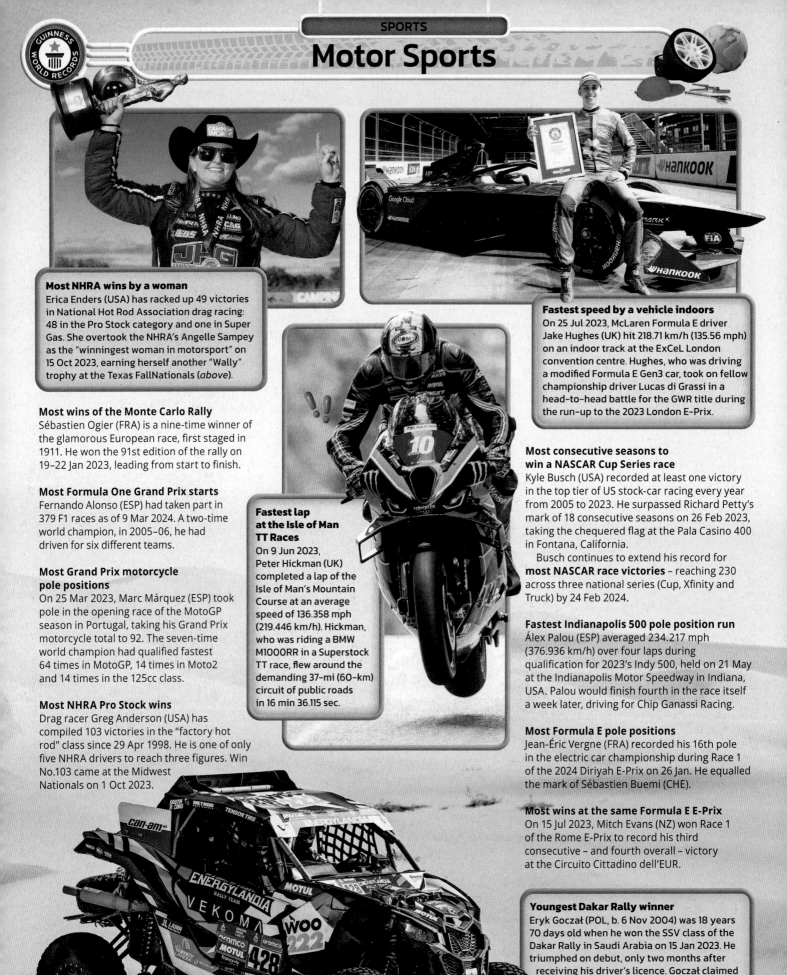

Most NHRA wins by a woman
Erica Enders (USA) has racked up 49 victories in National Hot Rod Association drag racing: 48 in the Pro Stock category and one in Super Gas. She overtook the NHRA's Angelle Sampey as the "winningest woman in motorsport" on 15 Oct 2023, earning herself another "Wally" trophy at the Texas FallNationals (*above*).

Most wins of the Monte Carlo Rally
Sébastien Ogier (FRA) is a nine-time winner of the glamorous European race, first staged in 1911. He won the 91st edition of the rally on 19–22 Jan 2023, leading from start to finish.

Most Formula One Grand Prix starts
Fernando Alonso (ESP) had taken part in 379 F1 races as of 9 Mar 2024. A two-time world champion, in 2005–06, he had driven for six different teams.

Most Grand Prix motorcycle pole positions
On 25 Mar 2023, Marc Márquez (ESP) took pole in the opening race of the MotoGP season in Portugal, taking his Grand Prix motorcycle total to 92. The seven-time world champion had qualified fastest 64 times in MotoGP, 14 times in Moto2 and 14 times in the 125cc class.

Most NHRA Pro Stock wins
Drag racer Greg Anderson (USA) has compiled 103 victories in the "factory hot rod" class since 29 Apr 1998. He is one of only five NHRA drivers to reach three figures. Win No.103 came at the Midwest Nationals on 1 Oct 2023.

Fastest lap at the Isle of Man TT Races
On 9 Jun 2023, Peter Hickman (UK) completed a lap of the Isle of Man's Mountain Course at an average speed of 136.358 mph (219.446 km/h). Hickman, who was riding a BMW M1000RR in a Superstock TT race, flew around the demanding 37-mi (60-km) circuit of public roads in 16 min 36.115 sec.

Fastest speed by a vehicle indoors
On 25 Jul 2023, McLaren Formula E driver Jake Hughes (UK) hit 218.71 km/h (135.56 mph) on an indoor track at the ExCeL London convention centre. Hughes, who was driving a modified Formula E Gen3 car, took on fellow championship driver Lucas di Grassi in a head-to-head battle for the GWR title during the run-up to the 2023 London E-Prix.

Most consecutive seasons to win a NASCAR Cup Series race
Kyle Busch (USA) recorded at least one victory in the top tier of US stock-car racing every year from 2005 to 2023. He surpassed Richard Petty's mark of 18 consecutive seasons on 26 Feb 2023, taking the chequered flag at the Pala Casino 400 in Fontana, California.

Busch continues to extend his record for **most NASCAR race victories** – reaching 230 across three national series (Cup, Xfinity and Truck) by 24 Feb 2024.

Fastest Indianapolis 500 pole position run
Álex Palou (ESP) averaged 234.217 mph (376.936 km/h) over four laps during qualification for 2023's Indy 500, held on 21 May at the Indianapolis Motor Speedway in Indiana, USA. Palou would finish fourth in the race itself a week later, driving for Chip Ganassi Racing.

Most Formula E pole positions
Jean-Éric Vergne (FRA) recorded his 16th pole in the electric car championship during Race 1 of the 2024 Diriyah E-Prix on 26 Jan. He equalled the mark of Sébastien Buemi (CHE).

Most wins at the same Formula E E-Prix
On 15 Jul 2023, Mitch Evans (NZ) won Race 1 of the Rome E-Prix to record his third consecutive – and fourth overall – victory at the Circuito Cittadino dell'EUR.

Youngest Dakar Rally winner
Eryk Goczał (POL, b. 6 Nov 2004) was 18 years 70 days old when he won the SSV class of the Dakar Rally in Saudi Arabia on 15 Jan 2023. He triumphed on debut, only two months after receiving his driver's licence. Goczał claimed four of the 14 stages in the SSV class (four-wheel vehicles with two-abreast seating), alongside co-driver Oriol Mena.

The **oldest Dakar Rally winner** is Carlos Sainz (ESP, b. 12 Apr 1962), who won the 2024 car class aged 61 years 282 days.

MOST CONSECUTIVE FORMULA ONE RACE WINS

On 3 Sep 2023, Max Verstappen (NLD, b. BEL) took the chequered flag at the Italian Grand Prix to seal an unprecedented winning streak of 10 F1 races in a row. The Red Bull driver claimed his third consecutive world championship in dominant fashion, winning 19 out of 22 races to beat his own record for the **most Grand Prix wins in a season**. He received the championship trophy at a ceremony on 8 Dec (*top right, with FIA president Mohammed Ben Sulayem*).

Verstappen (b. 30 Sep 1997) has amassed numerous GWR titles since making his F1 debut – including the **youngest Grand Prix winner** (*right*), which he achieved at the Spanish Grand Prix on 15 May 2016 aged 18 years 228 days.

Only 17 drivers have won more F1 races in their entire career than Verstappen won in 2023.

Most pole positions at a Formula One Grand Prix

Lewis Hamilton (UK) has qualified fastest nine times at the Hungarian Grand Prix. Despite a difficult couple of seasons for his Mercedes team, the seven-time world champion bounced back to produce a sensational lap at the Hungaroring circuit on 22 Jul 2023, extending his overall record for the **most pole positions** to 104.

The **most consecutive pole positions at a Grand Prix** is seven, by Ayrton Senna (BRA) at San Marino in 1985–91.

Water Sports

Fastest women's 400 m freestyle (S7)

On 1 Aug 2023, at the World Para Swimming Championships in Manchester, UK, Morgan Stickney (USA) took gold in 4 min 54.28 sec. Stickney, who underwent below-the-knee amputations in 2018 and 2019, smashed the 11-year-old record in the event by nearly 5 sec.

Most women's 10 m diving gold medals at the World Aquatics Championships

Chen Yuxi (CHN) secured her third consecutive 10 m platform title on 19 Jul 2023. The 17-year-old also teamed up with Quan Hongchan to claim gold in the 10 m synchronized. China won an astonishing 12 of the 13 diving events in Fukuoka.

Fastest women's 400 m individual medley

Summer McIntosh (CAN) touched home in 4 min 25.87 sec at the Canadian swimming trials in Toronto on 1 Apr 2023. It was the 16-year-old's second world record of the meet, having already set the **fastest 400 m freestyle** in 3 min 56.08 sec. This mark fell on 23 Jul 2023 to Ariarne Titmus (AUS) at the World Aquatics Championships; Titmus powered to victory in 3 min 55.38 sec, with McIntosh finishing in fourth.

Fastest men's 100 m butterfly (S11)

On 1 Aug 2023, Danylo Chufarov (UKR) claimed his first swimming world title in style, winning the final in 1 min 0.66 sec at the World Para Swimming Championships in Manchester, UK. The S11 classification is for blind swimmers.

Most men's water polo titles at the World Aquatics Championships

Hungary claimed their fourth water polo world title in dramatic fashion at the 2023 championships, beating Greece 14–13 in the final after a penalty shoot-out on 29 Jul. Hungary equalled the record of Italy, who were champions in 1978, 1994, 2011 and 2019.

Fastest 2,000 m women's lightweight double sculls

On 17 Jun 2023, Emily Craig and Imogen Grant (both UK) won their semi-final at the World Rowing Cup II regatta in Varese, Italy, in 6 min 40.47 sec. Grant also holds the **single sculls** record of 7 min 23.36 sec, set on 9 Jul 2022.

Fastest 2,000 m mixed double sculls (PR3)

Nikki Ayers and Jed Altschwager (both AUS) posted a time of 7 min 7.02 sec at the World Rowing Cup in Varese on 18 Jun 2023. PR3 rowers have functional use of legs, trunk and arms, and can use a sliding seat when performing strokes.

Farthest women's freediving dynamic apnea without fins

On 13 Jun 2023, Julia Kozerska (POL) swam 213 m (698 ft 9 in) – more than four lengths of an Olympic pool – underwater on a single breath. She was competing at the 30th AIDA Pool World Championship in Jeju, South Korea.

Fastest men's windsurfing speed (nautical mile)

On 30 Jun 2023, Antoine Albeau (FRA) achieved a speed of 44.12 knots (50.77 mph; 81.71 km/h) at the Prince of Speed event in La Palme, France. Heidi Ulrich (CHE) broke the **women's** record at the same event, hitting 38.44 knots (44.23 mph; 71.19 km/h) on 15 Jun. Both records were verified by the World Sailing Speed Record Council.

Most points for men's waterskiing tricks

Patricio Font (MEX) tricked his way to a score of 12,690 on 12 May 2023 at a Masters Qualifying Series event in Winter Garden, Florida, USA. He beat his own world record from 2022 by 100 points.

Deepest women's constant weight freedive

On 24 May 2023, Alessia Zecchini (ITA) swam to a depth of 123 m (403 ft 6 in) on a single breath off the Philippines. The subject of the 2023 Netflix documentary *The Deepest Breath*, Zecchini has broken 11 world records across four different categories under the auspices of the AIDA International diving federation.

Most individual gold medals at the ICF Canoe Slalom World Championships

Jessica Fox (AUS, b. FRA) has won 10 solo world championship titles: four in the kayak (K1), four in the canoe (C1) and two in kayak cross. She claimed her latest gold, in the K1, on 23 Sep 2023 in London, UK. Kayakers use a double-bladed paddle and remain seated in the boat, while canoeists kneel and use a single-bladed paddle.

FASTEST MEN'S 400 M INDIVIDUAL MEDLEY

On 23 Jul 2023, Léon Marchand (FRA) won the final of the 400 m individual medley in 4 min 2.50 sec at the World Aquatics Championships in Fukuoka, Japan. The event comprises four 100-m legs, each swum using a different stroke: butterfly, backstroke, breaststroke and freestyle. The previous best of 4 min 3.84 sec, set at the 2008 Olympics, had been the longest-standing record in swimming. The man responsible, US legend Michael Phelps, was on hand to present Marchand with his gold medal (*inset*).

FUKUOKA 2023
WORLD AQUATICS CHAMPIONSHIPS

Marchand took 1.34 sec off Michael Phelps's record, which had stood for 5,460 days.

Fastest men's 200 m breaststroke

In Fukuoka, Qin Haiyang (CHN) became the first swimmer to win all three events – 50 m, 100 m and 200 m – in the same stroke at a world championships. He finished with a record-breaking swim in the 200 m breaststroke final on 28 Jul 2023, clocking 2 min 5.48 sec.

Fastest women's 200 m freestyle

On 26 Jul 2023, Mollie O'Callaghan (AUS) won her second individual world title in 1 min 52.85 sec. The 19-year-old claimed five gold medals and set four world records (three in relays) in Fukuoka, despite dislocating a kneecap just six weeks earlier.

Most individual swimming gold medals at the World Aquatics Championships

Katie Ledecky (USA) won the women's 800 m and 1,500 m freestyle titles in Fukuoka to take her career championships tally in solo events to 16. She passed Michael Phelps's total of 15, amassed from 2001 to 2011.

Athletics

Most appearances at the World Athletics Championships

On 19 Aug 2023, race walker João Vieira (PRT) competed at his 13th world championships. He finished 33rd in the men's 20 km in Budapest, Hungary, at the age of 47. Vieira equalled the appearance record set by Jesús Ángel García (ESP), also in the race walk (1993–2019).

The **women's** record is 11, and is also shared by two race walkers: Susana Feitor (PRT), between 1991 and 2011; and her compatriot Inês Henriques, between 2001 and 2023.

Youngest winner of a Diamond League women's event

Founded in 2010, the Diamond League is an annual series of elite one-day track and field meetings. Birke Haylom (ETH, b. 6 Jan 2006) was 17 years 160 days old when she won the Dream Mile at the Bislett Games in Oslo, Norway, on 15 Jun 2023. Haylom also acted as a pacemaker for Gudaf Tsegay's 5,000 m world record run at the Diamond League Final (*see opposite*).

Farthest men's shot put

Ryan Crouser (USA) launched the shot 23.56 m (77 ft 3 in) on 27 May 2023 in Los Angeles, California, USA. The 2.01-m-tall (6-ft 7-in) Olympic champion unleashed a series of monster puts at Drake Stadium, using a new technique dubbed the "Crouser Slide". It adds a step to his approach inside the circle, enabling him to generate more speed and power.

Ryan Crouser's father, uncle and cousin have all represented the USA in throwing events.

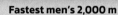

Fastest men's 2,000 m

On 8 Sep 2023, Jakob Ingebrigtsen (NOR) ran 2,000 m in 4 min 43.13 sec in Brussels, Belgium. The previous record, by Hicham El Guerrouj (MAR), had stood since 1999 – just over a year before the 22-year-old Ingebrigtsen was born. The Norwegian middle-distance star also has designs on El Guerrouj's records in the **1,500 m** (3 min 26 sec) and **mile** (3 min 43.13 sec).

Fastest men's 3,000 m steeplechase

An Olympic event since 1900, initially over varying distances, the steeplechase is the only distance event in which athletes have to clear obstacles – a total of 28 barriers and seven water jumps. On 9 Jun 2023 in Paris, France, Lamecha Girma (ETH) ran a time of 7 min 52.11 sec. The previous world record had stood for 19 years.

Fastest mixed 4 x 400 m relay

On 19 Aug 2023, the US team of Justin Robinson, Rosey Effiong, Matthew Boling and Alexis Holmes won gold at the World Athletics Championships in Budapest in 3 min 8.80 sec. The event was introduced in 2017; since 2022, teams must run in the order "man-woman-man-woman".

Farthest men's long jump (T64)

On 25 Jun 2023, "Blade Jumper" Markus Rehm (DEU) leapt 8.72 m (28 ft 7 in) on home soil in Rhede, Germany. This is a metre farther than any other para athlete and placed Rehm, who competes using a carbon-fibre prosthesis, ninth on the all-time list of long jumpers.

Highest men's pole vault

Armand Duplantis (SWE, b. USA) soared to 6.23 m (20 ft 5 in) at the Diamond League Final on 17 Sep 2023 in Eugene, Oregon, USA. Duplantis – nicknamed "Mondo" – is a pole-vaulting prodigy who first tried the sport in his back garden at the age of three. He was 20 when he broke the men's world record for the first time, clearing 6.17 m (20 ft 2 in). He has gone on to raise the bar a further six times.

Fastest women's 100 m (T34)

Hannah Cockroft (UK) powered to victory in 16.31 sec at the Nottwil Grand Prix in Switzerland on 27 May 2023. She competes in the T34 class, one of seven for wheelchair athletes. A seven-time Paralympic champion, Cockroft also holds T34 records in the **200 m** (28.90 sec), **400 m** (52.80 sec), **800 m** (1 min 44.43 sec) and **1,500 m** (3 min 21.06 sec).

FIRST COMPLETION OF ["TRIPLE CROWN"]

In the space of just 10 w[...]
Dauwalter (USA) becam[...]
history to win three pr[...]
races: the Western Stat[...]
and the Ultra-Trail du [...]
310.7 mi (500 km) and [...]
elevation gain – almos[...]
Everest from sea level[...]

Dauwalter's quest be[...]
smashed the record fo[...]
Western States 100, n[...]
the mountains of Sierr[...]
in 15 hr 29 min 33 sec ([...]
she followed up with t[...]
Hardrock 100 – 26 hr [...]
fourth overall in Silve[...]
Dauwalter completed [...]
du Mont-Blanc in Eur[...]
and stomach issues to[...]
2 Sep, 40 min ahead o[...]

FASTEST WOMEN'S 1,500 M

In 2023, Faith Kipyegon (KEN) blitzed world
records in three different events in just
49 days. She began on 2 Jun in the 1,500 m,
clocking 3 min 49.11 sec in Florence, Italy.
Next to fall was the **5,000 m**, seven days
later. Kipyegon ran 14 min 5.20 sec in Paris,
despite saying that she felt tired in the
build-up to the race. On 21 Jul, she added
the **mile** record to her collection with a
time of 4 min 7.64 sec in Monaco (*below*).

Kipyegon capped her golden summer at
the 2023 World Athletics Championships in
Budapest, Hungary, where she extended
her record for the **most women's
1,500 m world championship titles**
to three (*bottom*).

Fastest women's 5,000 m

On 17 Sep 2023, Gudaf
Tsegay (ETH) ran 5,000 m
in 14 min 00.21 sec at the
Diamond League Final
in Eugene, Oregon, USA.
She took five seconds off
Faith Kipyegon's record,
set three months earlier.
Tsegay was competing
at Hayward Field, where
she had won a world
championship gold in
the same event in 2022.

Consultants

Each year, we collaborate with dozens of experts who know their subjects inside out. Learned specialists who contributed to *GWR 2025* excel in everything from movie costumes, AI and railways to astronomy, numismatics, cacti, fungi, twins and gigantism, to name just a few categories. For a full list, visit **www.guinnessworldrecords.com/records/partners.**

Tom Beckerlegge is an award-winning writer whose books have been translated around the world. He is also *GWR*'s lead sports consultant, updating hundreds of new records every year across athletic disciplines and liaising with sporting federations to keep abreast of the latest stories. This year has seen him learning about racquetball, ski flying and the trailblazing players of the Copa '71 women's soccer tournament.

Randall Cerveny is a professor of geographical sciences at Arizona State University, USA. He serves as Rapporteur on Extreme Records for the UN and World Meteorological Organization, and in this connection is responsible for researching and verifying global weather records. He is contributing editor for the magazine *Weatherwise*, and has authored journal articles and several books including *Judging Extreme Weather* (2024).

Hugh Ferguson is a professional civil engineer who has worked as a contractor, consulting engineer, journalist and editor. After graduating with a civil-engineering degree, he worked in the industry before joining *New Civil Engineer* magazine, which he managed from 1976 to 1990. He is author (or co-author) of several books, including *Constructionarium* (2016) and *The Consulting Engineers* (2020).

Kathryn Brown is a specialist in modern and contemporary art and art markets. She is the author of many articles and books, including *Women Readers in French Painting 1870–1890* (2012) and *Dialogues with Degas: Influence and Antagonism in Contemporary Art* (2023). Kathryn is the series editor of *Contextualizing Art Markets* for Bloomsbury Academic and is Associate Professor of Art History at Loughborough University, UK.

Mike Chrimes retired as Director of Engineering Policy and Information at the Institution of Civil Engineers in 2014, after 37 years. A professional librarian and information scientist, he has contributed to many books and papers on engineering history and information services. He has an American Society of Civil Engineers History and Heritage Award, and was honoured with an MBE for services to engineering in 2011.

David Fischer is GWR's senior US sports consultant. He has written for *The New York Times* and *Sports Illustrated for Kids*, and worked at *Sports Illustrated, The National Sports Daily* and NBC Sports. His books include *Tom Brady: A Celebration of Greatness on the Gridiron* (2021), *The New York Yankees of the 1950s: Mantle, Stengel, Berra, and a Decade of Dominance* (2019) and *The Super Bowl: The First Fifty Years of America's Greatest* Game (2015).

Yvette Cendes is an assistant professor of physics at the University of Oregon, USA, specializing in radio astronomy and signals that vary over time, ranging from exoplanets to black holes that shred stars. Yvette has written for publications such as *Astronomy* magazine and *Scientific American*, and is active on Reddit as /u/Andromeda321, where her "astronomer here!" comments are read by millions around the world.

Gareth Dennis is a writer for the railway and national press and regularly appears on the TV and radio explaining engineering and transport ideas, as well as fulfilling his day job as a railway design engineer. He is a lecturer in transport systems and presents a weekly show called *Railnatter* on YouTube. He is also a founding member of the Campaign for Level Boarding.

Stephen Follows is a world-leading film-industry analyst and data researcher. He seeks to discover how the motion-picture industry operates and to use that knowledge to help moviemakers get their productions made and seen. His work has covered gender equality, applied creativity, AI innovation and film education.

To help investigate and verify records across a broad spectrum of disciplines, GWR also works with clubs, institutions and federations. A few that assisted with this edition are included here. For a full list, visit **www.guinnessworldrecords.com/records/partners.**

8000ers.com
Eberhard Jurgalski has developed the system of "Elevation Equality", a method of classifying mountain ranges and peaks. His website has become the main source of altitude statistics for the Himalayas and Karakoram ranges.

American Numismatic Society
The ANS is dedicated to the study of currency, medals and related objects from all cultures, past and present. The Society's headquarters in New York City has the foremost research collection and library related to numismatics in the USA. Its resources are used to support research and education in this subject area.

Antiquarian Horological Society
The AHS was formed in 1953 to encourage the study of all matters relating to the art and history of time measurement and to encourage the preservation of examples of the horological and allied arts. Its quarterly journal, books and public lectures are aimed at anyone interested in the story of time.

CANNA UK National Giant Vegetables Championship
The annual Malvern Autumn Show held in Worcestershire, UK, is a pinnacle in the calendar of competitive giant fruit and vegetables growers across the country. Taking over the duties as head judge in 2023 was Sebastian Suski, who himself cultivated the **longest cucumber** in 2022.

Council on Tall Buildings and Urban Habitat
Headquartered in Chicago, Illinois, USA, the CTBUH is the world's leading resource for professionals focused on the design, construction and operation of tall buildings and future cities.

Fungi Foundation
The Fungi Foundation works for fungi, their habitats and the people who depend on them. It is a global organization that explores fungi to increase knowledge of their diversity, promote innovative solutions to contingent problems, educate about their existence and responsible applications, as well as recommending policy for their conservation.

Gerontology Research Group
Established in 1990, the GRG's mission is to slow and ultimately reverse ageing via the application and sharing of scientific knowledge. It also keeps the largest database of supercentenarians (i.e., people aged over 110), which is managed by GWR's senior gerontology consultant, Robert Young.

Great Pumpkin Commonwealth
The GPC cultivates the growing of giant pumpkins – among other prodigious produce – by establishing universal standards and regulations that ensure quality of fruit and fairness of competition.

International Ice Swimming Association
Founded by Ram Barkai, the IISA was established in 2009 with a vision to formalize swimming in icy water – i.e., below a threshold of 5°C (41°F). It has put in place rules to allow for maximum safety measures, and to regulate swim integrity in terms of distance, time and conditions. The body also oversees a series of ice-swimming meets and competitions.

The IRONMAN® Group
The IRONMAN Group is the largest operator of mass-participation sports in the world. It provides more than a million participants annually the benefits of sport through its vast offerings across triathlon, cycling, running and trail/dirt events.

The Kite Society of Great Britain
Founded in 1979, and currently administrated by Jon and Gill Bloom, the society has over 3,500 members worldwide. Its aim is to promote kite flying as a pastime for all. It arranges festivals around the UK, actively works with local organizations and publishes its own quarterly magazine, *The Kiteflier*.

Ocean Rowing Society International
The ORSI was established in 1983 by Kenneth F Crutchlow and Peter Bird, later joined by Tom Lynch and Tatiana Rezvaya-Crutchlow. The organization documents all attempts to row the world's oceans and major bodies of water, and classifies, verifies and adjudicates ocean-rowing achievements.

Parrot Analytics
Parrot Analytics is the leading global content demand analytics company for the modern multi-platform TV business. It tracks more than 1.5 billion daily expressions of demand in over 100 languages and 200 countries.

Polar Expeditions Classification Scheme
PECS is a grading and labelling system for extended, unmotorized polar journeys that is overseen by a committee of polar-expedition specialists, managed by Eric Philips. Polar regions, modes of travel, routes and forms of aid are defined under the scheme, giving expeditioners guidance on how to classify, promote and immortalize their journeys.

The Numbers
The Numbers is the web's biggest database of cinema box-office information, with figures on 50,000 movies and 200,000 people in the film industry. It was founded in 1997 by Bruce Nash and is visited by more than 8 million people every year.

UK & International Timing Adjudication
The UK&ITA was established in 2013 when Straightliners Ltd and SPEE3D Ltd united to enhance and promote land-speed record-breaking in Britain and Europe. It ensures that land-speed contenders can compete under all governances.

World Cube Association
The WCA governs competitions for mechanical puzzles that are operated by twisting groups of pieces, such as the Rubik's Cube. Its mission is to have more competitions in more countries, all participating under fair and equal conditions.

World Jigsaw Puzzle Federation
The WJPF is an international organization dedicated to jigsaw puzzles and oversees the World Jigsaw Puzzle Championship. It establishes a standard on rules and regulations for competitions and strives to have jigsaw-puzzle competitions acknowledged as a sport. The current chair is Alfonso Álvarez-Ossorio.

World Freestyle Football Association
Founded in Canada in 2017, the WFFA is the global governing body for the sport of freestyle football. It organizes iconic events including the World Freestyle Football Championship, the Pulse Series and the Super Ball, plus an array of regional and national events, in more than 100 countries.

World Meteorological Organization
Based in Geneva, Switzerland, this UN body is the global authority on weather, climatology and hydrology, for both the purposes of science and advising governmental policy.

World Open Water Swimming Association
Founded in 2005, WOWSA is an international governing body for the sport of open-water swimming. It provides membership and certification programmes as well as publications and online resources.

World Sailing Speed Record Council
The WSSRC was recognized by the International Yacht Racing Union (now World Sailing) in 1972. Its experts are drawn from Australia, France, Great Britain and the USA.

World Ultracycling Association
WUCA is a non-profit organization dedicated to supporting ultracycling across the world. It holds the largest repository of cycling records for all bike types, and certifies successful rides for its members.

Giuliana Furci is the foundress and CEO of the Fungi Foundation. She is an associate at Harvard University, a National Geographic Explorer, a Dame of the Order of the Star of Italy and the deputy chair of the IUCN Fungal Conservation Committee. Her published work includes a series of field guides to Chilean fungi. She is also co-author of *1st State of the World's Fungi* (2018), which delimits the term "funga" and the 3F Proposal (Fauna, Flora & Funga).

Nancy L Segal is Professor of Psychology and Founder and Director of the Twin Studies Center at California State University in Fullerton, USA. She has penned nine books on twin-related topics, with one (*Born Together–Reared Apart*) earning her the 2013 William James Book Award from the American Psychological Association. Her most recent titles are *Gay Fathers, Twin Sons* and *The Twin Children of the Holocaust* (both 2023).

Matthew White is *GWR*'s music, cricket and tennis consultant. From 2009 to 2023, he scrutinized 60,000-plus published records as proofreader for the world's **best-selling annual**. After training as a journalist, Matthew landed his dream job in the team that made the final four editions of the *Guinness Book of British Hit Singles & Albums*. He has also worked on projects for the likes of EMI, Universal Music Group and the Official UK Charts Company.

Wouter W de Herder is Professor of Endocrine Oncology at the Erasmus MC/Erasmus University Rotterdam, Netherlands. His interests are (neuro-) endocrine tumours, pituitary disorders and the history of endocrinology, in particular the history of acromegaly and gigantism.

Karl P N Shuker has a PhD in Zoology and Comparative Physiology from the University of Birmingham, UK, and is a Scientific Fellow of the Zoological Society of London, a Fellow of the Royal Entomological Society and a Member of The Society of Authors. He has penned 25 books and hundreds of articles about natural history. Karl's work has an emphasis on anomalous animals, including new, rediscovered and unrecognized species.

Sam Willis is one of the UK's best-known historians. He has made more than 10 television series for the BBC and National Geographic, and penned more than 15 books, many of them centring on maritime and naval history. Sam is also the presenter of two chart-topping history podcasts: *Histories of the Unexpected* and, for those interested in the history of all things maritime, *The Mariner's Mirror Podcast*.

Jesse Kraft is the Resolute Americana Assistant Curator of American Numismatics at the American Numismatic Society, which focuses on the history of coins, tokens, medals and paper currency. Additionally, he is a member of the Editorial Committee of *The Journal of Early American Numismatics*, and the Treasurer for the International Committee of Money and Banking Museums.

Eliza Strickland is a senior editor for *IEEE Spectrum*, the magazine and website for technology insiders. She manages *Spectrum*'s coverage of AI, and takes particular interest in AI ethics, AI alignment and the societal impacts of AI. Eliza has reported on science and technology for more than 20 years and holds a master's degree in journalism from Columbia University.

Robert D Young is GWR's lead consultant for gerontology – the study of various aspects of ageing. He has maintained lists of the world's oldest people for the Gerontology Research Group (GRG) since 1999, and has worked with the Max Planck Institute for Demographic Research and the International Database on Longevity. Robert became Director of the Supercentenarian Research Database Division for the GRG in 2015.

Park Nobel has a PhD in Biophysics. He honed his research on ion and water flow for chloroplasts in Tokyo, Japan, and London, UK, and finally as a faculty member at the University of California, Los Angeles, USA. A switch to studying air boundary layers around rigid-plant parts led him to focus on agaves and cacti in the field worldwide. His seminal textbooks include *The Cactus Primer* (1986) and *Cacti: Biology and Uses* (2002).

Colin Stuart is a multi-award-winning astronomy author and speaker. His books have sold over 400,000 copies globally and have been widely translated. Colin has written more than 250 articles for publications such as *New Scientist* and *The Wall Street Journal*, as well as for the European Space Agency. In recognition of his work to popularize astronomy, asteroid 15347 Colinstuart is named after him.

Cassidy Zachary is a fashion historian specializing in the social and cultural significance of dress throughout history right up to today. She is the creator and co-host (along with April Calahan) of the award-nominated podcast *Dressed: The History of Fashion* and the founder of the popular blog turned Instagram account *The Art of Dress*, which has more than 300,000 followers worldwide.

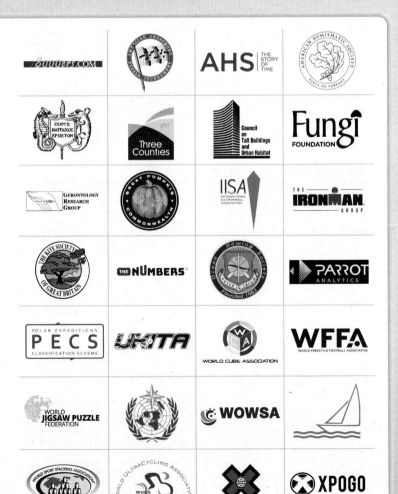

Thanks also to…

Evan Ackerman; American Museum of Natural History (Nancy B Simmons); American Society of Ichthyologists and Herpetologists (Prosanta Chakrabarty); Jeremy Angel; Aris Apollonatos; Mark Aston; Scott D Banks; Serena Bassaler-Bielfeld; BCSA (Tom Evans); Eric Berger; Zach Blank; Nick Buckenham; Minette Butler; Classic Tetris World Championship (Vincent Clemente); CLDSA (Shoneé Cornelissen); Colorado State University (Phil Klotzbach); Cornell Lab of Ornithology/eBird (John Fitzpatrick); Margaret F Docker; Dundee Heritage Trust (Julie Cumming, Ashleigh Pink); Durham University (Chris Stokes); Pádraig Egan; Etches Collection (Ash Hall); European Space Agency (Anne Daniels, Iris Nijman); Paul Frame; Friends of Ironwood Forest (Tom Hannagan); Fungi Foundation (Marios Levi); Taylor Geall; Gen Con (Peter Adkison, Stacia Kirby); Thomas Haigh; Bob Hoke; Aurélien Houard; Mark Hutchinson; ILDSA (Jacqueline McClelland); Jean Jeffries; JOIDES Resolution (Susan Q Lang, Andrew McCaig, Maya Pincus); James Kempster; Karen Krizanovich; Emily Lakdawalla; Large Pelagics Research Center (Chi Hin Lam, Molly Lutcavage); Nick Letzkus; Adam Lindquist; LPSA (Adherbal de Oliveira); Kirstie Macleod; Scott Manley; Jonathan McDowell; Michael A Morgan; Neil Morrison; NASA (D C Agle, James Anderson, Steve Garber, Brian C Odom, Katherine Schauer, Joshua Schmidt, David Woods); National Motor Museum (Patrick Collins, Michelle Kirwan, Jon Murden); Natural History Museum Los Angeles County (Christine Thacker); Natural History Museum, University of Oslo (Jørn Harald Hurum); NIST (Alexandra Boss, Andrew Ludlow); New Mexico Highlands University and *Journal of Herpetology* (Jesús A Rivas); NOAA (Monica Allen, Joe Cione); NZMSF (Philip Rush); NZOWSA (Simon Olliver); Lori Oschefski; Peter Lynn Kites (Craig Hansen); Royce Peterson; Robert Riener; Roller Coaster DataBase / *First Drop Magazine* (Justin Garvanovic); Royal Life Saving Society (Charlotte Knowles); RNLI (Laura Haslam, Emily Hazard); RSPCA (Tess Macpherson-Woods, Catherine Peerless); Elisabeth and Norbert Sarnes; Brian Schmidt; *Ships Monthly* (Nicholas Leach); SLAC National Accelerator Laboratory (Manuel Gnida, Travis Lange, Regina Matter); Stamford Museum and Nature Center (Chase Brownstein); *The Cactus and Succulent Journal* (Peter Breslin); University of Alaska Museum of the North (Patrick Druckenmiller); University of Bristol (Gareth Jones, Andre J Rowe, Judyth Sassoon); University College London (Susan Evans); University of Göttingen (Stephan Getzin); University of Illinois Urbana-Champaign (Milton Tan); University of Wisconsin-Madison (Chris Barncard, Shimon Kolkowitz, Kelly Tyrrell); University of Wolverhampton (Mark O'Shea); Jenn Virskus; Tom Wagg; World Cube Association; World Freestyle Football Association (Jordi Mestre, Dan Wood); World Sport Stacking Association (Lisa Berman); Mike Wray; Wesley Yinn-Poole; John Zacharias

Acknowledgements

SVP Global Publishing
Nadine Causey

Editor-in-Chief
Craig Glenday

Managing Editor
Adam Millward

Senior Editors
Tom Beckerlegge,
Ben Hollingum

Junior Editor
Caitlin Hyem

Layout Editor
Rob Dimery

**Proofreading
& Fact-Checking**
Matthew White

Picture Editors
Alice Jessop, Abby Taylor

**Director of Publishing
& Book Production**
Jane Boatfield

**Production & Distribution
Director**
Patricia Magill

**Production & Distribution
Manager**
Thomas McCurdy

Talent Researchers
Charlie Anderson, Hannah
Prestidge

Design
Paul Wylie-Deacon
and Richard Page at
55design.co.uk

Cover Design
Chris Labrooy

Indexer
Marie Lorimer

**Head of Commissioned
Content**
Michael Whitty

Original Photography
Brien Adams, Alberto
Bernasconi, Ian Bowkett,
Bob Croslin, James Ellerker,
Santiago Garcés, Gabriel
Gurrola, Krishnendu Halder,
Paul Michael Hughes,
Erik Isakson, Shinsuke
Kamioka, John F Martin,
Kevin Scott Ramos

Original Artwork
Daniel Clarke, Julio Lacerda,
The Maltings Partnership

Production Consultants
Yannick Laag, Astrid
Renders, Kevin Sarney,
Maximilian Schonlau,
Dennis Thon

Printing & Binding
Mohn Media Mohndruck
GmbH, Gütersloh, Germany

Global Marketing Director
Nicholas Brookes

**Head of Publishing &
Brand Communications
(UK & International)**
Amber-Georgina Maskell

**PR Manager
(UK & International)**
Madalyn Bielfeld

**PR Executive
(UK & International)**
Alina Polianskaya

**Marketing Executive
(UK & International)**
Nicole Dyer-Rainford

**Senior Content Manager
(UK & International)**
Eleonora Pilastro

**Senior PR Manager
(Americas)**
Amanda Marcus

**Senior PR Executive
(Americas)**
Kylie Galloway

CRM Marketing Manager
Jody Ho

Global Sales Director
Joel Smith

**Senior Key Account
Manager**
Mavis Sarfo

**International Sales
Manager**
Aliona Ladus

Reprographics
Resmiye Kahraman
and Louise Pinnock
at BORN Group

British Library Cataloguing-in-publication data:
a catalogue record for this book is available from the
British Library

UK: 978-1-913484-55-2
US: 978-1-913484-56-9
CAN: 978-1-913484-57-6
AUS: 978-1-913484-60-6
MENA: 978-1-913484-63-7
Trade Paperback: 978-1-913484-64-4

Records are made to be broken – indeed, it is one of the key
criteria for a record category – so if you find a record that
you think you can beat, tell us about it by making a record
claim. Always contact us before making a record attempt.

Sustainability

At Guinness World Records, we continue to run our
business in the most sustainable,
environmentally conscious way we can.
As part of that commitment, the pages of
this book are printed on a fully recycled
paper, made of 100% reclaimed paper
and post-consumer de-inked pulp.
No chlorine bleaching is used in the
paper production process. It has been
awarded the Blue Angel and EU Ecolabel
recognition.

This paper is produced at the Steinbeis Papier mill in
Germany, which is one of the most energy-efficient and
low-emission paper mills in Europe. The mill is focused
on ecological balance throughout the production process
– from the regional procurement of reclaimed paper as a
raw material, to production with an almost entirely closed
energy and water cycle.

GWR is committed to ethical and responsible sourcing of
paper, as well as ink. We also work to ensure that all our
supply-chain partners meet the highest international
standards for sustainable production and energy
management. For more information, please contact us.

GWR has a very thorough accreditation system for records
verification. However, while every effort is made to ensure
accuracy, GWR cannot be held responsible for any errors
contained in this work. Feedback from our readers on any
point of accuracy is always welcomed.

GWR uses metric and imperial measurements. Exceptions
are made for some scientific data where metric
measurements are universally accepted, and some sports
data. Where a specific date is given, the exchange rate is
calculated according to the currency values at the time.
Where only a year date is given, the exchange rate is
calculated from 31 Dec of that year.

Appropriate advice should always be taken when
attempting to break or set records. Participants undertake
records entirely at their own risk. GWR has complete
discretion over whether or not to include a record attempt
in any of its publications. Being a GWR record holder does
not guarantee you a place in any Guinness World Records
publication.

Printed in Germany by Mohn Media

Guinness World Records Limited's authorized
representative in the European Union is Mohn Media
Mohndruck GmbH, Carl-Bertelsmann-Straße 161M,
33311 Gütersloh, Germany

www.mohnmedia.de

Registered address: Ground Floor,
The Rookery, 2 Dyott Street,
London, WC1A 1DE

Global President
Alistair Richards

Governance
Alison Ozanne

Global Finance
Elizabeth Bishop, Jess Blake,
Arianna Cracco, Lisa Gibbs,
Kimberley Jones, Jacob Moss,
Bhavik Patel, Ysanne Rogers
Business Partnering: Sian Bhari,
Lorenzo Di Sciullo, Thomas Jones,
Maryana Lovell

eCommerce
Sara Kali, Athina Kontopoulou,
Scott Shore

Global Legal
Mathew Alderson, Greyson Huang,
Matthew Knight, Maria Popo,
Jiayi Teng

IT & Global Operations
Rob Howe
Project Management:
Caroline Brouwer, Vivian Peter
Digital Technology & IT: Anita Casari,
Mohamed Hanad Abukar, Oliver Hickie,
Veronica Irons, Joshua Jinadu, Apon
Majumder, Sohail Malik, Benjamin
McLean, Ajoke Oritu, Cenk Selim,
Gerry Sweeny, Roelien Viljoen,
Alex Waldu

Central Records Services
Mark McKinley
Record Content Support:
Lewis Blakeman, Amelis Escalante,
Clea Lime, Will Munford, Mariana
Sinotti, Dave Wilson, Melissa Wooton
Records Curation Team: Nana Asante,
Erin Branney, Megan Bruce, Dominic
Heater, Esther Mann, Thomas Marshall,
William Sinden

Global People & Culture
Stephanie Lunn
London: Eleonora Angelova, Jackie
Angus, Gurpreet Kaur, Monika Tilani
Americas: Jennifer Olson,
Mariama Sesay
China: Crystal Xu, Nina Zhou
Japan: Emiko Yamamoto
UAE: Monisha Bimal

Brand & Digital
Katie Forde
Brand Strategy & Communications
Jack Brockbank, Juliet Dawson,
Lucy Hunter, Doug Male
TV & Digital
Karen Gilchrist
Social Media: Josephine Boye,
Dominic Punt, Dan Thorne
Website Content: Sanj Atwal,
Vassiliki Bakogianni, Vicki Newman
Commissioned Content:
Michael Whitty
Video Production & Design: Callum
Dean, Rebecca Fisher, Jessica Hargrave,
Orla Langton, Rikesh Mistry, Fran
Morales, Matthew Musson, Joseph
O'Neil, Catherine Pearce, Aaron Quinn,
Emma Salt
Content Licensing: Kirsty Clark,
Kathryn Hubbard, Kate Stevenson

GWR Entertainment
Alexia Argeros, Fiona Gruchy-Craven,
Paul O'Neill, Alan Pixsley

Global Consultancies
Marco Frigatti
Global Demand Generation:
Angelique Begarin, Melissa Brown
Global Product Marketing: Catherine
Blyth, Aled Mann, Rebecca Ward
Americas Consultancy
Carlos Martinez
Commercial Account Services: Isabella
Barbosa, Mackenzie Berry, Brittany
Carpenter, Carolina Guanabara,
Ralph Hannah, Kim Partrick, Michelle
Santucci, Joana Weiss
Commercial Marketing: Nicole Pando,
Ana Rahlves
Records Management: Raquel Assis,
Lianett C Fernandez, Maddison
Kulish, Alba (Niky) Pauli, Callie Smith,
Carlos Tapia Rojas
Beijing Consultancy
Charles Wharton
Content Licensing: Chloe Liu
Editorial: Angela Wu
Commercial Account Services:
Catherine Gao, Linda Li, Xiaona Liu,
Tina Ran, Amelia Wang, Elaine Wang

Commercial Marketing: Theresa Gao,
Nicole Kang
Events Production: Fay Jiang
Brand Comms: Echo Zhan,
Yvonne Zhang
Records Management: Vanessa Tao,
Kaia Wang, Richard Xie, Alicia Zhao

Dubai Consultancy
Talal Omar
Commercial Account Services:
Sara Abu-Saad, Khalaf Badi,
Naser Batat, Danny Hickson,
Mohammad Kiswani, Kamel Yassin
Commercial Marketing: Shaddy Gaad
Brand & Content Marketing:
Mohamad Kaddoura, Alaa Omari
PR: Hassan Alibrahim
Records Management: Reem Al
Ghussain, Sarah Alkholb, Dina
Charafeddine, Hani Gharamah,
Karen Hamzeh

London Consultancy
Sam Prosser
Commercial Account Services:
Nick Adams, Monika Drobina,
Sirali Gandhi, Shanaye Howe,
Nick Hume, Spoorthy Prakash,
Nikhil Shukla, Lucia Sinigagliesi,
Nataliia Solovei
Commercial Marketing: Amina Addow,
William Baxter-Hughes
Records Management: Muhammad
Ahmed, Shreya Bahuguna, Andrew
Fanning, Apekshita Kadam, Ted Li,
Francesca Raggi

Tokyo Consultancy
Kaoru Ishikawa
Commercial Account Services:
Saif Alamannaei, Minami Ito, Takuro
Maruyama, Yumiko Nakagawa,
Nana Nguyen, Yuki Sakamoto,
Wei Watanabe, Masamichi Yazaki
Commercial Marketing: Momoko
Cunneen, Hiroyuki Tanaka, Eri Yuhira
Event Production: Yuki Uebo
Brand Comms: Kazami Kamioka,
Masakazu Senda
Records Management: Aki Makijima,
Mai McMillan, Momoko Omori,
Naomi-Emily Sakai, Lala Teranishi

Picture Credits

1 GWR, Alamy, Shutterstock, NASA, Blue Origin/Alamy; **1 (US)** Shutterstock, Alamy, Blue Origin/Alamy, GWR, NASA, World of Wonder Productions/Alamy, Paul Michael Hughes/GWR; **2** Shutterstock; **3** Shutterstock; **4** Shutterstock, Millennium House Australia, Alamy, Gary Null/NBCUniversal/Getty Images, Getty Images; **5** Shutterstock, "Damien Hirst and Science Ltd/DACS 2024", "Prudence Cuming Associates Ltd/Damien Hirst and Science Ltd/DACS/Artimage 2024", NPL, Todd Simpson/Western University; **6 (UK)** Shutterstock, BBC, Channel 4, Abby Taylor/GWR; **8 (UK)** Shutterstock, Tom Jackson, BBC, Abby Taylor/GWR; **9 (UK)** Alamy, Shutterstock, RTÉ One, MSC Cruises, Abby Taylor/GWR; **4 (US)** Shutterstock, MSC Cruises; **5 (US)** Shutterstock, GWR, Marisa S Cohen; **6 (US)** Zak Krill Photography, Shutterstock; **7 (US)** Shutterstock, Alamy; **8 (US)** Alamy, Shutterstock; **9 (US)** Mario Formisano, Getty Images, Kevin Scott Ramos/GWR, Shutterstock; **6 (Can)** Ripley's Aquarium of Canada, Shutterstock; **7 (Can)** Wallace Wong, Shutterstock; **8 (Can)** Getty Images, Shutterstock; **9 (Can)** Shutterstock, Getty Images; **6 (Aus/NZ)** Shutterstock; **7 (Aus/NZ)** Shutterstock; **8 (Aus/NZ)** Rebekah Marie/Australia Zoo, Ben Beaden/Australia Zoo, Kate Berry/Australia Zoo; **9 (Aus/NZ)** Shutterstock, Getty Images, Alamy; **6 (MENA)** Shutterstock; **8 (MENA)** Shutterstock, Getty Images; **9 (MENA)** Shutterstock, Getty Images; **10** U.S. Navy; **11** Getty Images, Shutterstock, Edd Thomas/HistoricTech.com, Alamy; **13** Richard Bradbury/GWR, Shutterstock, Alamy, Getty Images, NASA; **14** GWR, Shutterstock; **15** Alamy, Kodak, Getty Images, Shutterstock; **16** Nintendo, Getty Images; **17** Getty Images, Alamy, Dan Winans; **18** Alamy, Reuters, Getty Images, eBay, Shutterstock, NASA; **19** Jan Ove Moen/Equinor, Namco/Sony, Reuters, Alamy; **20** Jawed Karim/YouTube, Kerras Jeffery; **21** Shutterstock, Disney/Alamy; **22** Shutterstock, Paul Michael Hughes/GWR, Alamy, Robyn Crowther/Natural History Museum; **23** Shutterstock, Kevin Scott Ramos/GWR, Ranald Mackechnie/GWR; **24** Shutterstock, GWR; **25** Shutterstock, GWR; **26** GWR, Alamy, Getty Images; **27** Getty Images, Robert K. Graul for the *Alton Telegraph*. Courtesy of The Hayner Public Library District (Alton, Illinois); **28** Shutterstock; **29** Chien Lee Photography (photos.chienclee.com), Chris Thorogood, Shutterstock; **30** Shutterstock; **31** Shutterstock; **32** Shutterstock, Alamy, ZSSD/Minden/Naturepl.com; **33** Shutterstock; **34** Alamy, Shutterstock, L. Sullivan/USFWS; **35** Alamy, Getty Images, Shutterstock; **36** Shutterstock, Blue Planet Archive, Kim Taylor/Warren Photographic, Olin Feuerbacher/USFWS/Wiki, Naturepl.com, Getty Images; **37** Blue Planet Archive/Shedd AQ/Brenna Hernandez, Alamy, Great Lakes Fishery Commission, Alan Jamieson, Shutterstock; **38** Shutterstock, Alamy, Mokele/Wikimedia Commons, Daniel Crisman; **39** Shutterstock, Marineland Melanesia; **40** Queensland Department of Environment and Science, Alamy, Arne Hodalič/Wikimedia Commons, Shutterstock; **41** Alamy, Shutterstock; **42** Shutterstock, Nuytsia@Tas, Minden Pictures; **43** Shutterstock, Alamy; **44** Shutterstock, Alberto Bernasconi/GWR, Jeff Cohen; **45** Shutterstock, Paul Michael Hughes/GWR; **46** Shutterstock, RSPCA, Getty Images for Paramount Pictures, Bob Croslin/GWR, Joseph O'Neil/GWR; **47** Shutterstock, Daniel Berchtold/pomona.media, Kevin Scott Ramos/GWR, GWR; **48** Shutterstock, Pamla J. Eisenberg/Wiki, Giacomo Vallicelli, Alamy; **49** Shutterstock, Niksokol/Wiki, Alamy, Michael Wolf/Wiki; **50** Alamy, Shutterstock, Lisa Barlow, Lohit YT/WWF-India; **51** Shutterstock, Alamy, Daniel Winkler; **52** Shutterstock, Getty Images, Alamy, Science Photo Library, Andrew Miller/Capture North Studios, NASA Earth Observatory; **53** Shutterstock, Getty Images, Alamy, Arctic Images; **54** Shutterstock, NWS Aberdeen, SD/Wiki, NOAA, Deanna Dent, Getty Images; **55** Alamy, Shutterstock; **56** Shutterstock, Dr Stephan Getzin, Australian Reptile Park, The Etches Collection, Julia d'Oliveira; **57** RZSS, Alamy, Shutterstock; **58** Kevin Scott Ramos/GWR; **59** Jennifer Waters, GWR; **60** Shutterstock, Alberto Bernasconi/GWR; **61** Simon Ashton/dmg media Licensing; **62** Shutterstock, Daniel Clarke; **63** Shutterstock, Daniel Clarke; **64** Shutterstock, Ranald Mackechnie/GWR, GWR, Matthew Musson/GWR; **65** Shutterstock, Mustapha Azab/GWR, Paul Michael Hughes/GWR; **66** Shutterstock, Alamy, Ryan Schude/GWR; **67** Alamy, Shutterstock; **68** Shutterstock, Tom Jackson, Jon Enoch/GWR; **69** Shutterstock, Gabriel Gurrola/GWR; **70** Shutterstock, Bryan Nelson/Beard Team USA; **71** Shutterstock, Alberto Bernasconi/GWR; **72** Shutterstock, Gemini Untwined, Newsteam SWNS, Getty Images; **73** Shutterstock, GWR; **74** Shutterstock, Marc Suarez/GWR; **75** Shutterstock, John F. Martin/GWR; **76** Getty Images, Alamy, Shutterstock; **77** Shutterstock, Ryan Schude/GWR; **78** Shutterstock, GWR, Images of Life by Ashli; **79** Shutterstock, Alamy; **80** Kevin Scott Ramos/GWR; **81** Kevin Scott Ramos/GWR; **82** Kevin Scott Ramos/GWR; **83** Kevin Scott Ramos/GWR; **84** Shutterstock, Getty Images; **85** Shutterstock; **86** Shutterstock, Alamy, Getty Images; **87** Shutterstock, Alamy; **88** National Museum of American History, Heritage Auctions, Getty Images, Shutterstock, Alamy, Classical Numismatic Group; **89** Jens Mohr/The Norwegian State Museums of History, Shutterstock; **90** Shutterstock, Alamy, LEGO®; **91** Mack Trucks; **92** Alamy, Getty Images, Shutterstock; **93** Shutterstock; **94** Shutterstock, Sarah Kaufmann; **95** Shutterstock, Getty Images, Alamy, Gloucester City Museums/Bridgeman; **96** Shutterstock, James Ellerker/GWR, James Ellerker/GWR; **97** Shutterstock, Shinsuke Kamioka/GWR, Shinsuke Kamioka/GWR; **98** Alamy, Shutterstock; **99** Shutterstock; **100** Shutterstock, Alamy; **101** Shutterstock; **102** Shutterstock; **103** Shutterstock, Paul Michael Hughes/GWR, Erik Isakson/GWR, Shutterstock; **104** Shutterstock, Oksana Kret; **105** Shutterstock, Paul Michael Hughes/GWR; **106** GWR, Shutterstock, Alamy; **107** Shutterstock, Alamy; **108** Shutterstock, Cris Burckauser, Marjan Radovic/Red Bull Content Pool, Mateusz Odrzygóźdź/WFFA; **109** Shutterstock, Paul Michael Hughes/GWR, WFFA; **110** Shutterstock, Alamy; **111** Penh Alicandro/Eckerd College, Shutterstock, Cheryl Clegg; **112** Shutterstock, Ben Thouard/Red Bull Content Pool, Dave Ledbitter; **113** Davide Canella, Richard Bradbury/GWR, Shutterstock; **114** Alamy, Shutterstock; **115** Santiago Garcés/GWR, Shutterstock; **116** Shutterstock; **117** Shutterstock; **118** Ian Bowkett/GWR, Shutterstock, Alicia Beaudoin; **119** Shutterstock, Paul Michael Hughes/GWR, Amaury Guichon, Erik Isakson/GWR, Brien Adams/GWR; **120** Paul Michael Hughes/GWR; **121** Caters News; **122** Ilaria Cariello, Shutterstock; **123** Ilaria Cariello, Shutterstock; **124** Maltings Partnership, Shutterstock; **125** Shutterstock, Maltings Partnership, Getty Images; **126** GWR, Shutterstock, Alamy, Abiral Rai; **127** Shutterstock, RealityMaps, Getty Images; **128** Shutterstock, Johnny Green, Studio Tomás Saraceno; **129** Shutterstock; **130** Shutterstock, Alamy, Crown Copyright, Ministry of Defence, Garth Milan/Red Bull Content Pool, Andreas Schaad/Red Bull Content Pool, Eros Maggi/Red Bull Content Pool; **131** Keith Breazeal, Rich Beketa, Guy Clifton/*Reno Gazette-Journal*; **132** Shutterstock, Alamy; **133** Shutterstock; **134** Shutterstock, Simon Price/First Pix; **135** Shutterstock, Tim Kothlow; **136** Shutterstock, Getty Images; **137** Shutterstock, World's Toughest Row; **138** Shutterstock; **139** Shutterstock, Predrag Vučković/Red Bull Content Pool, Naim Chidiac/Red Bull Content Pool, Ian Avery-Leaf/Red Bull Content Pool, Mirja Geh/Red Bull Content Pool, Christian Pondella/Red Bull Content Pool; **140** Shutterstock, Alamy, Christopher P. Michel, Rhys Newsome, Jason South/*The Age*, Felipe Molina, Andrés Moncada; **141** Polheim Expedition; **142** Shutterstock, Alamy, Rouven Christ/Hylo Sports; **143** Shutterstock; **144** Alamy; **145** Shutterstock; **146** Shutterstock, Max Evans; **147** Shutterstock; **148** Shutterstock, artefacts-berlin.de; Material: German Archaeological Institute (this image is a "reconstruction proposal" and was made in 2012), Turbosquid, Carola Schelle-Wolff, Getty Images; **149** Getty Images, Turbosquid, Shutterstock; **150** Shutterstock, Division of Rare and Manuscript Collections, Cornell University, Obvious, Gil Weinberg, Cruise, Waymo; **151** Noah Berger, Shutterstock, Division of Work and Industry, National Museum of American History, Smithsonian Institution; **152** Danjaq/Eon/UA/Shutterstock, SL Rasch, Shutterstock, NIST; **153** Shutterstock, Patek Philippe, National Maritime Museum, Greenwich, London; **154** Shutterstock, International Gemini Observatory/NOIRLab/NSF/AURA/J. da Silva/Spaceengine/M. Zamani, ESA/Hubble, M. Kornmesser, Koichi Itagaki, Dennis Normile, NASA, ESA, CSA, and STScI, ESA–D. Ducros, 2013, Northrop Grumman; **155** Shutterstock, NASA, ESA, CSA, M. Zamani (ESA/Webb), ALMA (ESO/NAOJ/NRAO), B. Saxton (NRAO/AUI/NSF), GWR; **156** Shutterstock, Erick Bravo, IODP JRSO, Gabriel Tagliaro & IODP, Alberto Gamazo/SLAC National Accelerator Laboratory, F4E QST, F4E; **157** Shutterstock, TRUMPF/Martin Stollberg, Aurélien Houard; **158** Shutterstock, ~P A EVANS, Alamy, Paul Michael Hughes/GWR; **159** Shutterstock, Krishnendu Halder/GWR; **160** Alamy, Ben Hollingum/GWR, Shutterstock; **161** David Jarvis/Wiki, Shutterstock; **162** Shutterstock, Alamy; **163** Shutterstock, Overview Collective, DEWA; **164** Shutterstock, RLSS UK, Sikorsky Historical Archives, RNLI, Alamy; **165** Shutterstock, RNLI; **166** Dddeco/Wikimedia Commons, Federal Office of Transport BAV/Wikimedia Commons, Alamy, Andersen Viel Bjerkeset/DACS 2024, Shutterstock; **167** Bouygues Construction, Herrenknecht AG, Shutterstock; **168** Shutterstock; **169** Shutterstock; **170** Shutterstock, Alamy, Michael Lyrenmann; **171** Shutterstock, Maxar Space Systems; **172** MrBeast, Nick Elwell, Feastables, Nickelodeon; **173** Mark Rober, Bryce France; **174** Shutterstock, Paul Michael Hughes/GWR; **175** Paul Michael Hughes/GWR; **176** Paul Michael Hughes/GWR, Shutterstock; **177** Paul Michael Hughes/GWR, Shutterstock; **178** Alamy, Shutterstock; **179** Shutterstock, Paul Michael Hughes/GWR; **180** Kevin Scott Ramos/GWR, "Basic Fun!/K'NEX UK Ltd", Paul Michael Hughes/GWR, Shutterstock, Alamy; **181** Kevin Scott Ramos/GWR, The Troll Hole Museum, Mattel, Shutterstock, Hasbro; **182** Shutterstock, GWR; **183** Shutterstock; **184** Shutterstock; **185** Shutterstock; **186** Shutterstock, Shinsuke Kamioka/GWR; **187** Shutterstock, Trew Photography; **188** Shutterstock, Paul Michael Hughes/GWR; **189** Shutterstock, Selina Metcalfe, Hallmark; **190** Courtesy Sotheby's, Alamy, Mojang Studios, Shutterstock; **191** Mojang Studios, Shutterstock; **192** Mattel; **193** Mattel, Springer Publishing, Ranald Mackechnie/GWR, Warner Bros./Alamy; **194–195** Alamy; **196** The Metropolitan Museum of Art, Shutterstock, The J. Paul Getty Museum, Los Angeles, Neue Galerie New York/Art Resource/Scala, Florence; **197** Sotheby's, Shutterstock, Alamy, Succession Picasso/DACS, London 2024, "The Willem de Kooning Foundation/Artists Rights Society (ARS), New York and DACS, London 2024", Alamy; **198** Getty Images, Alamy, Shutterstock; **199** Alamy, Shutterstock, Getty Images; **200** Shutterstock, David MacDonald/CTWC, Activision/Games Press; **201** Shutterstock, Roblox/Games Press, Nintendo/Games Press, Mojang Studios/Games Press, Larian Studios/Games Press; **202** Shutterstock, Getty Images; **203** Getty Images, Rimas, Shutterstock; **204** Shutterstock, Alamy, Romina Amato/Red Bull Content Pool, Little Shao/Red Bull Content Pool; **205** Shutterstock, Alamy, Getty Images; **206** Shutterstock, Netflix, Paramount+, FXP/Alamy, HBO/Alamy, Paramount/Alamy; **207** HBO/Alamy, StarPlus, Apple TV+, Showtime/Alamy, Shutterstock, BBC Studios, Netflix/Alamy, Lucasfilm/Disney, HBO, TOHO Animation, Marvel/Disney, Netflix, HBO; **208** Alamy, Shutterstock, Getty Images; **209** Alamy, Shutterstock; **210** Shutterstock, Marvel/Disney/Kobal/Shutterstock, United Artists/Alamy, DC Entertainment/Warner Bros./Alamy, Sony Pictures/Apple Originals/Alamy, Sony Pictures/Apple Originals; **211** Sara Tautuku Orme, Shutterstock; **212** Warner Bros./Shutterstock, MGM/Shutterstock, Disney/Shutterstock, Netflix/Shutterstock, Netflix/Alamy, Shutterstock; **213** Getty Images, Disney/Pixar/Alamy, Universal/Alamy, Paramount/Shutterstock, Paramount/Alamy, Universal/Shutterstock, Paramount/Shutterstock, Shutterstock; **214** Shutterstock; **215** Shutterstock, Heritage Auctions, Sony/Getty Images; **216** Alamy, Shutterstock; **217** Alamy, *TIME*, Beth Garrabrant, Shutterstock; **218** Shutterstock, Terry Ratzlaff/*New York Times*/Redux/eyevine, Nebraska Athletic Communications Office; **219** Shutterstock, New Black Films ltd/Colour Artist Marina Amaral; **220** Getty Images, Inter Milan, Alamy, Shutterstock; **221** Getty Images, Shutterstock, Alamy; **222** Shutterstock, Getty Images, Alamy; **223** Shutterstock, Alamy; **224** Getty Images, Shutterstock, Sportsfile; **225** Shutterstock, Getty Images, Alamy; **226** Alamy, PSA World Tour, Shutterstock, GWR; **227** Alamy, Shutterstock; **228** Shutterstock, NHRA, Isle of Man TT, Alamy; **229** Getty Images, FIA, Paul Michael Hughes/GWR, Shutterstock; **230** Getty Images, World Karate Federation @wkf.net, Shutterstock; **231** Shutterstock, Getty Images, Alamy; **232** Getty Images, Kurt Wang, Shutterstock; **233** Shutterstock, Alamy, Getty Images; **234** Shutterstock, Alamy, IMAGO; **235** Alamy, Shutterstock; **236** Shutterstock, Howie Stern, Jacob Zocherman, iRunFar.com, Comrades Marathon Association; **237** Sportograf, Alexis Berg; **238** Getty Images, Shutterstock; **239** Getty Images, Alamy, Shutterstock; **240** Alamy, Getty Images, Shutterstock; **241** Shutterstock, Getty Images, Alamy; **242** Shutterstock, Getty Images; **243** Shutterstock, Alamy; **244** Getty Images, Alamy; **245** Alamy, Warner Bros./Alamy, Getty Images; **246** Shutterstock; **247** Shutterstock; **248** Shutterstock; **249** Shutterstock; **250** Shutterstock; **251** Shutterstock; **252** Shutterstock; **253** Shutterstock; **254** Shutterstock; **255** Shutterstock

Every effort has been made to trace copyright holders and gain permission for use of the images in this publication. We welcome notifications from copyright holders who may have been omitted.

Acknowledgements

55Design (Hayley Wylie-Deacon, Tobias Wylie-Deacon, Rueben Wylie-Deacon, Linda Wylie, Vidette Burniston, Lewis Burniston, Paul Geldeart, Sue Geldeart, Jay Page, Ellice Page, Bruno, Zeus, Macy), Arizona Science Center (Sari Custer, Guy Labine, Matthew Schwartz), Atmosphere Inc (Sebastian Quinn and team), Banijay Group Italia & Mediaset (Gabriela Ventura, Silvia Martini and teams), Susan Bender, Big Yellow Self Storage Liverpool (David Reason, Bev Rose), Linda Blyth, Lance Burnett, Cepac Ltd, City Museum (Kieran Burke, Maria Cassilly, Hue Eichelberger, Katy Enrique, Rick Erwin, Eric Gilbert, Joel Heckaman), Codex Solutions Ltd, Copenhagen GWR Museum (Phyllis Calloway, Henri Sokou), DataWorks Plus, Definition Group, Ezoic (Claire Johnson), FJT Logistics Ltd (Ray Harper), Grafit Display Hire Ltd (Paul Harrison, Antonia Johnston), GWR Kids (Pip Anderson, Clara Capgras, Juliet Capgras, Max Capgras, Georgia Grisdale, Samuel Holder, Isaac Holder, Frederick Lazell, Millicent Hume, Harriet Hume, Ellie Jones, Mylo Louw, Willow Sparkle Flower Marsh, Sydney Quince, Derrick Reynolds, Ivy Roelien, Adam Roelien, Michael Sarfo, Thea Simpson, Kaiden Testler Jagpal, Sapphire Testler Jagpal, Isabella Whitty, Clara Walker Knight, Suhana Tilani, Vesna Velkova Djurdjevic, Grace Wild, Sam Wild), Duncan Hart, Roger Hawkins, Matt Hillman, Hollywood GWR Museum (Nick Norman, Kirin Sundher, Raubi Sundher, Tej Sundher), IMG Media (Tim Ball) and ITV, Kidoodle (Brenda Bisner), Left Brain Games, Chris Lumb, Meta (Dan Biddle), Mintaka (Torquil Macneal, Tim Stuart), Mirage Entertainment (David Draves, Debra Draves), Mohn Media (Yannick Laag, Astrid Renders, Kevin Sarney, Maximilian Schonlau, Jeanette Sio, Dennis Thon), MSC Cruises (Mihaela Carlan, Andrea Correale, Biagio De Girolamo, Steve Leatham, Carlos Ponzetto, Thiago Lucio Santos Vieira), Orchard Wales and S4C (Jessie Lewis, Maisy Williams and team), Papercup (Luis, Idil), Parque de las Ciencias (Xavier A Colon Rivera, Jorge Jorge, Katherine Otero), Robert Partis, Ping Leisure Communication Ltd (Claire Owen), Precision Proco, Prestige Design (Jackie Ginger), Production Box (Milad Khalil, Christy Semaany), Propworks (Emma Banwell, Dan Lee, Annie Lumby, Pauline McGrath, Flo Minchella, Charlie Stoddart, Jess Way, Rosie Young), RCSSD (Clara Clark, Kristen Gilmore, Sophie Williams, Dot Young), Ripley's Office (William Anthony, Tacita Barrera, John Corcoran, Todd Hougland, Jim Pattison Jr., Brian Relic, Clay Stewart), Devonte Roper, Science North (Marc Gareau, Kris Gurnsey, Ashley Larose, Chris Theriault, Pamela Therrien), Liz Smith, Snap Inc (Lucy Luke), Stark RFID, Steinbeis Papier GmbH, The Production Suite (Jo Boase Zoe, Vaux-Thompson, Beverley Williams, Lorna Williamson), Tinizine (Luca Fiore), Julian Townsend, Sally Treibel, Uplause (Veli-Pekka Marin, Jussi Marin)

Official adjudicators

Osman Alwaleed, Camila Borenstain, Thomas Bradford, Emma Brain, Joanne Brent, Sarah Casson, Hannah Choi, Marc Cote, Swapnil Dangarikar, Brittany Dunn, Kanzy El Defrawy, Michael Empric, Pete Fairbairn, Fumika Fujibuchi, John Garland, Şeyda Subaşı Gemici, Andrew Glass, Iris Hou, Monica Hu, Kazuyoshi Kirimura, Lena Kuhlmann, Maggie Luo, Mike Marcotte, Karen Mazarello, Chloe McCarthy, Rishi Nath, Mbali Nkosi, Hannah Ortman, Pravin Patel, Justin Patterson, Glenn Pollard, Susana Reyes, Alfredo Arista Rueda, Emi Saito, Paulina Sapinska, Carl Saville, Tomomi Sekioka, Tina Shi, Brian Sobel, Hanane Spiers, Richard Stenning, Sheila Mella Suárez, Natalia Ramirez Talero, Raafat Tawfik, Anouk De Timary, Aynee Toorabally, Sonia Ushirogochi, Lorenzo Veltri, Xiong Wen, Peter Yang, Jacob Yip

Abbreviations

AFG	Afghanistan
ALB	Albania
AND	Andorra
ARG	Argentina
ARM	Armenia
ASM	American Samoa
AUS	Australia
AUT	Austria
AZE	Azerbaijan
BEL	Belgium
BGD	Bangladesh
BGR	Bulgaria
BHR	Bahrain
BHS	The Bahamas
BIH	Bosnia and Herzegovina
BLR	Belarus
BOL	Bolivia
BRA	Brazil
BRB	Barbados
CAN	Canada
CHE	Switzerland
CHL	Chile
CHN	China
CIV	Côte d'Ivoire
CMR	Cameroon
COL	Colombia
CPV	Cape Verde
CRI	Costa Rica
CUB	Cuba
CZE	Czechia
DEU	Germany
DJI	Djibouti
DNK	Denmark
DOM	Dominican Republic
DZA	Algeria
ECU	Ecuador
EGY	Egypt
ERI	Eritrea
ESP	Spain
EST	Estonia
ETH	Ethiopia
FIN	Finland
FJI	Fiji
FRA	France
GEO	Georgia
GHA	Ghana
GIN	Guinea
GRC	Greece
GTM	Guatemala
GUY	Guyana
HND	Honduras
HRV	Croatia (Hrvatska)
HTI	Haiti
HUN	Hungary
IDN	Indonesia
IND	India
IRL	Ireland
IRN	Iran
IRQ	Iraq
ISL	Iceland
ISR	Israel
ITA	Italy
JAM	Jamaica
JOR	Jordan
JPN	Japan
KAZ	Kazakhstan
KEN	Kenya
KHM	Cambodia
KOR	Korea, Republic of
KWT	Kuwait
LBN	Lebanon
LKA	Sri Lanka
LTU	Lithuania
LVA	Latvia
MAR	Morocco
MCO	Monaco
MDA	Moldova
MDG	Madagascar
MEX	Mexico
MLI	Mali
MMR	Myanmar
MNE	Montenegro
MNG	Mongolia
MOZ	Mozambique
MRT	Mauritania
MUS	Mauritius
MWI	Malawi
MYS	Malaysia
NAM	Namibia
NGA	Nigeria
NIC	Nicaragua
NLD	Netherlands
NOR	Norway
NPL	Nepal
NZ	New Zealand
PAK	Pakistan
PER	Peru
PHL	Philippines
PNG	Papua New Guinea
POL	Poland
PRI	Puerto Rico
PRT	Portugal
PRY	Paraguay
QAT	Qatar
ROM	Romania
RUS	Russian Federation
SAU	Saudi Arabia
SDN	Sudan
SEN	Senegal
SGP	Singapore
SHN	Saint Helena
SMR	San Marino
SOM	Somalia
SRB	Serbia
SSD	South Sudan
SVK	Slovakia
SVN	Slovenia
SWE	Sweden
SWZ	Eswatini
SYC	Seychelles
SYR	Syrian Arab Republic
THA	Thailand
TKM	Turkmenistan
TON	Tonga
TTO	Trinidad and Tobago
TUN	Tunisia
TUR	Türkiye
TZA	Tanzania
UAE	United Arab Emirates
UGA	Uganda
UK	United Kingdom
UKR	Ukraine
URY	Uruguay
USA	United States of America
UZB	Uzbekistan
VEN	Venezuela
VNM	Vietnam
VUT	Vanuatu
WSM	Samoa
YEM	Yemen
ZAF	South Africa
ZWE	Zimbabwe

THE
GUINNESS
BOOK
OF
RECORDS
WORLD BEST SELLER

The New
Guinness
Book of
Records
1995

new
THE
GUINNESS
BOOK OF
RECORDS
1996

THE GUINNESS
BOOK OF
RECORDS
1991

GUINNESS
WORLD RECORDS
2002

GUINNESS
WORLD
RECORDS
2003

GUINNESS
WORLD
RECORDS
2004

GUINNESS
WORLD
RECORDS
2005
50

GUINNESS
WORLD
RECORDS
2010
THE BOOK OF THE DECADE

GUINNESS
WORLD
RECORDS
2011
EXPLODING WITH
THOUSANDS OF NEW RECORDS

GUINNESS
WORLD
RECORDS
2012
BURSTING WITH
AMAZING NEW RECORDS

GUINNESS
WORLD
RECORDS
2013
DISCOVER A WORLD
OF NEW RECORDS

GUINNESS
WORLD
RECORDS
2018
MEET
REAL
SUPER
THOUSANDS OF AMAZING NEW

GUINNESS
WORLD
RECORDS
2019

GUINNESS
WORLD
RECORDS
2020

GUINNESS
WORLD
RECORDS
2021